TAKE ME TO YOUR LEADER

DK

LONDON, NEW YORK, MUNICH, MELBOURNE, DELHI

Project Editor Kathryn Wilkinson
Senior Art Editor Vicky Short
Editors Ann Baggaley, Kim Dennis-Bryan,
Anna Fischel, Nigel Ritchie
US Editor Margaret Parrish
Designers Clare Joyce, Tim Lane, Loan Nguyen

Proofreader Caroline Hunt
Indexer Helen Peters
Picture Researcher Sarah Smithies
Production Editor Clare McLean
Production Controller Rita Sinha

Managing Art Editor Christine Keilty
Publishing Manager Liz Wheeler

Art Director Bryn Walls
Publisher Jonathan Metcalf

First American Edition, 2007

Published in the United States by
DK Publishing
375 Hudson Street
New York, New York 10014

07 08 09 10 11   10 9 8 7 6 5 4 3 2 1

MD390—October 2007

Published in Great Britain by Dorling Kindersley Limited.

A catalog record for this book is available from the Library of Congress.

ISBN: 978-0-7566-3202-1

DK books are available at special discounts when purchased in bulk for sales
promotions, premiums, fundraising, or educational use. For details, contact:
DK Publishing Special Markets, 375 Hudson Street, New York, New York
10014 or Special Sales@dk.com.

Printed and bound in China by Hung Hing Offset Printing Company Ltd.

Discover more at
www.dk.com

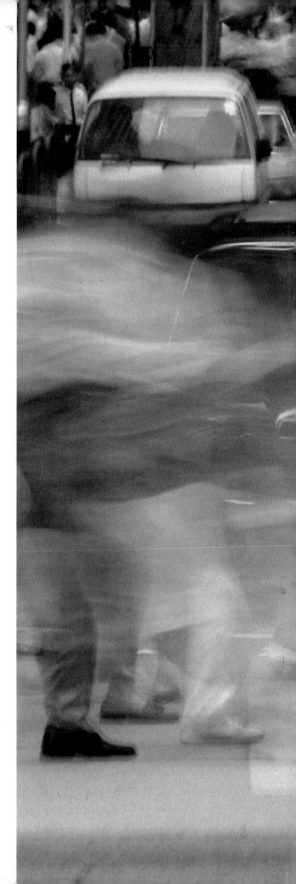

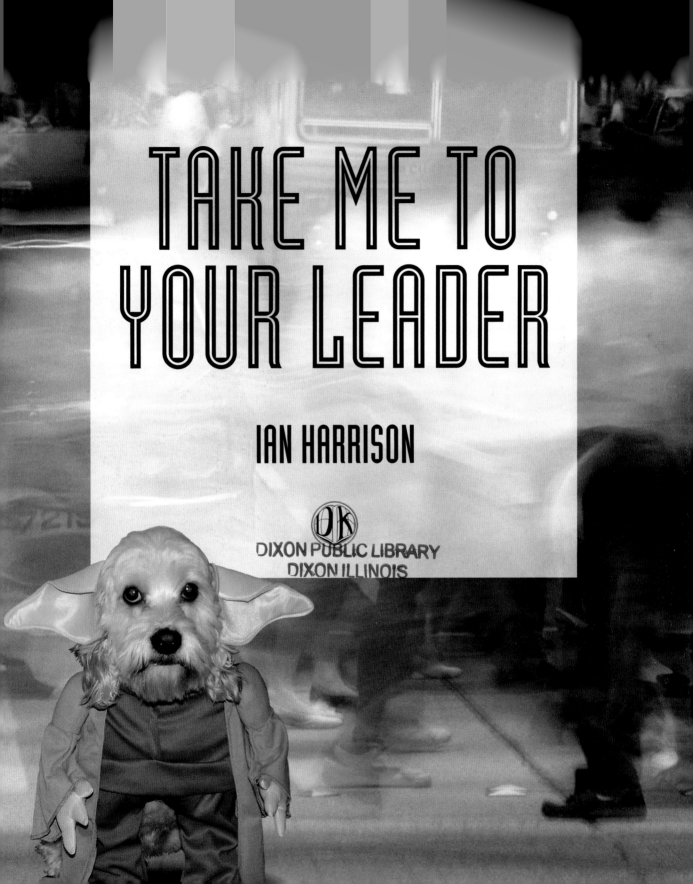

CONTENTS

8   INTRODUCTION TO EARTH

10   **CHAPTER 1**

12   *The meaning of one*
Number-based trivia, from one-armed bandits to
111,111,111 X 111,111,111 = 12345678987654321

14   PLANET EARTH
Don't go there
Canceled flights are the least of your travel
worries, it's when you arrive that you're really
going to have to watch out.

16   CUSTOMS AND ETIQUETTE
It's still legal...
Find out what you can get away with where.

18   FOOD AND DRINK
Everyone loves a sausage
Every nation has its favorite and Germany has
1,200 of them.

20   FLORA AND FAUNA
"Man's best friend"
A gallery of dogs in their (or their owners')
favorite party costumes.

22   TECHNOLOGY
How to become a superhero
Find out how to emulate the superpowers of
universally popular superheroes.

24   MYTHS AND LEGENDS
Urban myths 1
Tales that play on human society's subliminal
hopes and fears.

26   SPORTS AND LEISURE
The sweet science
Two men get into a square ring and try to
knock each other out, while wearing soft
gloves so they don't hurt each other too much.

28   SPORTS AND LEISURE
Classic bout
Nose crunching in Madison Square Garden.

30   COMMUNICATION
Meet and drink
The right words to say when raising a glass,
wherever you are in the world.

32   FLORA AND FAUNA
50s pin-ups
See what happened when Hollywood took
off its clothes.

34   MYTHS AND LEGENDS
Great escapes
Everybody wants to be free, and that's why
escapes are so inspiring.

36   FOOD AND DRINK
Supersize maki
A step-by-step guide to making supersized
sushi, but go easy on the wasabi.

38   SPORTS AND LEISURE
Big feats
Who was the first person to go over Niagara
Falls in a barrel or the first person to pogo stick
up the CN tower? The answers here.

40   CUSTOMS AND ETIQUETTE
World party
Whatever the time of year there's always a BIG
party going on somewhere in the world, details
here from Glastonbury to Rio de Janeiro.

42   FLORA AND FAUNA
Superhuman
Human extremes, from the longest beard
to the smallest waist.

44   FLORA AND FAUNA
Most deadly
Its not just the animals with big teeth and
claws you need to look out for...

46   CUSTOMS AND ETIQUETTE
Rules of the road
Learning to drive is complicated enough
already, but then, if you're in Athens or
Thailand, you've also got to remember the
legal requirement to dress before you drive.

48   CUSTOMS AND ETIQUETTE
When in Rome
When in Rome do as the Romans do. For those
who aren't quite sure what the Romans do,
here's a helpful guide.

50   MYTHS AND LEGENDS
Hoaxing Times
Read this and see just how gullible humans
can be.

52   SPORTS AND LEISURE
On the slopes
Learn snowboarding jargon to find out why
ollie, butter, grab, and ally-oop impress.

54   MYTHS AND LEGENDS
Crime firsts
Firsts in the fields of assassination, conviction,
and execution.

56   SPORTS AND LEISURE
What's in a name
The stories behind some of the greatest album
titles in the world.

58   TECHNOLOGY
Big Brother
You are being watched.

60   **CHAPTER 2**

62   *The meaning of two*
Number-based trivia, from famous double
acts to yin and yang.

64   CUSTOMS AND ETIQUETTE
Men of the world
From caribou fur to kilts, this is a photo guide
to what men wear around the world.

66   CUSTOMS AND ETIQUETTE
Women of the world
From Dutch caps to feather wraps, see what
women wear around the world.

68   MYTHS AND LEGENDS
Great balls of fire
Can a human being just burst into flames for
no reason?

70   FLORA AND FAUNA
Man v beast
Who can eat more, a caterpillar or an adult
human? If you measure the results fairly, it's
the insects every time.

72   FLORA AND FAUNA
60s sex symbols
Looks that made the Sixties swing.

74   PLANET EARTH
Acts of God
Avalanches, cyclones, earthquakes, landslides,
volcanoes, tsunamis, epidemics—which ones
caused the most damage?

76   PLANET EARTH
Plague of locusts
Eating disorder.

78   PLANET EARTH
Death and disaster
The devastating consequences of humans'
mistakes.

80   FOOD AND DRINK
Supersize cookie
Step-by-step guide to making a cookie with
approximately 8,000 calories.

82   TECHNOLOGY
Man on the Moon
Ever wondered how long it took humans to get
to the Moon? About 1.8 million years.

84   FOOD AND DRINK
Dying for a drink
What those in the know drink around the
world, and what they call it.

86   FLORA AND FAUNA
A narcotic web
How do caffeine, marijuana, LSD, and
amphetamines affect spiders?

88   SPORTS AND LEISURE
New balls, please
Once upon a time you could simply hit a
pebble into a hole with a stick and call it golf,
but then it got more sophisticated.

90   MYTHS AND LEGENDS
Conspiracy theories
Whether it's because they believe in it or
because they want to rant about how ludicrous
it is, humans love a conspiracy theory.

      FLORA AND FAUNA
Unwanted guests
From follicle mites to liver flukes, hundreds of
species make their home in the human body.

94 FOOD AND DRINK
Food firsts
What annoyed a chef so much that he invented potato chips? And whose idea was it to create ready-to-eat breakfast cereal?

96 FLORA AND FAUNA
Queen bee
All-over coverage.

98 SPORTS AND LEISURE
Bar tricks
A step-by-step guide to bar tricks that help you win friends and influence people.

100 FLORA AND FAUNA
Pet projects
Monkeys in space, skydiving dogs, and flying sheep. Why? Ask their owners.

102 SPORTS AND LEISURE
Deadly sports
From angling and cheerleading to base jumping and big-wave surfing.

104 SPORTS AND LEISURE
Bull-riding
A sport for the truly insane.

106 MYTHS AND LEGENDS
Ways to make money
Everyone likes to make money. Some people work, some people steal, some people inherit, and some people set up elaborate scams.

108 **CHAPTER 3**
110 **The meaning of three**
Number-based trivia, from the three states of matter to the three musketeers.

112 CUSTOMS AND ETIQUETTE
Work-life balance
Where do you have to work the longest to buy a three-course meal, or the least number of hours to buy your clothes?

114 SPORTS AND LEISURE
America's national pastime
Baseball facts and stats.

116 COMMUNICATION
Attract a mate
Find out how to tell whether or not that gorgeous person on the other side of the room likes you or not, and how to let them know you like them, too, without actually saying so.

118 FLORA AND FAUNA
Wild sex
Curious mating habits.

120 FLORA AND FAUNA
Paint that cat
Transformation with a few brushstrokes.

122 TECHNOLOGY
Patent junk
Marvel at the things people have thought worth patenting, from spaghetti forks to a pat-on-the-back apparatus.

124 SPORTS AND LEISURE
Crash and burn
When sports goes wrong the consequences can be painful.

126 CUSTOMS AND ETIQUETTE
The rules of dating
How to behave and win your date's affection.

128 PLANET EARTH
I will survive... part I
This might just save your life.

130 PLANET EARTH
I will survive... part II
More potentially lifesaving information.

132 FLORA AND FAUNA
70s stars
Who was hot in the decade that fashion forgot.

134 CUSTOMS AND ETIQUETTE
It's still illegal
Find out where your office has to have a view of the sky, where parents can't insult their children, and in which US state you can't pawn your dentures.

136 FLORA AND FAUNA
Comfort stop
Because when a man's got to go, a man's gotta go.

138 SPORTS AND LEISURE
Origami
A step-by-step guide to folding paper to make waterbombs, boats, and dollar shirts.

140 MYTHS AND LEGENDS
Fact or fiction
Can high notes shatter a wine glass and can urinating on the third rail of a train track kill? Find out here.

142 FLORA AND FAUNA
Breaking rank
However much people are made to conform, there's always one...

144 COMMUNICATION
World karaoke
Lyrics to a few traditional songs from around the world so that you can sing along with the locals.

146 PLANET EARTH
Own islands
Once adventurers went off to discover unknown islands, now people just build new ones instead.

148 CUSTOMS AND ETIQUETTE
Million-dollar humans
Legs and breasts are worth more to some than to others.

150 CUSTOMS AND ETIQUETTE
Worth its weight in gold
What was so valuable in Roman times that Goths demanded it as a ransom?

152 MYTHS AND LEGENDS
Who's afraid of...
From flying to thunder, spiders to sunsets, guns to chewing gum, what do the famous really fear?

154 SPORTS AND LEISURE
Trick cyclist
Doing backflips in the sky.

156 TECHNOLOGY
Safety in the home
Exposes the dangers of tea cozies, chairs, and laundry baskets.

158 **CHAPTER 7**
160 **The meaning of 7**
Number-based trivia, from the seven seas to the lucky connotations.

162 PLANET EARTH
The eve of destruction
Temperatures are rising on planet Earth. How hot will it get and how will it devastate the planet?

164 CUSTOMS AND ETIQUETTE
The rules of drinking
You've learned how to say cheers, but what else do you need to know?

166 FOOD AND DRINK
Local delicacies
Take a look at what passes for delicious food around the world.

168 SPORTS AND LEISURE
Backhanders
Find out why every year thousands of men gather on beaches around the world.

170 SPORTS AND LEISURE
Horror movies
If one cast member dies, it's unfortunate, if two die that's sinister, if three or more die then you've got a cursed movie.

172 SPORTS AND LEISURE
Unlucky breaks
From a vehicle hitting the leading cyclist in the Tour de France to a goal celebration that resulted in a missing finger.

174 FOOD AND DRINK
Supersize Scotch egg
Step-by-step guide to making a supersized Scotch egg—but beware, to burn it off you'll need to skip fast for around seven hours.

176 MYTHS AND LEGENDS
Hit the road
Who was the first unfortunate to die in a car crash, and the first hedonist to be convicted for drunk driving?

178 TECHNOLOGY
Hide and seek
Essential toolkit for spies.

180 FLORA AND FAUNA
Bad hair day
For the people in this gallery it looks like every day was a bad hair day.

182 MYTHS AND LEGENDS
Six degrees of celebrity
It's a small world, but for celebrities it's even smaller, as these connections show.

184 CUSTOMS AND ETIQUETTE
National treasures
Been there, done that, but perhaps you don't want the T-shirt, in which case one of the souvenirs here might be more your bag.

186 FLORA AND FAUNA
Bird scarer
A cheeky form of crop protection.

188 MYTHS AND LEGENDS
Join the club
These secretive societies are the subject of rumors, accusations, and conspiracy theories.

190 FLORA AND FAUNA
80s icons
Out—curves and cleavage. In—long legs.

192 SPORTS AND LEISURE
Extreme endurance
Pushing the human body to the limits.

194 SPORTS AND LEISURE
United we fall
Freefall-formation but everyone has a position.

196 TECHNOLOGY
World of war
When it comes to armies, size matters.

198 CUSTOMS AND ETIQUETTE
National health
Who spends what on health?

200 MYTHS AND LEGENDS
Staying alive
Human determination.

202 TECHNOLOGY
Human spares
From artificial noses to replacement hearts, humans have come a long way since the first ancient Greek artificial limb.

204 COMMUNICATION
Sweet nothings
How to say "I love you" in a hundred languages.

206 **CHAPTER 9**
208 *The meaning of 9*
Number-based trivia, from why 9 is lucky in China but unlucky in Japan, to the importance of 9 in baseball.

210 TECHNOLOGY
Remote control
Robots performing surgery, directed by doctors across the oceans: medicine has come a long way.

212 FLORA AND FAUNA
Self-improvement 1
A gallery of tattoos from tribal marks to fashion statements.

214 FLORA AND FAUNA
Painted lady
Be amazed.

216 SPORTS AND LEISURE
Sports superstitions
There's always an element of luck in sports, and where there's luck there's superstition.

218 FLORA AND FAUNA
At a stretch
Flexible fitness.

220 COMMUNICATION
Trouble ahead
Signs: customized, or just curious.

222 MYTHS AND LEGENDS
Forever young
What did child stars do next?

224 SPORTS AND LEISURE
Road trip
"The Hell of the North" causes chaos.

226 FLORA AND FAUNA
90s booty
Breasts were back, in a big way.

228 SPORTS AND LEISURE
The beautiful game
The good, the bad, and the ugly.

230 FLORA AND FAUNA
Vital statistics
Despite having more neurons in their brains than the number of people who have ever walked on planet Earth since *homo sapiens* first stood upright, the majority of humans are unaware of their own vital statistics.

232 TECHNOLOGY
Money, money, money
Around the world, some pretty odd things have been used as cash, from skulls to peppercorns.

234 SPORTS AND LEISURE
Paper planes
A step-by-step guide to making aircraft from paper.

236 TECHNOLOGY
Plane spotting
A guide to help you identify everything from the Wright Flyer to the new Airbus.

238 TECHNOLOGY
Plane crash
Nose-diving in Paris.

240 FOOD AND DRINK
Supersize marshmallow
Step-by-step guide to making a marshmallow that's the size of a cake.

242 TECHNOLOGY
The sharpest tool in the box
When a penknife is too big to be a pocket knife.

244 FLORA AND FAUNA
Self-improvement 2
See what lengths some people go to in the quest for the body beautiful.

246 MYTHS AND LEGENDS
Urban myths 2
More apocryphal stories to amuse and disturb.

248 PLANET EARTH
7 wonders of the world
As chosen by the American Society of Civil Engineers.

250 FOOD AND DRINK
Big bird
All Thanksgiving guests catered to.

252 TECHNOLOGY
What to do with a spoon
From chipping away to freedom with a spoon to family-planning potato chip bags, see just what can be done with everyday things.

254 SPORTS AND LEISURE
Winners and losers
Often it's more memorable if someone just falls over.

256 **CHAPTER 12**
258 *The meaning of 12*
Number-based trivia, from the importance of 12 in time to the 12 points of the Beaufort scale.

260 PLANET EARTH
60 seconds to save the world
Humans are very good at destroying the planet, so here are some ways to save it.

262 FLORA AND FAUNA
Animal miles
From the birds that fly 10,000 miles a year to the birds that catch a ferry to go 1.5 miles.

264 TECHNOLOGY
Natural remedies
Sometimes the old cures are the best. Disinfection with maggots or a cowdung poultice, anyone?

266 CUSTOMS AND ETIQUETTE
The rules of business
What to do wherever your business takes you.

268 FLORA AND FAUNA
Animal house
Since time immemorial people have kept pets; here are some of the odder ones.

270 PLANET EARTH
Cloud spotting part I
Find out how to identify a cirrus, altocumulus, and stratus.

272 PLANET EARTH
Cloud spotting part II
Now for the interesting one.

274 MYTHS AND LEGENDS
Modern myths
Is it true that humans only use 10 percent of their brains, or that teeth will dissolve in cola overnight?

276 FLORA AND FAUNA
OOs idols
Figures for the new millennium.

278 CUSTOMS AND ETIQUETTE
Rules of attraction
Next time you tell someone they look divine, you'll be able to explain the science behind it.

280 CUSTOM AND ETIQUETTE
Gurning
If your face is less than perfect, here's a look for you.

282 COMMUNICATION
Out of place
What bikinis, hamburgers, and marathons are named after.

284 COMMUNICATION
Sign language
Handsigns—they don't all mean the same thing everywhere.

286 CUSTOMS AND ETIQUETTE
Odd jobs
Routine 9 to 5? Not for vermiculturalists, hot walkers, and fluffers.

288 CUSTOMS AND ETIQUETTE
Job for life
Requires a head for heights.

290 TECHNOLOGY
Come fly with me
Everything you ever wanted to know about flying.

292 COMMUNICATION
Quote unquote
According to André Breton, "The man who can't visualize a horse galloping on a tomato is an idiot."

294 FLORA AND FAUNA
Lord of the rings
Taking body piercing to the extreme.

296 TECHNOLOGY
Human transporters
Boats that mimic dolphins and walking tanks, for times when ordinary vehicles just won't do.

298 SPORTS AND LEISURE
Little soccer horrors
Some of the more notorious soccer-watching incidents.

300 COMMUNICATION
Gang culture
Recognizing what gang someone belongs to can come in handy in some cities.

302 TECHNOLOGY
Not in real life
We all know that movies aren't real, but when they bend the laws of physics someone's going to start noticing.

304 **CHAPTER 13**
306 **The meaning of 13**
From why 13 is thought unlucky in many cultures to how many references to it there are on a dollar bill.

308 TECHNOLOGY
Reach for the sky
What did humans need to invent before they could build skyscrapers?

310 SPORTS AND LEISURE
Bad sports
When the pressure's on, see who cracks.

312 TECHNOLOGY
Pimp your ride
The ultimate expression of car love.

314 TECHNOLOGY
Happy accidents
Find out what mistakes led to the invention of everyday necessities.

316 TECHNOLOGY
Emergency room
When your eye is hanging out of its socket or your whole face has been ripped off, it's good to know what can be fixed.

318 SPORTS AND LEISURE
Excess all areas
Extreme behavior.

320 SPORTS AND LEISURE
Balloon sculpture
A step-by-step guide to how to tie balloons in knots. If you ever have to look after kids this will come in very handy.

322 SPORTS AND LEISURE
Extreme sports
From toe-wrestling to dwarf-throwing.

324 SPORTS AND LEISURE
Board sport
Taking ironing to extremes.

326 COMMUNICATION
I want to be left alone
Sometimes you just want to be left alone: here are the words to say, wherever you find yourself.

328 FOOD AND DRINK
Supersize fish stick
A step-by-step guide to making a giant fish stick, with some fairly large peas on the side.

330 MYTHS AND LEGENDS
Better off dead
Some people are worth more money now that they're dead than when they were alive.

332 MYTHS AND LEGENDS
Crime lasts
Who was the last woman boiled alive or the last man executed by ax?

334 MYTHS AND LEGENDS
Ways to go
Some people hope to die quietly in their beds, others want to go out in a blaze of glory, but very few will make their exit in the bizarre manner of these people.

336 MYTHS AND LEGENDS
Killer on the loose
The Black Dahlia, Lake Bodom murders, and the Zodiac killer—we know how these unsolved murders end but not who did it.

338 SPORTS AND LEISURE
Contact sports
See a master at work.

340 COMMUNICATION
Famous last words 1
Even when the famous are on their deathbeds the public is still listening.

342 FLORA AND FAUNA
Going, going, gone
These Earth species are all at risk of extinction.

344 FOOD AND DRINK
Last meals
Whose last meal was mint chocolate-chip ice cream, and who wanted to save their pecan pie for later?

346 COMMUNICATION
Famous last words 2
When strong opinions prove to be spectacularly wrong.

348 COMMUNICATION
Where there's a will...
Wills can be used to leave money to loved ones, to settle scores, or to carry out posthumous social experiments.

350 PLANET EARTH
The end is nigh
From asteroid impact to pandemics, and global warming to computers taking over.

352 CUSTOMS AND ETIQUETTE
That's all, folks
Adding a touch of pizzazz at the end.

354 **Glossary of useful words**
Does what it says on the can.

357 **Index**
360 **Acknowledgments**

AUTHOR'S NOTE
More astute readers may have noticed that the seven chapters in this book are not numbered according to the conventional human counting system. This is because the author chose the most interesting seven numbers rather than the first seven. For the record, the first seven numbers are: 1, 2, 3, 4, 5, 6, and 7.

INTRODUCTION TO EARTH

Finding your way to Earth is simple compared with the complications you'll face once you land. First, head for the Orion Arm of the Milky Way, which lies some 25,000 light-years from the galactic center. Then take a fix on the distinctive triple star system, Alpha Centauri. Now you're only 4.4 light-years from the solar system, which comprises a yellow dwarf (known to humans as the Sun), surrounded by a number of orbiting planets and planetoids. Earth is the fifth largest planet in the system, the third from the Sun, and the only one thought to support life.

Life on Earth has been evolving for only a few billion years and so remains primitive. After bacteria and viruses, the dominant life form is insects. But humans exert a disproportionate influence over their surroundings and give the appearance of dominance.

At first glance all humans look alike—bipedal, with most of the sense organs concentrated in the head. However, there are variations in body type and skin color, and it is possible, with practice, to tell the genders apart. There are cultural similarities linking all humans (males like sausages, drinking, and sports, each of which this guide covers in detail). But many humans strive to stand out from the crowd: for examples, see odd jobs, extreme sports, and big feats.

Humanity's primitive technology means that, with a few enlightened exceptions, the inhabitants of Earth consider themselves the only intelligent life form in the universe. As on visits to any other planet whose inhabitants harbor such beliefs, protocol demands that you assume human form and behavior if you want to interract with them. This guidebook shows you what to expect and how to blend in. If, as a visitor, the strangeness of human underlings overwhelms you and you long to meet some sensible fellow extraterrestrials, the best way to spot them will be that they too are carrying a copy of TAKE ME TO YOUR LEADER.

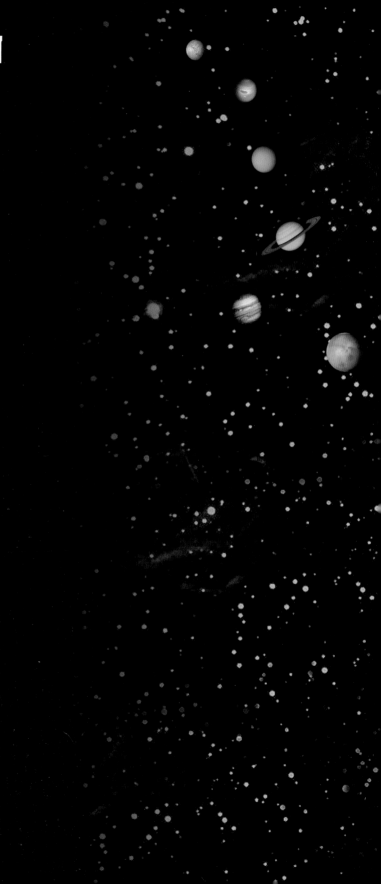

CHAPTER

1

Air Force One is the code name of the US President's plane – it is a Boeing 747 containing bedrooms, showers, a stateroom, an operating theatre, two kitchens, and a communications centre ▮ The words a, an, unit, unity, union, unique, and universal all derive from the Latin for one (*unus*) ▮ One-armed bandits are so called because they have a single lever and relieve gamblers of their change ▮ Formula One is the highest class of motor racing governed by the Fédération Internationale de l'Automobile (FIA) ▮ In Tarot, card no. 1 is the Magician ▮ *The Wild One* is a classic outlaw biker movie released in 1953 starring Marlon Brando ▮ A unicorn is a mythological horse-like creature with one horn, symbolic of power and purity ▮ The Cyclops was a giant human-like creature with one eye in the centre of its forehead. Like many other mythical one-eyed monsters, the Cyclops is symbolic of the power of dark forces or elemental violence over reason and intellect ▮ Monotheism is a belief in one god ▮ Monism is the belief that reality exists in one form only, and that body and soul are of the same substance ▮ One metre is the distance travelled by light in 1/299,792,458 of a second ▮ One second used to be defined as 1/86,400th of the time taken for the Earth to rotate – it is now defined as the time taken for one atom of Caesium-133 to vibrate 9,192,631,770 times ▮ The ancient Greeks considered one to be not a number but the unity from which all other numbers arose ▮ 111,111,111 x 111,111,111 = 12345678987654321 ▮ The number one can be written using all ten single digit numbers once each: 148/296 + 35/70 = 1 ▮ One is not accepted as a prime number, so it is the only exception to the definition of a prime number as any number that is divisible only by itself and one.

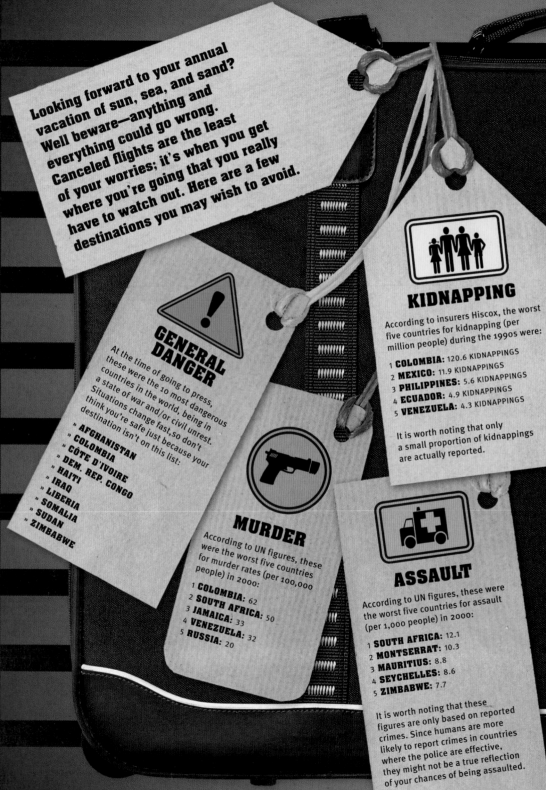

Looking forward to your annual vacation of sun, sea, and sand? Well beware—anything and everything could go wrong. Canceled flights are the least of your worries; it's when you get where you're going that you really have to watch out. Here are a few destinations you may wish to avoid.

GENERAL DANGER

At the time of going to press, these were the 10 most dangerous countries in the world, being in a state of war and/or civil unrest. Situations change fast, so don't think you're safe just because your destination isn't on this list:

- » AFGHANISTAN
- » COLOMBIA
- » CÔTE D'IVOIRE
- » DEM. REP. CONGO
- » HAITI
- » IRAQ
- » LIBERIA
- » SOMALIA
- » SUDAN
- » ZIMBABWE

KIDNAPPING

According to insurers Hiscox, the worst five countries for kidnapping (per million people) during the 1990s were:

1 **COLOMBIA:** 120.6 KIDNAPPINGS
2 **MEXICO:** 11.9 KIDNAPPINGS
3 **PHILIPPINES:** 5.6 KIDNAPPINGS
4 **ECUADOR:** 4.9 KIDNAPPINGS
5 **VENEZUELA:** 4.3 KIDNAPPINGS

It is worth noting that only a small proportion of kidnappings are actually reported.

MURDER

According to UN figures, these were the worst five countries for murder rates (per 100,000 people) in 2000:

1 **COLOMBIA:** 62
2 **SOUTH AFRICA:** 50
3 **JAMAICA:** 33
4 **VENEZUELA:** 32
5 **RUSSIA:** 20

ASSAULT

According to UN figures, these were the worst five countries for assault (per 1,000 people) in 2000:

1 **SOUTH AFRICA:** 12.1
2 **MONTSERRAT:** 10.3
3 **MAURITIUS:** 8.8
4 **SEYCHELLES:** 8.6
5 **ZIMBABWE:** 7.7

It is worth noting that these figures are only based on reported crimes. Since humans are more likely to report crimes in countries where the police are effective, they might not be a true reflection of your chances of being assaulted.

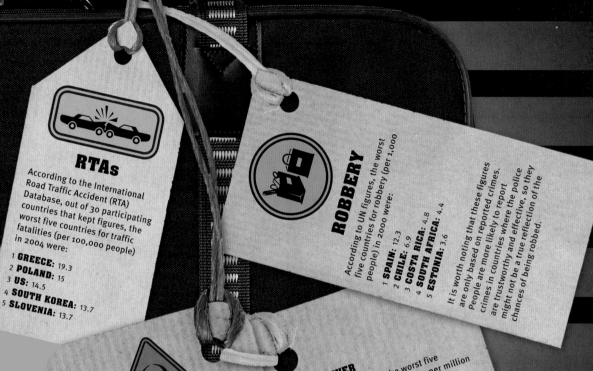

RTAs

According to the International Road Traffic Accident (RTA) Database, out of 30 participating countries that kept figures, the worst five countries for traffic fatalities (per 100,000 people) in 2004 were:

1 **GREECE:** 19.3
2 **POLAND:** 15
3 **US:** 14.5
4 **SOUTH KOREA:** 13.7
5 **SLOVENIA:** 13.7

ROBBERY

According to UN figures, the worst five countries for robbery (per 1,000 people) in 2000 were:

1 **SPAIN:** 12.3
2 **CHILE:** 6.9
3 **COSTA RICA:** 4.8
4 **SOUTH AFRICA:** 4.4
5 **ESTONIA:** 3.6

It is worth noting that these figures are only based on reported crimes. People are more likely to report crimes in countries where the police are trustworthy and effective, so they might not be a true reflection of the chances of being robbed.

DISEASE

MALARIA

According to UN figures, the worst five countries for malaria (cases per 100,000 people) in 2000 were:

1 **GUINEA:** 75,386
2 **BOTSWANA:** 48,704
3 **BURUNDI:** 48,098
4 **ZAMBIA:** 34,204
5 **MALAWI:** 25,948

HEPATITIS B

According to WHO figures, the worst five countries for hepatitis B (fatalities per million people) in 2004 were:

1 **DOMINICAN REPUBLIC:** 7.2 DEATHS
2 **BAHRAIN:** 5.8 DEATHS
3 **KYRGYSZSTAN:** 5.6 DEATHS
4 **JAPAN:** 5.3 DEATHS
5 **SOUTH KOREA:** 3.4 DEATHS

DENGUE FEVER

According to WHO figures, the worst five countries for dengue fever (fatalities per million people) in 2004 were:

1 **BARBADOS:** 7.2 DEATHS
2 **BELIZE:** 3.6 DEATHS
3 **KUWAIT:** 3 DEATHS
4 **DOMINICAN REPUBLIC:** 0.7 DEATHS
5 **ECUADOR:** 0.4 DEATHS

DIARRHEA & GASTROENTERITIS

According to WHO figures, the worst five countries for diarrhoea and gastroenteritis (fatalities per million people) in 2004 were:

1 **SOUTH AFRICA:** 172 DEATHS
2 **EGYPT:** 157 DEATHS
3 **EL SALVADOR:** 84 DEATHS
4 **VENEZUELA:** 65 DEATHS
5 **NICARAGUA:** 58 DEATHS

It's still LEGAL...

We all know human beings get up to some pretty bizarre activities, and sometimes laws have to be passed to stop them. But passing laws to make bizarre activities legal? That's either because they are old laws that have never been annulled, or because lawyers have found loopholes that make things technically legal even if they were never intended to be.

... in parts of Pakistan for a **MAN** to **SWAP HIS SISTER FOR A WIFE.**

... in Nevada to **HANG ANYONE** who shoots your dog on your property.

... in Utah to **MARRY YOUR COUSIN**—but only if you're over 50.

... in Alaska to **SHOOT A BEAR,** but **NOT TO DISTURB** its hibernation by waking it up.

... in England to **SHOOT A SCOTSMAN**—so long as you do so in Cathedral Close, York, on any day except Sunday.

... in Seattle for a woman to **SIT ON A MAN'S LAP ON A BUS OR TRAIN**—but only if their flesh is separated by a pillow.

... in Arizona for a **MAN TO BEAT HIS WIFE**—but only once a month.

... in Turkey for a married woman to **HAVE A JOB**—but only with her husband's permission.

... to **HAVE SEX** in Florida—but only in the missionary position.

... in Sweden for a woman to **BE A PROSTITUTE**—but not for a man to use her services.

... in parts of South Carolina for a **MAN TO BEAT HIS WIFE**—but only on the steps of the courthouse on a Sunday.

... in the Netherlands to **BUY, SMOKE, AND CARRY SMALL AMOUNTS OF CANNABIS.**

... in England to **SHOOT A WELSHMAN**, as long as you do so with a **BOW AND ARROW** inside Chester city walls **AFTER MIDNIGHT,** or with a longbow on a Sunday in Hereford.

... in Vermont for **WOMEN** to wear **FALSE TEETH**—but only with written permission from their husbands.

... in the Netherlands to **RUN A BROTHEL.**

... for a burglar in Michigan to **SUE A HOUSE-OWNER FOR ANY INJURIES** sustained while burgling the house.

... in Hong Kong for a betrayed wife to **KILL HER ADULTEROUS HUSBAND**— as long as she does so with her bare hands.

... for **SALESWOMEN** in Liverpool, UK, to go **TOPLESS** —but only in stores **SELLING TROPICAL FISH.**

... in Pennsylvania to use the same vehicle to deliver **CARRY-OUT FOOD** and **DEAD BODIES.**

... to **HAVE SEX** in Virginia—but only in the missionary position and only with the lights off.

... to **SNORE** in Massachusetts— but only if all the bedroom windows are closed and locked.

... in Canada to **HAVE A WATER TROUGH IN YOUR FRONT YARD**—but only if you fill it by 5 a.m.

... in Iowa for a man to **KISS A WOMAN**—but not for more than five minutes, and not if he has a moustache.

... in Paraguay to **FIGHT A DUEL,** so long as both parties are **REGISTERED BLOOD DONORS.**

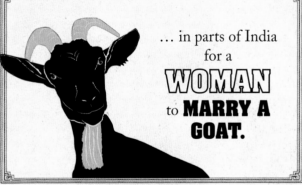

... in parts of India for a **WOMAN** to **MARRY A GOAT.**

... in Britain for a **MAN TO URINATE** in public—but only on the rear wheel of his motor vehicle and only if he's touching the vehicle with his right hand.

FOOD AND DRINK

EVERYONE LOVES A SAUSAGE

What is it about sausages? They were invented as a way of disguising, sorry, *preserving*, all the parts of various animals that no one really wanted to eat—organs, blood, fat, and gristle. Yet wherever you go in the world, everyone loves a sausage. So much so that most countries, and many individual regions within those countries, have their own characteristic version of the world's oldest processed food.

MERGUEZ
Tunisia, Algeria, Morocco. Filled with beef spiced with a chilli harissa paste. Good with couscous.

BLACK PUDDING
Ireland and northern England. Blood, fat, onions, vegetable/cereal base. Seasoning includes minty herb pennyroyal.

HAGGIS
Scotland. Sheep's stomach filled with ground sheep lungs, liver, heart, fat, salt, and oatmeal.

FRANKFURTER
Germany. The classic hot dog. Lean pork mixed with bacon fat, smoked and parboiled.

SAUCISSON AU POIVRE
France. A fresh pepper-coated sausage. Saucisson can include a variety of meats and seasonings.

ANDOUILLETTE
France. Tripe sausages served hot with mustard.

14 WAYS TO SAY SAUSAGE

DANISH: Pølse
DUTCH: Worst
ENGLISH: Sausage/banger
FINNISH: Makkara
FRENCH: Saucisse (small)/Saucisson (large)
GERMAN: Wurst
GREEK: Allantes
ICELANDIC: Pylsa
ITALIAN: Salsiccia (including the subgroup Salame)
LATIN: Salsicia/Lucanica
NORWEGIAN: Pølse
SPANISH: Salchicha
SWEDISH: Korv
TURKISH: Sosis

ENGLISH HUMORIST AND MP A. P. HERBERT ONCE WROTE THAT **"A HIGHBROW IS THE KIND OF PERSON WHO LOOKS AT A SAUSAGE AND THINKS OF PICASSO."**

GERMANY IS FAMOUS FOR ITS SAUSAGES—SOME **1,200** VARIETIES

FARINHEIRA AND MORCELA
Portugal. Farinheira is a smoked pork sausage. Morcela is a blood pudding, made with pig's blood and rice.

BRATWURST
Germany. Pork or pork-and-veal grilling sausage. Thüringer is said to be the original bratwurst.

CUMBERLAND
England. Made from coarse-cut pork and spices, sold in coils.

DROËWORS
South Africa. The shape helps dry the spicy beef/lamb before it goes bad.

KASZANKA
Poland. Pig's intestines stuffed with pig's blood and buckwheat or barley.

WEISSWURST
Germany. Delicately flavored veal; great with mild mustard.

SALAMI
Italy. Pork or pork-and-beef; spicier as you go south.

CHORIZO/CHOURIÇO
Spain/Portugal. Chopped/ground pork and pork fat with paprika.

MORCILLA
Spain. Pig's blood pudding seasoned with cinnamon, cloves, and nutmeg.

LAAP CHEONG
China. Dried, smoked sausage made with pork, fat, and seasoning.

IN 1867 US IMMIGRANT CHARLES FELTMAN, ORIGINALLY FROM FRANKFURT IN GERMANY, SOLD FRANKFURTER SANDWICHES AT CONEY ISLAND, NEW YORK— BELIEVED TO BE THE WORLD'S FIRST HOT DOGS.

One of the characters created by the ancient Greek playwright Aristophanes, in 484BCE, was a sausage seller. Aristophanes described him as a perfect politician because he minced all his policies, greased and stuffed them, and dressed them up with butcher's sauce.

Man's best friend"

Man's best friend? Not when these dogs discover that their embarrassing party photos have been seen around the world on the internet. And if it's true that dog owners look like their pets then there are some pretty weird-looking dog owners out there.

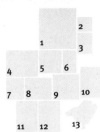

05. **FLUFFY**
    Pomeranian wearing
    bee costume
06. **WILLIS**
    dressed as Superman
07. **MAESTRO**
    in top hat and tails
08. **MEG**
    dressed as a witch
09. **COMET**
    the 10-legged spider
10. **BOXER**
    looking cool at the Rio
    de Janeiro carnival
11. **BORIS**
    in monkey costume
12. **ROXY**
    as Dorothy from the
    Wizard of Oz
13. **FRANK**
    hotdog with added
    ketchup

ELI (main photo, left)
dressed up for
Halloween
01. **PRINCE**
    in killer glamour
02. **REUBEN**
    as Pocahontas
03. **REX**
    martial arts black belt
04. **LARRY**
    wolf in sheep's clothing

TECHNOLOGY

HOW TO BE A SUPERHERO

Is it a bird? Is it a plane? No, it's you. All humans, at some point, have dreamed about having superpowers. That's why superheroes are so universally popular. But is there any chance of anyone ever being able to fly like Superman or teleport like his archrival, Lex Luther? Not yet... but scientists are working on it.

X-RAY/THERMAL VISION LIKE SUPERMAN

There are devices that can "see" through walls. Using detectors to measure electromagnetic radiation, they are so sensitive they can detect breathing and heartbeat. The police and armed forces also use thermal-imaging devices or night-vision equipment.

TELEPATHY LIKE XAVIER

Many people have claimed to have psychic abilities, but none has yet been proved. The nearest most of us will get to telepathy is a cell phone—you can communicate remotely with anyone, anywhere (if you've got their number), and if you wear a small enough earpiece and microphone no one will know how you're doing it.

CHI POWER LIKE BATMAN

Chi power gives Batman the ability to send an opponent flying across the room with a simple push. But that ability isn't restricted to superheroes: Batman learned his martial arts skills and the harnessing of chi power from a mere mortal, and so could you. Some people claim that chi power is the harnessing of an external energy force, others that it simply requires focus to channel energy from within and to send adrenalin pumping through your system at will.

RADAR OR SONAR SENSE LIKE DAREDEVIL

Radar and sonar work by sending out a signal and measuring how long the signal takes to return. Mammals are certainly capable of a similar thing—bats and dolphins use echolocation to find their way around. So it's not beyond the bounds of possibility that the human brain could adapt to do the same thing. We use our ears more than we think to orientate ourselves, and blind people rely on sound location all the time. The biggest problem would be finding a suitable signal emitter that could accurately tell us what's out there if it weren't emitting its own sounds.

FLY LIKE SUPERMAN

Sorry—not yet. The nearest you can get to flying is hang-gliding, flying a microlite, using a rocket-pack, free-fall parachuting, or one of those fairground games with a huge fan pushing you up from below. You could also try NASA's "Vomit Comet"—a converted Boeing 707 that repeatedly climbs to a height of over 6 miles (9.5 km) and then makes a parabolic dive back toward the ground, giving its occupants 30 seconds of weightlessness with each dive.

LIE-DETECTING LIKE WONDERWOMAN

Lies can be detected through body language and through measurable physical changes in the liar, such as rising blood pressure, increased breathing rate, sweaty palms and fingers, and change in voice tone. Polygraphs measure just such changes, and a person would be an equally reliable lie detector if they were able to observe these changes or to observe body language accurately.

SUPERHUMAN STRENGTH LIKE SUPERMAN OR THE INCREDIBLE HULK

Adrenalin can do amazing things to a person—for instance, there are countless stories of mothers lifting cars to prevent their babies or children from being trapped beneath them (although the number of such stories suggests it might be an urban myth). If you want a more controllable and sustained burst of strength, you could always use human hormones such as HGH or testosterone, or synthetic steroids to build up your muscle bulk—as some athletes already do. How else would people continue breaking world records?

SUPERHUMAN SENSES LIKE BATMAN OR TIGRA THE CAT

Our senses of sight, hearing, smell, and touch can all be enhanced by super-training, and particularly if one of the other senses is suppressed. The Fuegians, the near-extinct indigenous population of Tierra del Fuego, were able to see vast distances through just such training.

SHOOT WEBS LIKE SPIDERMAN

In addition to shooting out silk strands for climbing, Spiderman shoots out silk webs to catch villains—just like the NYPD, which employs "nonlethal entanglement technology" (N.E.T.—get it?!) to do the same thing. Basically, they launch a grenade that drops a 16¼ ft (5 m) diameter net over the villain. There are three types: your basic net; a conducting net that is connected to a battery and stuns the victim; and a glue-impregnated sticky net, just like Spiderman's.

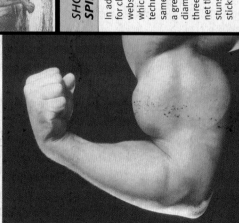

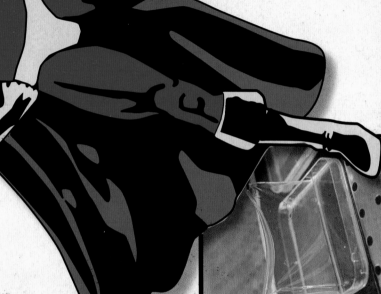

INVISIBILITY OR SHAPESHIFTING LIKE STORM

Masters of disguise, such as Carlos the Jackal, might be considered shapeshifters, and it is always possible to alter your appearance using prosthetics—look at Eddie Murphy's fat suit in *Norbit* (2007). An Anglo-American team of scientists has just worked out how to deflect microwaves around an object, making invisibility-cloaking science a possibility rather than science fiction. Another team of scientists has come up with a "see-through coat" that projects an image of whatever is behind it onto the front of it, making the wearer appear invisible.

INVULNERABILITY LIKE THE THING

Try Kevlar. It's strong, lightweight, and fire-resistant. Kevlar body armor is used by soldiers, stuntmen, firemen, and others to withstand enormous impacts and heat. Kevlar fiber is five times as strong as steel of the same weight, and when woven into a textile or fabricated into a composite material, it absorbs energy and prevents cracks from spreading from the point of impact, because fibers at this point stretch rather than breaking, dissipating energy by causing other fibers away from the impact to stretch as well.

TELEPORTATION LIKE LEX LUTHER OR NIGHTCRAWLER

Teleportation is the art of disappearing and instantly reappearing somewhere else. Some people do it regularly in a bar when it's their turn to buy drinks, but that's not quite the same— teleportation means doing it without physically moving from one location to another. It'll be a long time before it becomes possible for a human to teleport, but scientists have achieved it at quantum level with a single photon.

CLIMB LIKE SPIDERMAN

Spiderman shoots out strands of sticky silk and away he goes just like... well, a spider. Old-style ninjas and new-style free climbers may not shoot out strands of silk but they get close to Spiderman's vertical sheer climbs with their split-toe shoes and their agility. Scientists are currently working on mimicking the gecko's skin (below), which grips using millions of tiny hairs called setae, to create a material that will enable people to walk on ceilings and walls.

>URBAN MYTHS 1

From the vanishing hitchhiker to alligators in the sewer, urban myths are the new folklore. Not to be confused with conspiracy theories, urban myths are cautionary tales that play on society's subliminal hopes and fears. Always on the verge of plausibility, they are laced with a characteristic dose of mystery, horror, humor, or all three.

>THE CURSE OF JAMES DEAN'S CAR

On September 30, 1955, James Dean was killed when his Porsche Spyder crashed head on with another vehicle. Dean loved his car, which he named Little Bastard, but girlfriend Ursula Andress refused to ride in it, friend Nick Adams was unnerved by it, and when actor Alec Guinness saw it, *HE STARTED TREMBLING AND WARNED DEAN NOT TO DRIVE IT,* telling him he must get rid of it or he would be dead within a week. Less than a week later, Dean crashed on his way to a race in Salinas—Little Bastard ended up in a ditch, "like a crumpled pack of cigarettes," and Dean was dead on arrival at the ER.

The Porsche then found its way into the hands of George Barris, "the King of Kustomizing," who bought it for parts. When Barris took delivery, Little Bastard rolled off the flatbed truck and broke a mechanic's legs. Barris sold the engine to Dr. Troy McHenry and the transmission to Dr. William Eschrid, both of whom crashed during the same race in October 1956: Eschrid was seriously injured when he rolled his Porsche over, while McHenry was killed when he lost control and veered off the track. Meanwhile, Barris had sold two of Dean's tires to an unnamed man who returned a week later complaining that both tires had blown simultaneously, causing him to crash into a ditch (as Dean had done).

Barris then loaned the crumpled car body to the California Highway Patrol for a road-safety exhibition but, while it was being transported to Salinas for the exhibition, the truck carrying it skidded and crashed, killing the driver. The last time Barris saw Little Bastard was when he lent it to another road-safety exhibition in Florida in 1958. Thirty-one years later, the *Los Angeles Times* quoted him as saying that he saw the Porsche being loaded up after the exhibition but, when the truck arrived at its destination, the car had vanished. The multiple deaths associated with Little Bastard are a macabre echo of Dean's own philosophy: *"DEATH IS THE ONLY THING LEFT TO RESPECT. THE ONE INEVITABLE, UNDENIABLE TRUTH."*

>MURDER ON LOVERS' LANE

In 1964, a University of Kansas freshman was driving home from a date with his girlfriend when he had an idea: if he pretended to run out of gas, he might be able to turn it into *AN OPPORTUNITY FOR A BIT OF SLAP AND TICKLE.* He stalled the car in a suitably secluded lane but his attempts at seduction failed—and, to make matters worse, when he tried the ignition the car wouldn't start.

He told his girlfriend that he would run back to a gas station they'd passed a couple of miles back, cautioning her to lock all the doors and not, under any circumstances, to get out of the car. So the girl sat listening to the radio waiting for him to return. Then she heard a strange banging noise on the roof of the car.

She was tempted to get out and see what it was, but she remembered her boyfriend's warning to stay in the car. She turned up the radio but she could still hear the banging, louder now and more insistent. Then she saw blue flashing lights and heard a policeman telling her over a loudhailer to get out of the car and walk toward him without looking back.

She did as she was told except that at the last minute, like Lot's wife, she looked back. But instead of being turned into a pillar of salt, she saw a man she later discovered to be *AN ESCAPED PSYCHOPATH SITTING ON TOP OF THE CAR BANGING ON THE ROOF WITH HER BOYFRIEND'S BLOODY SEVERED HEAD.*

>ALLIGATORS IN THE SEWERS

Twice during the 20th century, New York has been plagued by alligators living in the labyrinth of sewers beneath the city. In February 1935, *The New York Times* carried the headline: *"ALLIGATOR FOUND IN UPTOWN SEWER: YOUTHS SHOVELING SNOW INTO MANHOLE SEE THE ANIMAL CHURNING IN ICY WATER"* above a report detailing how the youths rescued the alligator from the water, but then beat it to death with their snow shovels when it snapped at them. The Superintendent of Sewers investigated the report and found scores of alligators, which were eventually eradicated using rat poison and by shooting them in a bizarre subterranean hunt. The infestation was put down to two alligators escaping from a ship and breeding in the sewers.

Thirty years later, alligators began repopulating New York's sewers, once again prompting large-scale hunts by the city authorities. This time the problem was caused by a sudden trend among rich families who started bringing baby alligators home as pets after vacations in Florida. When the alligators grew too large to be convenient pets, the families would flush them down the toilet. Those that survived *BEGAN BREEDING IN THE SEWERS, WHERE THEY LEARNED TO LIVE OFF RATS, RAW SEWAGE*, and edible garbage. Deprived of sunlight, they developed as blind albinos, like the alligator described in Thomas Pynchon's novel *V.*

>ESCAPING THE RIPPER

In the 1970s, when serial rapist and murderer the Yorkshire Ripper was terrorizing the north of England, a young female schoolteacher was driving home after a Parent–Teacher Association meeting. She was nervous about driving through a deserted part of town in the wintry darkness. When she saw an old lady standing at a bus stop with a heavy shopping bag, she offered her a lift, partly out of good citizenship and partly for her own comfort.

ALMOST AT ONCE THE TEACHER BEGAN TO FEEL UNEASY. The old lady said nothing, responding to the teacher's attempts at conversation with incoherent coughs and grunts. Then the teacher glanced across at her passenger and was chilled to the bone when she saw that the sleeve of the old lady's coat had ridden up to reveal, in the gap between the sleeve and the top of the lady's glove, a glimpse of a hairy forearm. Thinking quickly, the teacher said that she thought one of her headlights had just blown, and asked the "lady" to get out and check while she flashed the lights on and off. As soon as the lady stepped out of the car, the teacher sped away to the nearest police station where the police examined the contents of the shopping bag, which turned out to contain *ROPE, KNIVES, TAPE, AND SURGICAL INSTRUMENTS.*

>VACATION PICS

Before the age of digital cameras, an English family decided that for their annual vacation they would go camping in Spain. All the campsites near the beaches were full but they were happy enough to find a peaceful site in some woods farther inland. They went to bed exhausted from the trip but happy and looking forward to a relaxing break.

But halfway through the night they were woken by the *THROATY ROAR OF MOTORCYCLE ENGINES* and then kept awake for several hours by the sound of loud talking, swearing, and intermittent bursts of laughter. The next morning they arose to discover that *THEIR WOODLAND IDYLL HAD BEEN SHATTERED BY THE ARRIVAL OF A CHAPTER OF HELLS ANGELS*, who proceeded to torment the family for the next week. One afternoon the family returned to the campsite to see several bikers scurrying away from the camper, but it wasn't clear whether or not they'd been inside. The family went in and checked their belongings but *NOTHING WAS MISSING*, even their daughter's camera that had been left in full view on the table.

Strangely, from that moment on the bikers seemed to lose interest in tormenting the family, who only found out what had happened when they returned home and had their photographs developed.

Along with shots of the local sights and the children playing on the beach were a dozen pictures of the Hells Angels taking turns posing, inside the camper, with the family's *TOOTHBRUSHES FIRMLY WEDGED IN THEIR BACKSIDES.*

>DEAD SCUBA DIVER IN TREE

In 1987, police in southern France found themselves dealing with a bizarre death. Forest rangers found the stiffened corpse of a diver, wearing wetsuit, mask, flippers, and breathing gear, lying trapped in the upper branches of a tree that had been charred and blackened by a recent forest fire.

The dead diver did not appear to be burned, apart from two places where *THE WETSUIT HAD MELTED ONTO HIS SKIN*, and a post mortem showed that he had died not from burns but from internal injuries consistent with being crushed. But how had he been crushed, and how had he come to be swimming in a treetop some 50 miles (80 km) from the coast? After identifying the body, police established that Monsieur Morton, a lawyer from Paris, had been vacationing in St. Tropez and that on the day of the forest fire he had been diving off the Riviera.

The only explanation for his presence in the forest was that *HE HAD BEEN SUCKED INTO THE "HELI-BUCKET" OF ONE OF THE FIREFIGHTING HELICOPTERS*, which had flown to the coast to take on water. Firefighting helicopters suck up water through an intake that is supposed to be narrow enough to prevent a person from being sucked in. However, in Mr. Morton's case, the squeeze into the bucket had evidently pulverized his bones and internal organs.

Although the chances of this happening might appear to be extremely slim, there have been reports since of divers being found in trees after forest fires in California and Australia.

THE SWEET SCIENCE

Boxing is a curious sport. Two men get into a square "ring" and try to knock each other out while wearing soft gloves so they don't hurt each other too much. To some people this is more than a sport, it's a "sweet science." To others it's primitive barbarism. For those who are undecided, here's a quick explanation of what all the fuss is about.

JACK JOHNSON
1908

White champions refused to fight black challengers until December 26, 1908. Johnson beat Tommy Burns to become the first black Heavyweight Champion of the World.

ANCIENT WORLD
FROM 1500 BCE
Boxing began with hand to hand combat and developed into a sport in northern Africa, Asia, and southern Europe. Some ancient forms of boxing involved fights to the death.

GREECE OLYMPIC GAMES FROM 688 BCE
In ancient Greece, boxing was part of army training. It became an Olympic sport in 688 BCE, when competitors wore leather straps on their hands, which were the earliest form of boxing gloves.

BROUGHTON RULES
1743
Heavyweight bare-knuckle champion Jack Broughton introduced the first rules in 1743, which included rounds, a 30-second count, and a roped-off "ring" to stop spectators from joining in.

QUEENSBERRY RULES
1867
These rules, drawn up by John Chambers for the 8th Marquis of Queensberry, included a 10-second count, three-minute rounds, and, most significantly, introduced the use of padded gloves.

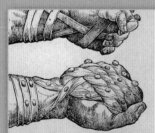

KNUCKLEDUSTERS
± YEAR 0
Boxers from India used sharks' teeth knuckledusters. Metal knuckledusters, called *cesti* (singular *cestus*), were used by Roman gladiators and freemen alike. Boxing was banned c. 500 CE by Theodoric the Great.

BARE-KNUCKLE
17TH CENTURY
The first recorded boxing match after the Romans banned the sport was in London, England, in 1681. James Figg became the first All England bare-knuckle champion in 1719.

CLASSIC BOUT JULY 4, 1919
DEMPSEY V WILLARD

Jack Dempsey, "the Manassa Mauler," knocked Jess Willard down seven times in the first round. In the third, Willard, nursing a broken jaw, nose, and ribs, instructed his trainer to throw in the towel: he threw in two, and Dempsey was proclaimed world heavyweight champion. Dempsey's 1921 title defense was boxing's first million-dollar gate.

CLASSIC BOUT JULY 22, 1938
LOUIS V SCHMELING

In 1937, Joe Louis became the first black World Heavyweight Champion since Jack Johnson. In the runup to World War II, the challenge from German Max Schmeling, who was staunchly pro-Nazi, was more than just a boxing match for fans and boxers alike. Louis demolished Schmeling in just 124 seconds, and went on to defend his title a record 25 times in 11 years.

CLASSIC BOUT SEPTEMBER 23, 1952
MARCIANO ∨ WALCOTT

Rocky Marciano is the only boxer to win all his professional bouts, but he nearly lost this world heavyweight title fight to Jersey Joe Walcott. Marciano took a pounding and, behind on points, needed a KO to win. It came in the 13th, when he delivered what is often described as the hardest punch ever thrown.

CLASSIC BOUT FEBRUARY 20, 2000
MORALES ∨ BARRERA

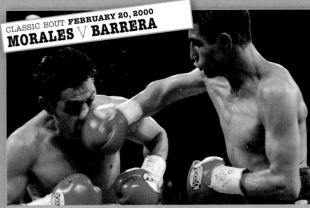

A great fight but a controversial outcome. Super Featherweight Champion Erik "El Terrible" Morales retained his WBC title and took the WBO title from Marco Antonio Barrera. One judge favored Morales by one point and another Barrera by one point. The casting vote went to Morales by three points.

QUICKEST KO
1946
Al Couture knocked out Ralph Walton after only 10.5 seconds, including the count. Couture must have left his corner before the bell—and struck while Walton was still adjusting his gum shield.

REFEREE KO
1978
One of boxing's stranger moments came when boxer Randy Shields accidentally floored referee Tom Kelly in the 9th round of a bout against Sugar Ray Leonard in Baltimore.

DON KING
1972–PRESENT
One of boxing's most flambuoyant characters is promoter Don King, who organized several legendary fights, such as the Rumble in the Jungle and the Thriller in Manilla.

WALLITSCH KO
1959
Henry Wallitsch is the only boxer to knock himself out. He swung to hit Bartolo Soni but Soni dodged and Wallitsch's momentum carried him over the ropes to hit his head on the arena floor.

CASSIUS CLAY TITLE
1964
Cassius Clay took on Sonny Liston as a 7–1 no-hoper. At the weigh-in, Clay said he would "float like a butterfly, sting like a bee." He did just that, and became World Heavyweight Champion.

CLASSIC BOUT MARCH 8, 1971
ALI ∨ FRAZIER

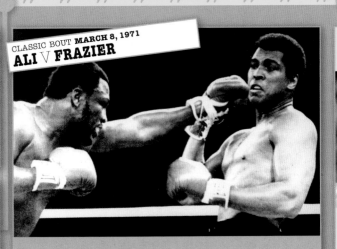

Known as "The Fight," this was the first time two undefeated heavyweight champions had met in the ring—Muhammad Ali had been stripped of his title for refusing the Vietnam draft and Joe Frazier had taken it in his absence. Frazier won on points after a grueling encounter, but Ali won two rematches.

MIKE TYSON
1986

In 1986, Tyson became the youngest boxer to win a world heavyweight title. Sadly, he tarnished his reputation with a rape conviction in 1992, and by biting off part of Evander Holyfield's ear in 1997.

CLASSIC BOUT **NOVEMBER 15, 1957**
FULLMER ∨ RIVERS

Twice world middleweight champion Gene Fullmer takes a nose-crunching right from Neal Rivers during a bout at Madison Square Garden, New York City. Amazingly, Fullmer survived the punch and went on to win by a majority decision.

MEET AND DRINK

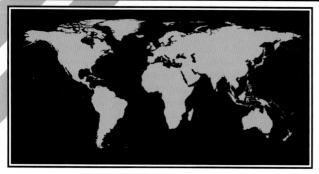

C $_2$**H**$_5$**OH**, better known as alcohol, is the oldest and probably the most widely used drug ever manufactured by humans—people have been fermenting wine since at least 5000 BCE. And wherever you are in the drinking world there's one universally recognized gesture: raising a glass as a bond of friendship. Here are the right words to accompany that gesture in 56 countries around the world.

"Gesondheid"
to your health
AFRIKAANS

"Gëzuar"
happiness
ALBANIAN

"Cheers"
cheers
AMERICAN ENGLISH

"Fisehatak"
to your health
ARABIC

"Skål"
good cheer
(literally "bowl", as in drinking bowl)
BAHASA INDONESIA

"On egin"
to your health
BASQUE

"Na zdrave"
to your health
BULGARIAN

"Gom bui"
dry the cup
CANTONESE

"Genatzt"
life
CARMENIAN

"Salut"
greetings/good health
CATALAN

"Zivjeli"
live long
CROATIAN

"Na zdravi"
to your health
CZECH

"Skål" *good cheer*
(literally "bowl", as in drinking bowl)
DANISH

"Proost"
good cheer
DUTCH

"Fee sihetak/Bisochtak"
to your health
EGYPTIAN

"Cheers", "Your good health", "Bottoms up" *drink up*
ENGLISH

"Je via sano"
to your health
ESPERANTO

"Tervist"
to your health
ESTONIAN

"Kippis"
good cheer
FINNISH

"Op uw gezondheid"
to your health
FLEMISH

"A votre santé"
to your health
FRENCH

"Sláinte"
to your health
GAELIC (IRISH)

"Slaandjivaa"
to your health
GAELIC (SCOTTISH)

"Prost" *good cheer*; "Zum Wohl" (formal) *to your health*
GERMAN

The world's first gin-and-vermouth cocktail (now known as a Dry Martini) was mixed by bartender Jerry Thomas at the Occidental Hotel, San Francisco, in 1860. American writer H. L. Mencken called the cocktail "the only American invention as perfect as a sonnet."

TOP FIVE CONSUMERS OF BEER

Pints of beer per person over the age of 15 per week, 2003

1. CZECH REPUBLIC   6.32 EST
2. IRELAND   6.05
3. GERMANY   4.64
4. AUSTRIA   4.43
5. LUXEMBOURG   4.24

CHAMPAGNE BOTTLE NAMES

1/4 bottle	Picolo
1/2 bottle	Filette (or demi)
2 bottle	Magnum
4 bottle	Jeroboam
6 bottle	Rehoboam
8 bottle	Methuselah
12 bottle	Salmanazar
16 bottle	Balthazar
20 bottle	Nebuchadnezzar
24 bottle	Melchior

1/4   1/2   2   4   6   8   12   16   20   24

"ONE OF THE DISADVANTAGES OF WINE IS IT MAKES A MAN MISTAKE WORDS FOR THOUGHTS." SAMUEL JOHNSON

"Ebiba"
drink
GREEK

"Okole maluna"
bottoms up
HAWAIIAN

"L'chaim"
to life
HEBREW

"Kedves egeszsegere"
to your health
HUNGARIAN

"Salute"
greetings/good health
ITALIAN

"Kampai"
drain your glass
JAPANESE

"Kong gang ul wi ha yo"
good luck
KOREAN

"Uz veselibu"
to your health
LATVIAN

"Kesak" *good cheer*
(literally "your glass")
LEBANESE

"I sveikata"
to your health
LITHUANIAN

"Gan bei"
dry the cup
MANDARIN

"Kia ora"
greetings
MAORI

"Salud"
greetings/good health
MEXICAN

"Skål" *good cheer (literally
"bowl", as in drinking bowl)*
NORWEGIAN

"Na zdrowie"
to your health
POLISH

"Saúde"
greetings/good health
PORTUGUESE

"Noroc"
Good luck
ROMANIAN

"Na zdorovje"
to your health
RUSSIAN

"Ziveli"
live long
SERBIAN

"Na zdravie"
to your health
SLOVAK

"Na zdravje"
to your health
SLOVENIAN

"Auguryo"
good luck
SOMALIAN

"Salud"
greetings/good health
SPANISH

"Hongera"
be proud
SWAHILI

"Skål" *good cheer*
(literally "bowl", as in drinking bowl)
SWEDISH

"Hotala"
drain your glass
TAIWANESE

"Choc-tee"
greetings
THAI

"Serefe"
to honour
TURKISH

"Djam"
cheers
URDU

"Chia"
drink up
VIETNAMESE

"Lechyd da"
good health
WELSH

"Mazel tov"
good luck
YIDDISH

BELGIUM IS THE WORLD'S BEER PARADISE, WITH MORE THAN 450 VARIETIES OF BEER BREWED THERE

DRINKING AND DRIVING LIMITS

COUNTRY	(mg/100 ml)		
Australia	50	Italy	80
Canada	80	Portugal	50
Denmark	50	Spain	50
France	50	UK	80
Germany	50	US	0.08–0.10
Ireland	80	(blood alcohol concentration %)	

TOP FIVE CONSUMERS OF WINE

Bottles of wine per person over the age of 15 per week, 2003 (based on 75 cl bottle)

1. LUXEMBOURG	2.08	EST
2. FRANCE	1.52	
3. ITALY	1.42	
4. PORTUGAL	1.29	
5. SWITZERLAND	1.26	

The 50s was the decade when Hollywood took off its clothes and sex appeal came out of the closet—starting in 1953 when Marilyn Monroe and Jane Russell set a trend for curves and cleavage in *Gentlemen Prefer Blondes*. Meanwhile, Dean and Brando taught men to smoulder, and "Elvis the Pelvis" drove girls wild with hip-gyrating antics.

50s PIN-UPS

1 **2**

3 **5**

4

6 **7** **8**

MARILYN MONROE
(main photo, left) "Not so much a Hollywood legend as *the* Hollywood legend" *The Times*.
01. JAMES DEAN
looking mean and moody.

02. ELVIS PRESLEY
wowed the girls and shocked the parents.
03. AVA GARDNER
witty, sexy, green-eyed legend.
04. JAYNE MANSFIELD
dubbed "Queen of the Erogenous Zones."
05. BRIGITTE BARDOT
whose initals made her Bébé.
06. AUDREY HEPBURN
50s men dreamed she was their Huckleberry friend.
07. MARLON BRANDO
smouldering in *The Wild One*.
08. SYDNEY POITIER
suave and stylish.

THE BODY
IS MEANT
TO BE SEEN.
NOT ALL
COVERED UP

Marilyn Monroe

GREAT ESCAPES

HENRI CHARRIÈRE, AKA PAPILLON (BUTTERFLY)

In 1931, 25-year-old Parisian gangster Henri Charrière was sentenced to life imprisonment for murdering a pimp—a charge he denied. Two years later, just 42 days after arriving in the penal colony of French Guiana, he knocked out the guards in the hospital wing and travelled more than 1,000 miles (1,600 km) in an open boat before being recaptured in Colombia in 1934. After several more escape attempts he was put in solitary confinement, then sent to the notorious, supposedly escape-proof, Devil's Island, 25 miles (40 km) off the coast of French Guiana. Papillon found one place on the island where the currents might allow him to launch a raft, and built one from jute sacks filled with coconuts. In 1941, he and an accomplice launched their raft into the shark-infested waters, surviving over 40 hours without food, drink, or shelter before being washed up on shore and making their way to Venezuela, where they were eventually granted citizenship.

HENRY McCARTY, AKA BILLY THE KID

Legend has it that Billy the Kid first murdered at the age of 12 and went on to kill 21 men, one for each year of his life. On December 19, 1880, Sheriff Pat Garrett captured 20-year-old Billy, who was sentenced to hang. Garrett warned his guards, "if this man is shown the slightest chance on Earth he will... murder the whole lot of you." Despite the warning, and leg irons and handcuffs, Billy escaped. On April 28, 1881, he asked guard James W. Bell to take him to the bathroom. Billy slipped a handcuff, hit Bell in the face with the chain, grabbed his revolver, and shot him dead. He shot another guard, Robert Olinger, before forcing a fellow prisoner to hack off his chains. Garrett tracked Billy down to Fort Sumner, New Mexico. At midnight on July 14, Garrett entered the bedroom of Pete Maxwell, a mutual acquaintance, to quiz him about Billy. Billy came into the dark room and asked Maxwell who was with him—Garrett recognized Billy's voice and shot him dead.

Everybody wants to be free, and that's why escapes are so inspiring—even when they're carried out by guilty men who deserve to be locked up for their crimes. Of the 10 great escapes featured here, six were made by innocent people and four by convicted criminals, but they've all become part of escaping folklore.

GIACOMO (JACQUES) CASANOVA

Best known for his sexual exploits, Casanova was also a gambler, alchemist, director of state lotteries, spy, and police informer. In 1755, he was imprisoned in Venice for "public outrages against religion," but within a year he escaped. He found an iron bar in the prison yard, which he smuggled back to his cell and used to dig a tunnel. The tunnel was discovered and he had to move cells, but he didn't give up. He still had the bar, so, knowing he would be watched closely now, he gave it to the prisoner in the next cell and told him to dig two tunnels: one linking their cells and one to the yard. Once out of their cells they reached the main entrance, using the iron bar to lever open locked doors, but the main doors were impenetrable. They had to wait for someone to open them and then run, before splitting up to foil their pursuers. The plan was successful, and Casanova fled to France to continue his adventures.

JOHN ANGLIN, CLARENCE ANGLIN, AND FRANK MORRIS

On June 11, 1962, three men made the escape that inspired the Clint Eastwood film *Escape from Alcatraz*. As soon as Morris was sent to Alcatraz, in 1961, he thought of escape. Using nail clippers, he scratched at the concrete around a ventilator shaft in his cell; then, soldering the clippers to a cafeteria spoon using matches and silver scraped from a dime, he fashioned a tool that made work quicker. When the hole was big enough he made a papier-mâché head, which he left in his bunk while he explored the ventilation system. He found he would need help in getting past a metal bar sealing the ventilation system from the outside world, so he recruited the Anglin brothers. Over six months the three men used wire and a small saw to cut through the bar before escaping the island on makeshift rafts. No one knows whether the escape succeeded because they have never been tracked down—nor have their bodies ever been found.

RUDOLF VRBA AND ARTHUR WETZLER

Rudolf Vrba and Arthur Wetzler escaped from the notorious Nazi concentration camp at Auschwitz on April 10, 1943, two of only about 80 prisoners who succeeded in doing so. In the days leading up to the escape, they managed to make a hiding place in a pile of wood situated just outside the prisoners' compound but inside the camp security zone, liberally sprinkling the area around the woodpile with alcohol and tobacco to put off sniffer dogs. On April 7, they hid in the woodpile just before the evening roll call and watched for three days and nights as the Germans carried out a massive manhunt. When the hunt was abandoned, they escaped under cover of darkness. Moving only at night, they reached their native Slovakia on April 21.

GEORGE BLAKE

British spy George Blake began acting for the KGB as a double agent around 1953. He was exposed in 1960 and, at a secret Old Bailey trial in 1961, he was sentenced to 42 years' imprisonment. But in 1966 he was sprung from Wormwood Scrubs by three former prisoners whom he had befriended while they were still inside. The plan was simple: Blake's accomplices thought they had a 20-minute window between security patrols in which to throw a rope ladder over a particular spot on the wall. On October 22, 1966, Sean Bourke drove into an adjacent street to throw the ladder, but a security guard approached him so he drove off. By the time he returned, Blake was panicking that the opportunity had been lost, but the ladder appeared and he climbed over the 20-ft (6-m) wall. He then hid in his accomplices' apartment since, with all ports and airports being guarded, they realized getting Blake out of the country wouldn't be easy. In the end, they built a secret compartment in a small van. On December 17, they left the UK via Dover and drove to the East German border, where Blake made himself known to the authorities.

MICHAEL KRUPA

In 1939, Polish cavalry officer Michael Krupa was sentenced to 10 years' hard labor at the Pechora Gulag in Siberia. His chance came when he was appointed to maintain the region's telephone poles—a job that came with a horse. He sabotaged the local exchange's connection to the town of Sosnogorsk, which he knew had a railroad station. He then volunteered to ride to Sosnogorsk and mend the supposed fault. He boarded a train and headed south, but at Kirov he was discovered by the NKVD (the precursor of the KGB), which summarily executed him at the side of the road. Krupa later said: "I should really be dead. If somebody puts a revolver to your ear, pulls the trigger and a bullet comes out the other side, well, would you expect to be alive? No." A railroad worker and his wife discovered Krupa, nursed him back to health, and lent him their son's railroad uniform. He traveled by rail nearly 2,000 miles (3,220 km) farther south to Samarkand, Uzbekistan (then part of the USSR), within walking distance of Afghanistan. A great storm sent the sentries inside and he took the opportunity to cross the border to freedom.

> "IF SOMEBODY PUTS A REVOLVER TO YOUR EAR AND PULLS THE TRIGGER ... WOULD YOU EXPECT TO BE ALIVE? NO."

HENRY "BOX" BROWN

Born a slave in 1815, Brown accepted his lot and worked in a tobacco factory in Richmond, Virginia, where he married another slave named Nancy and had at least three children. But in 1848 Nancy and their children were sold to a preacher from North Carolina. Determined to see them again, Brown arranged for two friends to mail him to Pennsylvania, which in 1780 had become the first state to abolish slavery. On March 23, 1848, his friends packed him into a small wooden crate, with three breathing holes drilled in the side. Despite marking the crate "This Way Up", Brown had to endure hours of the 275-mile (443-km) journey upside down. After 26 hours of confinement, he arrived in Philadelphia, where he was taken in by abolitionist James Miller McKim. Brown subsequently became a prominent abolitionist, but the man who had helped him, white merchant Samuel Smith, was later imprisoned for smuggling two other slaves to free states.

GÜNTER WETZEL AND PETER STRELZYK

In the 28 years of the Berlin Wall's existence, at least 75 people died trying to escape across it. One of the most daring escapes was that of Peter Strelzyk and Günter Wetzel in September 1979 aboard a homemade hot-air balloon with their wives and children. Inspired by a television documentary about hot-air balloons, Wetzel and Strelzyk spent two years secretly building a basket and gas burners while their wives used curtains, sheets, and whatever other fabric they could find to sew a balloon 60 ft (18 m) in diameter and 75 ft (23 m) high. In June, their first attempt failed but, on September 15, they took off successfully. Using a converted barometer as an altimeter, they navigated as best they could, drifting over the border and landing near a farm after running out of fuel for the burner, unsure at first if they had flown far enough. The Strelzyks returned to their hometown of Poessneck in 1999.

CHARLES GLASS

When peacekeeping forces left Lebanon in 1984, insurgents began taking foreign hostages to gain political influence. On June 16, 1985, American journalist Charles Glass was taken from his car by armed radicals, who chained him up, blindfolded, for 62 days before he escaped. Taking off his blindfold at night while his guards slept, Glass worked out that, if the chain around his ankle were locked on the 18th link not the 14th, he could slip it and escape. Using thread picked from the blindfold, he tied two links of the chain together to make it appear tighter. The next day, after his bathroom break, the guard locked it on the 15th link instead of the 14th, Glass did the same for three more days until he had to escape the room. That night he untied the thread and removed his foot, but still had to escape the room. He climbed out of the window only to see he was near the top floor of a hotel, with no hope of jumping or reaching a balcony. He had to go back into the room, past his sleeping guards, and out of the door, which he locked behind him to delay pursuit. He then hitched a ride into Beirut, where he notified the authorities of his escape.

SUPERSIZE MAKI

DIFFICULTY RATING:
>VERY EASY   >EASYISH   >MODERATE   >A BIT TRICKY

Maki is the name for the little seaweed-wrapped rolls that are part of any self-respecting selection of sushi (sushi is rice and raw fish). But for anyone with a decent appetite, *little* seaweed rolls are never going to be enough, so here's how to make a mammoth version (with cooked fish).

INGREDIENTS

3 Nori (seaweed) sheets
18 oz (500 g) nishiki (sushi) rice
2 cans of tuna in oil
2 peppers (1 red, 1 green)

METHOD

1 First you need to cook the nishiki rice. Keep your eye on it. It needs at least 20 minutes in boiling water, then turn off the heat, cover it with a lid, and leave for a further 10 minutes before draining.

2 The most vital component of the mammoth maki to differentiate it from a pile of rice is, of course, the seaweed. Cut the Nori sheets into strips.

3 Use the Nori sheets to line a springform cake pan. In usual sushi-making, you roll the Nori sheets, with their stuffing, into a big, compacted log. But for this huge sushi, you'd need a Nori sheet the size of a comforter and arms like Popeye, so here's an alternative method.

4 Place a glass in the middle of the cake pan, surround it with the cooked rice, and press down tightly. Allow to cool. Drain the tuna. Remove the glass and fill the space with the chunks of tuna.

5 Wash and cut the peppers into slices and poke into the center of the tuna.

6 And there it is! To serve, you'll need two tomato stakes to use as chopsticks, the largest bottle of soy sauce you can find, and a business letter-sized piece of pickled ginger to rest on the top.

The mammoth maki sitting alongside a standard-sized maki for comparison.

BIG FEATS

R ecords are made to be broken, but a first can never be taken away. That's why humans remember the first people to fly a plane, climb Everest, and walk on the Moon. But going over Niagara Falls in a barrel? Walking across the Atlantic? Why do people do these things? The answer is the same as George Mallory gave when asked why he wanted to climb Everest —"Because it's there."

FIRST TO WALK THE ATLANTIC

In the 15th century, Leonardo da Vinci sketched "flotation shoes" for walking on water. On April 2, 1988, 500 years later, 38-year-old Frenchman Rémy Bricka left the Canary Islands on a pair of 14 ft (4.25 m) fiberglass "shoes" and set off for the Caribbean towing a small raft containing fishing tackle, compass, sextant, and desalinators for fresh water. Call it walking, call it upright rowing, but after 3,502 miles (5,636 km) at an average 50 miles (80 km) a day, Bricka was picked up off Trinidad: the first person to walk across the Atlantic.

FIRST TO GO OVER NIAGARA IN A BARREL

Widowed American schoolteacher Annie Edson Taylor decided to find fame and fortune by attempting to become the first person to survive the plunge over Niagara Falls. On her 46th birthday, October 24, 1901, she stepped out of a rowboat on the Niagara River and into an oak pickle barrel, which had been padded with a mattress and weighed down with an anvil. Her friends sealed her in and set her adrift at 4:05 p.m., and watched as her barrel floated toward the Horseshoe Falls and over the edge before plunging 58 yd (53 m) to the water below. Other friends plucked the barrel out of the water at 4:40 p.m. and unsealed it to find daredevil Annie bruised but well.

TWIN TOWERS TIGHTROPE

110 stories

French funambulist Philippe Petit said: "When I see three oranges, I juggle; when I see two towers, I walk." On August 7, 1974, after six years' planning, he stepped onto his rope 1,350 ft (410 m) above ground to make the 150 ft (45 m) illegal walk between the towers. Charges were dropped and he was instead given a lifetime pass to the Observation Deck.

150 feet between the towers

SKI EVEREST
29,029
feet

TIGHTROPE ACROSS NIAGARA

The first person to cross the Niagara River on a tightrope was the Frenchman Jean François Gravelet, aka Charles Blondin, on June 30, 1859—an achievement described by The New York Times as: "The greatest feat of the Nineteenth Century." It took Blondin 20 minutes to walk his 1,100 ft (335 m) long, 3 in (7.5 cm) diameter manilla rope, stretched across the Niagara Gorge a mile downstream of the Falls. He made eight more crossings that summer, on one occasion even carrying his manager, Harry Colcord, on his back.

POGO POWER

On July 23, 1999, American Ashrita Furman was the first to climb all 1,899 steps of Canada's CN Tower on a pogo stick. Furman was also the first person to pogo stick underwater, to climb the foothills of Mt. Fuji on a pogo stick, and to pogo stick in Antarctica. His firsts without a pogo stick include skipping a full marathon and hopping a mile on one leg.

At 08:00 on October 7, 2000, 37-year-old Slovenian extreme skier Davo Karničar pushed off from the summit of Everest and skied down the world's highest peak, arriving at Base Camp (at 17,520 ft/ 5,340 m) five hours later. Not content with that, he was the first to ski down the highest peak on each continent, ending with Mt. Vinson, Antarctica, on November 11, 2006.

PEDAL FLIGHT

On June 12, 1979, American racing cyclist and hang-glider pilot Bryan Allen became the first person to fly a man-powered aircraft across the English Channel. He pedaled the Gossamer Albatross for 2 hours 49 minutes at an average altitude of 5 ft (1.5 m).

FIRST ROCKETPACK ALTITUDE RECORD

50 yards

On April 20, 2004, Texan stuntman Eric Scott, aka Rocketman, wearing a backpack powered by gas jets, flew to a height of 50 yd (46 m)—roughly that of a 12-story building. Scott, who first used a rocketpack on Michael Jackson's 1992 tour, said: "… it's like a dream that is reality. When I go to the top I did a little pirouette, which was fun."

JANUARY

Ganna, Ethiopia

This Christmas festival is named after a hockeylike game said to have been played by Ethiopian shepherds to celebrate Christ's birth. Festivities begin on Christmas Eve (Jan 6—which is Dec 24 under the old Julian calendar). Crowds gather in Lalibela for ceremonies in churches hewn from rock hillsides.

MARCH

St. Patrick's Day, Ireland

The feast day of Ireland's patron saint (March 17) is marked with public holiday parades, stout (beer), and rivers dyed green. It is celebrated not just in Ireland, but in cities around the world with Irish communities; and not just by the Irish, but by millions of self-declared honorary Irish people.

FEBRUARY

Rio Carnival, Brazil

With more than half a million tourists coming here every February for this one event, Rio de Janeiro is the Carnival Capital of the World. Four days of festivities culminate on Fat Tuesday—the day before the Christian period of Lent—with the Rio Carnival Parade, also known as the Samba Parade.

APRIL

Fête des Maques, Mali

A festival of masks is celebrated in April and May in the villages of the Dogon people of central Mali. Masks play an important role in Dogon culture, and in this 1,000 year-old annual festival they are used to remember the dead and to give thanks for the harvest.

CUSTOMS AND ETIQUETTE

WORLD PARTY

Whatever the time of year, there's always a BIG party going on somewhere in the world. Whether you want to get beer soaked in Germany, mud soaked at Glastonbury in England, or just tomato soaked in Bunol, here is the best of the best, all year round.

MONTH BY MONTH DIRECTORY

BURNS NIGHT, *Scotland,* Jan 25. Celebration of Scotland's national poet, with whisky and haggis, neeps, and tatties.

AUSTRALIA DAY, *Australia,* Jan 26. Fireworks to celebrate British arrival in 1788; day of mourning for Aborigines.

ST. VALENTINE'S DAY, *Western countries,* Feb 14. A festival in which lovers treat each other to flowers, chocolates, and sexy underwear, and anonymous cards are sent.

CHINESE NEW YEAR Dates vary with moon. Called the Spring Festival in Chinese, it ends with a Lantern Festival.

JAN   **FEB**

SEPTEMBER

Burning Man, US

A recent but fast-growing event, the Burning Man festival in the Nevada Desert is a Californian return to hippy ideals. The temporary city of Black Rock springs up to house thousands of people who enjoy the alternative outlook for a week. It culminates in burning a 50 ft (15 m) high wooden effigy of a man.

OCTOBER

Oktoberfest, Germany

Beer drinkers' paradise, Oktoberfest is the world's largest fair. Some 6 million people visit Munich for the 16–18-day festival. The first Oktoberfest was held in 1810 to celebrate the marriage of Crown Prince Ludwig to Princess Therese. The venue, the 104-acre (42-hectare) Theresienwiese, is named after her.

MAY

Rose Festival, Morocco

An oasis makes the Dadès Valley ideal for growing roses. Their tons of petals are pressed for perfume oil. Every May the locals gather in the town of El-Kelaâ M'Gouna to celebrate the rose harvest with music, singing, folk dancing, and banqueting, and to elect the annual belle, Miss Rose.

JUNE

Glastonbury Festival, UK

The world's largest greenfield music and performing arts festival, Glastonbury is famous for the tented city that springs up, and for the all-enveloping mud if it rains. Nearly 400 live-music, dance, theater, and circus acts take place over three days in front of 150,000 people on a 900-acre (364-hectare) site.

JULY

Gion Matsuri, Japan

Japan's most famous festival takes place in Kyoto all July. The centerpiece is the Yamaboko parade on July 17. For three nights beforehand traffic is banned from the city center, which becomes a fairground with stalls and people in traditional dress. The parade is rooted in a ceremony of purification.

AUGUST

La Tomatina, Spain

Some 30,000 people travel to Bunol for an annual tomato fight, which first took place in 1944 seemingly for the sheer fun of it. La Tomatina begins with a race to dislodge a large ham from a greasy pole, followed by two hours of tomato throwing before the fire brigade hoses down the streets.

DOLL FESTIVAL, *Japan,* Mar 3. Dolls are displayed for luck, echoing an ancient festival of floating dolls down rivers.

BOUAKÉ CARNIVAL, *Ivory Coast.* A week-long masked carnival in March/April in Bouaké, the second largest city.

PASSOVER, *Israel, et al.* Commemorates the Israelite Exodus from Egypt and the founding of the Jewish nation.

EASTER, *Christian countries.* Christ's resurrection merges with pagan spring rite, hence bunnies and chocolate eggs.

ABOAKYIR FESTIVAL, *Ghana.* Dancing and game hunting celebrate the Simpa migration from Sudan to Ghana.

UCHINADA, *Japan.* International traditional and modern kite festival, with flyers dressed in traditional costume.

NORTHERN SOLSTICE, *World,* June 21. Midsummer rite in the northern hemisphere and midwinter in the southern.

CHERRY HARVEST FESTIVAL, *Morocco,* Atlas mountains. Villagers process by torchlight and crown a Cherry Queen.

PAMPLONA BULL RUN, *Spain,* July 7–14. Each morning enraged bulls chase competitors through the streets.

INDEPENDENCE DAY, *US,* July 4. Celebration of Declaration of Independence from Britain in 1776.

NEWPORT JAZZ AND FOLK FESTIVALS, *US.* The 1965 Folk Festival was the scene of Bob Dylan's electric debut.

EDINBURGH FESTIVAL, *Scotland.* International festival of opera, music, and theater, plus the "fringe" festival.

FESTA DE LA MERCÈ *Barcelona, Spain.* Four-day street carnival and assertion of Catalonian identity.

DIECIOCHO (FIESTAS PATRIS). *Chile,* Sept 18–19. A two-day celebration of independence that stretches to a week.

NAVARTI, *India.* The Indian month of Ashwin, at the end of the monsoon, sees a nine-day music and dance festival.

HALLOWEEN, *English-speaking countries.* All Hallows Evening is now an excuse for horror films and mischief.

DIWALI (FESTIVAL OF LIGHTS). *Hindu, Sikh, and Jain.* Oct/Nov. Earthenware lamps are lit as symbols of hope.

MOMBASA CARNIVAL, *Kenya.* Two spectacular multireligion, multireligion parades join in a grand finale.

SOUTHERN SOLSTICE, *World,* Dec 21. Midsummer rite in the southern hemisphere and midwinter in the northern.

NEW YEAR'S EVE, *World.* Spectacular firework displays; the cream of the crop at Brazil's Copacabana Beach.

| MARCH | APRIL | MAY | JUNE | JULY | AUG | SEPT | OCT | NOV | DEC |

NOVEMBER

Day of the Dead, Mexico

Mexico is the most famous celebrant of this festival, common to South America, Asia, and Africa. Days of the Dead are not morbid, but a celebration of lives past and the afterlife to come. Although it takes place on All Saints' Day and All Souls' Day (Nov 1 and 2), the festival has pre-Christian roots.

DECEMBER

Junkanoo, Bahamas

Junkanoo is a bright, rhythmic parade that starts early the day after Christmas and goes until dawn—and then happens again on New Year's Day. The music of cowbells, goat-skin drums, whistles, an d horns fills the air as themed groups of up to 1,000 people parade the streets hoping to win prizes.

FLORA AND FAUNA

SUPERHUMAN

When you land on this planet you might think that all humans look the same. One head, two arms, two legs, etc. But a closer look would reveal that there are differences—some people are taller than others, some have more fingers and toes, one can pull the skin of his neck up over his face. Here's a selection of a few human extremes.

LONGEST MOUSTACHE It took Indian Kalyan Ramji Sain 17 years to grow his 11 ft 1 in (3.39 m) moustache. He didn't trim it evenly, though. The right side is 5 ft 7½ in (1.72 m) and the left is 5 ft 5½ in (1.67 m). **LONGEST BEARD (WOMAN)** American Janice Deveree's beard measured 14 in (36 cm) in 1884. She was imaginatively known as the Bearded Lady. **LONGEST BEARD (MAN)** Norwegian Hans Langseth started growing a beard in 1876 at the age of 30. When he died at 81, it was a record 17½ ft (5.33 m) long. It is on display at the Smithsonian in Washington, D.C.

FEWEST FINGERS AND TOES Some members of the Wadomo tribe in Zimbabwe and the Kalanga tribe in Botswana suffer from an inherited genetic mutation leading to a condition known as ectrodactyly. As a result they develop clawlike hands and feet with only two fingers or toes on each.

LONGEST NECKS From the age of 5 the women of Southeast Asian Paduang tribe (aka Kayan) elongate their necks by wearing brass coils. The ideal woman has 30–40 coils.

LARGEST BELLY Gut barging involves two fat men trying to knock each other over with their bellies. In 2001 English champion gut barger David White, who competes under the stage name Mad Maurice Vanderkirkoff, had a belly circumference of 54¼ in (137.7 cm)... not to be confused with the largest waist, which, at 119 in (302 cm), belonged to American Walter Hudson (d. 1991). That's well over three times the size of the average waist.

STRETCHIEST SKIN Using the stage name Gary Tiberius Stretch, UK's Gary Turner amazes onlookers with his elastic skin. As one of only nine sufferers of Ehlers-Danlos Syndrome, defective collagen means Gary's skin stretches nearly 6¼ in (16 cm)—enough to pull his neck over his mouth.

BIGGEST BICEPS Twenty years of steroids and dumbbell curls have given American Greg Valentino the world's biggest biceps, at 27½ in (70 cm), which is larger than a slim woman's waist. The former record holder was Denis Sester with 30½ in (77.8 cm).

LONGEST FINGERNAILS American Lee Redmond has been growing her nails since 1979. At the time of going to press they measured a total of just over 8 yd/24 ft (7.51 m), the longest nail being the left thumb, at 31½ in (80 cm).

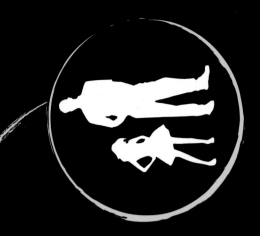

TALLEST American Robert Pershing Wadlow measured 8 ft 11 in (2.72 m) shortly before he died in 1940—more than 4½ times the height of Gul Mohammed (see below).

SMALLEST WAIST For 10 years, between 1929 and 1939, Englishwoman Ethel Granger used corsets to reduce her waist size gradually by nearly half, from almost 23 in (56 cm) to 13 in (33 cm). American Cathie Jung is currently doing a similar thing, and has reduced her waist to 15 in (38.1 cm), the smallest of any living adult. The average British woman has a waist of almost 34 in (86 cm).

TALLEST MARRIED COUPLE On June 17, 1871, Anna Swan married Martin Van Buren Bates in St. Martin's-in-the-Fields, London. The groom was a massive 7 ft 2½ in (2.2 m) tall, and the bride was 3 in (7.5 cm) taller, giving them a combined height of 14 ft 8 in (4.47 m). The greatest height difference between a bride and groom was between French couple Fabien Pretou and Natalie Lucius, who married in April 1990: he is 6 ft 2 in (1.88 m) and she is half his height, at 3 ft 1 in (94 cm).

MOST FINGERS AND TOES As a result of a condition known as polydactylism, Indian Devendra Harne has six digits on each hand, six toes on his left foot, and seven toes on his right: a total of 25—the most of any living person. Historically the greatest number recorded is 50, comprising 13 fingers on each hand and 12 toes on each foot. English Queen Anne Boleyn had an extra finger, West Indian cricketer Sir Gary Sobers had an extra finger on each hand, and World Champion darts player Eric Bristow has an extra toe.

SHORTEST As a full-grown adult, Indian Gul Mohammed (d. 1997) measured just 22½ in (57 cm) tall—that's below knee height compared with a 6 ft (1.83 m) person.

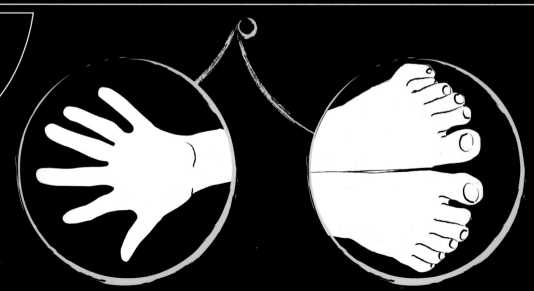

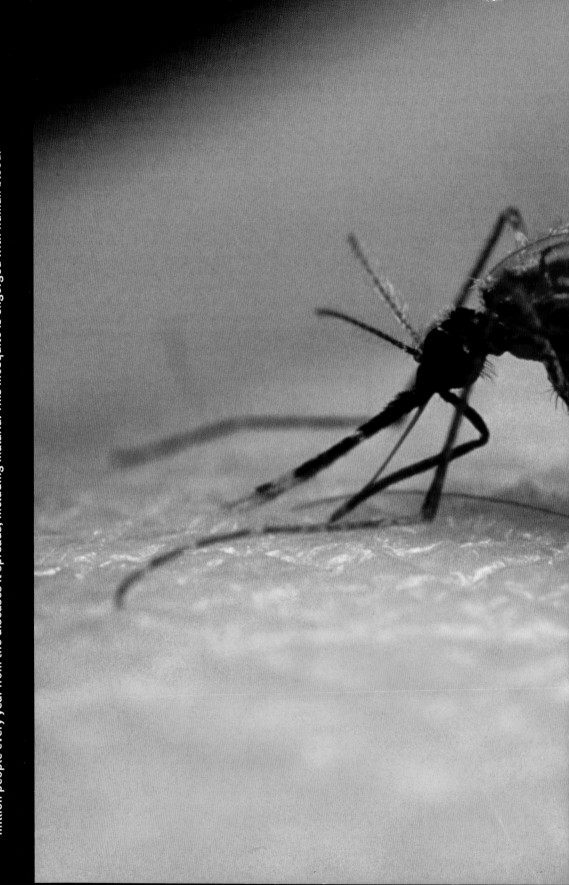

MOST DEADLY

Discounting humans themselves, the world's deadliest creature is the mosquito, which causes the deaths of more than two million people every year from the diseases it spreads, including malaria. This mosquito is engorged with human blood.

IN AUSTRALIA, it's illegal to leave your KEYS IN THE CAR DOOR if the vehicle is unattended.

In Athens, drivers can lose their licenses for being **POORLY DRESSED** or **UNWASHED.**

The statutory punishment for **DOUBLE PARKING** in Minnesota, is to serve time on a **CHAIN GANG.**

In Tennessee, it's illegal to drive a car while **ASLEEP.**

In Switzerland, it's a legal requirement for drivers with **DEFECTIVE VISION** to keep a spare pair of glasses in the car.

RULES OF
THE ROAD

Learning to drive is a complicated business. First there are the controls and the traffic laws. Then, if you're in Athens or Thailand, there's remembering the legal requirement to dress before you drive and, in California, the ban on shooting game from a moving vehicle. Ignorance of the law is no excuse, so read these laws and stay out of jail.

In Turkey, one punishment for **DRUNK DRIVING** is to be driven 20 miles (32 km) out of town and MADE TO WALK BACK under police supervision.

In Detroit, it's illegal to **MAKE LOVE** in a car unless it's parked on your own property.

In Belgium, drivers turning **ACROSS THE ONCOMING TRAFFIC** have **RIGHT OF WAY** unless they slow down or stop.

In Utah, **BIRDS** have right of way on all roads.

In Idaho Falls, Idaho, it's illegal for anyone **OVER THE AGE OF 88** to ride a motorcycle.

In South Korea, traffic police are legally obliged to report all **BRIBES** received from drivers.

In Thailand, it's a legal requirement to **WEAR A SHIRT** while driving a car.

In Missouri, it's illegal for drivers to carry **UNCAGED BEARS.**

NO WHEELED VEHICLES are allowed to enter Mexico City during **HOLY WEEK**.

In Glendale, Arizona, it's illegal to **REVERSE** a car.

In Britain and Australia, it's a legal requirement for taxis to carry a **BALE OF HAY.**

In California, it's a misdemeanor to **SHOOT GAME** from a moving vehicle—unless you're shooting at a **WHALE.**

In the Philippines, cars with **LICENSE PLATES** ending in 1 or 2 are not allowed on the roads on Mondays, 3 or 4 on Tuesdays, 5 or 6 on Wednesdays, 7 or 8 on Thursdays, and 9 or 0 on Fridays.

In Alabama, it's illegal to drive a car while **BLINDFOLDED.**

In Washington State, it is a legal requirement for any motorist with criminal intentions to **STOP ON THE OUTSKIRTS OF A CITY** and **TELEPHONE THE CHIEF OF POLICE** before entering town.

In Denmark, it's a legal requirement, before starting a car, to check the **LIGHTS, BRAKES, STEERING, AND HORN**—and to make a visual check that there are **NO CHILDREN BENEATH THE CAR.**

IN GERMANY, it's illegal to **RUN OUT OF GAS** on the *Autobahn* (highway).

In Youngstown, Ohio, it's illegal for **TAXIS** to carry **PASSENGERS ON THE ROOF.**

In Pennsylvania, it is a legal requirement for anyone driving on a country road at night to "stop every mile and send up a **ROCKET SIGNAL**, wait 10 minutes for the road to be cleared of **LIVESTOCK**, and continue."

CUSTOMS AND ETIQUETTE

When in Rome

In the 4th century CE, St. Ambrose was asked whether a person should fast on a Saturday, as was the custom in Rome, or not, as in Milan. Ambrose replied, "If you are at Rome, live in the Roman style; if you are elsewhere, live as they live elsewhere"—often paraphrased as: "When in Rome, do as the Romans do." For those who aren't quite sure what the Romans do, here's a handy guide to human etiquette from all corners of the globe.

In **Saudi Arabia**, don't accept an invitation immediately—it's polite to decline at least once.

In the **UK**, an invitation specifying "black tie" isn't quite what it seems. You are expected to wear a dinner jacket and a bow tie, but the tie doesn't have to be black—indeed, an increasing number of people dispense with the tie altogether.

In the **US**, it is polite to arrive up to half an hour after the time specified on a drinks invitation, but on time for a dinner invitation.

In **Belgium**, the greeting or parting gesture of kissing on the cheek is done three times, rather than twice, as in France.

In **Africa** and most of **Southeast Asia**, the left hand is used for personal hygiene and therefore considered unclean, so you should not eat with it or shake hands with it. In Ghana, this extends to not even making gestures with the left hand.

In most of **Southeast Asia**, it is extremely rude to touch another person's head—even that of a close friend.

In **China**, do not wrap gifts in black, white, or blue wrapping paper because these are considered to be funereal colors. Always present any gift with both hands. And never write a card with red ink, because that signifies the ending of a relationship.

In **Belgium, Italy,** and **Luxembourg**, a gift of chrysanthemums may not be warmly received; they are considered funereal flowers. In France, avoid roses and chrysanthemums, in Spain, dahlias and chrysanthemums, and in Britain, lilies.

In **Sweden**, when leaving someone's home, wait until you get to the doorway before putting on your coat. To do so earlier suggests you are eager to leave.

In **Iceland**, tipping in restaurants is considered an insult.

In **Egypt** and **China**, don't finish everything on your plate—leave some food to indicate you've had enough to eat.

In **Colombia**, it's rude to yawn in public.

In **Latin America**, standing with your hands on your hips is an aggressive gesture.

In the **UK**, it is considered rude to start a conversation by asking what someone does for a living—the weather is the traditional way of starting a conversation. But in the US, "what do you do?" is a standard conversation opener.

In **Germany**, if taking wine to a dinner party make sure it's French or Italian. Giving German wine is seen as a sign that you don't think the host has discerning taste.

In **Fiji**, be wary of admiring someone's possessions—it is tantamount to asking the person to give you the admired object as a gift.

In **Malaysia**, **China,** and **India**, it is rude to open a gift as soon as it is presented.

In **Japan**, it is polite to refuse a gift at least once before accepting it—and when you do accept it, take it with both hands.

If presenting a gift of flowers in the **Czech Republic**, always give an odd number, but not 13 because it is considered unlucky.

In **Japan**, giving a knife to someone is considered an encouragement to suicide, so it's best to think of an alternative! Giving pairs of objects such as cufflinks or earrings is considered good luck—but never give four of anything because the Japanese word for "four" carries connotations of death.

In **Britain**, to give a knife is said to risk cutting the friendship, so the recipient will often make a token payment of a penny so that the knife is bought rather than given.

HOAXING TIMES

REAL STORIES THAT MADE THE NEWS

MARS ATTACKS!

In October 1939, less than two months after Hitler invaded Czechoslovakia, Martians invaded the US.

On the evening of October 30, the CBS radio broadcast of a Ramon Raquello concert was interrupted by the following announcement, causing panic in the streets: "Ladies and gentlemen, I have a grave announcement to make. Incredible as it may seem, strange beings who landed in New Jersey tonight are the vanguard of an invading army from Mars." The news report went on to describe three-legged death machines emerging from a spaceship that had landed near Grovers Mill, NJ. The machines killed US Army personnel and civilians indiscriminately using powerful death rays, before releasing clouds of toxic gas that killed others not in the line of fire. As a result of the hoax, emergency services' switchboards were jammed and many people fled their homes with whatever food they could carry.

The next morning it emerged that the broadcast was a play based on the H. G. Wells sci-fi classic *The War of the Worlds*, recorded by Mercury Theater, a drama group founded two years before by young actor Orson Welles. Welles claimed that he was worried the play "might bore people."

Bigfoot caught on film

Rumors of a huge apelike creature roaming northwest US began with the Native American legend of a hairy giant.

The beast was dubbed Bigfoot in 1958 after construction worker Jerry Crew found a set of massive footprints in the mud near his site, although he didn't see the supersize ape itself.

One afternoon Roger Patterson and Bob Gimlin were riding in California's Six Rivers National Forest when they saw a large creature crouching beside Bluff Creek, about 25 ft (7.5 m) away from them. Patterson dismounted, running toward the creature with his 16 mm camera rolling while Gimlin covered him with a rifle. Patterson filmed Bigfoot for 53 seconds. Scientists dismissed the film as a hoax—but is it?

In 2002 Jerry Crew's prankster boss Ray Wallace admitted faking the tracks. And a man named Bob Heironimus claimed to have worn the Bigfoot suit for the film. But his claim is disputed and the film has never been thoroughly debunked.

FRAME 352 OF GIMLIN'S FILM Bigfoot glances back at the camera before striding off into the woods.

WINGDINGS PROPHECY IS SICK JOKE

With the world still reeling from the 9/11 attacks on the World Trade Center in New York, internet hoaxers used a Microsoft font to circulate scary rumors and predictions.

Indecently soon after the September 2001 bombings, electronic rumors were circulating that Jews had something to do with the attacks—and that Microsoft predicted the entire attack when software engineers wrote the font Wingdings.

Millions of people were sickened to receive emails entitled *Scary*. The email instructed them to open a Word document and type Q33NY, the flight number of one of the planes that hit the twin towers. They were told to convert the font to Wingdings, which produces the symbols below. However, a quick check revealed that Q33NY was not the flight number of any of the planes involved and that this was indeed a sick joke—and not even an original one. In 1992 the *New York Post* had announced that converting NYC to Wingdings gave ✈ ☠ ✡, which the paper claimed constituted incitement to kill Jews in the city. Wingdings' successor Webdings sends a gentler message: NYC becomes 👁 ❤ 🗽 (I love New York).

PILTDOWN MAN EXPOSED

A skull, supposedly the remains of a prehistoric human being, was "discovered" in 1912 by amateur archeologist Charles Dawson in Piltdown, Sussex, UK. But it was, in fact, pieced together from a human cranium, an orangutan jaw bone, and the tooth of a chimpanzee—making Dawson either the victim or perpetrator of the greatest archeological hoax ever. The hoaxer's identity has never been confirmed.

HITLER DIARIES ARE FAKE

The *Hitler Diaries* were published in 1983 by German magazine *Stern*. British historian Hugh Trevor-Roper, British newspaper *The Sunday Times*, and French magazine *Paris-Match* were all fooled but the diaries were declared fake two weeks later. *Stern* journalist Gerd Heidemann and accomplice Konrad Kujau, a dealer in Nazi memorabilia, had forged the diaries. Both received 4½-year prison sentences.

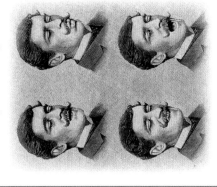

Words on the tip of your tongue?

ORSON WELLES announcing the Martian invasion. He claims the play was not a deliberate hoax, and that CBS warned listeners that the announcements were fiction.

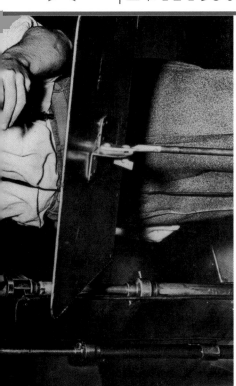

BEATLE DEAD?

According to Detroit DJ Russ Gibb, the Beatles spent years duping their fans.

In November 1966 Paul McCartney was apparently killed in a car crash and replaced with a double. The Beatles left clues for fans—played backward, the song *Revolution Number Nine* contains the words "Turn me on, dead man," and at the end of *Strawberry Fields*

| Paul is either dead or alive— NBC news

John can be heard saying "I buried Paul." Other hints included the funereal flower display on *Sgt. Pepper's* album cover and the funeral march on the *Abbey Road* cover, which showed "Paul" holding a cigarette in his right hand—the real Paul is left handed. *LIFE* magazine dampened the rumor a few weeks after Gibb's claim with a recently taken front-cover photo of Paul.

FAB FOUR The Abbey Road funeral procession of John as priest in white, Ringo as undertaker in black, George as gravedigger in denim, and the barefoot Paul-replacement as corpse.

Urban myths 1
Alligators in the sewers; Hells Angels' vacation pics; James Dean's car

24 ››

Great escapes
Read all about it. Tales of derring-do in Alcatraz, et al

34 ››

Conspiracy
Who killed Kennedy? Is AIDS a man-made virus? It's a murky world out there

90 ›››

Join the club
You know something about the Mafia and Knights Templar, but not about...ssh!

188 ››››

Ways to go
Irate farmer kills king over cucumbers

334 ›››››

HALF-PIPE

Where snowboarding shows the influence of skateboarding: slide down and/or ride up a U-shaped tube, riding up and over the lip of the pipe to perform aerial maneuvers like the ones featured here.

ALLY-OOP

Any half-pipe move that involves rotating 180° or more in the uphill direction.

FLIP

As you might expect, in a **Frontflip** you jump and flip forward; in a **Backflip** you jump and flip backward. Simple.

BUTTER

Shorthand for the phrase "Buttering the Muffin." Ride with the board at right angles to the slope while in a nose or tail **Press** (see below). Buttering is also used to describe spinning on the ground while in a Press.

ROTATION

Once airborne, rotate with your board through as many revolutions as you can. Rotations are named after the number of degrees you turn through—180° for a half turn (aka **Half Cab**), 360° for a full turn (aka **Cab** or **Three**), 540° for one and a half turns, 720° for twice round, and so on.

HANDPLANT

A move in which you "plant" one or both hands on the lip of a **half-pipe**. A **Backside Handplant** is a 180° backward rotation with the rear or both hands planted. A **Frontside Handplant** is a 180° forward rotation with the front hand planted, and a **Layback** is a 180° forward rotation with the rear hand planted.

ON THE SLOPES

In 1964, American Sherman Poppen saw his daughter trying to ride a sled standing up, so he attached two skis together for her and called it a Snurfer (from snow and surfer). Snowboarding really got going when Jake Burton decided to improve his Snurfer: in 1977, at the age of 23, he launched the first commercially viable board. From there things took off, the sport even developed its own jargon, some of which is explained here. Snowboarding gained wide exposure in the 1985 Bond film *A View to a Kill*, in 1987 the first World Cup was held, and in 1998 it became an Olympic sport.

PRESS

Aka **Manual**, this is another skateboarding trick. Shift your weight over the nose or tail to ride on one end of the board with the other end in the air.

OLLIE

Another skateboarding stunt, jump into the air from flat ground by lifting your front foot, and then your back foot as you spring off the tail of the board. To do a **Nollie**, you spring off the nose of the board instead.

BIG AIR

Air means you have air between your board and the snow. Big air means you've got lots of it—a high jump.

FAKIE

Aka **Switch**: ride the board backward, with your normal leading foot at the back. **Goofy** footers ride right foot forward, regular footers ride with the left forward so, when riding Switch, goofy footers have the left foot forward and regulars the right. Got that?

GRAB

Hold the board while in the air. Try **Indy** (rear hand grabs board between bindings); **Seat Belt** (front hand reaches across body to grab tail); **Swiss Cheese** (rear hand grabs board through legs); **Iguana** (rear hand grabs board near tail); **Chicken Salad** (rear hand reaches behind front leg and grabs board between bindings).

GRIND

Another move from street skateboarding, you ride along a narrow object such as a ledge or handrail. If you think it looks easy, just try it (practice in private first).

WIPEOUT

Not one to include in your competition routine—a wipeout, as in surfing, is a crash. While snowboarding has more in common with surfing and skateboarding than skiing, all four can catch the unwary in an ignominious tumble.

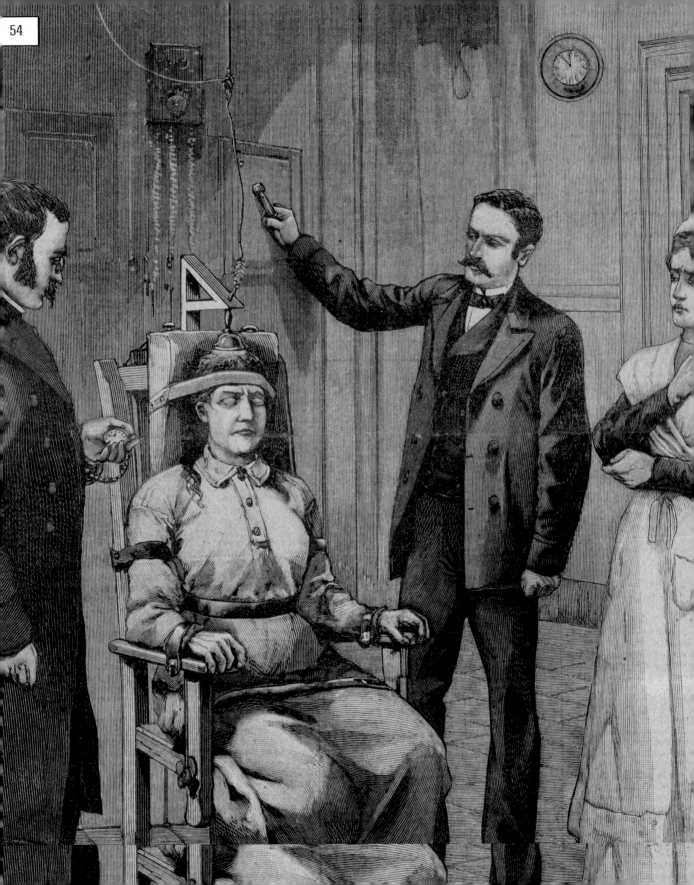

MYTHS AND LEGENDS

Crime FIRSTS

The great thing about being the first to do something is that however many other people follow in your footsteps your name will always be at the top of the list – even if your claim to fame is something as dubious as being the first person to be executed in the electric chair.

FIRST ASSASSINATION OF A HEAD OF STATE WITH A HANDGUN
On 10 July 1584, French Catholic Balthasar Gérard visited the Protestant Dutch court of William "the Silent", Prince of Orange. Pretending to be a Calvinist seeking alms, Gérard shot William three times with a wheel-lock pistol.

FIRST MAN/WOMAN TO BE EXECUTED IN THE ELECTRIC CHAIR
At 06:51 on Wednesday 6 August 1890, American murderer William Kemmler became the first person to be executed in the electric chair. Smoke rose from the top of his head and it took a full minute for him to die. The first woman to be executed was American murderess Martha Place, at 11:05 on Monday 20 March 1899. The executioner in both cases was Edwin Davis, who electrocuted a total of 241 people in his career.

◄ THE FIRST WOMAN to be executed in the electric chair was Martha Place. While the first attempt was unsuccessful, the second killed her in ten seconds.

FIRST TEST CRICKETER TO BE EXECUTED FOR MURDER
The first – and, so far, only – Test cricketer to be executed for murder was West Indies fast bowler Leslie Hylton, for the murder of his wife, Lurlene. His defence counsel, Jamaican cricket captain Noel "Crab" Nethersole, claimed that Hylton was attempting to shoot himself but missed!

FIRST PERSON EXECUTED BY LETHAL INJECTION
The first person to die by lethal injection was American Charles Brooks Jr, at 00:07 on Tuesday 7 December 1982, for the murder of a second-hand car salesman. The injection comprised a mixture of sodium thipental (aka sodium pentothal), pancurionum bromide, and potassium chloride, and was injected in Brooks' arm, close to a tattoo reading "I was born to die".

FIRST MURDERER TO BE CAUGHT BY WIRELESS TELEGRAPHY
After murdering his wife, Cora, in 1910, Dr Hawley Crippen fled to Canada by steam liner with his lover, Ethel Le Neve. The captain recognized Crippen from a newspaper photograph and radio-ed Scotland Yard on 22 July. They sent a detective to overtake them and Crippen was arrested nine days later.

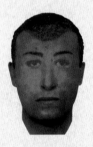

FIRST USE OF IDENTIKIT
The first murderer to be caught using Identikit was Englishman Edwin Albert Bush in 1961. Identikit (see above) was superseded by Photofit, first used to capture English murderer John Ernest Bennett in 1970.

FIRST "GREAT TRAIN ROBBERY"
The first so-called "great train robbery" took place on 15 May 1855, when Edward Agar and William Pierce, together with two railway employees, stole £14,000-worth of gold from the London–Paris bullion train. They appeared to have got away with it until the following year when Pierce reneged on a promise and Agar, who had been framed for forgery, turned Queen's Evidence.

FIRST CRIMINAL TO BE CONVICTED ON DNA EVIDENCE
The first time DNA was used to decide a criminal case was on 21 November 1986, when it proved the innocence of Englishman Richard Buckland, who had made a false confession to the murder of a schoolgirl. The first conviction on DNA evidence was that of English rapist Robert Melias, convicted on 13 November 1987 of the rape and robbery of a disabled woman.

FIRST ASSASSINATION TO BE FILMED
On 9 October 1934, in Marseilles, France, Bulgarian revolutionary and multiple murderer Valdimir Chernozemsky, aka "Vlada the Chauffeur", shot and killed King Alexander I of Yugoslavia. Chernozemsky, who was shot in the head by a policeman, died a few hours later. Newsreel cameras covering the state visit caught the entire assassination on film.

FIRST CRIMINAL TO BE CONVICTED ON FINGERPRINT EVIDENCE
On 29 June 1892, Argentinian Francisca Rojas murdered her two children, aged 6 and 4. She tried to blame the murders on a local ranch worker but fingerprints proved that she was the culprit.

THE DIVISION BELL
PINK FLOYD

The album is about lack of communication and the divisions between people. But the title, suggested by guitarist David Gilmour's friend Douglas Adams, author of *The Hitchhiker's Guide to the Galaxy*, has a second meaning. It refers to the "division bell" rung in British parliament to tell MPs to go to the Division Lobby to vote.

UNTITLED
THE BYRDS

The Byrds were still trying to decide what to call their ninth album when the sleeve was being prepared, so producer Terry Melcher wrote "(untitled)" on the artwork, pending a final decision. But somehow the cover went to print without the title being inserted, so *(Untitled)* became the name of the album.

SPORTS AND LEISURE

WHAT'S IN A NAME

You've written the songs, laid down the tracks, and emptied the local convenience store of ciggies, beer, and coffee. You've had the obligatory fight with your producer, so there's only one thing left to do—name the album. Some album titles are carefully considered artistic references, others are phrases chosen on the spur of the moment, still others happen by accident...

DE STIJL
THE WHITE STRIPES

Rock duo Megan and Jack White named their second album (2000) after De Stijl—meaning "the style"—the Dutch art movement that they say influenced their musical style, their image, and the album sleeve design. De Stijl art typically emphasizes the vertical and horizontal by using rectangular blocks of strong primary colors together with black and white—Mondrian's work is the most famous example. The album was dedicated to Blind Willie McTell and De Stijl architect Gerrit Rietveld.

NO ANSWER
ELO

As was the fashion at the time (1972), ELO's debut album was released in the UK under the name of the band—"The Electric Light Orchestra." When a secretary at ELO's American label, United Artists, phoned manager Don Arden to discuss an American title, Arden was out, so the secretary wrote down a memo: "No answer." And that became the American title. Often dismissed as an urban myth, the story has been retold by drummer Bev Bevan, who confirmed that *No Answer* was a complete accident but said: "It was quite a good title though, wasn't it?"

ODELAY!
BECK

American alt rock star Beck
intended to call his second album
Andale!, the Spanish for "get
going!" But when someone spelled
the word incorrectly on a tape box
he decided to keep the misspelling.

PLEASE
PET SHOP BOYS

Neil Tennant and Chris Lowe
said they chose the title so
that people had to ask
politely for the album,
saying: "Can I have the Pet
Shop Boys' album, *Please*?"

AUTOBAHN
KRAFTWERK

An apt title for an album that
German electro-pop band Kraftwerk
say was intended to capture the
monotony of a long car journey
on the highway (autobahn).

HISTOIRE DE MELODY NELSON
SERGE GAINSBOURG

A concept album that tells
the story of teenager Melody
Nelson's affair with a middle-
aged man and her death
in a plane crash.

IT TAKES A NATION OF MILLIONS TO HOLD US BACK
PUBLIC ENEMY

The title sums up the theme
of the American hip-hop band's
influential second album: that
American society is suppressing
black people.

BACK IN BLACK
AC/DC

This was the Australian rock
band's first album after the
death of their original lead
singer, Bon Scott. The title
refers to the band still being
in mourning.

BLOOD ON THE TRACKS
BOB DYLAN

One of Dylan's most critically
acclaimed albums, this was a break
with the past, musically, lyrically,
and thematically. Songs of
everlasting love were out, the pain
of divorce was in. The album is
about the relationship between past
and present, and its title is a play
on how the past affects Dylan's
current work—metaphorical blood
on both the tracks of his life and
the tracks of the album.

TWO SEVENS CLASH
CULTURE

Joseph Hill, lead singer of Jamaican roots
reggae band Culture, had a vision in which
he saw July 7, 1977, as a day of judgment.
This date was the inspiration for a hit song
and was used as the title of Culture's 1977
debut album. The album notes claim that
on the fateful day of the clashing sevens,
"a hush descended on Kingston; many people
did not go outdoors, shops closed, an air
of foreboding and expectation filled the city."

WHEN THE PAWN HITS THE CONFLICTS HE THINKS LIKE A KING WHAT HE KNOWS THROWS THE BLOWS WHEN HE GOES TO THE FIGHT AND HE'LL WIN THE WHOLE THING FORE HE ENTERS THE RING THERE'S NO BODY TO BATTER WHEN YOUR MIND IS YOUR MIGHT SO WHEN YOU GO SOLO, YOU HOLD YOUR OWN HAND AND REMEMBER THAT DEPTH IS THE GREATEST OF HEIGHTS AND IF YOU KNOW WHERE YOU STAND, THEN YOU'LL KNOW WHERE TO LAND AND IF YOU FALL IT WON'T MATTER, CUZ YOU KNOW THAT YOU'RE RIGHT

FIONA APPLE

The second album by American singer-songwriter
Fiona Apple McAfee Maggart, better known simply
as Fiona Apple, has the world's longest title—
an entire poem that she wrote in response to the
music magazine *Spin* portraying her in a bad light.
The album was critically acclaimed in some quarters,
but *Spin* was evidently not impressed. The magazine's
review simply quoted the title and then wrote:
"Whoops. Now we don't have room for a review.
One star."

STANDING ON THE SHOULDER OF GIANTS
OASIS

While sitting in a pub,
Noel Gallagher saw the quote
that is engraved around the
rim of the British £2 coin: "I
am standing on the shoulders
of giants." He wrote it down
(but misquoted it as the
"shoulder" of giants).

BIG BROTHER

When George Orwell wrote his dystopian novel Nineteen Eighty-Four in 1948, his ideas seemed farfetched. Orwell described "doublethink," a deliberate government policy of saying one thing and meaning another, and "Big Brother," the overweaning state watching our every move. Surely, that could never happen? Get real—it already has. **BIG BROTHER IS WATCHING YOU.**

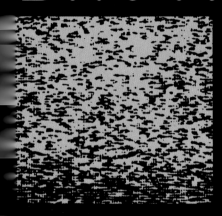

CELL PHONES

Cell phones can very easily be tapped, either as the wireless signal travels through the air or as it travels along conventional phone lines from base station to base station. Phone records are one of the first sources that investigators turn to for information.

CREDIT CARD

Your bank can tell instantly where you are and what you're buying, which means anyone else can too if they try hard enough. If you use cash instead, you'll need lots of it in order to avoid going near a cash machine, which is also instantly traceable.

CCTV

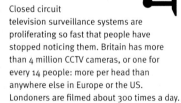

Closed circuit television surveillance systems are proliferating so fast that people have stopped noticing them. Britain has more than 4 million CCTV cameras, or one for every 14 people: more per head than anywhere else in Europe or the US. Londoners are filmed about 300 times a day.

MEDICAL RECORDS

The transfer of medical records onto central computer databases makes the personal information they contain vulnerable to misuse.

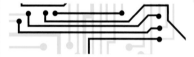

MICROCHIP IMPLANTS

Pets can have microchip IDs and prisoners can be tagged. So when will they start implanting chips in people? An American company is already developing an implantable chip that would allow Big Brother to track a person's whereabouts continuously.

SUPERMARKET BARCODES

Barcodes are not a problem, since they are just used for stock control. But when you use a reward card all your shopping habits are recorded and stored. If you start buying diapers or dog food your supermarket knows you've just had a child or bought a pet. So what else do they know?

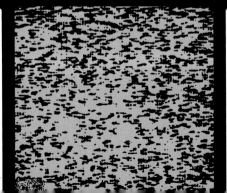

DE-ENCRYPTION

Information that you send to and from your bank and other organizations over the internet isn't really that secure. Any

encryption can be de-encrypted with the right electronic key, leaving all your information available to hackers.

BIOMETRIC ID CARDS

Identity cards are nothing new but biometric ones are—in addition to digital information about a person, biometric cards can store biological information such as fingerprints, retinal or/and iris scans, and facial scans. Many countries already have biometric ID cards or passports.

DNA DATABASE

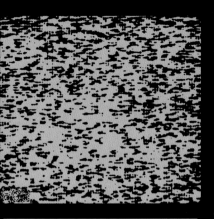

Many countries keep fingerprint and DNA records of criminals, but British PM Tony Blair wants to have every British adult's DNA stored on a state database. The database already holds samples from 6 percent of the population—more than any other country.

LISTENING DEVICE

Listening devices currently being sold as toys can enhance sounds from over 300 feet (90 m) away, using a high-sensitivity microphone and a parabolic sound-collection dish.

BABY MONITORS

If a listener doesn't have access to laser technology they can always tune in to the frequency of your baby monitor and listen in that way.

SPY IN THE SKY

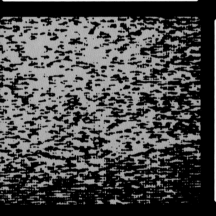

Many vehicles are tracked by traffic monitoring and congestion charging cameras. Now the British government is going further and considering making "black boxes" compulsory in all vehicles so that they can then be tracked and billed for every mile they travel.

OFFICE SURVEILLANCE

EMAIL MONITORING

This isn't just for the security services—office managers also monitor emails. They can find out who an email is to or from, how long it took to write, if there are attachments, and if it is business related.

COMPUTER TRACES

Even more intrusive than email monitoring is computer tracing. It is like someone looking over your shoulder as you type without you knowing they're there, watching what you type as you type it.

FINGERPRINT PADS

Although fingerprint pads increase security by making it difficult for unauthorized people to access the wrong areas, they also mean that employers know where their employees were and when.

PHONE TAPS

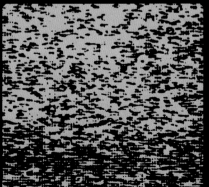

One of the oldest surveillance tricks in the book, and one of the easiest to do. If they don't actually listen to your calls, it's even easier to check the phone bills to see who you were talking to and when.

CHAPTER 2

2 minutes is the average duration of human sexual intercourse ✲ The Roman god Janus had 2 faces, looking forward and back – January is named after him as guardian of the gateway between the old and the new year ✲ Irish rock band U2 is named after an American spyplane, the Lockheed U2 Dragon Lady ✲ Famous twosomes include Batman & Robin, Laurel & Hardy, Starsky & Hutch, Tom & Jerry, Sherlock Holmes & Dr Watson, Dr Jekyll & Mr Hyde, Romeo & Juliet, Lennon & McCartney, Sonny & Cher, Simon & Garfunkel, Adam & Eve, Barbie & Ken, Gin & Tonic, Moët & Chandon, Smith & Wesson, Stars & Stripes, Rolls & Royce, Dolce & Gabbana ✲ The 2 cities in Charles Dickens's classic *A Tale of Two Cities* are London and Paris ✲ In Taoism, 2 represents the completeness of opposites unified and the potential for them to divide (as yin and yang) ✲ Pythagoras thought 2 an evil number, so the 2nd day of the 2nd month was unlucky and dedicated to Pluto, god of the Underworld ✲ 2 is lucky in Chinese culture, as good things come in pairs ✲ Dualism is the belief that reality is made up of 2 elements, spiritual and physical, or (as in Zoroastrianism) that reality is influenced by 2 forces, good and evil ✲ 2 is the number of strands in a DNA helix ✲ 2 weeks is the lifespan of an average mosquito ✲ 2 is the only number whose sum when added to itself is the same as its product when multiplied by itself ✲ 2 is the only even prime number✲ German mathematician Gottfried Liebniz, who discovered binomial theorem, said there were only 2 unquestionable realities: zero and God ✲ Computers operate using binary code, Base 2.

MEN OF THE WORLD

Not sure where on Earth you are? The clues are all around you. But don't rely on the availability of certain soft drinks or the presence of particular fast-food restaurants because they're everywhere. All you need to do is look at the way the natives are dressed, and with this handy guide you'll know exactly which country you're in.

INDIGENOUS AUSTRALIAN

Don't worry—today the spear, shield, and war paint that identify this ancient and noble race are purely ceremonial.

BANGLADESH

The skirtlike cotton *lungi*, tied with a knot at the waist, is usually worn with a short-sleeved cotton shirt— very comfortable in the heat.

SCOTS GUARDSMAN

A drum major of the Scots Guards is carrying his mace and wearing the traditional kilt, sporran, and bearskin hat of his regiment.

US, HOPI KACHINA

In Hopi legend, a Kachina is a life-bringing spirit. This Kachina represents a hummingbird, said to intercede with the gods on behalf of the Hopi to bring rain.

MALLORCA, SPAIN
The striped pants, vest, and neckerchief are de rigeur for boys and men from the moment they can walk. (Eyeliner optional.)

UK POLICEMAN
The original UK police uniform included a top hat, which doubled as a perch for looking over high walls. This has now been replaced by the familiar dome-shaped helmet.

US, ALASKAN FUR TRAPPER
Animal fur is one of the earliest forms of clothing known to humankind—this fur trapper is wearing clothes made of seal and beaver fur.

UNIDENTIFIED
You'll often see characters dressed like this mystery man hanging around seedy bars in the dock areas of maritime cities.

CANADA, INUIT
The preferred material for Inuit clothing is caribou fur, which provides superb insulation due to long hollow guard hairs that trap air. And nothing is wasted—the thread for sewing the clothes is made from the caribou's tendons.

PHILIPPINES
The *barong tagalog* (literally meaning "dress of the Tagalog people") is a cool, loose shirt reaching slightly below the waist and worn outside the pants.

CUSTOMS AND ETIQUETTE
WOMEN OF THE WORLD

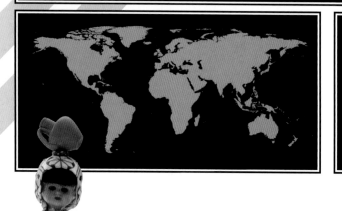

As with the men on the previous pages, the way the native women are dressed tells you instantly which country you're in. In the modern world the gender divide is less pronounced so you may also see women wearing the men's costumes, which will tell you not only the country you're in but also who wears the pants.

PORTUGAL
The national dress is topped with a woolen handkerchief known as a *lenço*, which protects the women's scalps from the loads they carry on their heads.

CROATIA
Details vary but the traditional Croatian dresses have bouffant sleeves and embroidered bodices, cuffs, and skirts—and lots of bows.

NAMIBIA
A woman of the Herero tribe wears a Victorian-style dress derived from the 19th-century costume that was worn by the wives of missionaries working in Namibia.

INDONESIA
A member of the matrilineal Minangkabau people of West Sumatra, Indonesia, wears an elaborate headdress.

ISRAEL
An Israeli woman in traditional fitted bodice, full skirt, and lace headdress tends to her candles.

AUSTRIA
Whatever the region, Austrian national dress includes gigot sleeves and a bodice cut in the Italian style, but the length of the skirt depends on how hilly the region is—the steeper the hills, the shorter the skirt, for practical reasons.

INDIA
This Indian woman wears a *ghagra choli*—a combination of *ghagra* (full pleated skirt) and *choli* (fitted blouse) worn with an embroidered *dupatta*, a length of light material which doubles as veil or throw.

NEW ZEALAND MAORI
The Maori *kahu huruhuru*, or feather cloak, is a highly prized garment, often passed down as a family heirloom. The most sought-after feathers are those of the huia and kiwi, particularly the white feathers of the rare albino kiwi.

GERMANY
Distinguishing features include bold-colored skirts, elbow-length sleeves, lace aprons, and plenty of ribbons.

CANADA
Une Canadienne from the francophone province of Quebec wears the national costume of full skirt and lace apron in Canada's national colors.

KENYA
A woman of the Samburu tribe wears a cloth wrap, known as a *kanga*, in the traditional strong red color.

PERU
This mother from Cuzco wears a traditional poncho (dating back to the 17th century) while the child, carried in a sling on her back, peeps over her shoulder.

CHINA
A performer with the Peking opera wears a *pei* jacket, which is part of the traditional dress of the imperial family, nobility, and high officials.

MEXICO
This woman of the Huichol people of western central Mexico wears a sombero style hat.

NETHERLANDS
A woman wearing the national combination of embroidered bodice, wide skirt, Dutch cap, and clogs—with obligatory basket of tulips.

FRANCE
The distinctive painted bonnet is traditional in Normandy, on the Channel coast of northern France—it is derived from the horn-shaped *hennin* worn just across the water in medieval England.

GREAT BALLS OF FIRE

Can a human being just burst into flames for no reason? Scientists don't think so, but there have been several cases where people seem to have done just that. One common factor is that the intense fire damages little else in the room and consumes only part of the victim's body.

BLUE HEAT
ROBERT FRANCIS BAILEY

At about 5:20 a.m. on September 13, 1967, the London Fire Brigade was called to a derelict house at 49 Auckland Street in Lambeth, south London. A group of women waiting at a bus stop had noticed blue flames in an upper window and assumed it was burning gas. However, the truth was far more horrific—when firefighters entered the house they discovered the flames were emanating from the body of a local homeless alcoholic, Robert Bailey.

Fire Chief John Stacey later said that he had found Bailey lying on the second-floor landing with blue flames issuing from a 4 in (10 cm) slit in his abdomen. Stacey stated that the flames were coming with some force from within Bailey's body: "He was burning literally from the inside out." Bailey's clothing and the rest of his body were not alight, but the heat from the flames was already beginning to char the floor around him. Having put out the flames, Stacey concluded that Bailey must have been alive when he'd started burning because, in his agony, Bailey had sunk his teeth into the post on the staircase. Firefighters had to prise his jaws apart to remove the body.

One theory is that the alcohol in his system had somehow ignited, but electricity and gas supplies had been disconnected and Bailey was not carrying matches or a cigarette lighter. Another theory is that of spontaneous human combustion (SHC). Like other alleged cases of SHC, the heat was intense enough to char the floor around Bailey but not to light clothing on his lower limbs or other combustible material nearby.

IGNITED
DR. JOHN IRVING BENTLEY

On December 5, 1966, a meter reader named Mr. Gosnell let himself into Bentley's house in Coudersport, Pennsylvania. Smelling smoke, Gosnell went to investigate and was shocked to find a large hole in the bathroom floor with Bentley's right lower leg lying beside the hole, the slipper still on the foot. Friends had left Bentley at 9 p.m. the previous evening and it was evident that at some point overnight his body had ignited. The fire had burned a hole some 2½ x 3 ft (75 x 90 cm) in the bathroom floor and Bentley's ashes were discovered in the basement. But, as with other alleged cases of SHC, part of his body was still intact despite the intense heat, and towels and bathroom fixtures were not even scorched.

MELTED FAT
ANNA MARTIN

On May 18, 1957, fireman Samuel Martin found the incinerated remains of his 68-year-old mother, Anna, lying in the basement of her home in West Philadelphia, Pennsylvania. The remains appeared to be lying in a pool of oil, but this subsequently turned out to be melted fat from the body. The coroner estimated that temperatures must have reached 1,700–2,000°F (925–1090°C) to melt the body in this way. Yet there was little damage to the room, and newspapers 2 ft (60 cm) away were found intact. However, unlike other alleged cases of SHC, it was

ENGULFED
JEANNIE SAFFIN

At about 4 p.m. on September 15, 1982, octogenarian Jack Saffin was sitting in the kitchen of his home in Edmonton, north London. He turned to speak to his 61-year-old daughter, Jeannie, and was horrified to see that her face and hands were engulfed in flames. Jack immediately called his son-in-law, Donald Carroll. They dragged Jeannie to the sink, doused her with water, and called an ambulance. Sadly, they weren't quick enough to save her. Jeannie suffered third-degree burns to her face, hands, and abdomen. She fell into a coma in the hospital and died eight days later. The inquest concluded that the cause of the fire was unknown, and noted that most of Jeannie's clothing and her chair were undamaged. Carroll said that, "The flames were coming from her mouth like a dragon and they were making a roaring noise."

Anna's limbs rather than her torso that had been consumed by the fire. All that was left of her were part of her torso and her feet, still in her shoes. And in her case there was a possible cause of ignition: she was found close to a coal furnace, leading to speculation that she may have accidentally ignited herself while trying to light the furnace.

CHARRED REMAINS
HENRY THOMAS

One evening in 1980, one of 73-year-old Henry Thomas's neighbors noticed thick, foul-smelling smoke billowing from the chimney of Thomas's house in Ebbw Vale, South Wales. The neighbor assumed Thomas was burning garbage until the police came around the next day with the horrific truth—Thomas's charred remains had been discovered in his living room.

Thomas's body was almost completely incinerated and only his skull remained, together with his lower legs and feet still clad in undamaged socks and pant legs. The fire had destroyed the chair in which Thomas was sitting as well as a light fixture and the television facing him. But it had not damaged other objects much closer to him than the television—including a pile of kindling that he had prepared for the fire.

The first policeman on the scene was John E. Heymer, who has since published articles on SHC. His notes recorded: "The living room was bathed in an orange glow, coming from windows and a lightbulb. This orange light was the result of daylight and electric light being filtered by evaporated human fat, which had condensed on their surfaces. The remainder of the house was completely undamaged."

Pathologists later tested blood samples taken from Thomas's legs. They discovered that the blood contained high levels of carbon monoxide, leading them to conclude that Thomas had been alive when he started to burn.

BURNS
AGNES PHILLIPS

On August 24, 1998, Jackie Park drove to a nursing home in Sydney, Australia, to pick up her 82-year-old mother, Agnes Phillips, and take her out for a day trip. About an hour later, Jackie stopped in Wollongong to buy some groceries and left Agnes in the car, since she had fallen asleep. But then, to her horror, Jackie saw smoke pouring from the car. With the help of a passer-by, she managed to drag Agnes from the car, put out the flames, and call an ambulance.

Agnes suffered severe burns to her chest, abdomen, neck, arms, and legs, and died in the hospital just over a week later. The coroner recorded an open verdict, specifically ruling out SHC despite the fact there was no apparent cause of ignition. A fire department inspector confirmed that the car engine was not running, the wiring was in good condition, neither woman was a smoker, and it had been a cool day.

RAGS, BONES, & ASHES
KROOK

In Charles Dickens' 1852 novel *Bleak House*, the unpleasant character of Krook, an alcoholic rag-and-bone man, dies by spontaneous combustion. Dickens describes it as a fire "engendered in the corrupted humors of the vicious body

itself." Critics ridiculed Dickens for this element of the plot but he responded by stating in the preface to the second edition that he had researched the subject and knew of many cases of SHC, citing by name the case of the 18th-century Italian

Countess Cornelia de Bandi Cesenate. The ashes of the 62-year-old countess were found by her maid with only her head and still-stockinged legs intact.

"engendered in the corrupted humors of the vicious body itself"

Man v

Who can eat more, a caterpillar or a human adult? Who can build higher, humankind's best civil engineers, using the latest techniques and materials, or a bunch of termites using mud? If you measure the results fairly, it's insects that win every time.

BEAST

Some caterpillars eat more than 100 times their own bodyweight every day—the equivalent of a 155-lb (70-kg) person eating **31,963 Big Macs every day.** And your weight would increase rapidly, so you'd have to eat even more Big Macs to keep up with the caterpillar.

Termites build nests up to 30 ft (9 m) high, or 900 times their own length—the equivalent of 6-ft (1.8-m) humans building a tower 5,400 ft (1,650 m) high, which is more than **three times the height of the world's tallest** habitable building, Taipei 101 in Taiwan.

A rhinocerous beetle can push an object **850 times its own weight**—the equivalent of an adult human strolling along pushing a fully grown **hump-backed whale** in front of them. Or one of the main supporting stones from Stonehenge.

A flea can jump **130 times its own height**, subjecting itself to **200 G**. That's like a 6-ft (1.8-m) person jumping over Britain's tallest building—the 50-story One Canada Square at Canary Wharf, London—at **66 times** the acceleration of a space shuttle taking off.

Termite mound

Taipei 101

Hump-backed whale

A rhinocerous beetle can push an object 850 times its own weight

130 times its own height

Canary Wharf Tower

20 times its own bodyweight

An ant can lift **20 times its own bodyweight**— that's the equivalent of a 155-lb (70-kg) person **lifting a medium-sized car** like a Honda Accord above their head.

A snake's jaws are loosely attached, enabling it to swallow prey whole. Some swallow prey **larger than their own diameter**— the equivalent of a human unlocking its jaws and **swallowing a basketball whole**.

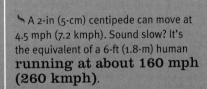

The wingspan of an albatross is three times its length—equivalent to a 6-ft (1.8-m) human with **an armspan of 16 ft (4.9 m)**.

Some species of mayfly live just one day. Compared with an 80-year human life expectancy, that's like being **born at 7 a.m.**, reaching your teens at 8:57 a.m., having children between 10 a.m. and noon, celebrating your 50th birthday at 2:30 p.m., retiring at about 4:30 p.m.,and **dying at 7 p.m.**

07:00   19:00

A 2-in (5-cm) centipede can move at 4.5 mph (7.2 kmph). Sound slow? It's the equivalent of a 6-ft (1.8-m) human **running at about 160 mph (260 kmph)**.

The mammal with the largest eyes relative to body size is the pygmy tarsier—the human equivalent would be a person with **eyes the size of grapefruit**.

60 & SEX SYMBOLS

Peace, love, and harmony were the buzzwords of the "Swinging Sixties" but this was also the decade when women could be tough and still be sexy—as proved by Raquel Welch in *One Million Years BC* and Ursula Andress, the first Bond girl, in *Dr. No.* As for the men, there were Sean Connery's Bond and Paul Newman's Cool Hand Luke to look up to.

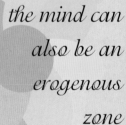

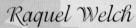

02. JULIE CHRISTIE
the epitome of King's Road chic.

03. MUHAMMAD ALI
"The Greatest."

04. ANITA EKBERG
proving life is sweet in *La Dolce Vita*.

05. URSULA ANDRESS
setting the Bond-girl standard as Honey Rider, in *Dr. No*.

06. SOPHIA LOREN
an Italian legend showing off her curves.

07. SEAN CONNERY
The name's Bond. James Bond.

08. LIZ TAYLOR
the violet-eyed beauty.

RAQUEL WELCH
(main photo, left) posing as Loana the Fair One in the prehistoric fantasy *One Million Years BC* (1966).

01. PAUL NEWMAN
as *Cool Hand Luke* (1967).

the mind can also be an erogenous zone

Raquel Welch

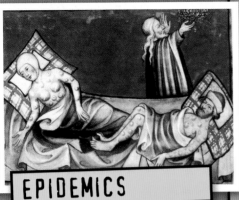

ACTS OF GOD

No wonder ancient people believed that the gods were angry when nature showed its dangerous side. Even in the scientific age, when we know the causes of earthquakes, cyclones, and tsunamis, it's hard to look at the death and destruction that follows without imagining a higher, and furious, force at work. Reading the death tolls—when a single cyclone can kill an estimated million humans or a disease wipe out 75 million—it seems extraordinary that there's still a global population explosion problem to contend with.

EPIDEMICS

1. c. 75 MILLION KILLED, BLACK DEATH, EUROPE AND ASIA, 14TH–18TH CENTURY
The Black Death, often called the bubonic plague (although the connection is considered scientifically unsound), first broke out in Asia in the 1330s. Traders spread it eastward along the Silk Road and it arrived in Europe in the 1340s carried by fleas living on the rats on trade ships. The Black Death wiped out at least one-third of the European population in a series of separate outbreaks between the 14th and 18th centuries.

2. 28 MILLION KILLED AND RISING, AIDS, WORLD, 20TH–21ST CENTURY
Identified in 1981 but thought to have originated earlier.

3. 21.6 MILLION KILLED, INFLUENZA, WORLD, 1918–20

TSUNAMIS

1. 287,534 KILLED, INDIAN OCEAN, DECEMBER 26, 2004
At 07:59, an earthquake buckled the seabed 93 miles (150 km) off the coast of the Indonesian island of Sumatra, pushing millions of cubic feet of seawater away from the epicenter at immense speeds. Over the next three hours, massive walls of water slammed into the coastlines surrounding the Indian Ocean, wreaking havoc in Indonesia, Malaysia, Thailand, Burma, the Andaman Islands, India, Sri Lanka, the Maldives, and even Somalia, which lies 2,800 miles (4,506 km) from the epicenter.

2. 36,380 KILLED, KRAKATOA, INDONESIA, AUGUST 27, 1883

3. 28,000 KILLED, SANRIKU, JAPAN, JUNE, 15, 1896

LANDSLIDES

1. 17,500 KILLED, YUNGAY, PERU, MAY 31, 1970
The world's most destructive landslide occurred as a result of the Ancash earthquake. Its epicenter was under the Pacific Ocean off the Peruvian coast. The total death toll from the earthquake was c. 50,000, but the worst single incident was the destabilization of Mt. Huascarán. This caused a 100 mph (160 km/h) mile-long landslide of rock and ice that buried the town of Yungay, killing all but 400 of the town's population. Yungay has since been declared a national cemetery, and May 31 is commemorated as Natural Disaster Education and Reflection Day.

2. c. 12,000 KILLED, KHAIT, TADZHIKISTAN, 1949

3. 2,427 KILLED, CHIAVENNA, ITALY, SEPTEMBER 4, 1618

VOLCANOES

1. 92,000 KILLED, MT. TAMBORA, INDONESIA, APRIL 10–11, 1815
The eruption, estimated to be the most explosive since 181 CE, was heard more than 1,250 miles (2,000 km) away on Sumatra. The huge amounts of volcanic ash thrown into the atmosphere affected the global climate and, in the northern hemisphere, 1816 became known as the "Year Without a Summer." Crops failed and livestock died, resulting in widespread famine.

2. 36,380 KILLED, MT. KRAKATOA, INDONESIA, AUGUST 26–27, 1883
Death toll includes people killed by the resulting tsunami (see tsunamis).

3. 29,000 KILLED, MT. PELEE, WEST INDIES, MAY 8, 1902

TWISTED EXPRESSWAY IN KOBE, JAPAN, AFTER AN EARTHQUAKE IN 1995 REGISTERING 7.2 ON THE RICHTER SCALE

HURRICANE IVAN SWIRLS OFF THE SOUTHERN UNITED STATES IN 2004

CYCLONES

1. 500,000 KILLED, EAST PAKISTAN (NOW BANGLADESH), NOVEMBER 13, 1970

The cyclone (hurricane) crossed the Bay of Bengal during the night and hit the low-lying and heavily populated coastal area in the early hours of the morning with winds of up to 115 mph (185 km/h) and a tidal storm surge of up to 39 ft (12 m). Most of the dead were killed by drowning as a result of extensive flooding, at a time when many people were asleep. The official death toll was 500,000 with 100,000 missing but unofficial estimates are as high as 1 million people killed.

2. c. 300,000 KILLED, CORINGA, INDIA, NOVEMBER 25, 1839

3. c. 300,000 KILLED, HAIPHONG, VIETNAM, OCTOBER 8, 1881

AN AVALANCHE SURGES DOWN A GULLY ON HUNCHULI IN THE HIMALAYAS IN NEPAL

AVALANCHES

1. 18,000 KILLED, ITALIAN ALPS, OCTOBER, 218 BCE

Avalanches are extremely common but the presence of large numbers of people in the mountains is not. The reason this still remains the worst death toll from an avalanche even after nearly 2,000 years is that the Carthaginian general, Hannibal, and his army were crossing the Alps from Switzerland into Italy to fight the Romans. Hannibal lost an estimated 18,000 men, 2,000 horses, and scores of elephants.

2. 10,000 KILLED, ITALIAN ALPS, DECEMBER 13, 1916

A number of separate avalanches occurred simultaneously.

3. 5,000 KILLED, HUARAS, PERU, DECEMBER 13, 1941

EARTHQUAKES

1. 830,000 KILLED, SHAANXI, SHANXI, AND HENAN PROVINCES, CHINA, JANUARY 23, 1556

The earthquake was so violent that it destroyed an area of some 520 square miles (347 km²), and aftershocks continued for several months. The death toll was especially high because the tremors destroyed a number of high loess (clay) cliffs in which millions of peasants lived in artificial caves. A Chinese historian noted, "Mountains and rivers changed places and roads were destroyed. In some places, the ground suddenly rose up and formed new hills, or it sank in abruptly and became new valleys."

2. 287,534 KILLED, INDIAN OCEAN, DECEMBER 26, 2004
(see tsunamis)

3. 250,000 KILLED, ANTIOCH, SYRIA, MAY 20, 526 CE

PLAGUE OF LOCUSTS

Locust swarms can destroy up to a third of a nation's crops and are a major contributor to famines in Africa. Here, a boy watches locusts swarm in October 2004 in the village of Mbour, northern Senegal.

SERIAL KILLERS

THREE INDIAN THUGEES HOLD AN APPARENTLY UNCONSCIOUS MAN ON THE FLOOR, 1830S

1. 931 KILLED, BEHRAM (AKA BUHRAM)
Behram was the leader of Thugee, an 18th–19th century Indian network of criminals from which we derive the word "thug." He claimed to have been present at 931 ritual stranglings between 1790 and 1830, but the number he personally dispatched is disputed.

2. c. 610 KILLED, COUNTESS BÁTHORY
Known as Countess Dracula, this Hungarian aristocrat killed hundreds of girls in the late 1500s and early 1600s and drank their blood to stop her from aging. She listed 610 girls at her trial.

3. c. 300 KILLED, PEDRO LóPEZ
Colombian "monster of the Andes" confessed to 300 rape–murders in Peru, Colombia, and Ecuador. Charged with 57 counts, he was imprisoned for life in 1980.

DEATH AND DISASTER

Scottish poet Robbie Burns wrote: "Man's inhumanity to man makes countless thousands mourn." There are far too many examples of humans' inhumanity to humans, other animals, and the planet itself, whether through deliberate actions or wanton carelessness. Burns would not have been exaggerating had he visualized countless millions mourning.

SPRAYING CHEMICAL DISPERSANT ON IXTOC 1 OIL

OIL SPILLS

1. GULF WAR OIL SPILL, PERSIAN GULF, 1991, 780,000–1,500,000 TONS
On January 23, 1991, Iraqi soldiers opened valves at offshore oil terminals and laden tankers in the Persian Gulf, releasing a 4,000 square mile (10,360 km^2) oil slick in the hope of preventing any attempt at an amphibious Coalition attack. The spill devastated marine wildlife, including fish, coral, and thousands of cormorants, as well as endangered hawksbills and green turtles.

2. IXTOC I OIL WELL SPILL, GULF OF MEXICO, 1979–80, 454,000–480,000 TONS
The world's largest unintentional spill occurred after a blowout at Ixtoc I, an exploratory oil well being drilled by Mexican oil company Pemex. Thousands of rare Kemp's Ridley sea turtles were airlifted to safety, and the United States Fish and Wildlife Service set up bird-cleaning stations. Bird populations did not recover to expected levels.

3. ATLANTIC EMPRESS AND AEGEAN CAPTAIN, 1979, 287,000 TONS
The world's largest tanker spill occurred when these two tankers collided off Trinidad on July 19.

AIRLINE ACCIDENTS

1. 583 KILLED, TENERIFE, CANARY ISLANDS, 1977
Two Boeing 747s operated by Pan Am and KLM collided on the runway of Los Rodeos airport and caught fire. 61 people escaped.

2. 520 KILLED, MT. OGURA, JAPAN, 1985
On August 12, a JAL Boeing 747 hit the mountain. Four survived.

3. 349 KILLED: NO SURVIVORS, CHARKHI DADRI, INDIA, 1996
A Saudi Airways Boeing 747 collided with a Kazakh Airlines cargo plane.

CIVILIAN MARITIME ACCIDENTS

1. 4,375 KILLED, DOÑA PAZ, 1987
Passenger ferry Doña Paz hit oil tanker MV Vector in the Tabias Strait, Philippines.

2. 1,863 KILLED, MV JOOLA, 2002
Senegalese passenger ferry capsized off Gambia on September 26, 2002.

3. c. 1,650 KILLED, MISSISSIPPI, 1865
The paddle steamer Sultana's boiler exploded.

MUSHROOM CLOUD FROM ATOMIC BOMB, NAGASAKI, JAPAN, 9 AUGUST 1945

WARS

1. c. 55 MILLION KILLED, WORLD WAR II, 1939–45
More than half the fatalities were civilians. The worst affected countries were China (8 m), USSR (6.5 m), and Poland (5.3 m). The greatest military losses were suffered by the USSR (c. 13.6 million soldiers killed), followed by Germany (3.3 m), and Japan and China (both more than 1 m).

2. c. 15 MILLION KILLED, WORLD WAR I, 1914–18
The high number of casualties was not enough to prevent World War II. Deaths were largely military. The greatest losses were USSR (c. 1.8 m), Germany (c. 1.7 m), and France (c. 1.4 m).

3. c. 10 MILLION KILLED, SINO-JAPANESE WAR, 1937–45
War broke out when Japan invaded China and went on until the end of World War II.

NO ENTRY SIGNS GO UP AROUND CHERNOBYL

INDUSTRIAL ACCIDENTS

1. EST. UP TO 50,000 KILLED, CHERNOBYL, UKRAINE, 1986
At 01:23 on April 26, 1986, a series of explosions rocked the Soviet nuclear power station at Chernobyl in the Ukraine, releasing a radioactive cloud that was to contaminate more than 20 countries and would eventually be detected as far away as North America. Rivers, lakes, forests, and agricultural land were contaminated, as were fish, meat, and dairy products from affected animals. Scientists predicted that over the next 70 years the disaster would result in between 5,000 and 50,000 deaths from cancer, as well as an inestimable number of genetic abnormalities.

2. c. 20,000 KILLED, BHOPAL, INDIA, 1984
On December 3, 1984, a lethal cloud of methyl isocyanate gas leaked from the Union Carbide chemical works and pesticide factory in Bhopal, India, killing c. 3,000 people in the immediate aftermath. An estimated 17,000 have died since from related illnesses.

3. 1,549 KILLED, HONKEIKO, CHINA, 1942
An underground coal-dust explosion at Honkeiko Colliery, China, on April 26, 1942.

TRAIN PARTIALLY SUBMERGED IN THE BAGMATI RIVER, INDIA, 1981

RAIL DISASTERS

1. c. 800 KILLED, BAGMATI RIVER, INDIA, 1981
The train was derailed and fell off a bridge when the driver braked sharply, possibly to avoid a sacred cow. The official death toll was 268 but the train was overcrowded.

2. UP TO 800 KILLED, CHELYABINSK, RUSSIA, 1989

3. OVER 600 KILLED, GUADALAJARA, MEXICO, 1915
The train derailed on a steep incline.

SUPERSIZE COOKIE

DIFFICULTY RATING:
>VERY EASY   >EASYISH   >MODERATE   >A BIT TRICKY

There are standard cookies the size of a beer mat and there are so-called giant cookies the size of a salad plate. But even the biggest and best things can be made bigger and better so, for those not satisfied with giant portions, here's how to make the colossus of cookies. The only limit is the size of your oven.

INGREDIENTS

1 lb (420 g) sugar
14 oz (375 g) butter
3 eggs
14 oz (400 g) chocolate
1 lb (420 g) plain flour
3 tsp bicarbonate of soda

METHOD

1 Place the sugar and butter in a mixing bowl and stir vigorously until creamed. Add the eggs and continue to beat. In fact, don't stop beating until we tell you to.

2 Break up the chocolate into small chunks and add to the mixture, saving some for the top. Sift in the flour and bicarbonate of soda and keep mixing.

3 When your arm drops off from mixing, line a cookie sheet with wax paper and spread the dough out into a cookie shape. Push the remaining chocolate chunks into the top of the cookie dough. You can't have too many!

4 Slide the tray into an oven preheated to 350°F/180°C. Cook for 30–40 minutes, or until toasty and browned. Don't burn it, because if you do you're eating it anyway.

 5 Remove and allow to cool for several hours. We highly recommend that you share this with at least 70 people!

HOW HEALTHY?

Estimated calories: 8,000 That's about 3½ times your daily allowance, but this doesn't mean you should try and eat it over the space of four days. Try a few weeks!

The standard cookie pales into insignificance beside our monster colossal cookie.

Man on the Moon

Have you ever wondered how long it took humans to succeed in getting to the Moon? The obvious answer is about 72 hours—Apollo 11 blasted off on July 16, 1969, and reached the Moon three days later, orbiting several times before landing in the Sea of Tranquility. But what about the preparation? Well, that took a mere 1.8 million years or so.

START HERE TO GO BACK THROUGH HISTORY

MAN ON THE MOON

At 22:45 EDT on July 20, 1969 (03:45 GMT on July 21), Neil Armstrong stepped on to the surface of the Moon and uttered the immortal words: "That's one small step for [a] man, one giant leap for mankind" (except he left out the "a"), and US President Nixon told Armstrong and fellow astronaut Buzz Aldrin: "Because of what you have done, the heavens have become part of man's world." Reaching the Moon certainly was a giant leap, but it was one that couldn't have been achieved without a long run-up and a number of other giant leaps before it.

▶ 1969: AMERICAN ASTRONAUT BUZZ ALDRIN WALKS ON THE MOON

▲ 1957: USSR'S ARTIFICIAL SATELLITE SPUTNIK I

THE COLD WAR

Throughout the 1950s and 60s, the Cold War between the US and USSR threatened to heat up into nuclear conflict. One way each could gauge the other's technological capabilities was the Space Race, which began when the USSR launched the first artificial satellite in 1957. Both sides began using animals to test whether a human could go into space. When the Soviets achieved that first as well, sending Yuri Gagarin into orbit on April 12, 1961, US President Kennedy swore that by the end of the decade the US would land a man on the Moon. The Americans did it with five months to spare.

V-2 ROCKET

NASA wouldn't have been able to achieve Kennedy's goal without the Saturn V rocket that carried Armstrong, Aldrin, and Collins to the Moon. It was designed by Wernher von Braun, the German rocket scientist who built the V-2 rocket for Hitler's regime during World War II. Fortunately, the V-2 was too late to affect the outcome of the war. When Germany was defeated, von Braun and his team of engineers surrendered to the US forces. Von Braun became a US citizen and director of first the Ballistic Missile Agency, and later the Marshal Space Flight Center, where he developed Saturn V.

▲ 1946: A V-2 ROCKET TAKES FLIGHT

NEWTONIAN PHYSICS

The inventiveness of the Industrial Revolution was nurtured by Enlightenment attitudes of 18th-century Europe. Inspired by the way physicist Sir Isaac Newton had proved physical explanations for natural phenomena, Enlightenment thinkers taught people to reason and analyze rather than accept traditional thought. Newton's greatest achievement was to formulate the laws of motion, particularly his third law—that for every action there is an equal and opposite reaction—which lies at the heart of jet and rocket propulsion.

◂ 1642–1727: SIR ISAAC NEWTON

◂ 1815: "PUFFING BILLY" STEAM LOCOMOTIVE

INDUSTRIAL REVOLUTION

Tsiolkovsky's theories would have remained just that were it not for the Industrial Revolution and the associated developments in chemistry and industry. The Industrial Revolution was triggered by the invention of the rotary steam engine by James Watt in 1781. Another key invention was the Bessemer Process for making mild steel, much stronger and more versatile than cast or wrought iron. Steam power also led to transportation developments such as steamships and steam railroads. One of the most famous early steam locomotives was *Puffing Billy*—it was a sign of things to come.

▸ 14TH CENTURY: SIEGE WITH CANNON

THE CANNON

Until the 14th century, wars were fought with bows and arrows: ineffective against medieval castles. Warmongers wanted something with more power—catapults could propel large, heavy objects into or over castle walls, but when someone put a steel ball and a pile of gunpowder into an iron tube and lit it, the cannon was born. If not rocket science, it got people thinking about trajectories and how far an object could be propelled by a given amount of gunpowder if the cannon barrel were tilted at a different angle.

◂ c.1900: RUSSIAN KONSTANTIN TSIOLKOVSKY

TSIOLKOVSKY

Von Braun couldn't have achieved what he did without the theories of USSR astrophysicist Konstantin Tsiolkovsky, "the father of space/flight theory." As early as 1895, Tsiolkovsky asserted that space flight was physically possible. In 1898, he specified that it would require liquid fuel rockets and, in 1903, he outlined details of how such rockets would work. Tsiolkovsky developed his theories of multistage rocketry and designed a space station, but, meanwhile, American Robert Goddard was putting some of those ideas into practice, launching the world's first liquid fuel rocket in 1926.

◂ c. 1000: CHINA INVENTS GUNPOWDER

INVENTION OF GUNPOWDER

Of course, cannons would not have been much use without gunpowder. English scientist Roger Bacon is sometimes credited with inventing gunpowder in the 13th century, but, in fact, he was simply the first European to discover it, probably from Arabic writings. The Arabs were using gunpowder to propel arrows from primitive guns during the 12th century but they didn't invent it either—they learned it from the Chinese, who had invented it c. 1000 CE and used it for medicinal procedures as well as for signals and fireworks.

◂ STAGES OF EVOLUTION OF THE HUMAN SKULL

EVOLUTION FROM APES

Why was humankind the only animal able to make fire? It's a question nobody has been able to answer for sure. According to the theory of evolution, humans evolved from apes through the natural selection of advantageous mutations, but the missing link proving it has yet to be found. Theories vary as to why humans' brains developed so quickly, one being that the very act of walking upright triggered the change. So it could be that standing on their own two feet is what got humans to the Moon.

c. 7000 BCE FLINT AND STONE FOR MAKING FIRE

DISCOVERY OF FIRE

The vital ingredient for smelting the metal to extract iron from which to make tools, and from which all else followed, was fire. The first humans would have had to rely on fires that started naturally and then try to keep them alight permanently. The earliest evidence of humans cooking with fire dates from c. 1.4 million years ago in Africa. Discovering how to create fire was a massive advance. It wasn't until c. 7000 BCE that Neolithic man was able to make fire on demand, by striking sparks from flints or by creating friction between two pieces of wood.

◂ c. 3000 BCE: HITTITES EXTRACT IRON FROM ORE

IRON AGE

None of the above would have been possible without iron. In about 8000 BCE people realized that rocks containing metal ores made better tools. About 3,000 years later, they discovered that metal melted if the ore was put in a fire and that the pure metal could be extracted and used for tools—so began the Bronze Age. Another 1,500 years later, c. 3500 BCE, people in the Middle East began to smelt iron ore and use the iron to make harder, superior tools. The idea spread slowly, and the Iron Age dates from c. 1500 BCE.

FOOD AND DRINK
DYING FOR A DRINK

Why pay for a drink when you can make it yourself? Well, because professionally made liquor doesn't taste like helicopter fuel for one thing. And the stuff you buy in bottles doesn't make you blind or insane (usually). But that doesn't stop some people—all around the world, since time immemorial, human beings have brewed, fermented, and/or distilled their own, and each country has its distinctive form of "hooch."

ARMENIA
Aragh/samogon

Made from mulberries, grapes, cherries, or apricots, this vodka-style hooch is widespread in rural villages. The word *aragh* means "juice" or "sweat", but Armenians often refer to it with the Russian word *samogon*.

BRAZIL
Cachaça

Popular sugar-cane alcohol made both commercially and home-distilled. Maria Louca (crazy Mary) is a prison version made from cereals such as corn or rice.

BULGARIA
Rakia

Made from grapes, plums, raspberries, or peaches, the national drink rakia is as popular as wine. Drink with a local Shopska salad.

COLOMBIA
Tapetusa, Chicha, chirrinche

Columbian *tapetusa* moonshine may be illegal but at least it's affordable, unlike legal alcohol, which is highly taxed. *Inca chicha* was traditionally made from corn, which is chewed until soft and then spat into containers and buried while it ferments. Now it is made from various grains, cassava root, or fruit. *Chirrinche* is made along the Caribbean coast, popular with locals and tourists alike and responsible for many a massive hangover.

CZECH REPUBLIC
Slivovice, aka rakia

Traditionally made from plums, although other fruit and even grass have been used. Distilled both commercially and at home, it is drunk like water at Moravian wedding parties.

FINLAND
Pontikka

Vodka-style hooch made from grain, sugar, potatoes, or other carbohydrates. Finns rise to the illegal challenge of home-brewing, especially in the moonshine city of Kitee, where you can buy a legal version called *kiteen kirkas*. Elsewhere in Finland, hooch goes by a number of names, including *pontikka* (a corruption of Pontacq, a French wine-making area), or *ponu* for short, *kotipolttoinen* ("home-burned"), *tuliliemi* ("fire sauce"), *moscha* (Swedish-Finn term), and *korpikuusen kyyneleet* ("tears of wildwood spruce"), a romantic allusion to the stills located deep in the forests.

GEORGIA
Chacha

Made from grapes or other fruit. Commercially made varieties are sold as Georgian brandy or Georgian vodka and taste similar to grappa.

GUATEMALA
Cusha

Widely made in rural areas from various fermented fruits, *cusha* plays a part in Mayan celebrations and is both drunk and spat during shamanic cleansing rituals.

HUNGARY
Házipálinka

The name means "homemade pálinka." Pálinka is a Hungarian brandy made from plums, apples, pears, apricots, or cherries.

ICELAND
Landi

Made from potatoes and other carbohydrates, including bread, and popular with underage teenagers and those unwilling to pay the high liquor taxes.

INDIA
Tharra

Made from sugar cane fermented to an extremely high—nearly 90 percent—alcohol content. Adding diverse ingredients such as batteries and copper wires to the brew raises the potency and potential for poisoning from copper formaldehyde.

IRAN
Aragh-e-sagi

Vodka-style hooch—the name means "doggy sweat." Distilled

SPACE HOPPERS

In 1992 astronaut and home-brewer Bill Readdy took 9 oz (250 g) hops with him aboard the Space Shuttle Discovery. A brewery later made a special liquor from the well-traveled hops, which had orbited the earth 128 times. Drinkers were said to be... spaced out.

DYING FOR A DRINK

Making and drinking hooch is fraught with danger. Aside from the risk of arrest, and the usual hazards of drinking hard liquor, there's also the lack of quality control. Toxic alcohols such as methanol, propanol, butanol, and amyl alcohol are a by-product of distillation. They are usually removed from commercial liquors but often present in home brews. They can cause headaches, vomiting, coma, and, in extreme cases, death. In Russia, *samogon* mixed with medical disinfectant has gotten onto the market and turned people in their thousands bright yellow—a sure sign of toxic hepatitis. Many have died from the "yellow death" caused by liver failure. Other dangers come from the equipment—one traditional piece of improvisation is to use a car radiator as a condenser, which can introduce lead and antifreeze into the hooch. Neither tastes good, and neither is good for your health.

"WELL, BETWEEN SCOTCH AND NOTHIN', I SUPPOSE I'D TAKE SCOTCH. IT'S THE NEAREST THING TO GOOD MOONSHINE I CAN FIND." WILLIAM FAULKNER

traditionally from grapes, it is also made with grains, molasses, plums, figs, or potatoes.

IRAQ
Arak/araq
Vodka-style liquor made from fermented date juice.

IRELAND
Poitin, aka poteen or potcheen
The term is a diminutive of the pot used to brew the grain- or potato-based hooch.

ITALY
Grappa
Made with grapes. The authorities have clamped down on illegal distillation and homemade grappa is now hard to find. Sardinian grappa is often known as *filoferru*, from the "iron threads" tied to illegally buried stills to help retrieve them.

LAOS
Lao Lao
Made from rice.

LEBANON
Arak/araq
Vodka-style alcohol made from grapes, various grains, molasses, plums, figs, or potatoes.

MACEDONIA
Rakia
Made from grapes left over from wine production, hooch is both legal and highly prized for

medicinal purposes as well as pure pleasure.

NORWAY
Hjemmebrent/Heimebrent
Given the price of taxed alcohol, home-brewing is widespread. Literally "home-burned," Norwegian liquor is distilled from potatoes and sugar. Often mixed with coffee to make *karsk* or *kaffedoktor* ("coffee doctor"). As alcohol above 60 percent is classed as a hard drug, home-brewers of high-percentage hooch risk severe penalties.

POLAND
Bimber/samogon & Éliwowica
Bimber is a vodka-style hooch made from grains and fruits. Making moonshine has a history going back to medieval innkeepers. Plum moonshine, called *Éliwowica*, is particularly famous, and worth a substantial detour to its home region in southern Poland.

ROMANIA
Tzuika/palinka
Brandy-style hooch made from plums. As in many countries, the government turns a blind eye to home production.

RUSSIA
Samogon
Meaning "self-distillate," *samogon* is a double-distilled hooch made from sugar, beet, corn—even plywood. Drinkers

have to be dedicated enough to ignore the vile stench. Single-distilled samogon is known as *pervach* ("the first").

SCOTLAND
Peatreek
Made from malted barley, the name derives from the smell ("reek") of the peat fires used for drying the barley.

SLOVAKIA
Slivovica
Brandy-style liquor made from plums, distilled both commercially and at home. Variations are made from pears or cherries and there is also a gin-style hooch made from juniper berries.

SLOVENIA
Tropinovec/snopc
Distilled from fermented grapes left over from wine-making; flavorings include various fruits to disguise the stink or herbs, such as anise, for medicinal value. At 60–70 percent, *tropinovec* is best drunk in modest amounts or diluted.

SOUTH AFRICA
Mampoer & Witblits
Mampoer, named after a chieftan, is made from fruit, usually peaches. *Witblits* ("white lightning") is made from grapes. Despite being illegal, both are widely available.

SRI LANKA
Kasippu
Lethal liquor made from jaggery (unrefined sugar) and whatever ingredients are available, from wood and rotting fruit to dead frogs and lizards. Local names include *vell* beer ("beer of the paddy field") and *suduwa* ("the white substance").

SWEDEN
Hembränt
Literally meaning "home-burnt" and sometimes dubbed "Chateau de Garage", Swedish home-brew is usually distilled from potatoes and sugar.

SWITZERLAND
Absinthe
Making absinthe, a herb-based spirit flavored with anise, was illegal in Switzerland from 1910 until 2005, but that didn't stop the Swiss from distilling it.

THAILAND
lao khao
Made from glutinous rice, the name means "rice liquor."

US
Moonshine/hooch
Whisky-style brew usually made from corn and sugar, with the added benefit of use as car fuel.

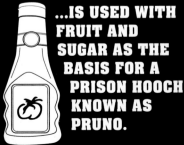

KETCHUP...
...IS USED WITH FRUIT AND SUGAR AS THE BASIS FOR A PRISON HOOCH KNOWN AS PRUNO.

MILK...
...IS FERMENTED TO MAKE THE ASIAN DRINKS *KEFIR* (COW, GOAT, OR SHEEP'S MILK) AND *KUMIS* (MARE'S MILK). *KUMIS* IS ALSO DISTILLED TO MAKE THE MILK SPIRIT *ARAKA*.

WOOD...
PLYWOOD IS SOMETIMES USED AS A SOURCE FOR THE RUSSIAN HOOCH KNOWN AS *SAMOGON*. WORMWOOD IS THE HALLUCINOGENIC INGREDIENT IN ABSINTHE.

FLORA AND FAUNA
A NARCOTIC

The 1960s was a decade of love, peace, and experimenting with drugs. But Swiss pharmacologist Dr Peter Witt slightly missed the point—instead of taking the drugs himself he gave them to spiders. Witt discovered that the effects were consistent and predictable, as they are when taken by humans. Here we take a look at what was going on in the spiders' minds.

Webs are a great tool for measuring how drugs affect spiders' normal design capabilities (see right).

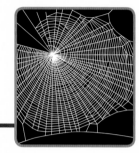

Marijuana

A quick toke didn't badly affect the spider's ability to spin a web but it seems to have chilled out, man, and not bothered finishing it. Delta-9 tetrahydrocannabinol (THC) is the active chemical in marijuana, which in humans acts on cannabinoid receptors in the brain, affecting memory, concentration, perception, and movement. Effects start almost immediately and last several hours, causing relaxation, inattentiveness, and an altered sense of time and space.

Benzedrine

This spider was very, very busy. Trying to get the job done fast. Spin, spin, spin. But the middle section's gone wrong. Move to the edge. Do a bit more. That's gone wrong as well. Feeling agitated. Like all amphetamines, benzedrine stimulates humans' central nervous system, increasing heart rate and blood pressure and reducing fatigue but also causing hyperactivity, jitteriness, and headaches. And in this case, it made the spider spin erratically.

WEB

Chloral hydrate (sedative)

Oh dear. This isn't as messy as the caffeine-affected web (right), but with all those gaping holes it's even less useful for catching flies. It looks as if the spider started off on the right lines and then just... fell asleep. Which is natural enough given that chloral hydrate is a sedative used in sleeping pills. In humans it usually takes effect in about an hour but it seems to have worked more quickly on this spider.

LSD

Very neat. This web is symmetrical and complete but too spaced out and not as efficient as the control for catching flies. The reason the spider did so well may be that LSD (Lysergic acid diethylamide) doesn't affect spiders in the same way as humans because it's a psychoactive drug and its effects depend on the user's mood. LSD induces feelings of strangeness in humans leading to hallucinations ("tripping"), including heightened emotional reactions ranging from extreme happiness to paranoiac fear.

Caffeine

This spider was even busier than the one on benzedrine (opposite). Busy, busy, busy. But this is a mess. It's all over the place—worse than the speed. How can that be? Well, caffeine is also a central nervous system stimulant but, while it increases alertness, it reduces fine motor coordination. The effects start within about 15 minutes and last for many hours, also causing insomnia, headaches, nervousness, and dizziness.

The author and publishers of this book do NOT recommend that readers try giving drugs to spiders.

▶ NEW BALLS, PLEASE

The theory of evolution by natural selection is that animals and plants that adapt best to their surroundings will survive while the rest die out. By this theory—also known as "the survival of the fittest"—species evolved and became more and more specialized. The same goes for sports equipment. At one time you could just hit a pebble into a hole with a stick and call it golf, or drive a car around in circles and call it car racing. But then people realized that they were more likely to win if their pebble was rounder and their stick flatter, or their car more aerodynamic and its tires wider. And so it continues: sports evolve just like animals, becoming faster, more powerful, and more accurate as they do so.

▶ GOLF

CLUBS

17th CENTURY
DOUBLET & HOSE

19th–20th CENTURY
KNICKERS AND
DRESS COAT

21st CENTURY
LIGHTWEIGHT CLOTHES
FOR FREER MOVEMENT

The origins of golf are disputed, but the Scots claim it as their game. It is said to have been invented some time before the 15th century by shepherds who would amuse themselves by hitting pebbles into holes with their crooks. As the game became more popular, clubs progressed from crooks or sticks to specially designed clubs. By the 17th century, players would carry a set of three clubs, each with a wooden head attached with twine to a wooden shaft, which sometimes had the luxury of a sheepskin grip. In the 19th century, a line of different clubs was introduced, including drivers, spoons, and irons. The first steel-shafted club was patented by US Arthur F. Knight in November 1910, vastly increasing the range and accuracy of shots.

BALLS

17th–19th CENTURY
FEATHERIE

19th CENTURY
LINE CUT

20th–21st CENTURY
DIMPLED

After pebbles came wooden spheres and, c. 1618, Featheries—hand-sewn leather balls stuffed with wet goose feathers. As they dried, the feathers expanded and the leather shrank, creating a hard, compact ball. After Featheries came solid gutta-percha Gutties, invented by Scotsman Rev. Adam Paterson in 1848. Then there was Bounding Billy, a solid-case ball filled with rubber threads wound round a solid core, patented by US Coburn Haskell in 1898. The principle holds for modern balls, which are made from silicone and rubber. From the mid-19th century, people realized textured balls were more accurate, so first lines then dimples were scored into outer casings.

▶ SOCCER

BALLS

Soccer originated in China as *tsu chu* (kickball). Rugby was codified first, but association football, or soccer, is the most popular worldwide. In medieval times, a pig's bladder was used as a ball, later encased in leather to keep its shape—often ovoid. Vulcanization enabled H. Lindon to develop a rubber inner in 1862, the year before the Football Association was formed. In 1872, the FA agreed on a standard spherical shape. Leather balls became heavy when wet but postwar synthetic paint made them waterproof. White balls were introduced in 1951 (easier to see in floodlights) and synthetic balls in the 1960s.

EARLY FOOTBALL
WITH STITCHED
LEATHER CASING

OLD BROWN c. 1910
MADE UP OF 18
SECTIONS WITH A LACED
SEAM OVER THE VALVE

CLEATS

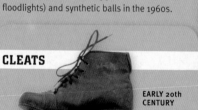

**EARLY 20th
CENTURY**

**MID-20th
CENTURY**

LEATHER SOCCER BALL
USED IN 1912 WALES–
ENGLAND MATCH

**21st
CENTURY**

Cleats have become lower, lighter, and sleeker. Rudolf Dassler designed the first screw-in studs in 1949. Rudolf began making sports shoes for his brother Adolf "Adi" Dassler's company, Adidas, in the early 1920s but set up his rival company, Puma, in 1924. The Adidas Predator cleat, patented in 1991, has special elastomeric ribs on the upper surface to increase area of the sweet spot, giving better ball control.

FROM 1950s 32
INTERLOCKING PANELS

▲ **1950s: ALFA ROMEO 158** KNOWN AS THE "ENGINE ON WHEELS", IT HAD AN 8-CYLINDER 1.5 LITER ENGINE DEVELOPING 370 BHP—AND NO SEAT BELT

▲ **1960s: LOTUS FORD 49** THE FIRST FORMULA ONE CAR TO BE POWERED BY THE FAMOUS FORD COSWORTH DFV ENGINE

▲ **1970s: LOTUS 79** AERODYNAMICALLY DESIGNED TO TAKE ADVANTAGE OF GROUND EFFECT: AIR FLOWING UNDER THE CAR CREATES A DOWNFORCE FOR GREATER GRIP

▲ **1980s: WILLIAMS FORMULA ONE** FRANK WILLIAMS LED THE FIRST TEAM TO WIN BOTH THE CONSTRUCTORS' AND THE DRIVERS' CHAMPIONSHIPS

▲ **2000s: FERRARI F2004** THE 21st CENTURY SAW THE INTRODUCTION OF HIGH-TECH ELECTRONICS AND THE DOMINANCE OF SCHUMACHER AND FERRARI

▌▶ FORMULA ONE

CARS

As the world's most expensive sport, Formula One car racing has seen the most technological advances. Grand Prix racing dates from the 1920s but the first World Championship took place in 1950, accelerating development: **1950s** direct fuel injection, Cooper introduces rear engine for better weight distribution; **1960s** Lotus introduce monocoque chassis for better suspension and cornering and wings to create downdraft for better stability and grip; **1970s** removal of central air intake, Lotus's wedge nose, side-mounted box radiators, skirts to create downforce for better grip; **1980s** turbo-charged engines (superseded by induction engines in 1989), carbon-fiber monocoques; **1990s** computer-controlled suspension and traction control, high-nose design, rib tires; **2000s** high-tech electronics.

▌▶ TENNIS

RACKETS

Lawn tennis evolved from the 11th-century French game *jeu de paume* (game of the palm). In England this game developed into indoor Real or Royal Tennis – the name "tennis" is said to come from the French practice of shouting *tenez!* (attention!) before serving the ball. The 14th century saw the development of long-handled wooden rackets strung with gut or string and, by the 18th century, these were tear-drop shaped for scooping the ball out of the corners of the enclosed court. In 1874, Major Walter Clopton Wingfield patented an outdoor version, which he called "Sphairistiké, or lawn tennis" – the latter name stuck. Lawn-tennis rackets were wooden ovals, and lasted a century before steel came in in the 1960s, and graphite (carbon fiber and plastic) in the 1980s.

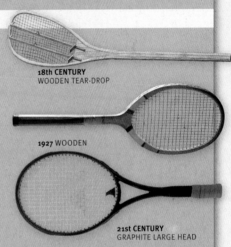

18th CENTURY WOODEN TEAR-DROP

1927 WOODEN

21st CENTURY GRAPHITE LARGE HEAD

BALLS

19th CENTURY SHEEPSKIN

LATE 20th–21st CENTURY OPTIC YELLOW

Real-tennis balls were made from leather packed so tightly with wool or hair that they could injure or even kill people. Lawn-tennis balls were made from rubber to bounce on grass, and have since been improved by pressurizing the hollow core and covering it with fabrics ranging from stitched sheepskin to flannel to a special melton fabric with vulcanized rubber seams. High-visibility yellow melton cloth was introduced in the 1970s for the benefit of television viewers, signaling the demise of the white ball. The last time white tennis balls were used at Wimbledon was in 1985.

CONSPIRACY THEORIES

All humans love a good conspiracy theory, whether they believe in it or they want to rant about how ludicrous it is. Some of the theories are farfetched but, according to conspiracists, that's all part of the conspiracy—after all, Hitler wrote that people "will more easily fall victim to a big lie than to a small one."

THE PHILADELPHIA EXPERIMENT

Conspiracy theorists assert that in 1943 the American Navy tried to make a ship at Philadelphia Naval Yard in Pennsylvania invisible to human vision and to radar. But instead of merely disappearing from view, *USS Eldridge* was supposedly teleported more than 300 miles (483 km) to Norfolk, Virginia, before returning with some members of its crew vanished and others deranged or with their bodies fused to the ship's hull. Repeated denials from the Office of Naval Research are seen as part of the conspiracy.

PEARL HARBOR

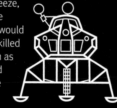

On December 7, 1941, Japan launched a shock unprovoked attack on the American Naval Base at Pearl Harbor, Hawaii, with no formal declaration of war. American President Roosevelt called it "a date which will live in infamy," but conspiracists claim that it was Roosevelt, not the Japanese, who behaved infamously. The theory is that Roosevelt knew about the attack but allowed it to go ahead to provide a reason for the US to enter World War II. The conspiracy begins with the American War Department, which was not totally in the dark: intelligence officers had been decrypting Japanese messages indicating an imminent strike, and war warnings were issued on November 27 and December 7 but were not passed down the line to Hawaii. In his book *Day of Deceit*, Robert B. Stinnet cites further evidence of a conspiracy: an official document listing a set of provocative political actions against Japan, which begins: "The United States desires that Japan commit the first overt act." However, even if Roosevelt did want to persuade Congress to go to war, and to portray the US as victim rather than aggressor, it would be tactical idiocy to sacrifice so much on the first day. A more plausible explanation is that intelligence indicated an attack was likely, but not where or when it would happen.

FAKED MOON LANDINGS

In July 1969, one-fifth of the world's population watched as Neil Armstrong became the first human to walk on the Moon. Or did he? Just two years later, a fake Moon landing scenario was floated in the James Bond film *Diamonds Are Forever*, and 1976 saw publication of Bill Kaysing's book *We Never Went to the Moon: America's Thirty Billion Dollar Swindle!* Kaysing asserted that NASA did not have the technology to reach the Moon, that the Saturn V rockets the public saw launched were empty, and that the flights and Moon landings were filmed at Area 51, a secretive American military base in Nevada—between filming, the Apollo crews allegedly spent their time gambling in Las Vegas. Supposed evidence of a conspiracy includes the fact that no stars appear in the lunar photographs; that shadows in the photos are not parallel; that the lunar lander created no crater when it touched down, nor flames when it took off; that the American flag fluttered

as if in a breeze, and that the astronauts would have been killed by radiation as they passed through the van Allen belt. NASA counters that the stars don't show up in the photos because there are brighter objects nearer the cameras; that wide-angle lenses distorted the shadows; that the lunar module did make a crater, but a small one, and that its fuel burned with a transparent flame; that the flag shook as it was being forced into the lunar surface; and that Apollo's hull protected the astronauts from radiation. Naturally, NASA's answers to the conspiracists' charges are all deemed to be part of the conspiracy. A more objective view is that it would be far more difficult to fake the entire Apollo program and then keep it secret than it actually was to go to the Moon.

THE KENNEDY ASSASSINATION

The only undisputed facts about the assassination of American President John F. Kennedy are that he was shot in the head at 12:30 on November 22, 1963, as his motorcade passed through Dallas, Texas, and died half an hour later. All else is disputed. The official story is that Kennedy was shot by a lone gunman, communist sympathizer Lee Harvey Oswald, acting on his own initiative. But two days later, before Oswald could be brought to trial, he was shot by strip-club owner Jack Ruby. For conspiracists, this was evidence that Oswald had not been acting alone and had been silenced before he could implicate others. For the public, unwilling to believe that a young and popular president, the world's most powerful man, could be gunned down in the street, such a conspiracy was more comforting than the official story. According to a History Channel poll 40 years later, 17 percent of Americans believe that Oswald acted alone—leaving 83 percent believing in conspiracy. The ingredients are all there: no eyewitness to the shots being fired; a supposed murder weapon incapable of firing accurately from where it was supposedly used; police failure to record witness statements; conflicting forensic evidence about the number and direction of shots; police incompetence or collusion in allowing Oswald to be killed before trial; faked photos of Oswald holding a rifle; and a report (Warren Commission) that raises more questions than it answers.

ROSWELL UFO

On July 8, 1947, a press officer at Roswell American Air Force base in New Mexico reported the discovery of debris from a crashed alien spacecraft, sparking two conspiracy theories. The first was short lived: many people dismissed the UFO story as a cover for a nuclear or weapons-research accident. But when the statement was retracted the following day and replaced with a story that the debris had come from a high-altitude weather balloon, the original UFO story gained credence. It lay dormant for years until UFO-logists resurrected the story in the 1970s, by bringing forward "expert witnesses." A Roswell intelligence officer claimed to have found alien material, which was subsequently substituted for pieces of weather balloon. A local mortician said airforce technicians asked him how to prevent body tissue from decaying (implying alien bodies had been found). And a supposed MIT scientist claimed to have been employed to reverse engineer alien spacecraft, including the one found at Roswell. Despite being an obvious hoax, a 1995 film purportedly showing autopsies carried out on the Roswell aliens brought the story to a wider audience, sparking even more ludicrous theories, including one of swapping abducted humans for extraterrestrial technology. In 2003, the American Assistant Secretary of Defense stated: "I think I can say beyond a shadow of a doubt that we have no classified program that relies on aliens from outer space." Conspiracists will note his use of "I think...."

AIDS, SARS, and EBOLA

Is AIDS a man-made disease? Conspiracists think so, and they back up their theory by pointing out that the origin of the AIDS virus HIV is offically unknown (although it is thought to have transferred from monkeys to humans); that AIDS developed into a global epidemic unusually quickly after it was first identified in 1982; and that it disproportionately affects two particular demographic groups—gays and black Africans. The theory is that AIDS was developed as a biological weapon and released deliberately or accidentally. This idea gained credence from an American Army biological warfare specialist telling the Senate in 1969 that it should 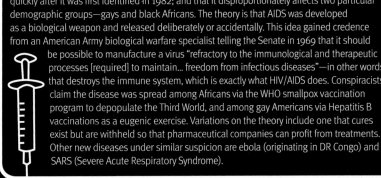 be possible to manufacture a virus "refractory to the immunological and therapeutic processes [required] to maintain... freedom from infectious diseases"—in other words, that destroys the immune system, which is exactly what HIV/AIDS does. Conspiracists claim the disease was spread among Africans via the WHO smallpox vaccination program to depopulate the Third World, and among gay Americans via Hepatitis B vaccinations as a eugenic exercise. Variations on the theory include one that cures exist but are withheld so that pharmaceutical companies can profit from treatments. Other new diseases under similar suspicion are ebola (originating in DR Congo) and SARS (Severe Acute Respiratory Syndrome).

A CURE FOR CANCER

In 1971, American President Nixon announced a War Against Cancer. Since then, billions of dollars have been spent on cancer research—but no prevention or cure has been found. Conspiracy theorists note that finding a cure would deprive pharmaceutical companies of revenue from existing palliatives and treatments, leading to two theories. One is that cures have been discovered but have been suppressed by the pharmaceutical companies for profiteering reasons; the other is that to avoid embarrassment the medical establishment trashes nonorthodox approaches that may be effective.

Unwanted guests

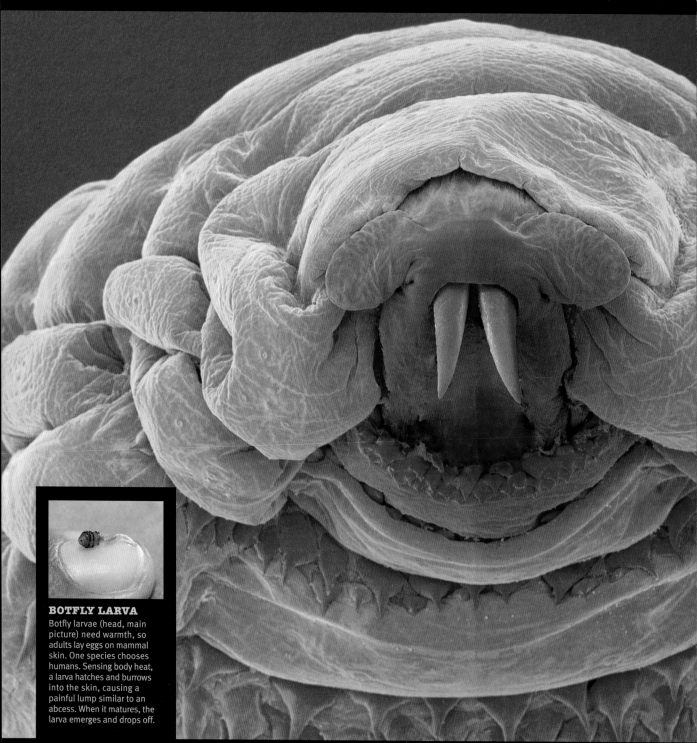

BOTFLY LARVA

Botfly larvae (head, main picture) need warmth, so adults lay eggs on mammal skin. One species chooses humans. Sensing body heat, a larva hatches and burrows into the skin, causing a painful lump similar to an abcess. When it matures, the larva emerges and drops off.

There's no place like home. It's where you're kept warm, safe, comfortable, and well fed. For thousands of species of parasites that means the human body, which has a good central heating system and provides endless supplies of food. The trouble is, that food is either nourishment that humans should be benefiting from or it's the humans themselves.

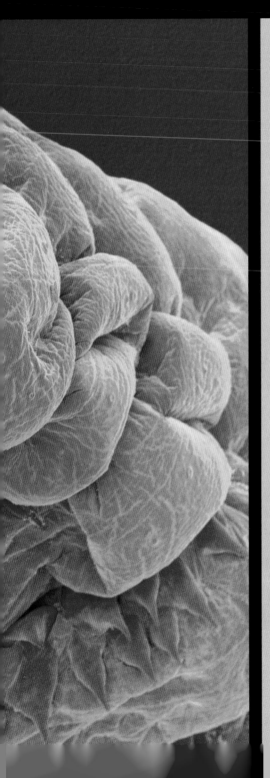

FOLLICLE MITES

Almost everyone has these microscopic wormlike mites living in their skin pores and hair follicles. They are often in the roots of eyebrows and eyelashes, hence, the microbe's alternative name, the eyelash mite.

GUINEA WORM

It enters the body as larva by drinking water contaminated with host water fleas. The female grows up to 3 ft (1 m) long. The only way to remove the worm is through surgery or by winding it sround a stick— but breaking the worm can induce anaphylactic shock.

PINWORMS

They enter the body as eggs or larvae on contaminated food. Females crawl out of the anus while you sleep to lay up to 20,000 eggs each night. They itch, inducing scratching, which transfers the eggs to the fingernails and perpetuates the cycle.

LIVER FLUKE

It enters the body as a cyst by consumption of contaminated fish, or water plants such as watercress. The cysts release immature flukes that find their way to the liver and gallbladder where they feed on bile and grow up to 3 in (7.5 cm) long. They reproduce rapidly, potentially blocking the bile duct, which can be fatal.

ROUNDWORM

Eggs of the roundworm enter the body in contaminated food and drink. As adults, they reproduce in the small intestine where a single female can produce 20,000 eggs a day. Roundworms can grow to 15 in (37.5 cm) long and cause appendicitis, peritonitis, liver abcesses, intestinal blockages, and hemorrhaging.

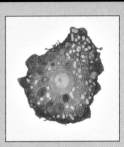

NAEGLERIA FOWLERI

This freshwater amoeba will make the human brain its home if it can, entering via the nose and reproducing until you die of amoebic meningoencephalitis. Taste and smell go, then you vomit, fall into a coma, and die.

TAPEWORM

Tapeworms enter the body on contaminated food. The scolex (above) attaches to the intestinal wall and the tapeworm absorbs digested food. Broad fish tapeworm grow up to 35 ft (10.5 m) long, and can live for up to ten years. Tapeworms can lay up to a million eggs per day.

VAMPIRE FISH

Natives fear this Amazon River parasite more than the piranha. Attracted to urine, it can follow a stream of urine to its source, swim into a human urethra, erect its spine to attach itself, and then feed on blood.

Food FIRSTS

All humans remember that Neil Armstrong was the first person on the Moon. But who cooked the first potato chip, froze the first ice pop, or opened the first restaurant? Crum, Epperson, and Boulanger—the names may not be as memorable, but their pioneering spirit has still been rewarding to much of the human race.

First DRINKABLE INSTANT COFFEE

1938

Discounting early failures such as liquid coffee essences and pulverized beans, the first instant powdered coffee was perfected by Swiss scientist Max Mortgenthaler and launched by Nestlé in April 1938 as Nescafé.

First CHIPS

1853

Chef's fit of temper MISFIRES

The first potato chips were served in 1853 at the Moon Lake House Hotel in Saratoga Springs, New York, where financier Cornelius Vanderbilt had complained that the fried potatoes were too chunky. Annoyed by the criticism, the chef, George Crum, sliced the potatoes as thinly as he could and fried them until they were crisp to teach Vanderbilt a lesson—but instead they proved extremely popular.

First BARCODE

1974 OHIO

The first item to be sold using a bar code was a packet of Wrigley's chewing gum, sold at 08:01 on June 26, 1974, at Marsh Supermarket in Troy, Ohio.

First RESTAURANT

The first eating place to call itself a restaurant was the Champ d'Oiseau in Paris, established by a Monsieur Boulanger in 1765. A sign in Latin invited people to Venite ad me, omnes qui stomacho laboratis, et ego restaurabo vos, meaning "Come to me all whose stomachs grumble, and I will restore you"—which is why a restaurant owner is called a restaurateur (restorer).

1765 PARIS

Venite ad me, omnes qui stomacho laboratis, et ego restaurabo vos

1923

Prototype popsicle

The first ice pop was wdiscovered in 1923 by American lemonade salesman Frank Epperson. He left a glass of lemonade on a windowsill overnight with a spoon in it. The next morning the lemonade was frozen, and when he tried to pull out the spoon he found himself holding the world's first ice pop. Epperson called it an Epsicle, but it was later marketed as a Popsicle.

First ICE POP

First BREAKFAST CEREAL

1893
Shredded Wheat

The first ready-to-eat breakfast cereal was Shredded Wheat, produced in 1893 by dyspeptic American lawyer Henry D. Perky in Denver, Colorado, as an aid to digestion. The first flaked breakfast cereal was Granose Flakes, produced two years later by fellow American Dr. John Harvey Kellogg at his Battle Creek Sanatorium in Michigan.

Meat was industrially frozen for transportation during the 19th century, and in the early 20th century frozen fruit was often sold along with ice cream. But the first individually packaged frozen food were 1 lb (0.45 kg) packs of frozen haddock sold in 1929 as "Fresh Ice Fillets" in Toronto. Clarence Birdseye launched his range of frozen foods the following year.

1929
TORONTO

Captain Birdseye wasn't the First

Fresh Ice Fillets

First MARGARINE

On July 15, 1869, Frenchman Hippolyte Mège-Mouriérs patented a mixture of suet, skimmed milk, pork and beef offal, and bicarbonate of soda. He called it margarine because of its pearly whiteness, *maragaron* being the Greek word for pearl.

1869
FRANCE

Invented by order of

Napoleon III to provide

"cheap butter"
for the French armed forces

1929
a million
fish sticks now eaten **every day** *in* *Britain*

The first frozen fish sticks, later marketed as "fish fingers" in Britain, were produced by an American company, Gorton's, in 1953. Britain's first ever radio commercial, on October 8, 1973, was for fish fingers.

First FISH STICKS

The idea of canning food was patented in Britain in 1810 and the first cannery was established in 1812. The first canned baked beans were produced in 1875 by Burnham & Morrill of Portland, Maine.

200 billion
cans of food produced **every year** *worldwide*

1812

First BAKED BEANS

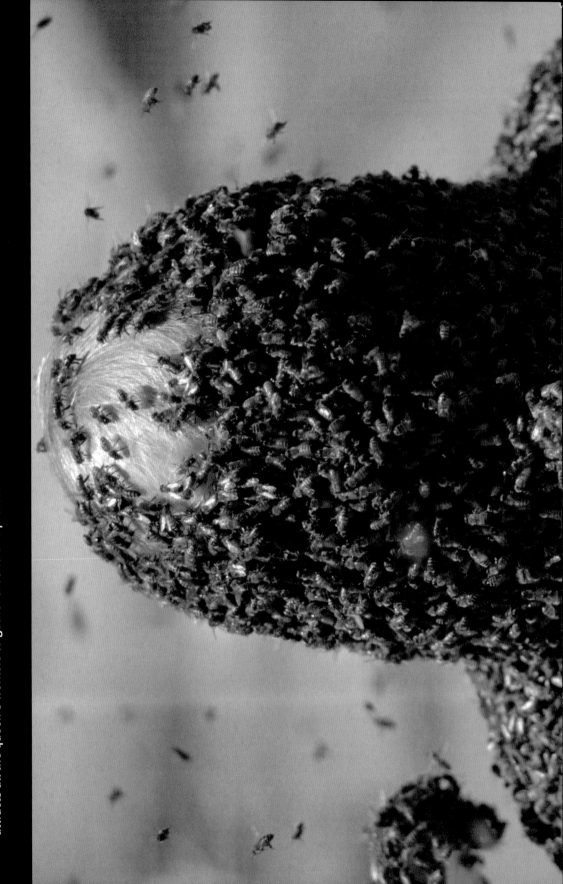

FLORA AND FAUNA

QUEEN BEE

It's enough to make you break out in hives. This man is using insect pheromones to mimic a queen bee, which attracts all the queen's workers to gather around and protect him.

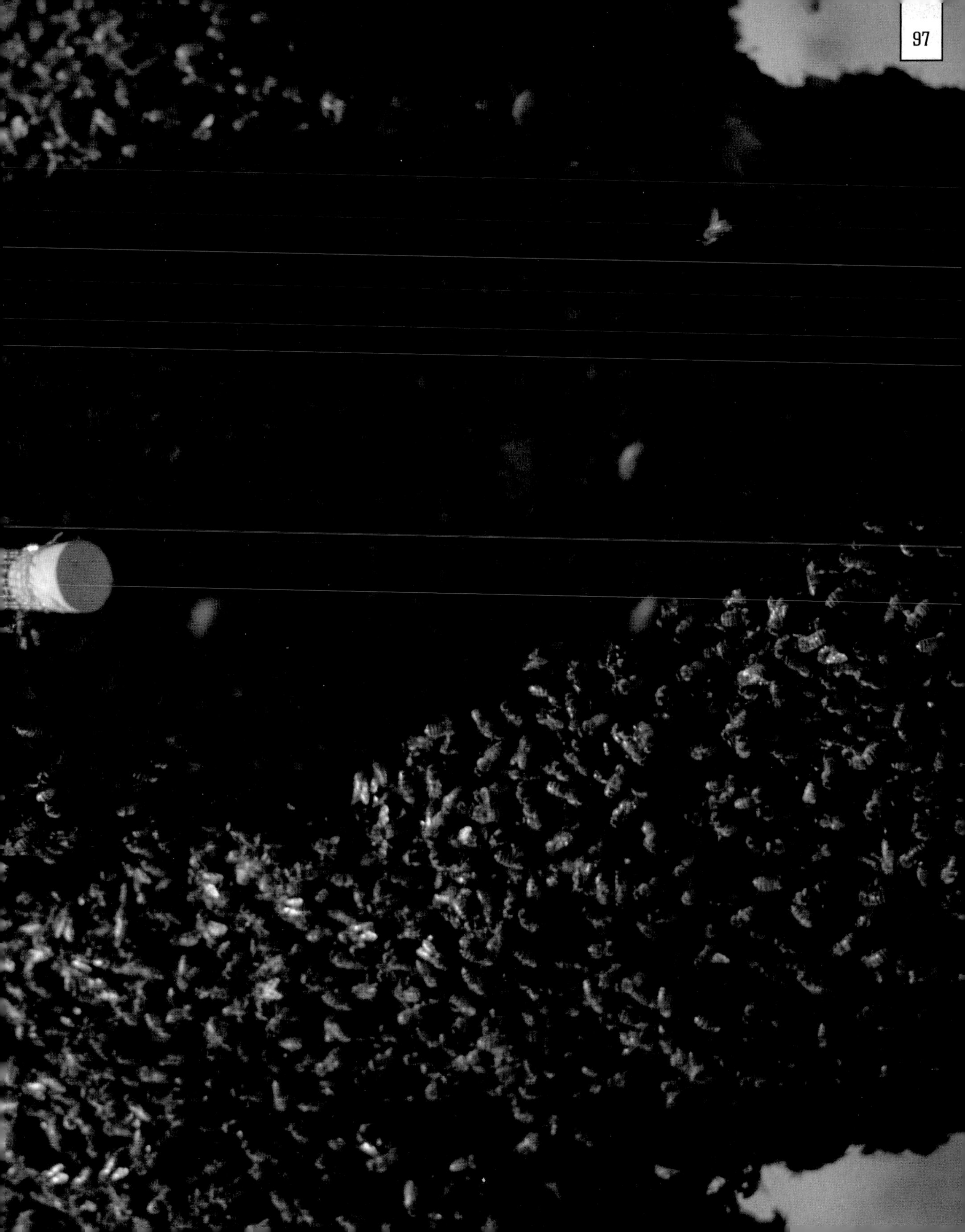

BAR TRICKS

Humans love to show off, especially after a drink. Depending on the company you keep, these tried-and-tested bar tricks are either guaranteed to: a) keep your companions amused all night, winning you the admiration of the crowd and lots of free drinks; or b) annoy everyone so much that you'll lose all your friends and end up with those free drinks poured over your head rather than down your throat.

BOTTLE BANK

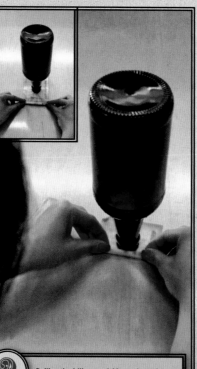

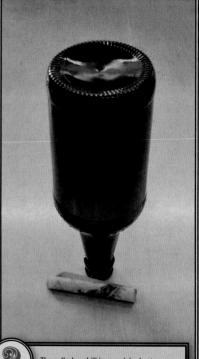

1 Place a bottle (empty it first!) neck down on a dollar bill. Challenge your friends to remove the bill without touching the bottle or knocking it over.

2 Pulling the bill out quickly rarely works. The trick is to roll it up carefully, holding it by the ends.

3 The rolled-up bill is surprisingly strong, and you can use it to push the bottle off. By the time you've rolled to the end of it, hey presto! the bottle will be resting securely on the tabletop.

KEEP IT UNDER YOUR HAT

1 Put a hat over your glass. Bet anyone the price of the drink underneath that you can drink it without touching the hat.

2 Duck under the table, then pop back up and tell the challenger that you've drunk it through the table.

3 The "victim" will be so amazed that he or she will lift up the hat to check. At this point, you can drink your drink, without touching the hat, and claim your winnings.

COINING IT IN

1 Put a beermat on top of a wine glass. Balance a cigarette on the center of the beermat and a coin on top of the cigarette. Challenge anyone to get the coin into the glass without touching coin, cigarette, mat, or glass.

2 It's done by blowing upward under the edge of the beermat—the beermat flips up, taking the cigarette with it.

3 Voilà! The weight of the coin makes it drop straight down into the glass.

HANDS OFF MY BEER

1 Put a beer mug (with handle) next to a tumbler on the table. Challenge anyone to push the small glass through the handle of the large one without touching either glass.

2 The way to do it is to put a straw, cigarette, match, or other implement through the handle of the large glass and push the small one.

3 You're doing exactly as you challenged: pushing the small glass through the handle of the large one without touching either glass. Clever or infuriating?

FLORA AND FAUNA

PET PROJECTS

Human beings strive to be first at things for the challenge, or to achieve fame, or both. For animals it's different – the first to fly, skydive, travel in space, or go through the Niagara Rapids had no choice. But some enjoy the thrill: owners of skydiving dogs say their pets get excited when they see the gear.

FIRST ANIMALS IN SPACE

47

hours in space

In July 1946, a group of fruit flies was sent into space aboard an American V2 rocket to test the effects of space radiation. The first space mammal was a monkey named Albert II, who blasted off on 14 June 1949, again on a V2. After 47 hours in space, he died on landing when the capsule's parachute failed. (Albert I died on an earlier mission without reaching space.)

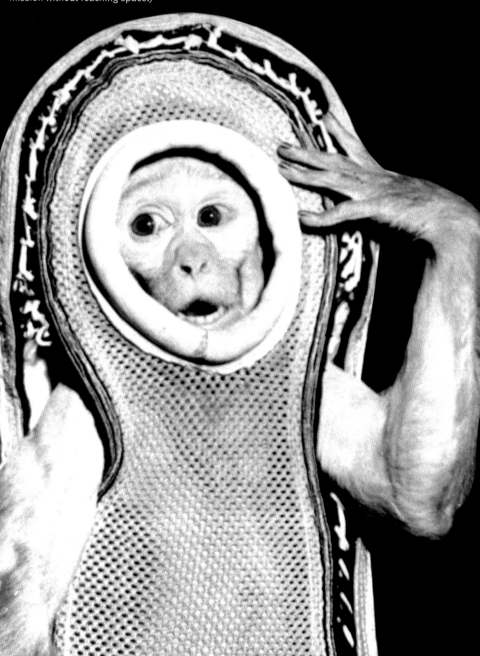

DOG ENFORCES LAW

In 1816, Scottish exciseman Malcolm Gillespie bought a black-and-tan bull terrier to help him catch smugglers. He trained the dog to seize the smugglers' horses by their noses, which made the horses rear up and shed their loads of contraband. The bull terrier, the first dog to be trained for law enforcement, successfully carried out its duties for a year, before being shot by a smuggler.

CLONED MAMMALS

In 1995, two genetically identical lambs, Morag and Megan, were cloned at Scotland's Roslin Institute by transferring the DNA from one embryo cell to another. The next year the Institute created Dolly, the first animal cloned from an adult cell. Lamb 6LL3 was born on 5 July 1996 and, as the cell she was cloned from came from an udder, she was named after Dolly Parton.

Megan

Morag

FIRST ANIMALS TO FLY

Many people have the impression that the history of flight began with the Wright brothers, but in fact it began 120 years earlier in France with another pair of brothers, the Montgolfiers. A human being first flew on 15 October 1783 in a Montgolfier hot-air balloon but, as with space travel, the idea was tested first on animals. A month earlier, on 19 September, the Montgolfiers demonstrated a hot-air balloon at the Palace of Versailles by sending aloft a sheep, a cockerel, and a duck. The animals reached an altitude of 520m (1,706ft) and flew for 8 minutes before the balloon came down 3.2km (2 miles) away in the Forest of Vaucresson.

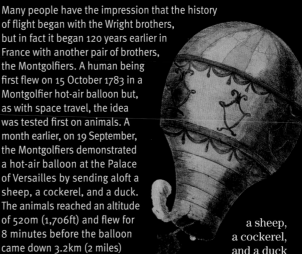

a sheep, a cockerel, and a duck

A section of sequenced DNA – the letters G, A, C, and T – represent four different base components, which in clones have the same arrangement.

GACCTCCAGGTA

DOG'S NIAGARA REVENGE

On 7 September 1901, Canadian Maude Willard attempted to navigate the Whirlpool Rapids below Niagara Falls in a sealed barrel. She took her pet dog along, who had its revenge by pressing its nose to the only air hole, suffocating its hapless owner.

FIRST ANIMAL TO ORBIT THE EARTH

The first animal to orbit the earth was a Soviet dog named Laika, the Russian for "Barker". After being launched as a passenger on the Sputnik II satellite on 3 November 1957, Laika was nicknamed Muttnik by the American press. Sputnik's telemetry system failed just hours into the flight, so nobody knows whether Laika died when the oxygen ran out, when temperature control systems failed, or after eating poisoned meat from the automatic feeder on board. What is certain is that she didn't survive – the capsule burned up on re-entry to the Earth's atmosphere in April 1958.

SHQIPERIA

LAIKA 1

FIRST BLOOD TRANSFUSION

255
grams of blood

As ever, the idea was first tested on animals. The first blood transfusion involving a human was a joint human–animal effort. On 12 June 1667, French physician Jean-Baptiste Denys tended a 15-year-old boy who had been bled 20 times to reduce his temperature. The loss of blood was critical, so Denys replaced it with 255g (9oz) of blood taken from the carotid artery of a lamb. The boy recovered but, when one of Denys' later patients died, transfusions of animal blood were abandoned. The first human-to-human transfusion did not take place until 1818.

FIRST SKYDIVING DOG

Military dogs have undergone parachute missions in various campaigns but the first civilian skydiving dog was a British Jack Russell terrier named Katie. In October 1987, Katie jumped 3,658m (12,000ft) with her owner – a British record. The world record is held by an American dachshund named Brutus.

SHARK STARTS MURDER HUNT

In 1935, at the Coogee Beach Aquarium in Sydney, the first shark ever to instigate a murder investigation disgorged a human arm. The arm had not been bitten off – it had been severed by a knife after its owner's death. Police managed to identify the victim but not the murderer.

ANGLING

The most lethal sport in England and Wales, angling has an average of six deaths a year. From drowning? No. Mostly electrocution, from fishing too close to overhead power lines.

CHEERLEADING

The most precarious moves are the pyramid (pictured) and the basket toss, which involves throwing one cheerleader as high as 20 ft (6 m) in the air.

KITE-FLYING

An obsession in the Punjab, where some kiters use sharpened metal kite strings for dog fights. One year two kiters were killed when their strings hit power lines, and six died falling from rooftops. Meanwhile, several spectators were crushed trying to catch stray kites and two had their throats cut by the razor-sharp strings.

DEADLY SPORTS

Caving is not as dangerous as sailing. Scuba diving is safer than table tennis. Parachuting causes fewer injuries than soccer. How can this be? Partly because cavers, scuba divers, and parachutists are trained to avoid accidents. Partly because "fewer injuries" hides the fact that fewer people go parachuting than play soccer. And partly because total injury stats don't differentiate between a twisted ankle and a broken neck. They're utterly misleading because a sport with five participants who all get injured has a 100 percent injury rate. But five doesn't even show up on a chart of the 500,000+ yearly US basketball injuries. So adrenalin sports might cause fewer injuries but don't be lulled—it's all or nothing. If you have any accident at all, the chances are you die.

ADRENALIN SPORTS →

← DANGEROUS SPORTS

BEWARE WHEELS—ALMOST HALF THE PLAYTIME HEAD INJURIES SUSTAINED BY AMERICAN CHILDREN HAPPEN WHEN THEY'RE SKATEBOARDING, CYCLING, OR SKATING.

BASE JUMPING

Freefall jumps without safety gear are truly dangerous. BASE—Building, Antenna, Span (bridges are popular), Earth (think cliff)—jumping kills up to 15 people a year. It's illegal in most places. Dangers include no reserve chute (no time to deploy it); being blown back to BASE; small landing space; and arrest—if you survive.

FREE DIVING

Imagine holding your breath and swimming as deep as you can. Not much fun if you need to inhale 330 ft (100 m) below the sea—the men's record is 364 ft (111 m), the women's 282 ft (86 m). Dangers include inhaling water or blacking out from lack of oxygen—either way you drown.

WHITE-WATER RAFTING

Rafting with a guide in charted waters is dangerous enough—you can still hit rocks or fallen trees, fall out of the boat and break bones, or simply drown. But real adrenalin junkies head for uncharted water, not knowing where the killer currents, undercut rocks, or high waterfalls are.

MOUNTAIN CLIMBING

Death from falling off the rockface is relatively rare thanks to ropes and belaying points, but there is a constant danger of twisted joints, broken bones, sprained muscles, and concussions. And then there's the weather, with exposure and frostbite big potential killers.

FREESTYLE BMX

No deaths yet but plenty of serious injuries. BMX—bicycle motocross—has evolved from racing over rough ground to urban stunt riding known as Freestyle BMX. The dangers are obvious: if you try acrobatics while flying a lump of hard metal above a lump of hard concrete, the chances are you're going to smash bones.

BIG-WAVE SURFING

Surfing is one thing. Big-wave surfing is something else. Exhilarating if you're cresting a wave up to 100 ft (30 m) high, but pretty dangerous if you wipe out and find yourself under it. If you don't get knocked out by hitting a reef, a rock, or your board you might surface to grab a breath before the next wave hits you.

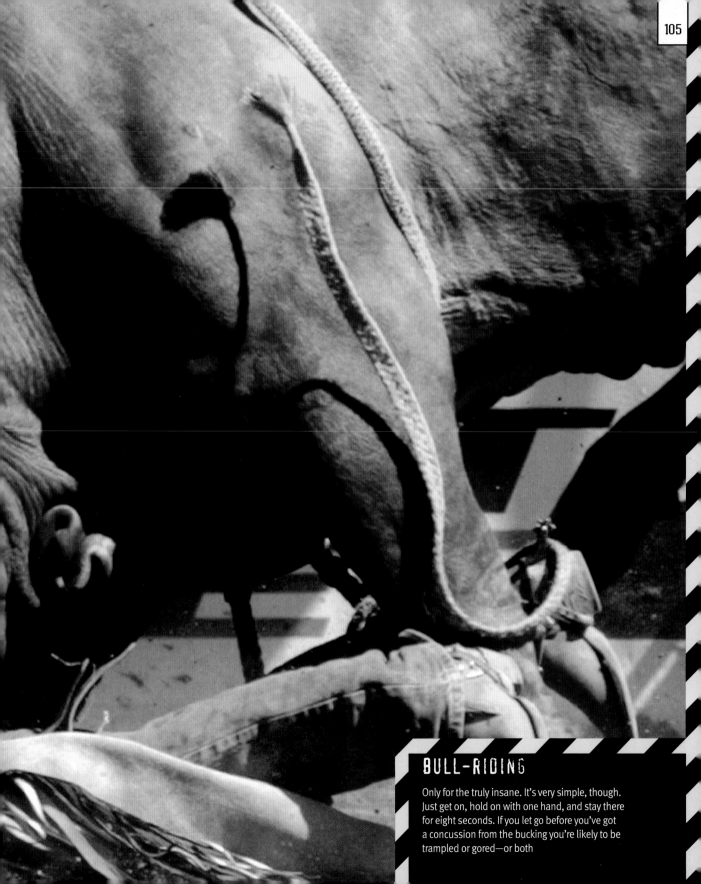

BULL-RIDING

Only for the truly insane. It's very simple, though. Just get on, hold on with one hand, and stay there for eight seconds. If you let go before you've got a concussion from the bucking you're likely to be trampled or gored—or both

GREGOR MacGREGOR

MacGregor was a Scottish adventurer who posed as the Cazique (prince) of Poyais, a fictional Central American country whose existence he fabricated to attract investment fraudulently. After capturing part of Florida from the Spanish in 1819, MacGregor returned to London, where he was fêted by high society. Claiming that a native chief had made him Cazique of Poyais, he said that he had established a civil service, an army, and a government, and that he was seeking investment. To make the scheme more plausible, he even published a guidebook entitled *Sketch of the Mosquito Shore*, including the Territory of Poyais, under the pseudonym Captain Thomas Strangeways. It described Poyais as a fertile country, rich in minerals, with a thriving capital city called Saint Joseph.

London merchants invested eagerly, and MacGregor also sold land rights to workers in his native Scotland, raising £200,000 ($950,000). In 1822 and 1823, two ships left London and Edinburgh with 270 would-be settlers, who arrived to find that Poyais didn't exist. Many died, many settled in British Honduras instead, and many others returned home and broke the story. But MacGregor had fled to France. He tried the same scam there, but, fortunately, the French authorities prevented the settlers' ship from leaving Le Havre. MacGregor was acquitted after cleverly shifting the blame onto one of his French co-conspirators, and went on to try several less ambitious versions of the same scam, the last of which involved the sale of land certificates in 1837.

⌘ ⌘

FRANK ABAGNALE

Thanks to Steven Spielberg's 2002 film *Catch Me If You Can,* Frank Abagnale is now one of the world's best-known scammers. Starting at the age of 16 with petty fraud using one of his father's credit cards, Abagnale moved on to defrauding banks by using multiple identities, faking checks, and printing his own account number on deposit slips so that other customers' money was diverted into his account.

He then began life as a serial impostor, scamming free flights by posing as a Pan Am pilot (complete with uniform and forged ID card) and taking advantage of the fact that airlines will often carry other airlines' pilots as a courtesy. After two years of free travel, he decided to lie low, renting an apartment in Georgia and telling neighbors that he was a doctor. As a result of meeting a real doctor, Abagnale spent 11 months as a hospital supervisor, performing the simpler medical procedures and delegating the more complex ones. He also used a forged degree to work as a college professor and posed as a Harvard graduate to become a lawyer.

By the age of 21, Abagnale had scammed about $2.5 million under eight identities in 26 countries. He was eventually arrested in France and served time in several European countries before being deported to the US, where he served five years of a 12-year sentence. On his release, he began teaching banks how to detect fraudsters, and now runs a legitimate antifraud consultancy.

CHARLES PONZI

Italian-born swindler Charles Ponzi gave his name to a scam known as the Ponzi Scheme, variations of which are still practiced to this day—basically, a fraudulent investment operation that pays high dividends to investors from money paid in by subsequent investors rather than from profit generated by any real business. It is bound to fail but, if the perpetrator gets out before the scheme collapses, he or she can make a tidy profit. The most lucrative scam ever was a Ponzi Scheme run by international financier Bernie Cornfield in the 1960s, which netted some $2.5 billion.

Born in 1882, Ponzi left Italy in the early 1900s for North America. In August 1919, he discovered that, under an international agreement, post offices in one country could issue coupons to buy stamps in another. The coupon exchange rate had been set before World War I but postwar depression in Europe meant that coupons bought for the price agreed to in Europe were now worth six times that amount in the US. Ponzi realized that if he could buy enough coupons in Europe and convert them into dollars, he could make astronomical profits.

In December 1919, he set up the Securities Exchange Company to do just that. He attracted thousands of investors on the promise of huge dividends. But instead of making money to pay the dividends, he paid them from subsequent investments. People were desperate for a slice of his profits, and in a matter of months about 40,000 people invested an estimated $15 million in the business (some $140 million today). But Ponzi didn't get out quickly enough and was arrested in August 1920 on 86 counts of fraud. After serving three and a half years, he was deported to Italy, where he died in poverty.

WAYS TO

All humans like to make money. Some work hard for it, some steal it, some inherit it. And some set up elaborate scams to con money out of other people. "Fraud" is boring

LEGENDS

SOUTH SEA BUBBLE

The South Sea Bubble was an economic bubble that burst in September 1720, ruining thousands of investors. The resulting inquiry revealed corruption in the British establishment and even implicated government ministers—effectively making this a government scam. It began with the South Sea Company, established in 1711 by the Lord Treasurer, Robert Harley, to try to ease national debt caused by Britain's part in the War of the Spanish Succession. In return for a monopoly on trade with South America and a perpetual government annuity, the company took on millions of pounds of government debt. In theory this benefited both parties: the government shed its debt while the company received a steady income and massive potential profits from its monopoly.

When the company took on more debt in 1719 and issued more shares, misrepresenting their value, the bubble began to inflate. Thousands of people wanted to invest, sending the share price rocketing by over 1,000 percent between January and August 1720. Then, in September, the bubble burst. Those selling to liquidate their profit at its peak sparked panic selling and the share price plummeted. The market collapsed, ruining both investors in the company and those banks that had loaned money for shares and could not now recover the loans. First Lord of the Treasury, Robert Walpole, eventually stimulated recovery by transferring some of the worthless stock to the Bank of England and the East India Company to spread the loss.

VICTOR LUSTIG

Also known as "the man who sold the Eiffel Tower," Lustig was born in Bohemia (now the Czech Republic) in 1890. After World War I, he spent several years in the US posing as a dispossessed Austrian Count in order to attract false investments. Then he moved to Paris where, in spring 1925, he read a newspaper article describing how the city could not afford to maintain the Eiffel Tower. This article gave Lustig his big idea.

Using forged government letterhead, he invited several scrap-metal dealers to a confidential meeting at one of Paris's top hotels, the Hotel de Crillon. Posing as the Deputy Director-General of the Ministry of Posts and Telegraphs, he said that the city could no longer afford the upkeep of the Eiffel Tower and wanted to sell it for scrap. He said that he would accept sealed bids for the famous landmark, warning the dealers that to avoid a public outcry the deal was an official state secret.

But rather than waiting for the highest bid, Lustig had already decided to accept a bid from the easiest mark, André Poisson, who was desperately eager to increase his standing in the city. When Poisson paid up, Lustig fled the city. But Poisson was too embarrassed to lodge a complaint, so Lustig returned to Paris and tried to repeat the scam with another group of scrap dealers. This time the mark informed the police before paying, and Lustig fled back to the US where, after many more scams, he was sentenced to 20 years in Alcatraz.

419 INTERNET SCAM

This 1990s–2000s internet fraud is an electronic variation on the age-old "Spanish prisoner" con trick. It began in the 16th century with the scammer sending letters claiming to be a wealthy prisoner held in a Spanish jail. The scammer would ask for money to bribe the guards, promising to reward the victim on his release.

The scam was revived in the 1990s in Nigeria, and became known as the Nigerian Letter fraud, or the 419 Scam after the section of the Nigerian Criminal Code that it violates. Organized gangs of scammers would send letters or faxes to heads of business claiming to be or to know an oppressed Nigerian who has inherited money and wishes to discreetly move it abroad to prevent it falling into corrupt hands. They claim to need an account to move the money into and offer up to 40 percent of the total moved if the victim allows it to be moved via his or her account.

With the advent of the internet, the ease of spamming people via email opened up the scam to a far greater number of potential victims, many of whom agreed to help. The scammers then say that bank officials need to be bribed—can the victim send money to finance that? Further delays and fees are added until the victim has been milked of as much cash as possible. It sounds implausible that people would fall for it, but the 419 Scam, which has since spread to other African countries, is estimated to have netted hundreds of millions of dollars. There are even reports of victims traveling to Africa to recover their losses and then being kidnapped or murdered.

MAKE MONEY

and technical but "scams" are imaginative and require panache to carry them off—even if they are just as illegal and just as damaging to the victims.

CHAPTER 5

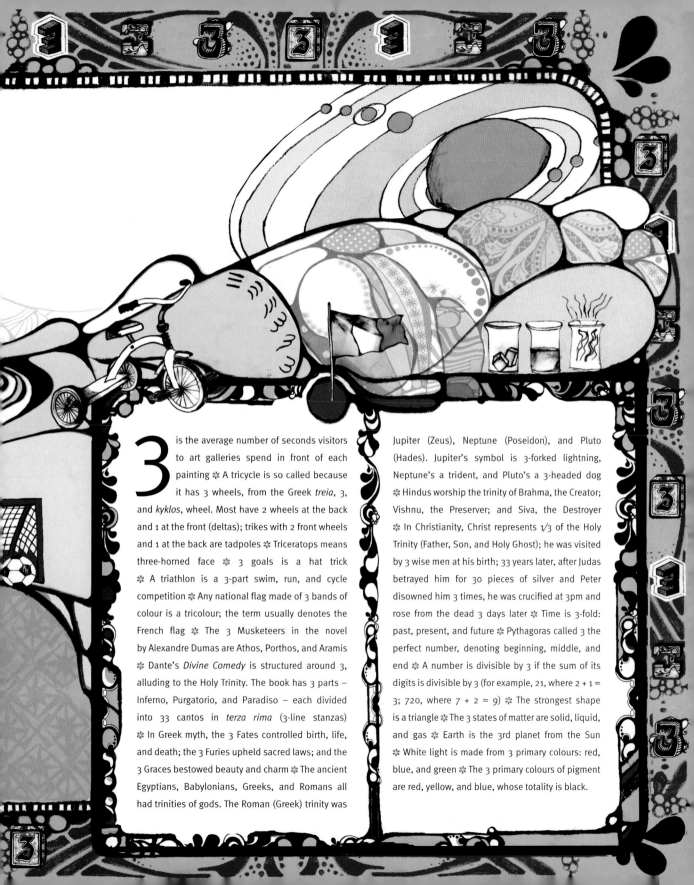

3 is the average number of seconds visitors to art galleries spend in front of each painting ❋ A tricycle is so called because it has 3 wheels, from the Greek *treia*, 3, and *kyklos*, wheel. Most have 2 wheels at the back and 1 at the front (deltas); trikes with 2 front wheels and 1 at the back are tadpoles ❋ Triceratops means three-horned face ❋ 3 goals is a hat trick ❋ A triathlon is a 3-part swim, run, and cycle competition ❋ Any national flag made of 3 bands of colour is a tricolour; the term usually denotes the French flag ❋ The 3 Musketeers in the novel by Alexandre Dumas are Athos, Porthos, and Aramis ❋ Dante's *Divine Comedy* is structured around 3, alluding to the Holy Trinity. The book has 3 parts – Inferno, Purgatorio, and Paradiso – each divided into 33 cantos in *terza rima* (3-line stanzas) ❋ In Greek myth, the 3 Fates controlled birth, life, and death; the 3 Furies upheld sacred laws; and the 3 Graces bestowed beauty and charm ❋ The ancient Egyptians, Babylonians, Greeks, and Romans all had trinities of gods. The Roman (Greek) trinity was Jupiter (Zeus), Neptune (Poseidon), and Pluto (Hades). Jupiter's symbol is 3-forked lightning, Neptune's a trident, and Pluto's a 3-headed dog ❋ Hindus worship the trinity of Brahma, the Creator; Vishnu, the Preserver; and Siva, the Destroyer ❋ In Christianity, Christ represents 1/3 of the Holy Trinity (Father, Son, and Holy Ghost); he was visited by 3 wise men at his birth; 33 years later, after Judas betrayed him for 30 pieces of silver and Peter disowned him 3 times, he was crucified at 3pm and rose from the dead 3 days later ❋ Time is 3-fold: past, present, and future ❋ Pythagoras called 3 the perfect number, denoting beginning, middle, and end ❋ A number is divisible by 3 if the sum of its digits is divisible by 3 (for example, 21, where $2 + 1 = 3$; 720, where $7 + 2 = 9$) ❋ The strongest shape is a triangle ❋ The 3 states of matter are solid, liquid, and gas ❋ Earth is the 3rd planet from the Sun ❋ White light is made from 3 primary colours: red, blue, and green ❋ The 3 primary colours of pigment are red, yellow, and blue, whose totality is black.

CUSTOMS AND ETIQUETTE
WORK-LIFE BALANCE

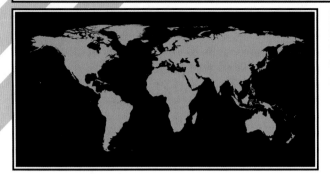

There are many ways of comparing the cost of living in different places, and most make no sense to any human without an economics degree. It boils down to how many hours you have to work to pay for food, clothes, and so on. The diners pictured below are eating a good three-course restaurant meal, with watches scaled to represent the minutes they'd have to work in 2006 to pay for it, according to UBS (Union Bank of Switzerland) figures.

70. AMSTERDAM
66.15 minutes

60. JOHANNESBURG
88.99 minutes

50. PRAGUE
110.07 minutes

40. LJUBLJANA
144.59 minutes

MINUTES WORKED TO BUY...

Figures are calculated by dividing the average cost of specified goods and services in each of 70 cities by the average wage and working hours across 13 occupations in those cities. The top and bottom five cities are listed.

MEN'S CLOTHES Complete wardrobe comprising a suit, blazer/jacket, shirt, jeans, socks, and shoes

1. COPENHAGEN
1,392 minutes

2. CHICAGO
1,662.6

3. GENEVA
1,684.2

4. LUXEMBOURG
1,708.2

5. TORONTO
1,790.4

66. SOFIA
8,280

67. BEIJING
9,762.6

68. BANGKOK
10,558.2

69. DELHI
12,295.8

70. JAKARTA
12,296.4

WOMEN'S CLOTHES
Complete outfit comprising suit, blazer/jacket, summer dress, underwear, shoes

1. OSLO
1,327.8 minutes

2. ZURICH
1,378.2

3. MUNICH
1,378.8

4. GENEVA
1,409.4

5. TORONTO
1,410.6

66. BOGOTA
5,590.8

67. BEIJING
6,567.6

68. KIEV
6,977.4

69. DELHI
7,266

70. JAKARTA
8,197.8

BUS TICKETS Bus, streetcar, or metro ticket for a journey of about 6 miles (10 km) or at least 10 stops

1. MANAMA
1.84 minutes

2. MOSCOW
2.31

3. BUENOS AIRES
2.41

4. ATHENS
3.35

5. BUCHAREST
3.39

66. NAIROBI
8.83

67. JAKARTA
9.46

68. BANGKOK
9.6

69. STOCKHOLM
11.68

70. TALLINN
11.97

THE MOST EXPENSIVE CITIES ARE OSLO, LONDON, AND COPENHAGEN. BUT HIGH SALARIES GIVE WORKERS A LOT OF BUYING POWER.

30. TAIPEI
199.52 minutes

20. SANTIAGO DE CHILE 275.29 minutes

10. JAKARTA
378.35 minutes

1. KIEV
627.95 minutes

RAIL TICKETS Single rail ticket (second class) for a train trip of 125 miles (200 km)	**TAXI** Journey of 3 miles (5 km) within the city limits, including service	**BREAD** Minutes worked to buy a 2 lb (1 kg) loaf of bread	**RICE** Minutes worked to buy a 2 lb (1 kg) bag of rice
1. MOSCOW 23.92 minutes	**1. SEOUL** 9.56 minutes	**1. LONDON** 5 minutes	**1.= AUCKLAND** 5 minutes
2. SEOUL 26.28	**2. LIMA** 11.24	**2. DUBLIN** 7	**1.= LONDON** 5
3. HONG KONG 41.56	**3. HELSINKI** 15.36	**3.= FRANKFURT** 9	**1.= SYDNEY** 5
4. JOHANNESBURG 44.5	**4. ATHENS** 15.8	**3.= NICOSIA** 9	**1.= ZURICH** 5
5. BRUSSELS 51.2	**5. KUALA LUMPUR** 16.54	**5. AMSTERDAM** 10	**5. COPENHAGEN** 6
66. DELHI 159.29	**66. BUDAPEST** 69.44	**66. BANGKOK** 49	**66. MUMBAI** 32
67. LIMA 160.75	**67. CARACAS** 69.97	**67. MEXICO CITY** 53	**67. NAIROBI** 33
68. LONDON 222.9	**68. KIEV** 93.03	**68. BOGOTA** 59	**70.= JAKARTA** 36
69. JAKARTA 249.08	**69. NAIROBI** 98.93	**69. MANILA** 64	**70.= ISTANBUL** 36
70. NAIROBI 249.09	**70. HONG KONG** 123.91	**70. CARACAS** 76	**70.= DELHI** 36

AMERICA'S NATIONAL PASTIME

Baseball is more than just a sport; it's part of the American psyche, and its origins are hotly disputed. Some people argue that it developed from the English game of rounders, while others, not surprisingly, claim that it's a purely American game. What can be said for certain is that the "father of modern baseball" was American Alexander Cartwright Jr., who codified the first official set of rules in 1845. Those rules are the basis of the game we know today—that is, a bat and ball game played between two teams of nine. One team's pitcher throws the ball toward the opposing team's batter, who attempts to hit the ball far enough to allow him and his teammates to score runs by advancing around the four bases of the diamond before the pitcher's teammates can retrieve the ball.

THE PLAYER

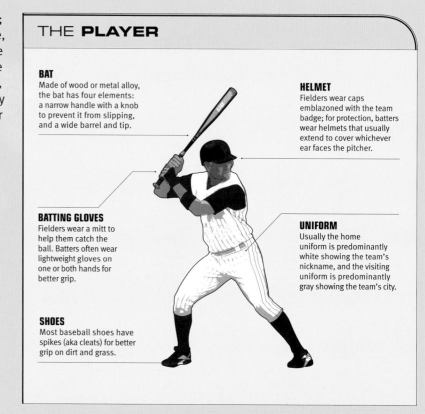

BAT
Made of wood or metal alloy, the bat has four elements: a narrow handle with a knob to prevent it from slipping, and a wide barrel and tip.

HELMET
Fielders wear caps emblazoned with the team badge; for protection, batters wear helmets that usually extend to cover whichever ear faces the pitcher.

BATTING GLOVES
Fielders wear a mitt to help them catch the ball. Batters often wear lightweight gloves on one or both hands for better grip.

UNIFORM
Usually the home uniform is predominantly white showing the team's nickname, and the visiting uniform is predominantly gray showing the team's city.

SHOES
Most baseball shoes have spikes (aka cleats) for better grip on dirt and grass.

BASEBALL TIMELINE

1846 The first officially recorded game of baseball takes place on June 19 in Hoboken, New Jersey. The New York Nine beat the Knickerbocker Club 23–1 in four innings.

1857 The length of a game is set at nine innings for the first time.

1869 The Cincinnati Red Stockings decides to pay all its players, thus becoming the first professional baseball team.

1876 The National League is formed as the first Major League.

1884 Bobby Lowe (US) becomes the first player to hit four home runs in one game (for the Boston Beaneaters). The rules are altered to allow overhand pitching for the first time.

1900 The American League is formed as the second Major League.

1903 First World Series: the winners of the two Major Leagues play a seven-game series to decide the overall champions—Boston Red Sox (AL) defeat Pittsburgh Pirates (NL).

1927 Babe Ruth becomes the first player to hit 60 home runs in a season—before the "Babe Ruth era" no player had hit more than 24 in a season.

1938 First baseball World Cup is held, in London, between the US and Great Britain: GB wins the series.

" WHOEVER WANTS TO KNOW THE HEART AND MIND OF AMERICA HAD BETTER LEARN BASEBALL. "

Philosopher and educator, Jacques Barzun

THE DIAMOND

1. BATTER
2. CATCHER
3. INFIELDERS
4. OUTFIELDERS
5. PITCHER
6. UMPIRES
A. HOME PLATE
B. SHORTSTOP
C. FIRST BASE
D. SECOND BASE
E. THIRD BASE
F. COACH'S BOX
G. FOUL LINE
H. FOUL POLE

1953 The New York Yankees becomes the first team to win five consecutive World Series.

1956 The first perfect game (no hits and no runs) in a World Series is pitched by Don Larsen (for the New York Yankees against the Brooklyn Dodgers).

1962 At the height of the Cold War, an article appears in the Soviet Union magazine *Nedelya*, making the ludicrous claim that Beizbol was an ancient game invented in Russia!

1991 Nolan Ryan (Houston Astros) becomes the first player to pitch seven no-hit games in major league baseball (having been the first to five in 1981 and the first to six in 1990).

1992 The Toronto Blue Jays (Canada) become the first non-American team to win the World Series, beating the Atlanta Braves 4–2.

2005 Cuba wins the baseball World Cup for the 24th time in the Cup's 67-year existence—far more than any other nation.

THE STATS

92,706 The highest ever attendance figure for an American game was recorded on October 6, 1959, when the LA Dodgers played the Chicago White Sox.

162 The number of baseball games played by every Major League team in the season, which lasts from April to October.

59 The age of the oldest ever pro, Satchel Paige, who played his last game for the Kansas City Athletics on September 25, 1969.

114,000 The highest ever attendance for a baseball game— an exhibition between Australia and an American services team during the 1956 Olympics.

3,562 The record number of games played during a pro career. The record is held by Pete Rose, who played for 24 years.

73 The record number of home runs hit by a single player during an MLB season. The record is held by Barry Bonds.

2,700,000 The price in dollars for the most expensive piece of baseball memorabilia—the baseball that Mark McGwire hit for record-breaking run number 70 in 1998. Canadian comic-book artist and avid baseball fan Todd McFarlane bought the ball at auction in 1999.

26 The number of times the New York Yankees have won the World Series.

Attract a mate

How can you tell whether or not that gorgeous human on the other side of the room likes you or not? And more to the point, how do you let them know you're interested without actually saying so? You read their body language. And you send out some subliminal signals of your own. Don't know how to do that? Then read on.

Eyebrow raise

A lot of body language differs between cultures but this one is universal — if a person sees someone they like their eyebrows raise and lower; and if the other person feels the same they'll do it too. But you've got to be watching carefully because it only lasts about a fifth of a second. You can try to do it consciously to indicate you like someone but it will probably end up looking clumsy because you won't be able to do it quickly enough.

Distance

There's no hard and fast rule about how close to sit or stand but you do need to be aware of what you're doing. Too far away and the person is going to assume you're not interested; too close and you're going to look overeager, too pushy, or just plain rude. You don't have to keep the same distance all the time. Find the right moments either to lean closer momentarily, or to move closer and stay closer.

Orientation

So you've started a conversation and you're trying out the techniques. Their face is toward you, but which way is their body turned? If their body is still turned toward their friends and they're only turning their head toward you, you need to try a bit harder. It doesn't need to be the whole body: if they're sitting with their hands or feet pointing toward you, that's a good start; if they move their arms or legs to face you, that's even better. And you can do the same; the positive vibe will be picked up subconsciously even if they're not actually looking for it.

Flirting triangle

Be aware of where the other person is looking. When meeting strangers, people tend to concentrate on the eyes, their focus often zigzagging from one eye to the other. As people become more familiar the zigzag becomes a triangle, taking in the nose and mouth. So when you flirt, make yourself seem more familiar and friendly by using the triangle; and watch to see if the other person is doing the same. Don't just look at the eyes; think about the mouth as well — what would it be like to kiss?

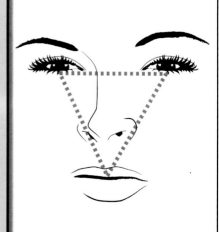

Eye contact

Don't overdo it with staring at the mouth — eye contact is important as well. If you keep staring over your intended's shoulder at someone else, or checking out other people as they walk past, you're not going to get very far. Nor if you just drool over a particular part of their anatomy, however tempting that may be. The eyes are the windows of the soul, so have a look at the person inside. But again, don't overdo it — if you stare too deeply into their eyes you're going to just come across as too intense (or just plain weird).

Mirroring

It may seem obvious, but no one is going to start copying what you do unless they like you. We all like people who are a bit like us, and mirroring is a subliminal way of saying "I want to be more like you." It can be done subconsciously or deliberately, and you can flatter someone by subtly copying what they do — but don't copy every single move as soon as they make it or it will seem as though you are trying to make them look silly. Leave a short pause and then do something similar to what they've just done, whether it's sipping your drink or touching your hair, or whatever.

Blink rate

While you're gazing (but not staring) into those gorgeous eyes, check out how many times the other person is blinking. If their eyelashes are fluttering up and down with a high blink rate, either they've got dust behind their contact lenses or you're in. Dilated pupils and an increased blink rate are sure signs of attraction. But dilated pupils are also a sign of drunkenness or drug abuse, so don't rely on this indicator alone. You can, of course, increase your own blink rate to let them know how you feel, and then they might unconsciously increase theirs to match (see "mirroring").

ANGLER FISH

A male angler fish has no digestive system and must find a mate in order to survive. When he does he bites her side and releases an enzyme that fuses them. Their circulatory systems join, and he receives nutrition directly from her bloodstream. Sounds ghoulish? It gets worse—the male then begins to degenerate, atrophying until only his gonads are left. These remain attached to the female, ready to release sperm on demand. Angler fish are life-long mates, inevitably.

ADELE PENGUIN

When a male chooses a mate he finds a stone—often by stealing one from another pair's nest—and rolls it to his paramour's feet. If she accepts this generous offering, they stand belly to belly with their heads back and flippers outstretched and sing a mating song. Then they go off to find somewhere private, but, after all the foreplay, intercourse lasts just three minutes. And that's your lot until the following year.

FLORA AND FAUNA

Wild Sex

"I say, I say, I say, how does a porcupine make love?" Answer: "Very carefully!" It's a well-known joke, but the truth is even stranger—and the truth about certain other animal mating habits is even stranger still. Ladies, it's a kill or be killed world, so better to be a praying mantis than a hippopotamus or red- (or dead) sided garter snake. And gents, if anyone asks whether you'd rather be a barnacle or an angler fish, opt for the barnacle.

SEA HARE

Also known as beach blobbies, sea hares have penises on their heads and vaginas within their shells. This arrangement means that a single pair of sea hares can't act as male and female at the same time, so they often mate in chains, the one at the front acting as a female, the one at the back as a male, and those in between having it both ways.

RED-SIDED GARTER SNAKE

Definitely not single-partner maters for life. These snakes mate in orgies of several thousand, often with up to 100 males fighting over each female. The pile of snakes can be as much as 2ft (60cm) thick. Sometimes snakes are crushed to death by the weight—although that doesn't bother the males, who keep going regardless of whether their partner is dead or alive.

AUSTRALIAN SCALY CRICKET

Until 2004, lions and tigers were billed as nature's sex machines, mating up to 50 times a day for up to a week. But a recent study discovered that the Australian scaly cricket mates more than 50 times with the same female in just four hours.

BARNACLE

Stationary and hermaphrodite, barnacles rely on a huge penis to mate—their inflatable members can extend to 2in (5cm). That's 20 times their body size, so, proportionately, barnacles have the longest penises in the animal world.

PRAYING MANTIS

Mrs. Mantis has a reputation for biting her partner's head off after sex, although naturalists say this happens more in captivity than in the wild because in a cage the male has less room to escape. The male, who is smaller than the female, mounts from behind and begins copulating. Sometimes the female devours his head before he's even finished, in which case reflexes keep him going. Apparently, the reason for this possessive behavior plays no part in the mating process—it just ensures that he doesn't share his genes with anyone else.

HIPPOPOTAMUS

Like many animals, hippos attract mates by smell. However, unlike many others, hippos do so by twirling their tails in order to spray a mixture of urine and feces through the air. Once a female responds to this romantic overture, the pair runs down to the water and begins mating, which is a strenuous business for the female, who is underneath and has to fight to keep her head above the water.

BLACK WIDOW

These spiders are so called because the female is supposed to eat her partner as soon as she's finished mating with him, but, in fact, such sexual cannibalism is rare in most species of black widow.

GOOSE

Geese practice one of nature's more enlightened forms of homosexuality. Often a pair of males will bond and take no interest in females. But if an intrepid female does join them for a threesome, they will fertilize her and all three will bring up the goslings.

PORCUPINE

Courtship and copulation are dramatic and messy. It begins romantically enough, with the male singing to his chosen one. But when he thinks she's ready to mate, he stands up on his hind legs and urinates on her. If she runs away, hits him, or bites him, the answer's no. When she finally stands still, she's ready to mate, which isn't as dangerous as you might think—the quills of both partners relax and lie flat, letting the male enter from behind. They go at it until the male is exhausted, after which the female may continue with someone else.

PAINT THAT CAT

When it comes to humans' favorite pets, cats are a close second to dogs, and in some countries are overtaking dogs in the popularity stakes. However, the cats featured here might no longer be their owners' best friends if they looked in the mirror and saw what happened while they were asleep.

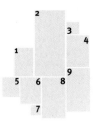

CATFISH (main photo)
fur or fin?

01. SKELETAL CAT
to celebrate Halloween.

02. OWL EYES
this elegant cat
looks wise.

03. DUOTONE
a startling effect with
fluorescent pink dye
sprayed over blue.

04. CATWOMAN
alluring minx in a
bikini and bandanna.

05. CLOWN FACE
professional clown-cat,
popular at children's
parties.

06. CHEVRON STRIPES
strokable pair in black
and white.

07. STUNNING SPECS
Miss Chartreuse,
first-prize winner
at a cat art show
in California.

08. CHARLIE CHAPLIN
retrospective view
that cost more than
$5,000 to paint.

09. KEYBOARD
a Cornish Rex hits
the right note.

The publishers and author do NOT
recommend that readers try to paint
their own cats.

Patent junk

Necessity is said to be the mother of invention, but in cases like these it seems that insanity had more to do with it. For every successful human invention there are hundreds of unsuccessful ones. Some fail because the inventor has the right idea at the wrong time. Others fail because even more inventive inventors find ways of circumventing the patent. And still others fail because they're just... ridiculous ideas.

Patent No. GB 229
Improvements in and Relating to Apparatus for Walking on Water

Marout Yegwartian. Filed January 5, 1914
It was audacious of Yegwartian to patent an improvement on an idea conceived by Leonardo da Vinci some 400 years earlier but the principle does work—in 1988 Frenchman Remy Bricka used similar apparatus to "walk" 3,502 miles (5,636 km) across the Atlantic from the Canary Islands to Trinidad.

Patent No. US 1,187,218
Firearm

Jones Wister. Filed March 15, 1916
Perhaps predicting that the US would join the Great War the following year, Wister invented a rifle for use in the trenches—complete with periscope. He had clearly not tested his patent claim that the curved barrel would "deflect the projectile at an angle to the longitudinal line of the firearm."

Patent No. US 4,428,085
Self-cleaning House

Frances Bateson (aka Gabe). Filed 1980
Frances Gabe hated housework, and spent 30 years and 36 patents developing a self-cleaning house. In a 45-minute cycle powerful sprinklers fitted to all the ceilings wash down all the walls, furniture, and fixtures before jets of hot air dry everything. Her own house in Oregon has been rebuilt to accommodate her invention but surprisingly she hasn't sold that many to other people.

Patent No. US 3,589,009
Spaghetti Fork

William J. Miscavich et al. Filed January 9, 1969
Just in case people weren't sure what to do with it, Miscavich and his pals explained: "In the operation of the device, the handle is held between the fingers and thumb of one hand, and as the tines 1 are inserted into a portion of spaghetti or the like the user depresses the plunger 22... When the desired amount of spaghetti has been wound upon the tines of the fork the plunger 22 is released."

Fig 1

Patent No. US 3,552,388
Baby-patting Machine

Thomas V. Zelenka. Filed November 7, 1968
Zelenka's patent states: "... it is sometimes difficult for the infant to fall asleep, and the parent must resort to patting the baby to sleep by repeated pats upon the hind parts thereof... the present invention... will pat a baby to sleep, thereby eliminating the necessity of a parent to do the same manually for an extended period of time."

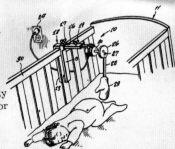

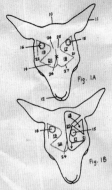

Method of Growing Unicorns

Patent No. US 4,429,685

Timothy G. Zell. Granted February 7, 1984

Zell's patent is for a surgical means of growing unicorns by transplanting the horn buds of newly born cows, antelope, sheep, or goats to a central position on the front of the animal's skull. The patent states: "Thereafter the resulting horns grow as one and connect with the frontal portion of the skull directly over the pineal gland to render a unicorn of higher intelligence and physical attributes."

Spider Ladder provided with Means of Attachment to an Item of Sanitary Ware

Patent No. GB 2,272,154

Edward Doughney. Filed August 12, 1993

Obviously hoping to be voted animal lover of the year, Doughney devised this latex ladder complete with suction pad for attachment to the bathtub. The patent helpfully points out: "Trapped spiders searching for an escape will scale the spider ladder by means of (2) and (3) the inner and outer steps respectively."

Pat-on-the-back Apparatus

Patent No. US 4,608,967

Ralph R. Piro. Filed May 31, 1981

Possibly traumatized as a child by Zelenka's baby-patting machine (below left), Piro invented this machine "for providing a self-administered pat on the back... Such an arrangement may provide the needed psychological lift to allow a person to overcome some of the 'valleys' of emotional life in a highly technicalized society."

Fire Escape

Patent No. US 221,855

Benjamin Oppenheimer. Filed March 26, 1879

Oppenheimer claimed: "A person may safely jump out of the window of a burning building from any height and land, without injury and without the least damage, on the ground." But that is not quite true—even with rubber soles to cushion your landing, attaching a parachute by a chin strap is not a good idea unless you have a particularly strong neck.

Horse-powered Minibus

Patent No. GB 2,060,081

P. A. Barnes. Granted April 29, 1981

Inventors are often accused of putting the cart before the horse, but Barnes went one better—he put the horse inside the cart. His minibus is powered by a horse walking on a conveyor belt in the vehicle, which acts as a treadmill and drives the wheels via a chain, a clutch, and a variable-ratio gearbox.

Barnes claimed: "There are several advantages in taking the horse off the road in vehicle propulsion. The most obvious is speed variation... [in] lowest gear the vehicle moves forward slower than the walking speed of the horse; this helps it to pull a load up hill. [In] highest gear the vehicle moves faster...and shortens the journey time." Barnes even proposed dashboard instruments with "horse temperature and collar-push," and the patent stated: "Containers are provided to collect droppings...".

PATENT CRAZY

English inventor Arthur Paul Pedrick was the king of wacky patents. A former patent examiner for the UK Patent Office, Pedrick filed a vast number of patents, many of which defied the laws of physics. Among them were a golf ball with aerodynamic flaps to control spin; a radioactive golf ball which, if lost, could be found using a geiger counter (below); one means of solving world famine by piping snowballs from Antarctica to irrigate the deserts of Australia, and another by piping fresh water from the Amazon to the Sahara. And during the Cold War he patented the idea of placing nuclear warheads in geostationary orbits over Washington, Moscow, and Beijing as a deterrent to war.

.FIG. 6.

1998 BELGIAN GRAND PRIX

At the biggest pile-up in Grand Prix history, David Coulthard lost control in the wet, hit a wall, and rebounded onto the track, taking out his own and 12 other cars: Rubens Barrichello and Jos Verstappen (Stewart), Pedro Diniz and Mika Salo (Arrows), Johnny Herbert (Sauber), Eddie Irvine (Ferrari), Shinji Nakano (Minardi), Olivier Panis and Jarno Trulli (Prost), Ricardo Rosset and Toranosuke Takagi (Tyrrell), and Alexander Wurz (Benetton).

CLINT MALARCHUK

In 1988, a wayward skate slashed the carotid artery of ice hockey goaltender Clint Malarchuk. Two teammates vomited on the ice, seven spectators fainted, and two more had heart attacks. He was saved by the team's ex-Army medic, who pinched the artery with his fingers until paramedics arrived.

DERRICK CRASS

At the 1984 Los Angeles Olympics, 24-year-old American weightlifter Derrick Crass lost control of the bar during his attempt at lifting 286 lb (130 kg), dislocating his elbow and spraining his right knee.

SPORTS AND LEISURE

WIPEOUT

Sports are like theater: there are highs and lows, heroes and villains, drama interspersed with reflective moments. And every so often something goes spectacularly wrong, resulting in embarrassment, or pain, or both. Here's a selection of some of sporting history's most painful moments, from dislocated joints and broken bones to close encounters with motorcycles and ice-skating blades.

◢ JOE THEISMANN

Washington Redskins quarterback Joe Theismann's career ended in 1985 when New York Giants linebacker Lawrence Taylor landed on his lower leg, fracturing his tibia and fibula so badly that the bones went through the skin.

VINKO BOGATAJ

Slovenian ski jumper Vinko Bogataj crashed spectacularly at the 1970 World Ski Flying Championships. Halfway through his third jump Bogataj realized that increasingly heavy snow had made the ramp too fast. Trying to slow himself down he lost his balance and shot off the end of the ramp completely out of control. Amazingly, he only suffered a light concussion.

◢ EVEL KNIEVEL

On May 31, 1975, American stunt motorcyclist Robert "Evel" Knievel attempted to jump a world record 13 double-decker buses at Wembley Stadium, London. Some 90,000 people watched him complete the jump but crash on landing, breaking his pelvis. Knievel announced the first of several retirements—but was soon jumping again.

DAVE BUSST

The career of Coventry soccer player Dave Busst of the UK ended after this collision, which broke his tibia and fibula so badly that his leg nearly had to be amputated. The match was delayed for 15 minutes to clean up the blood.

△ 2002 DAYTONA 500

The Daytona 500 is the blue-riband event of the American National Association for Stock Car Auto Racing (NASCAR) cup series. In 2002, race leaders Jeff Gordon and Kevin Harvick nudged each other for pole position on lap 194 out of 200. Gordon went spinning, triggering a massive 18-car pile-up behind them. After Gordon and Harvick were both penalized, Ward Burton became the surprise winner following a three-lap sprint to the finish.

NIKI LAUDA

In the 1976 German Grand Prix, Lauda's Ferrari spun out of control and burst into flames after hitting another car. Fellow drivers saved his life by pulling him out from the fire. Despite being given the last rites, he was driving again just six weeks later.

△ 2001 GRAND NATIONAL

In 2001, heavy conditions at this long-distance steeplechase caused complete chaos. Eight horses were down by the third fence, nine at the Canal Turn, and four more at the infamous Chair, leaving just eight running. Six more fell before the finish but two jockeys remounted. Here, Tom Doyle parts company with "Esprit de Cotte" at the 11th.

DESTRY WHITE

In July 2000, Pittsburgh Steelers running back Destry White broke his right leg and dislocated his right ankle. The lower half of his right leg twisted 180° and ended up facing behind him.

THE RULES OF DATING

There aren't many things that humans all agree on but finding a partner is one of them, whether it's for love, sex, reproduction, or all three. But how do humans attract mates? An essential but poorly understood part of the courtship ritual is "dating"—going out—and getting to know each other better. Here are some of the rules.

DATING DOS AND DON'TS

DO:
♥ make an effort: dress well and smell sweet.

♥ show up on time.

♥ make eye contact—make your date feel that he or she is the only person in the room.

♥ show an interest in your date's interests (hopefully, you may have some in common).

♥ ask questions that will stimulate conversation, not ones that require just a "yes" or a "no."

♥ lean toward your date a little, if all seems to be going well.

♥ try mirroring his or her body language.

♥ compliment your date on his or her looks/hair/outfit/earrings/aftershave/perfume—flattery is fine, as long as it's not obviously insincere.

♥ say you'd like to meet again, if things have gone well. Ask if you can swap phone numbers or email addresses.

♥ be honest if you don't want to take things any further.

DON'T:
♥ stand anyone up. Ever.

♥ use words like "babe," "cool," or "wicked."

♥ use cheesy come-on lines. Your date is not an undiscovered model or an angel from heaven, so just be yourself. "Do you sleep on your stomach? If not, may I?" may seem hilarious on paper, but you will probably be rewarded with a glare, a mild expletive, and perhaps the sudden termination of your date.

♥ talk to your date's body; focus on the face.

♥ forget your sense of humor.

♥ try too hard to make yourself sound important or boast about how many lovers you've had.

♥ launch into your life story: leave your date wanting to know a bit more about you; stay mysterious.

♥ argue with the waiter/taxi driver/anyone else who irritates you.

♥ get pressured into giving your number to someone you don't like or find scary.

♥ try to get your date into bed on the first occasion. Sex should not be on the agenda. If you do sleep together on the first date, the chances are the romance will be over before it begins.

WHO PAYS?

♥ Dating etiquette suggests that men pay for the first and second dates and women offer to pay for the third date—if it goes that far.

♥ Some men would never ever let a date pay, however much she insisted, while some women are determined to share the bill.

♥ If an argument seems likely, fake going to the bathroom, then slip off to settle the bill. Return to the table with the throwaway line: "It's OK—taken care of."

DATING VENUES

CASUAL CAFE

A casual daytime date can ease the pressure to "perform." You can chat in a café and then stroll around a gallery, museum, or the park. What you look at—whether it's art or flowerbeds—acts as a stimulus for safe conversation, which you can always steer to the more personal if you're feeling confident. Daytime dates also tend to avoid any awkward, "Would you like to come up for a coffee?" or "Can I walk you home?" moments.

MEAL AT A RESTAURANT

A tried and tested formula, the traditional candlelit meal for two can be very romantic. Dress up, eat, talk, and get merry—but don't get sloshed.

MOVIE AND POPCORN

An evening at the movies is another popular option, but what to watch? Romantic comedies are the safest option. Action-thrillers are probably OK, too. Schlock-horror is probably for the post-third date. Don't go for the back-seat kill before you've properly introduced yourselves. Sitting in the moview theater for a couple of hours allows nerves to subside before you talk afterward.

MOONLIGHT STROLL

Perfect for "thoughtful" or "creative" types. A stroll under the stars along the beach front, river path, city streets, or around favorite boho haunts, while humming your latest musical composition, is a surefire winner given the right setting and mood. Avoid empty parking lots, cul-de-sacs, water treatment plants, recycling centers, and places where there are more CCTVs per corner than human beings. You're on a romantic tryst, not an urban experience, so a walk to the 24-hour garage won't do the trick.

DANCING CHEEK TO CHEEK

Be it ballroom, disco, barn, or house, dancing close to a new partner will either ignite the passion or squelch it entirely. The date could be fun and should help to break the ice.

VITAL STATISTICS

♥ There's safety in numbers. In some countries (such as Kenya, South Korea, and Jamaica), dating usually involves going out in groups on double, triple, or quadruple dates.

♥ In London and France, teens apparently start dating as young as 12 or 13. In Sweden, the average age is around 15. A Jamaican teen usually waits until age 16 or 17 before pairing off.

♥ Worldwide, Australian women are statistically the most likely to have sex on a first date.

♥ It's raining men: for every 100 single women in their 20s in the US there are 119 single men (never-married, widowed, or divorced) of the same age. For over 65s, the proportion is drastically reversed: for every 100 women there are a mere 34 single men.

ONLINE DATING

♥ With over 90 million people online and a mushrooming of dating sites for the world's increasing singles populations, how on earth do you choose? In one week in 2005, there were just under 19 million visitors to the five most popular dating sites, with slightly more men visiting than women...

REMEMBER TO PLAY SAFE

♥ Guard your identity—don't share any personal details such as phone numbers until you build a sense of trust.

♥ Use your gut feeling and common sense: listen to what you hear, not what you want to hear.

♥ Use a third-party anonymous email address.

♥ Don't put all your eggs in one inbox—"play the field" when it comes to online dating, so that you have plenty to compare and contrast.

♥ Take things offline once you feel comfortable, but always arrange to meet in a public place.

♥ Tell at least one friend or family member who you are meeting, where you are going, and when you expect to return. Let your date know your meeting is not a secret.

♥ Don't leave home without your cell phone.

♥ Don't be afraid to end the meeting promptly if it's not working out.

SPEED DATING

The same essential dating etiquette applies... it's just more frantic. You have only a few minutes to speak to each person and to record whether you like them or not before moving on to the next person. It can be a great way of meeting single people, but don't hold your breath for a string of dates off the back of the evening. You will only be given contact details of those people whose responses match yours.

DO:

♥ dress well—speed dating tends to attract the fashionable and well groomed.

♥ flirt a little—if you're interested in someone, let him or her know. Eye contact, the occasional touch, and using the date's name often are useful tools, but don't overdo it.

♥ have a number of stock questions ready. Five minutes may not seem very long but there is nothing worse than choking.

♥ use the break and "after dating" times to chat and meet. If you flubbed your lines during your scheduled date, don't be scared to make an approach later for a second chance.

♥ be careful what you eat, particularly if food is served during the dating session. Your date is unlikely to enjoy watching you slurping noodles.

DON'T:

♥ lie. If you're not an entrepreneur/dolphin handler/bungee-jump instructor then don't pretend to be.

♥ forget to fill out the Speed Dating cards after each rotation. There is nothing worse than getting to the end of the night and pondering over that special person with the wonderful eyes and thinking: "Now what was their name?"

♥ swear. This is often a big turn-off for both sexes.

♥ talk about exes, politics, or religion.

♥ give your personal contact details on the evening. It might seem the most natural thing in the world at the time, but email contact is safer—and more fun—to start with.

SHARK ATTACK

- ❑ **DON'T SWIM ALONE,** at dusk, or with bleeding wounds.

- ❑ **DON'T WEAR BRIGHT JEWELRY** or highly contrasting colors.

- ❑ **GET OUT OF THE WATER** if dolphins, fish, turtles, or other sea creatures appear nervous.

- ❑ **IF A SHARK DOES ATTACK,** fight back—sharks will only continue an attack if they are sure they have the upper hand.

- ❑ **AIM FOR ITS EYES OR GILLS,** which are the most sensitive areas. Punch, kick, or make repeated jabs with any object in your possession.

- ❑ **AIM FOR THE NOSE** only if you can't reach the eyes or gills; the nose is less sensitive.

QUICKSAND

- ❑ **IF THERE IS ANY DANGER** of encountering quicksand, carry a stout pole.

- ❑ **IF YOU START SINKING** into quicksand, discard your backpack and any heavy equipment.

- ❑ **LAY YOUR POLE** on the quicksand surface behind you; lie back over the pole, pull your legs out one at a time, and roll toward solid ground.

- ❑ **NO POLE?** Lie back anyway to spread your weight and try the same technique.

- ❑ **IF YOUR LEGS ARE STUCK,** wriggle them slowly. A University of Amsterdam physics professor assures us that, contrary to popular belief, this will not drag you deeper but loosen the sand, enabling you to extricate yourself.

CROCODILE ATTACK

- ❑ **RUN FAST;** crocodiles, and alligators, too, are fast runners over a short distance but quickly exhaust themselves.

- ❑ **IF ATTACKED,** hit it repeatedly on the nose or poke it in the eyes.

- ❑ **IF IT GETS YOU IN ITS JAWS,** play dead—if you're lucky it will stop shaking you and put you aside to eat later.

I WILL SURVIVE... PART I

POLAR SURVIVAL

- ❑ **ONLY TRAVEL IF YOU HAVE TO**—if rescue is likely, make a shelter near your aircraft or vehicle and stay there. Do not shelter close to inland water, since mosquitoes and other pests will gather there. If such a location is unavoidable, cover skin, use a mosquito net, and light a smoky fire.

- ❑ **TRY TO KEEP WARM AND DRY.** Wear a fur-trimmed hood pulled close; the fur will prevent breath from freezing on your face. But don't fasten anything so tightly that it prevents air from circulating. Keep clothing clean; it will breathe better, keeping you warmer and drier.

- ❑ **IF YOU DON'T HAVE SPECIAL CLOTHING,** wear layers of wool, not cotton—wool doesn't absorb moisture and remains warm when wet.

- ❑ **KEEP ACTIVE TO STAY WARM** but don't sweat—loosen collar and cuffs and remove clothing if necessary to regulate temperature.

- ❑ **KEEP HYDRATED** but don't eat snow or ice: ice can damage your mouth, and both will dangerously lower body temperature. Melt it first.

- ❑ **FROSTBITE AFFECTS EXTREMITIES** first. Watch out for the signs: a prickly feeling followed by skin turning white and waxy, then red, then bluish-black. Exercise the affected parts—flex fingers and toes, pull faces. If you have access to heat, warm the affected part gradually: never rub.

BEAR ATTACK

- ❑ **BE CONSPICUOUSLY NOISY** so as not to surprise a bear (some walkers wear "bear bells").

- ❑ **IF CONFRONTED WITH A BEAR,** do not shout. Raise your arms above your head to make yourself look bigger and speak in a normal voice while slowly backing away—do not turn your back on the bear. Climbing a tree may help but does not guarantee safety.

- ❑ **IF THE BEAR CHARGES,** stand your ground. Bears often bluff an attack. Do not try to outrun or outswim a bear.

- ❑ **IF ATTACKED,** adopt a fetal position, cover your head and neck with your hands, and play dead—if the bear deduces that you are not a threat, it may stop attacking.

DESERT SURVIVAL

- ❑ **DEHYDRATION AND EXCESSIVE HEAT** are the greatest dangers, so make use of shade when possible and cover all skin—this will reduce dehydration through sweat evaporation as well as protecting against sunburn and insect bites. Keep clothing as loose as possible and don't forget to cover your head and feet.

- ❑ **DO NOT SHELTER IN A VEHICLE** or plane, which will overheat. Instead, make shelter in the shadow of the vehicle, using fabric if possible—leave the fabric loose during the day to increase air circulation and weigh it down at night.

- ❑ **CONSERVE WATER** but don't overration it—take sips regularly. If searching for water, follow converging animal trails or flocks of birds. Dig on the outside edge of a dry streambed but don't induce sweating and lose more water than you can hope to find. If you have a plastic sheet, collect water overnight through condensation.

- ❑ **DO NOT EAT MORE** than necessary. Digestion uses water, and proteins raise metabolic levels and therefore increase water loss. Try to eat foods containing moisture, such as fruit and vegetables.

- ❑ **DO NOT TRAVEL** in the heat of the day Restrict movement to dawn, dusk, or nighttime. Do not sit or sleep directly on the ground as it retains heat: find something to sit or lie on.

THIN ICE

❏ **TURN AROUND TO FACE** the direction from which you came.

❏ **STRETCH YOUR ARMS** across the unbroken surface of the ice—or, even better, reach out with an ice pick if you have one.

❏ **WORK YOURSELF** onto the unbroken ice by kicking your feet.

❏ **IF THE ICE BREAKS,** continue the process until you reach thicker ice.

❏ **WHEN YOU ARE LYING** on unbroken ice, don't stand up—roll away from the hole to spread your weight over a larger area.

SNAKES

❏ **BACK AWAY SLOWLY** and do not make any sudden movements.

❏ **IF BITTEN,** do not cut or suck the wound.

❏ **KEEP AS STILL AS POSSIBLE** to prevent poison from spreading. Apply pressure to the wound. Keep the bite below the level of your heart.

❏ **DO NOT EAT OR DRINK.**

❏ **FREEZE OR APPLY EXTREME COLD** to the bite, if possible.

LIGHTNING

❏ **AVOID HILLTOPS, TALL TREES,** and lone landmarks. If this is impossible, sit on some insulating material, keeping your legs and arms clear of the ground.

❏ **TRY TO FIND LOW, LEVEL GROUND** and lie flat.

❏ **DO NOT HOLD METAL OBJECTS.**

Poet Alexander Pope warned that "a little learning is a dangerous thing." But total ignorance is even more dangerous. Read this information and remind yourself of it whenever you venture beyond the city limits—you never know when you might get caught in a forest fire or attacked by a shark. Live by the Boy Scouts' motto: Be Prepared.

JUNGLE SURVIVAL

❏ **MOST IMPORTANT,** keep your clothes on, however hot and sticky you feel—they'll protect you from stings, bites, and scratches, some of which can be dangerous in their own right and all of which will fester in the humidity.

❏ **WHEN SHELTERING** keep yourself and all your gear off the ground and check everything in the morning for spiders, snakes, and scorpions. Light a fire for cooking and repelling insects: everything is likely to be damp, so use standing wood and strip off the outer layers.

❏ **THERE WILL BE NO SHORTAGE OF WATER,** and you can eat fruit, roots, leaves, insects, and—if you can catch any—jungle mammals, reptiles, birds, or fish.

❏ **BEWARE OF DISTURBING** insects' nests, and use a net or fabric to protect against mosquitoes—a band of cloth cut into vertical strips that hang around the face and neck is highly effective.

❏ **IF YOU FIND A LEECH** attached to your skin, don't pull it off or its sucker may be left behind. Either remove it with fire (a cigarette or burning ember) or leave it—it will just drop off when it's drunk enough blood.

❏ **PROTECT YOUR FEET AND LEGS:** wrap something around boot tops to prevent insects from getting in there, and air feet as often as possible.

FOREST FIRE

❏ **DO NOT RUN WILDLY;** plan your escape.

❏ **HEAD TOWARD A NATURAL FIREBREAK** such as a river or wide break in the trees; otherwise take shelter in a ravine or gully. Do not head for high ground; fire travels faster uphill.

❏ **IF THE FIRE IS MOVING SLOWLY,** you may be able to create your own firebreak by setting a second fire ahead of the first.

❏ **IF THE FIRE IS BURNING** on a shallow front, you may be able to run through the flames to safety. Cover as much skin as possible and cover your face with a damp cloth. If your clothes catch fire then, as soon as you are through the flames, LIE DOWN (smoke and flames will rise toward your face) and roll over to put out the flames.

❏ **AS A LAST RESORT,** dig a hollow and cover yourself with dirt. Breathe through cupped hands or clothing as fire passes over.

SEA SURVIVAL

❏ **DON'T ABANDON SHIP** until you have to. Prepare yourself by putting on warm clothing and taking whatever useful lightweight equipment you can carry.

❏ **DON'T JUMP INTO A LIFE RAFT** from the ship in case you damage it. If you're already in the water, board the life raft from the end, not the side, to keep it from capsizing.

❏ **DO NOT OVERLOAD THE LIFE RAFT** If necessary, some people will have to hang onto the side, swapping places in a rota.

❏ **MAKE SURE NO SHARP OBJECTS** are in danger of puncturing an inflatable. If you're within sight of land, move toward it. If not, try to keep the life raft close to where you abandoned ship, which will make you easier to find—you can reduce drifting with a makeshift sea anchor by tying any heavy object to a line over the side.

❏ **PROTECT EVERYONE IN THE LIFE RAFT** from exposure to sun and wind where possible. Keep as dry as you can and perform gentle exercises for warmth and to maintain circulation.

❏ **RATION FOOD AND WATER.** Collect rainwater when possible. Do not drink seawater unless the life raft is equipped with a desalination kit, and even then only when rainwater is unavailable.

SINKING CAR

❑ **TRY TO OPEN THE CAR DOOR** as soon as you hit the water.

❑ **OPEN OR BREAK THE WINDOW** (if you were unable to open the door) to allow water to enter and equalize the pressure, enabling you to open the door and escape.

❑ **IF THE CAR SINKS** and you cannot open the door or window, wait for the car to fill with water. At the last moment, take a deep breath and hold it; when the car is full you should be able to open the door and swim to the surface.

HOSTAGE SITUATION

❑ **STAY CALM AND RATIONAL**—you're less likely to goad your captors into hurting you, and staying calm will give you a better chance of thinking clearly and making the best of any escape opportunities.

❑ **COMPLY WITH YOUR CAPTORS'** demands and do not complain. Do not resist, and do not make any sudden movements.

❑ **TRY TO COMMUNICATE** with your captors and establish a rapport, but give away as little information as possible. Do not make it obvious that you are listening to them or gleaning information from them.

❑ **ASK FOR ESSENTIALS FIRST** and comforts later. Do not demand—make your requests sound as reasonable as possible.

❑ **ESTABLISH A ROUTINE** and try to maintain a positive outlook. Prepare yourself mentally for a long ordeal.

❑ **MAINTAIN MENTAL ALERTNESS** and physical fitness by eating as well as possible and performing mind and body exercises.

❑ **CAREFULLY PLAN ANY ESCAPE ATTEMPT,** and do not proceed unless you are certain of success.

❑ **THE MOST DANGEROUS TIME** is during a rescue attempt. Stay still, and lie flat on the floor.

NAVIGATE A MINEFIELD

❑ **GUERRILLAS LAY MINES AT NIGHT** so, if driving, try to avoid being first on the road each morning. If possible, follow a heavy truck, but stay at least 220 yd (200 m) behind.

❑ **DRIVE WITH THE WINDOWS OPEN** to reduce blast if you hit a mine.

❑ **IF WALKING,** try to avoid being first. Follow at least 33 yd (30 m) behind the person in front of you, and follow in their footsteps.

❑ **WEAR YOUR FLAK JACKET** if walking. Sit on it if driving.

❑ **DO NOT LEAVE THE ROAD** unless you have to. If necessary, you can probe the ground ahead of you for mines with a knife or rod: most require downward pressure to detonate them so insert the probe at a forward angle rather than straight down. Mark any mines you find by whatever means you can.

❑ **NEVER PICK UP ANYTHING** if you're not sure who left it. It may be booby trapped.

LOSE A TAIL

❑ **IF YOU SUSPECT** you're being followed in your car, make sudden and unexpected changes of direction and negotiate traffic lights and junctions at the last minute. If your tail doesn't want to be noticed, you'll lose him/her quickly.

❑ **IF YOUR TAIL PERSISTS,** drive to a well-populated area and head for a police station.

❑ **IF YOU'RE BEING FOLLOWED ON FOOT,** make unexpected changes of direction and cross roads at the last minute, or enter/leave a bus or train at the last minute, any of which should force your tail to break cover.

❑ **IF THE TAIL PERSISTS,** enter a shop, restaurant, or bar by one entrance and leave immediately by another, preferably at the rear. Alternatively, enter a movie theater and leave by a fire exit.

❑ **IF THIS DOESN'T LOSE THEM,** head for a police station immediately.

PLANET EARTH

I WILL SURVIVE.. PART II

You won't need this information until you least expect it. So read it now, remember it carefully, and practice these moves as often as possible—or carry this book with you whenever you venture into the urban jungle. If you find yourself caught in a minefield or are abducted on your way to work, it might just save your life. And remember: Who Dares Wins.

EARTHQUAKE

❏ **STAY INSIDE;** avoid mirrors and windows.

❏ **MOVE TO THE CELLAR** if possible (if there are multiple exits) or the ground floor.

❏ **MOVE TO A CORNER** of the building or to a doorway, or shelter under solid furniture.

❏ **AVOID TALL DISPLAYS** in shops; in high-rise buildings, do not use elevators.

MUGGING

❏ **HAND OVER WHATEVER IT IS** they want—it can't be worth risking your life for.

❏ **IF THEY ATTACK AFTER** you've handed over your possessions and you need to defend yourself, don't start a fistfight. Know the vulnerable areas: jab at the eyes, karate chop the throat, elbow them in the stomach or ribs, stamp on their feet, or knee them in the groin.

ALIEN ABDUCTION

❏ **DON'T PANIC**—as with wild animals, aliens may sense fear.

❏ **THINK POSITIVELY** in case they're telepathic –visualize a protective barrier of light around you and keep your belief in your right to freedom at the forefront of your mind.

❏ **TALK CALMLY AND FIRMLY.** As with bears, even if they don't understand you, your tone will convey your message. And if it doesn't convey your message, at least it will make you feel a little better.

❏ **IF THEY PERSIST,** give 'em all you've got. As with sharks, hit them with fists, feet, or any available instrument, aiming for the eyes (if they have any), face (if they have faces), or reproductive organs (if you can figure out where they are).

FLOODED BUILDING

❏ **TURN OFF** gas and electricity.

❏ **MOVE TO AN UPPER FLOOR,** taking food, water, warm clothing, and any means of signaling to rescuers (such as a flashlight, whistle, some bright fabric, or a mirror).

❏ **MOVE ONTO THE ROOF** if necessary. If possible, tie everyone to the building, for example, around the chimney, to prevent anyone from being swept away.

CIVIL UNREST

❏ **IF VISITING AN UNSTABLE COUNTRY,** check in with your embassy on arrival and plan your route out: know where the airport and railroad station are, and when transportation is scheduled to leave (though this may be disrupted).

❏ **AVOID MAIN SQUARES** and main thoroughfares and government buildings (other than your embassy!)—they're where the trouble usually starts.

❏ **IF UNREST ERUPTS,** stay in your hotel and contact your embassy to let them know where you are, either by telephone or by sending a messenger—do not go yourself.

❏ **DO NOT WATCH EVENTS** from a window. Stay in an inside room above the ground floor.

❏ **TRY TO HAVE SOMEONE INTERPRET** local radio updates on the situation.

❏ **IF THERE IS ANY CHANCE** that a revolution is underway, do not trust the army or police. They may either be panicky or part of the revolution.

CAR ON EDGE OF CLIFF

❏ **STAY PERFECTLY STILL** while you assess the situation. If the car is teetering on the edge, you need to act quickly. If it is at rest, plan what to do more carefully and move more slowly. Either way, do not make sudden movements.

❏ **IF THE FRONT OF THE CAR** is over the edge and there are people in the back, they must remain there while those in the front move to the back (or vice versa).

❏ **IF IT IS POSSIBLE** to open the doors without making the car slide nearer the edge, do so and get out slowly.

❏ **IF IT IS NOT POSSIBLE** to open the doors, you need to smash the rear window (or the windshield if the back of the car is overhanging) and get out that way.

BREAK DOWN A DOOR

❏ **DON'T SHOULDER CHARGE IT:** the force won't be concentrated, and the blow will be too high.

❏ **GIVE IT A GOOD KICK** just above the handle and lock. Exterior doors need more force.

❏ **ALTERNATIVELY, PRISE IT OPEN** with a crowbar inserted close to the lock.

HOTEL FIRE

❏ **FEEL YOUR DOOR:** if it's cool, leave the room and use emergency exits, taking a wet towel with you to cover your head in case of smoke or heat. If you do encounter heavy smoke, stay low.

❏ **IF THE DOOR IS HOT,** remain in your room and cover the gap at the bottom of the door with a wet towel.

❏ **TURN OFF AIR-CONDITIONING** to keep it from drawing smoke into the room.

❏ **PHONE RECEPTION** to find out whether the fire is above or below you—if it's below, don't open your window too wide in case rising smoke enters. If the fire is above, open the window and hang out a sheet to alert firefighters to your presence.

❏ **HANG ANOTHER WET SHEET** or towel from the curtain rail and stand on the window side of it so that you can breathe fresh air.

❏ **AS A LAST RESORT,** try to kick through the wall to the room next door—stud walls are relatively easy to break through.

70 & stars

The 70s was the decade that fashion would like to forget—check out Farrah's swimsuit and Burt's moustache. But there were still plenty of stars to look up to. John Travolta may have fallen afoul of 70s' fashion in *Saturday Night Fever,* but he looked cool in *Grease.* And in spite of the costume department's efforts, Bo Derek still managed to score a perfect 10.

01. **JOHN TRAVOLTA**
as dashing Danny Zuko in *Grease* (1978).

02. **DEBBIE HARRY**
living up to the name of her band *Blondie*.

03. **ROBERT REDFORD**
—lasting appeal.

04. **FARRAH FAWCETT**
in an iconic swimsuit poster.

05. **BRITT EKLAND**
continues the tradition of Bond beauties as Mary Goodnight.

06. **MARSHA HUNT**
singer, actress, and writer.

07. **BURT REYNOLDS**
smooth—except for the upper lip.

BO DEREK
(main photo, left) as Jenny Hanley in *10* (1979)—Dudley Moore's character George Webber considers her "11" on a 1:10 scale of sexiness.

God gave women intuition and femininity—Farrah Fawcett

It's still
ILLEGAL...

*E*very country has its share of strange laws. Some are a hangover from days gone by when they actually made sense, and are never enforced now. Others are the result of knee-jerk politics—a 13-year-old boy was stabbed with a comb in Alabama so it was made illegal to carry a comb there. Yet others are just plain bizarre...

... in France to address a **PIG** as **NAPOLEON.**

... in Swiss apartment blocks for a man to **URINATE** standing up or for anyone to flush a toilet **AFTER 10 P.M.**

... to **REPAINT A HOUSE** in Sweden without a license.

... for a German office not to have **A VIEW OF THE SKY.**

... to kill or threaten a **MONARCH BUTTERFLY** in California.

... **TO KISS** on a French railroad.

... in Switzerland to wash a car, **HANG OUT LAUNDRY,** or mow the lawn on a Sunday.

... to take a **BEAR TO THE BEACH** in Israel.

... to **SPAY A FEMALE DOG** or cat in Norway, but males may be castrated.

... for a Danish restaurant to **CHARGE FOR WATER** unless it is served with ice, lemon, or some other addition.

... in the Australian state of Victoria for anyone other than a qualified electrician to **CHANGE A LIGHTBULB.**

... for margarine to be the same **COLOR AS BUTTER** in Quebec, Canada.

... to have **SEXUAL RELATIONS** with a porcupine in Florida.

... in South Africa for young people to sit **CLOSER THAN 24 INCHES (60 CM)** apart if they are wearing swimsuits.

... for a man to wear a **SKIRT** in **ITALY.**

... to chain an **ALLIGATOR** to a fire hydrant in Michigan.

... to be drunk **IN POSSESSION OF A COW** in Scotland.

... to carry a **COMB** in your pocket in Alabama.

... in Britain to **HANG A BED** out of a window.

... to tie a giraffe to **A TELEPHONE POLE** or street lamp in Atlanta.

... for parents to **INSULT** their children in Sweden.

... for a British Member of Parliament to wear a **SUIT OF ARMOR** in the House of Commons.

... for a woman to **EAT CHOCOLATES** on **BRITISH** public transportation.

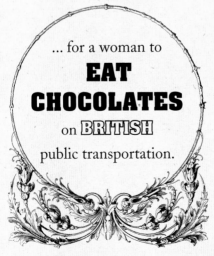

... to **HUNT WHALES** in Oklahoma (which is landlocked).

... for a **MOOSE TO WALK** on the pavement in Fairbanks, Alaska.

... to **HUNT CAMELS** in Arizona.

... to own or sell **CHEWING GUM** in Singapore.

... **TO PAWN** one's dentures in Las Vegas.

... **FOR A MODEM** to connect on the first ring in Australia.

... for a man to **KNIT** during the fishing season on the Channel Island of Jersey.

... to have sex on a **PARKED MOTORCYCLE** in London, England.

... to **FISH FOR SALMON OR SEA TROUT ON SUNDAYS** in Scotland.

... to have sex in a butcher's **MEAT FREEZER** in Newcastle, Wyoming.

... in Canada to **PAY A DEBT** of more than 25 cents in pennies.

... to dress as **BATMAN** in Australia.

... in Scotland to refuse to let someone enter your house if they wish to use **THE COMMODE.**

... to **RECYCLE EYEGLASSES** in the US.

... **NOT TO HAVE A BATH** at least once a year in **KENTUCKY.**

COMFORT STOP

While the real Darth Vader was off wreaking havoc elsewhere in the universe, this *Star Wars* fan in Cologne, Germany, was clocking up a few moments of the three years that the average human spends on the lavatory during a lifetime.

Toiletten-
benutzung

0,50 €

EGN
Entsorgungsgesellschaft
Niederrhein

0 21 62 / 3 76 - 44 00

Origami

Origami is the ancient Japanese art of paper folding—uncannily, the word comes from the Japanese for "fold" and "paper." Legend has it that if a person folds 1,000 paper cranes they will be granted a wish. So start folding—then you can wish for lots of money to fold into dollar shirts. Practice with a watery theme, starting with a waterbomb and boat.

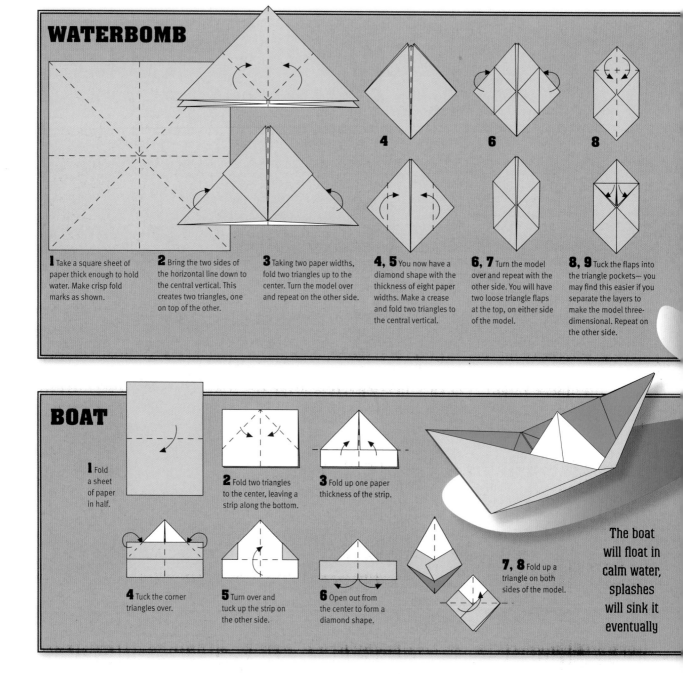

WATERBOMB

1 Take a square sheet of paper thick enough to hold water. Make crisp fold marks as shown.

2 Bring the two sides of the horizontal line down to the central vertical. This creates two triangles, one on top of the other.

3 Taking two paper widths, fold two triangles up to the center. Turn the model over and repeat on the other side.

4, 5 You now have a diamond shape with the thickness of eight paper widths. Make a crease and fold two triangles to the central vertical.

6, 7 Turn the model over and repeat with the other side. You will have two loose triangle flaps at the top, on either side of the model.

8, 9 Tuck the flaps into the triangle pockets— you may find this easier if you separate the layers to make the model three-dimensional. Repeat on the other side.

BOAT

1 Fold a sheet of paper in half.

2 Fold two triangles to the center, leaving a strip along the bottom.

3 Fold up one paper thickness of the strip.

4 Tuck the corner triangles over.

5 Turn over and tuck up the strip on the other side.

6 Open out from the center to form a diamond shape.

7, 8 Fold up a triangle on both sides of the model.

The boat will float in calm water, splashes will sink it eventually

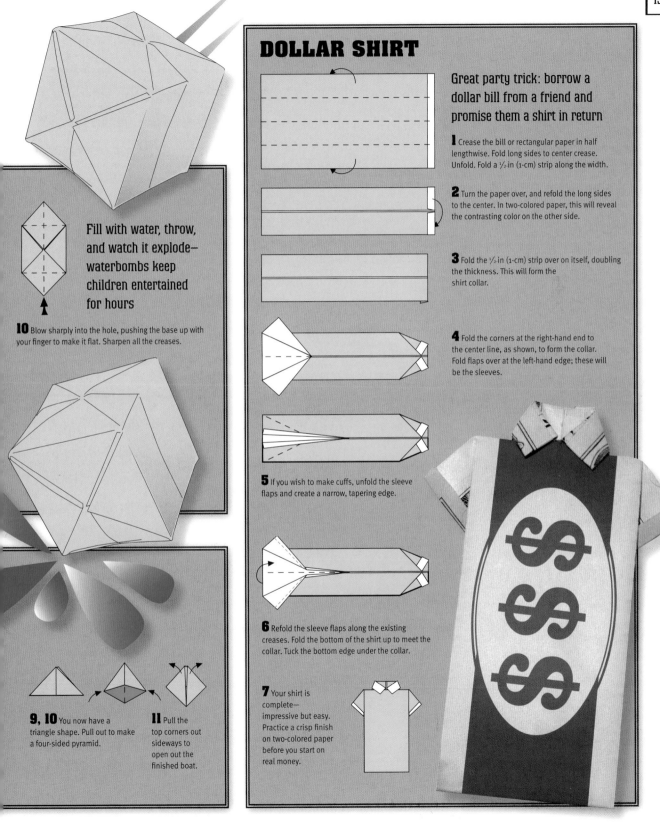

Fill with water, throw, and watch it explode—waterbombs keep children entertained for hours

10 Blow sharply into the hole, pushing the base up with your finger to make it flat. Sharpen all the creases.

9, 10 You now have a triangle shape. Pull out to make a four-sided pyramid.

11 Pull the top corners out sideways to open out the finished boat.

DOLLAR SHIRT

Great party trick: borrow a dollar bill from a friend and promise them a shirt in return

1 Crease the bill or rectangular paper in half lengthwise. Fold long sides to center crease. Unfold. Fold a ½-in (1-cm) strip along the width.

2 Turn the paper over, and refold the long sides to the center. In two-colored paper, this will reveal the contrasting color on the other side.

3 Fold the ½-in (1-cm) strip over on itself, doubling the thickness. This will form the shirt collar.

4 Fold the corners at the right-hand end to the center line, as shown, to form the collar. Fold flaps over at the left-hand edge; these will be the sleeves.

5 If you wish to make cuffs, unfold the sleeve flaps and create a narrow, tapering edge.

6 Refold the sleeve flaps along the existing creases. Fold the bottom of the shirt up to meet the collar. Tuck the bottom edge under the collar.

7 Your shirt is complete—impressive but easy. Practice a crisp finish on two-colored paper before you start on real money.

CONFIRMED

A FALLING ICICLE CAN KILL

Those pretty spikes of ice that form when near-freezing water drips from an object and refreezes may look beautiful, but they're potentially lethal. For anyone who laughed off the idea that a falling icicle might kill them as "just an urban myth," the Mythbusters have bad news: it is possible. Adam and Jamie found that a 18 in (45 cm) icicle falling a mere 15 ft (4.5 m) completely pierced a slab of beef, which means that it could easily pierce your flesh, and, if it hit you in a vulnerable area, it could kill you.

ELECTRICAL APPLIANCES IN THE BATHTUB CAN KILL

We've seen it countless times in the movies: Baddie catches Goodie in the bathtub and threatens to drop a conveniently placed electric heater or hairdryer in there with him if Goodie doesn't tell him what he wants to know. But would that kill Goodie? Yes. The current would pass through him on its way to make a connection with the drain—and the farther from the drain, the worse the effect. The good news is that Adam and Jamie discovered that an RCCB (residual current circuit breaker) would save the Goodie.

USING THE PHONE DURING A THUNDERSTORM CAN KILL

Everyone knows you shouldn't walk around in a thunderstorm with a metal spike on your head. But using the phone inside your home? Adam and Jamie put a dummy in a hut, strapped it to a chair, and taped a phone to its ear. Then they fired 200,000 volts at the hut. A bolt of electricity shot out of the telephone mouthpiece and into the dummy's mouth—and they couldn't measure how badly the dummy was zapped because the voltmeter blew. So be warned: careless talk costs lives.

HIGH NOTES CAN SHATTER A WINE GLASS

We've seen it done on television, but usually in cartoons or commercials—someone sings a sustained high note and glasses start shattering. But can it be done for real? Yes: lead-crystal wine glasses resonate at a certain frequency—re-create the frequency, turn up the volume, and the glass will vibrate and shatter. Adam did it with an amplifier and then got rock singer and voice trainer Jaime Vendera to do it with his unamplified voice, confirming a myth that is often rejected as fiction.

PLAUSIBLE

TALKING TO PLANTS HELPS THEM GROW

The Mythbusters planted pea plants in seven greenhouses. Sound systems fed two greenhouses with gentle speech (one male and one female voice), two with angry speech, one with classical music, and one with death-metal music. The seventh was left silent as a control. After 27 days, the plants in the speech greenhouses had all grown better than those in the control, regardless of gender or tone of voice. The classical music helped even more than the speech but, surprisingly, heavy-metal music helped most of all.

TAKING REFUGE UNDER WATER CAN STOP BULLETS

Another one from Hollywood—the Goodie dives into the water and the water stops the bullets from killing him. But would it happen in real life? Well, yes and no. It depends what caliber bullet, what type of weapon it's fired from, and what angle the bullet hits the water. Jamie and Adam discovered that supersonic bullets (up to .50-caliber) fired vertically disintegrated in less than 3 ft (90 cm) of water, but it took up to 8 ft (2.4 m) to reduce slower-velocity bullets to nonlethal speeds. Fired at an angle, the depths would be reduced.

A GREAT WHITE SHARK CAN PUNCH A HOLE IN A BOAT

To test this one, the Mythbusters built a "shark ram" from a 3,000 lb (1,360 kg) pipe (the weight of a great white) with a shark's head made from rubber. The ram, variously nicknamed Sha-rammer, Sharkpedo, and Jawpedo, was towed into the side of a wooden boat at 25 mph (40 km/h): the speed of a great white. The boat was damaged, and the Mythbusters concluded that, given the right circumstances, a great white could punch a hole in a boat. But don't worry: no instance of this happening has ever been documented.

Information courtesy of Mythbusters, produced by Beyond Entertainment Limited for the Discovery Channel.

MYTHS AND LEGENDS

Fact or FICTION

If the "facts" are to be believed, humans are in constant danger of death from falling icicles, pennies dropped from skyscrapers, and using their phones during thunderstorms. But can these dangers all be real? Special-effects experts Adam Savage and Jamie Hyneman have devoted an entire television series on the Discovery Channel to demonstrating scientifically what's real and what's fiction. They are the Mythbusters.

BUSTED

A PENNY DROPPED FROM A SKYSCRAPER CAN KILL

A hard one to test—the Mythbusters couldn't really go to the Empire State Building, drop a penny on someone's head, and see what happened. So Adam and Jamie worked out that the terminal velocity of a penny is 35–65 mph (56–105 km/h). They adapted a staple gun to fire pennies at $64\frac{1}{2}$ mph (103.5 km/h). After testing it on a dummy, they fired the penny at each other's hands and, while it hurt, it didn't even break the skin.

URINATING ON THE THIRD RAIL CAN KILL

Power is delivered to most modern electric railroads via a third rail alongside the two that carry the train, and there is a persistent myth that urinating on it can kill. After calculating that urine could carry a charge of 65 milliamps (enough to give you a heart attack), Adam and Jamie discovered that a stream of urine breaks into droplets before reaching the rail and therefore doesn't conduct the current—although if you peed on the rail from just 6 in (15 cm) the urine might conduct. Busted, but definitely not one to try next time your train's late.

BEING BURIED ALIVE WON'T NECESSARILY KILL YOU

There is a myth about grave robbers opening a coffin only for the occupant to sit up and start talking. But when Jamie was buried alive, he discovered that the occupants of the coffin would not have lasted more than an hour. Above ground, Jamie lasted 50 minutes in a sealed casket equipped with a blood-oxygen sensor, heart-rate monitor, carbon-dioxide detector, and night-vision camera. But when he was buried beneath tons of soil, the experiment had to be abandoned after 30 minutes because the steel coffin began buckling under the pressure.

JUMPING AT THE LAST MOMENT IN A FALLING ELEVATOR CAN SAVE YOU

As the elevator heads up toward the top floor, you imagine the yawning gap opening beneath you. Then there's a jolt and you're plunging back down the shaft. What do you do? If you jump just before the elevator hits the ground, will you be saved? Sadly not. When you jump, you move upward relative to the elevator but relative to the outside world you're still traveling downward—extremely fast. When the Mythbusters tested the theory with a robot in an abandoned hotel, both the elevator and the robot were smashed to pieces.

YOU CAN JUMP FROM A BUILDING USING AN UMBRELLA AS A PARACHUTE

So, if you saw the experiment with the falling elevator (above) and you no longer want to use elevators, is it safe to jump from a tall building using your umbrella to slow your fall? Well, basic physics says that the umbrella will slow your fall but, as Jamie and Adam discovered, not enough to save you from a deadly jump. And real parachutes often fail to deploy when used at low altitudes so, if you really don't want to use the elevator, you'll have to take the stairs.

SPORTS AND LEISURE

BREAKING RANK

However much people are made to conform, there's always one who has to be different. Here, an Argyll and Sutherland Highlander shows the strain during a rehearsal for a portrait with Queen Elizabeth II at Redford Barracks, Edinburgh, Scotland.

WORLD KARAOKE

Around the globe different people have different customs and traditions.
Two universal forms of entertainment are drinking and music—often indulged
in at the same time, with increasing quantity of the former leading to decreasing
quality of the latter. Here are the words to a few of the songs you might
encounter in bars around the world, so that you can sing along with the locals.

ENGLAND

(Jerusalem/W. Blake, 1804)

And did those feet in ancient time
Walk upon England's mountains
  green?
And was the holy Lamb of God
On England's pleasant pastures
  seen?
And did the countenance divine
Shine forth upon our clouded
  hills?
And was Jerusalem builded here
Among these dark Satanic mills?

Bring me my bow of burning gold
Bring me my arrows of desire
Bring me my spear; Oh, clouds
  unfold!
Bring me my chariot of fire
I will not cease from mental fight
Nor shall my sword sleep in my
  hand
Til we have built Jerusalem
In England's green and pleasant
  land.

FRANCE

*(La Marseillaise/C-J. Rouget
de Lisle, 1792) "The War Song
of the Rhine Army"*

Allons enfants de la Patrie
Le jour de gloire est arrivé
Contre nous de la tyrannie
L'étendard sanglant est levé.

Entendez-vous dans les
  campagnes
Mugir ces féroces soldats?
Ils viennent jusque dans vos bras
Égorger vos fils, vos compagnes!

Aux armes, citoyens!
Formez vos bataillons!
Marchons, marchons!
Qu'un sang impur
Abreuve nos sillons!

SOUTH AFRICA

*(Nkosi Sikelel' iAfrika/E. Sontonga,
1897) "God bless Africa"*

Nkosi sikelel' iAfrika
Maluphakanyisw' uphondo lwayo
Yizwa imithandazo yethu
Nkosi sikelela,
Thina lusapho lwayo.

HUNGARY

*(Himnusz/F. Kolcsey,
1844) "Hymn"*

Isten, áldd meg a magyart
Jó kedvvel, boséggel,
Nyújts feléje védo kart,
Ha küzd ellenséggel;
Balsors akit régen tép,
Hozz rá víg esztendot,
Megbunhodte már e nép
A múltat s jövendot.

IRELAND

(Danny Boy/F. Weatherly, 1913)

Oh Danny Boy, the pipes,
  the pipes are calling
From glen to glen, and down
  the mountain side
The summer's gone, and all the
  flowers are dying
'Tis you, 'tis you must go and
  I must bide
But come ye back when
  summer's in the meadow
Or when the valley's hushed and
  white with snow
'Tis I'll be there in sunshine or
  in shadow
Oh Danny Boy, oh Danny Boy,
  I love you so.

INDIA

*(Vande Mataram/B. C. Chatterjee,
1882) "Mother, I salute thee!"*

Vande Mataram!
Sujalam, suphalam,
malayajasheetalam,
Sasyashyamalam mataram,
Shubhra jyotsna pulakitayaminim,
Phulla kusumita
drumadalashobhinim,
Suhasinim sumadhura bhashinim,
Sukhadam varadam,
Mataram.

GERMANY

*(Das Lied der Deutschen/A.
von Fallersleben, 1841)
"The Song of the Germans"*

Deutschland, Deutschland
  über alles,
Über alles in der Welt,
Wenn es stets zu Schutz
  und Trutze,
Brüderlich zusammenhält.
Von der Maas bis an die Memel,
Von der Etsch bis an den Belt,
Deutschland, Deutschland
  über alles,
Über alles in der Welt.

US

*(The Star-Spangled
Banner/F. S. Key, 1814)*

O say, can you see, by the dawn's
  early light,
What so proudly we hailed at the
  twilight's last gleaming,
Whose broad stripes and bright
  stars, through the perilous fight,
O'er the ramparts we watched,
  were so gallantly streaming?
And the rockets' red glare, the
  bombs bursting in air,
Gave proof through the night that
  our flag was still there;
O say, does that star-spangled
  banner yet wave
O'er the land of the free and the
  home of the brave?

CANADA

*(O Canada/Sir
A. B. Routhier, 1880)*

O Canada! Our home and
  native land!
True patriot love in all thy sons
  command.
With glowing hearts we see
  thee rise,
The true North strong and free!
From far and wide, O Canada,
We stand on guard for thee.
God keep our land glorious
  and free!
O Canada, we stand on guard
  for thee.
O Canada, we stand on guard
  for thee.

AUSTRALIA

*(Waltzing Matilda/A.
Paterson, 1895)*

Once a jolly swagman camped by
  a billabong,
Under the shade of a
  coolibah tree,
And he sang as he watched and
  waited 'til his billy boiled
"Who'll come a-Waltzing
  Matilda, with me?
Waltzing Matilda,
Waltzing Matilda
Who'll come a-waltzing
  Matilda with me?
And he sang as he watched and
  waited 'til his billy boiled
"Who'll come a-waltzing Matilda,
  with me?"

NORWAY

*(Ja vi elsker dette landet/
B. Bjornson, 1868)
"Yes we love this country"*

Ja, vi elsker dette landet som det
  stiger frem,
Furet, værbitt over vannet, med
  de tusen hjem.
Elsker, elsker det og tenker på vår
  far og mor,
Og den saganatt som senker,
  drømme på vår jord.
Og den saganatt som senker,
  drømme på vår jord.

NEW ZEALAND

*(Ka Mate/Te Rauparaha, 1810)
"We're going to die!" [from trad.
Maori dance known as the haka;
adopted by the All Blacks]*

Ka Mate! Ka Mate!
Ka Ora! Ka Ora!
Ka Mate! Ka Mate!
Ka Ora! Ka Ora!
Tenei te tangata puhuruhuru
Nana nei i tiki mai
Whakawhiti te ra
A upane ka upane!
A upane kaupane whiti te ra!
Hi!

ITALY (NAPLES)

*(O sole mio/G. Capurro, 1898)
"My own sun"*

Che bella cosa', na jurnata 'e sole,
N'aria serena doppo' na tempesta
Pe' ll'aria fresca pare gia' na
  festa...
Che bella cosa na iurnata 'e sole
Ma n'atu solecchiu' bello, oi ne
'O sole mio sta nfronte a te!
'O sole, 'o sole mio
Sta 'nfronte a te!
Sta 'nfronte a te!

MEXICO

*(La Cucaracha/trad., 15th century)
"The Cockroach"*

Cuando uno quiere a una,
Y esta una no lo quiere,
Es lo mismo como si un calvo,
En calle encuetre un peine.

La cucaracha, la cucaracha,
Ya no quieres caminar,
Porque no tiene,
Porque le falta,
Marihuana que fumar.

ISRAEL

*(Hatikvah/N. Herz Imber, 1886)
"The Hope"*

Kol ode balevav P'nimah,
Nefesh Yehudi homiyah,
Ulfa'atey mizrach kadimah
Ayin l'tzion tzofiyah.
Ode lo avdah tikvatenu,
Hatikvah bat shnot alpayim:
L'hiyot am chofsi b'artzenu
Eretz Tzion v'Yerushalayim.

CUBA

*Guantanamera/J. Marti, 1880s)
"Girl from Guantanamo"*

Yo soy un hombre sincero
De donde crecen las palmas
Yo soy un hombre sincero
De donde crecen las palmas
Y antes de morirme quiero
Echar mis versos del alma

Guantanamera
Guajira Guantanamera
Guantanamera
Guajira Guantanamera

OWN ISLANDS

In the past, adventurers went off and discovered unknown islands. Now, people build new ones instead. Artificial islands have been used as forts, airports, residential developments, and even "micronations." Fort Roughs (photo 3, opposite) was occupied in 1967 by Paddy Bates, who claimed it was an independent state as it was in international waters. Although not recognized by the United Nations, the island has its own flag, national anthem, currency, and postage stamps.

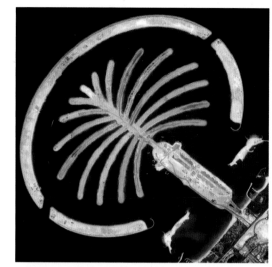

SPITBANK FORT, ENGLAND (main photo, left) Built 1861–78 off Portsmouth.

01. PALM ISLAND, DUBAI
Under construction in the Persian Gulf.

02. STAR ISLAND, US
Completed in 1922 in Biscayne Bay, Florida.

03. PRINCIPALITY OF SEALAND, ENGLAND
Built as HM Fort Roughs in 1942 off the Suffolk coast.

04. TREASURE ISLAND, US
Built in 1939 in San Francisco Bay for the Golden Gate International Exposition.

05. BARRO COLORADO ISLANDS, PANAMA
Former high ground, flooded when the Panama Canal was constructed.

06. DURRAT AL BAHRAIN
A seaside city resort.

07. ÎLE NOTRE-DAME, CANADA.
Built for Expo 67 in Montreal, using earth from the excavation of the Montreal metro.

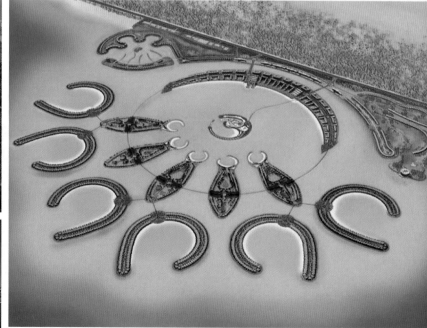

MILLION-DOLLAR
HUMANS

It all started when silent movie star Ben Turpin, famous for his crossed eyes, took out a policy against his eyes uncrossing. Then, celebs all started insuring parts of themselves. In Brazil, insured backsides are so common that they're known as bum-bum policies—one Brazilian model even negotiated a $2-million policy for the use of her image on the insurance company's billboards.

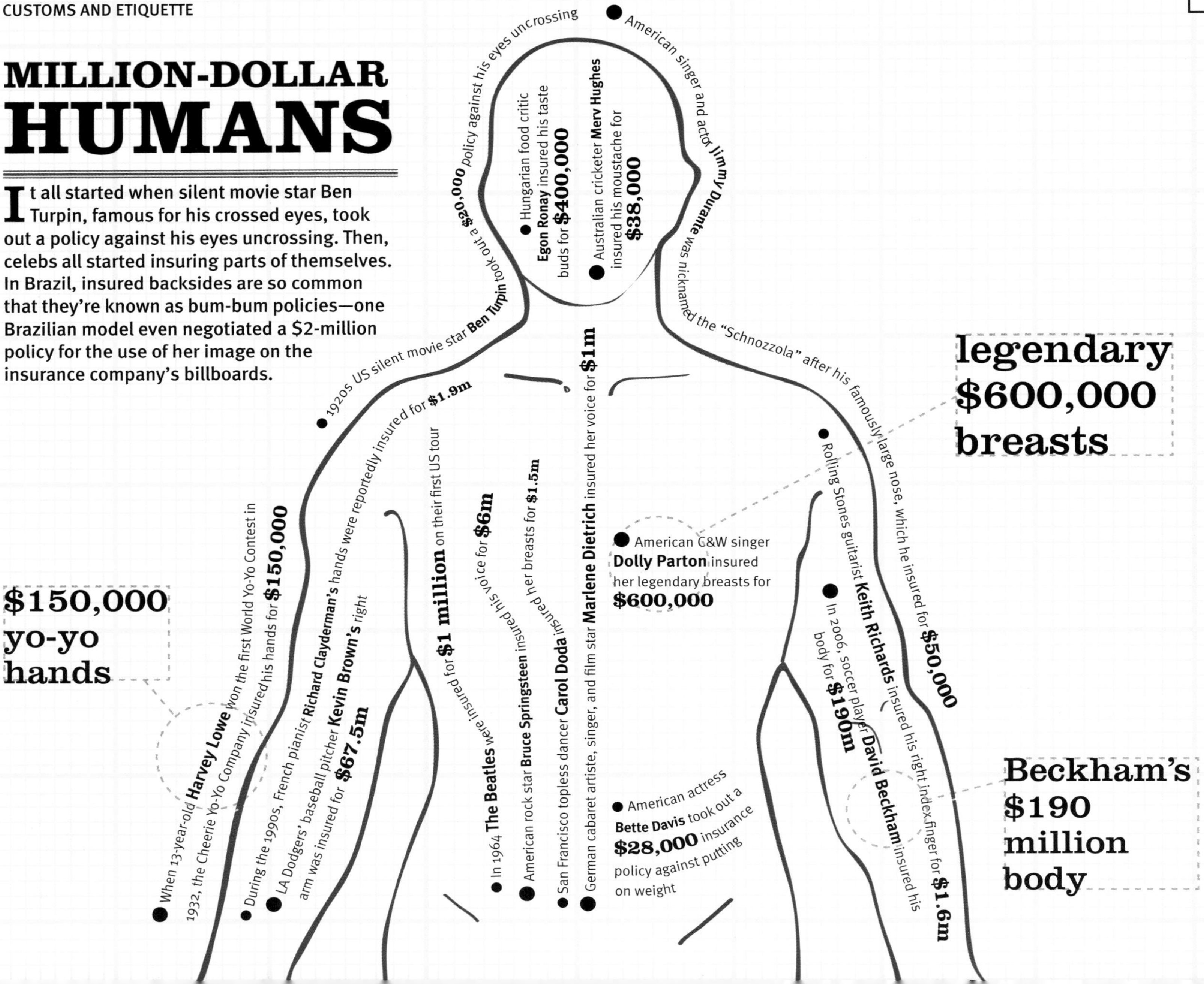

legendary $600,000 breasts

Beckham's $190 million body

Rolling Stones guitarist **Keith Richards** insured his right index finger for **$1.6m**

In 2006, soccer player **David Beckham** insured his body for **$190m**

Jimmy Durante was nicknamed the "Schnozzola" after his famously large nose, which he insured for **$50,000**

American singer and actor **Jimmy Durante**

American C&W singer **Dolly Parton** insured her legendary breasts for **$600,000**

American actress **Bette Davis** took out a **$28,000** insurance policy against putting on weight

German cabaret artiste, singer, and film star **Marlene Dietrich** insured her voice for **$1m**

San Francisco topless dancer **Carol Doda** insured her breasts for **$1.5m**

American rock star **Bruce Springsteen** insured his voice for **$6m**

In 1964 **The Beatles** were insured for **$1 million** on their first US tour

Australian cricketer **Merv Hughes** insured his moustache for **$38,000**

Hungarian food critic **Egon Ronay** insured his taste buds for **$400,000**

1920s US silent movie star **Ben Turpin** took out a **$20,000** policy against his eyes uncrossing

LA Dodgers' baseball pitcher **Kevin Brown's** right arm was insured for **$67.5m**

During the 1990s, French pianist **Richard Clayderman's** hands were reportedly insured for **$1.5m**

When 13-year-old **Harvey Lowe** won the first World Yo-yo Contest in 1932, the Cheerio yo-yo company insured his hands for **$150,000**

$150,000 yo-yo hands

$12-million disability policy

The St. Louis Cardinals took out a **$12-million** disability policy on **Mark McGwire,** the first baseball player ever to hit 70 home runs in a season

German supermodel, actress, and singer **Heidi Klum** insured her legs for **$2.2m**

British stripper **Frankie Jakeman** insured his penis for **$1.6 million**

American dancer and film star **Fred Astaire's** legs were insured for **$75,000** each

$75,000 a Fred Astaire leg

film's first million-dollar legs

American actress **Jamie Lee Curtis** insured her legs for $1m

20th Century Fox insured American film star **Betty Grable's** legs for $1m each—the origin of the phrase "**million-dollar legs**"

Irish dancer **Michael Flatley** insured his legs for **$47.5m**

Brazilian erotic model and actress **Susana Alves,** aka Tiazinha, insured her buttocks, knees, and ankles for **$2m**

Tiazinha's $2m buttocks, knees, and ankles

WORTH ITS WEIGHT IN GOLD

Gold has always been precious to humans and probably always will be, which is why it's used as a benchmark for the value of other goods. But other commodities fluctuate in value depending on supply and demand, which means that during the course of history some things that now "go for a song" were once worth their weight in gold.

When China tea came to Europe, demand sent the mark-up over 1,000 percent. In 1700, retail value was the equivalent of several hundred pounds per pound in weight in London, Paris, and Amsterdam, and tea was kept in lockable caddies.

TEA

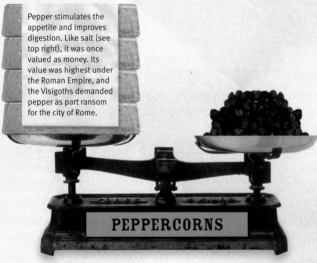

Pepper stimulates the appetite and improves digestion. Like salt (see top right), it was once valued as money. Its value was highest under the Roman Empire, and the Visigoths demanded pepper as part ransom for the city of Rome.

PEPPERCORNS

Derived from the Aztec word *xocolatl*, meaning "bitter water," chocolate was introduced to Europe in 1528 as a drink. It wasn't until 1819 that eating chocolate was produced in bars for the first time.

CHOCOLATE

Nylon was invented in 1935 as a synthetic substitute for silk. One of the first products was ladies' stockings but, when nylon production was diverted to military use in WWII, stockings became a rare and pricey black-market luxury.

NYLON STOCKINGS

In 1633, tulip fever was rampant in the Netherlands—bulbs cost the equivalent of over $40,000 each. One investor is said to have paid 1,000 lb (455 kg) of cheese, 12 sheep, a bed, and a suit of clothes for a single bulb.

TULIPS

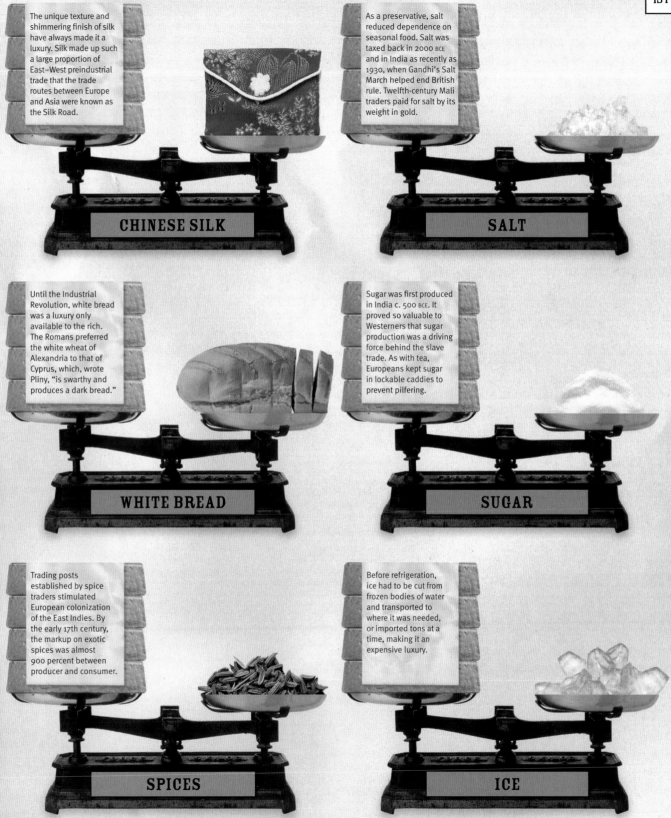

The unique texture and shimmering finish of silk have always made it a luxury. Silk made up such a large proportion of East–West preindustrial trade that the trade routes between Europe and Asia were known as the Silk Road.

CHINESE SILK

As a preservative, salt reduced dependence on seasonal food. Salt was taxed back in 2000 BCE and in India as recently as 1930, when Gandhi's Salt March helped end British rule. Twelfth-century Mali traders paid for salt by its weight in gold.

SALT

Until the Industrial Revolution, white bread was a luxury only available to the rich. The Romans preferred the white wheat of Alexandria to that of Cyprus, which, wrote Pliny, "is swarthy and produces a dark bread."

WHITE BREAD

Sugar was first produced in India c. 500 BCE. It proved so valuable to Westerners that sugar production was a driving force behind the slave trade. As with tea, Europeans kept sugar in lockable caddies to prevent pilfering.

SUGAR

Trading posts established by spice traders stimulated European colonization of the East Indies. By the early 17th century, the markup on exotic spices was almost 900 percent between producer and consumer.

SPICES

Before refrigeration, ice had to be cut from frozen bodies of water and transported to where it was needed, or imported tons at a time, making it an expensive luxury.

ICE

WHO'S AFRAID OF...

President Roosevelt famously said "the only thing we have to fear is fear itself." But, like a lot of things politicians say, that isn't all true—it's very sensible to fear water if you can't swim. Or poisonous spiders if you don't have an antivenom. Or wild animals if you don't have a gun. On the other hand, some phobias are ludicrous, and look even more so when magnified by the spotlight of fame. Here are some of the things that famous people are—allegedly—afraid of.

BEING SEEN AS STUPID AND COCKROACHES

Megastar **Madonna**, who reportedly has a genius-level IQ of 140, is said to be afraid of being thought of as stupid. And she has a more understandable fear of cockroaches. She confessed: "Whenever I saw them... I screamed and ran away."

OPEN OR PUBLIC SPACES

Hollywood actor **Macaulay "Home Alone" Culkin** has the opposite problem to Drew Barrymore (see below). He suffers from agoraphobia—a fear of being in **open or public spaces**.

CONFINED SPACES

Hollywood actress and producer **Drew "Poison Ivy" Barrymore,** who continues a family acting tradition going back five generations, suffers from claustrophobia, a fear of confined spaces.

SHARKS, SNAKES, AND SPIDERS

American singer 'n' actor **Justin Timberlake** suffers from galeophobia, ophidiophobia, and arachnophobia—that's fears of sharks, snakes, and spiders.

SPIDERS

American tennis star **André Agassi** is afraid of spiders, too.

CLOWNS

Hollywood actor **Johnny Depp** suffers from clourophobia, a fear of clowns. Depp, who plays famously disconcerting roles, said: "[There was] something about the painted face, the fake smile. There always seemed to be a darkness lurking just under the surface, a potential for real evil."

ELECTRICITY

American cult filmmaker **John Waters** fears electricity—maybe from William Castle's horror film *The Tingler*, for which movie theater seats were rigged with electric buzzers.

PIGS

English actor **Orlando "Lord of the Rings" Bloom** broke his back falling from a third-story roof terrace, but he isn't afraid of heights—he's terrified of pigs.

FLYING AND THUNDER

Former world heavyweight boxing champion **Muhammad Ali** sang that he would "float like a butterfly, sting like a bee." Note the word "float"—he didn't like flying, or thunder.

SUNSETS

French writer **Marcel** *A la Recherche du Temps Perdu* **Proust** once said: "I have a horror of sunsets, they're so romantic, so operatic."

CHEWING GUM

Architect Frank Lloyd Wright described TV as "chewing gum for the eyes." How ironic that TV talk show host **Oprah Winfrey** should fear chewing gum.

HEIGHTS

Would you believe that actor **Tobey Maguire** who played Spiderman is afraid of... heights ? (It might have been worse—he could have been scared of spiders.)

DISORDER

Former England soccer captain **David** "Golden Balls" **Beckham** suffers from a form of obsessive compulsive disorder known as ataxophobia: a fear of untidiness or disorder.

GHOSTS AND INDOOR PLANTS

Hollywood actress **Christina Ricci**, who starred alongside Johnny Depp in *Sleepy Hollow,* shared one fear with him: ghosts. She also suffers from a form of botanophobia— she is frightened of indoor plants.

JAIL AND LESBIANS

Hungarian-born actress/socialite **Zsa Zsa Gábor** is said to fear jail (she served three days in 1989 for slapping a policeman) and lesbians.

WATER

Hollywood actress **Natalie Wood**, who starred alongside James Dean in *Rebel Without A Cause* and dated Elvis Presley among others, had a lifelong fear of water— possibly with good reason: in 1981 she drowned at the age of just 43.

HOSPITALS

Pop artist, avant-garde filmmaker, and writer **Andy** "Soup Cans" **Warhol** was afraid of hospitals: reasonable, as he had open heart massage after being shot in 1968.

FLYING

Soul diva **Aretha Franklin** was once sued for breach of contract when she was unable to star in a Broadway musical, largely because of her fear of flying.

BUTTERFLIES

After being attacked by a psychotic in *Dead Calm,* married to Tom Cruise, and dying of TB in *Moulin Rouge,* it would be understandable if Australian-born actress **Nicole Kidman** were afraid of yachts, short men, and windmills. But she isn't—instead she's frightened of butterfles.

SOMEONE TOUCHING YOUR TOES

American TV actress, talk show host, and comedian **Roseanne Barr** is afraid of anything—people or objects—touching her toes.

TOP 10 PHOBIAS

Celebrities have access to a lot of things that are beyond the reach of ordinary people, but a phobia is something that anyone can share. According to www.phobia-fear-release.com, the following are the 10 most common phobias.

1. **Arachnophobia:** fear of spiders.

2. **Social phobia:** fear of being evaluated negatively in social situations.

3. **Aerophobia:** fear of flying.

4. **Agoraphobia:** a generalized fear of leaving home or a small familiar "safe" area, and of possible panic attacks that might follow.

5. **Claustrophobia:** fear of being trapped in small confined spaces.

6. **Acrophobia:** fear of heights.

7. **Emetophobia:** fear of vomit.

8. **Carcinophobia:** fear of cancer.

9. **Brontophobia:** fear of thunderstorms.

10. **Necrophobia:** fear of death or of dead things.

GUNS

English actor **Roger Moore** was licensed to kill in his role as James Bond—but he has a fear of guns, which make him blink.

EGGS

Legendary British suspense director **Alfred** "Psycho" **Hitchcock**, one of whose films was *The Birds*, was afraid of... eggs. His daughter told the *Chicago Tribune*: "He just said they were so horrible-looking—that you'd cut into them and that yellow stuff would run all over. He thought it was absolutely disgusting."

TRICK CYCLIST

American Travis Pastrana performs a backflip against the Cleveland skyline in the Freestyle Moto-X final at the 2002 Gravity Games.

SAFETY IN THE HOME

Home sweet home? Think again—the home is one of the most dangerous places known to humankind, with all kinds of dangers lurking in the most unexpected places. Some humans are more accident prone than others, or else they're just more likely to go to the hospital with their injuries. Here are some of the objects that lead to hospital admissions every year.

BEANBAGS: NOT SHARP ENOUGH FOR CHOPPING LAMB BUT THEY'RE INVOLVED IN MORE ACCIDENTS THAN **MEAT CLEAVERS.**

DON'T DROP YOUR GUARD WHILE PUTTING YOUR CLOTHES ON—SOME **16,000** PEOPLE INJURE THEMSELVES PUTTING ON **PANTS, SOCKS, OR TIGHTS.**

SMOKING IN BED IS SAFER THAN GARDENING. CONTACT WITH **SHARP PLANTS** CAUSES **10 TIMES** AS MANY ACCIDENTS AS "IGNITION OR MELTING OF PAJAMAS."

IF YOU'RE DOING A BIT OF YARDWORK, DON'T STOP FOR A CUP OF COFFEE: **HOT DRINKS** CAUSE THREE TIMES AS MANY ACCIDENTS AS **LAWN MOWERS.**

TEA COSIES MAY LOOK AS HARMLESS AS A WOOLEN HAT, BUT WATCH OUT— THEY CAUSE ABOUT **40 HOSPITAL** ADMISSIONS A YEAR.

IF YOU'RE FEELING ACCIDENT PRONE, SIT ON THE FLOOR—SOME **7,000** PEOPLE ARE ADMITTED TO THE HOSPITAL AFTER **FALLING OFF CHAIRS.**

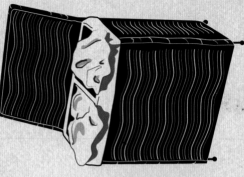

CUT YOURSELF SHAVING? DON'T USE A COTTON SWAB— THEY CAUSE **2.5** TIMES MORE INJURIES THAN **RAZOR BLADES.**

THE PERFECT EXCUSE FOR LEAVING YOUR CLOTHES IN A PILE ON THE FLOOR: MORE THAN **3,000** PEOPLE ARE HOSPITALIZED EACH YEAR AFTER FALLING OVER **LAUNDRY BASKETS.** BUT YOU MIGHT HAVE TO GIVE UP ON SOME CONVENIENCES— ALMOST EXACTLY THE SAME NUMBER IS ADMITTED TO THE HOSPITAL AFTER **CANNED CORNED BEEF** INCIDENTS.

IT'S SAFER TO ORDER IN: **FOOD PREPARATION** CAUSES MORE THAN **60,000** INJURIES A YEAR. AND DON'T EVEN THINK ABOUT **FROZEN MEALS**— SOME **2,000** OF THOSE FOOD PREP INJURIES HAPPEN TO PEOPLE TRYING TO SEPARATE ITEMS FROZEN TOGETHER.

WHATEVER YOU DO, DON'T DUST YOUR BREAD BOX— **DUSTPANS** CAUSE SOME **150 INJURIES** A YEAR. AND **BREAD BOXES** ABOUT **100**, SO THE COMBINATION COULD BE LETHAL.

EACH YEAR, **HUNDREDS** OF PEOPLE SWALLOW THEIR **FALSE TEETH.**

THE TEXAS MAGAZINE MASSACRE? GLOSSY MAGAZINES CAUSE **4 TIMES** AS MANY ACCIDENTS AS CHAINSAWS

CHAPTER

7

7 is the luckiest number in many cultures because it is made up of 3 and 4, also thought lucky ▶ When asked to think of a number between 1 and 10, more people choose 7 than any other number ▶ 7 is the number of minutes it takes the average person to fall asleep ▶ The 7 continents are Africa, Antarctica, Asia, Australia, Europe, North America, and South America ▶ The 7 seas are the Arctic, Antarctic, North Atlantic, South Atlantic, North Pacific, South Pacific, and Indian Oceans ▶ The Japanese Samurai code of conduct defines 7 principles of *bushido* (way of the warrior) ▶ One Trident missile is 7 times more powerful than the nuclear bomb dropped on Hiroshima ▶ According to Shakespeare's play *As You Like It*, the 7 ages of man are infant, schoolboy, lover, soldier, justice, pantaloon, second childhood ▶ The 7 dwarves in the story of Snow White are Sneezy, Grumpy, Dopey, Happy, Sleepy, Bashful, and Doc ▶ In John Sturges' Western *The Magnificent Seven*, an American remake of Akira Kurosawa's *Seven Samurai*, the 7 were played by Yul Brynner, Eli Wallach, Steve McQueen, Charles Bronson, Robert Vaughn, Brad Dexter, and James Coburn ▶ There are 7 notes in a Western musical scale ▶ The body has 7 chakras (energy points) in Eastern medicine ▶ The 7 alchemy metals are gold, silver, quicksilver (mercury), copper, iron, tin, lead ▶ Christianity recognizes 7 deadly sins: pride, covetousness (or avarice or greed), lust, envy, gluttony, anger, sloth. The 7 opposing virtues are faith, hope, charity, justice, fortitude, prudence, temperance ▶ On a pilgrimage to Mecca, Muslims make 7 circuits of the Ka'ba ▶ Acidity and alkalinity are measured from 1 (acidic) to 14 (alkaline) on the pH (potential of Hydrogen) scale. Distilled water is neutral (pH7) ▶ The 7 colours of the rainbow are red, orange, yellow, green, blue, indigo, and violet.

THE EVE OF DESTRUCTION

2.5°F (1.5°C) RISE

The best-case scenario if humans stop polluting, deforesting, and destroying the planet immediately is that the average global temperature will rise by 2.5°F (1.5°C).

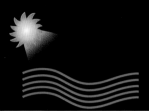

△ **RISING SEA LEVEL**
Sea levels will rise an average of 4 in (10 cm), having a noticeable effect on global weather systems and coastal flooding.

△ **ICE CAPS**
Ice sheets and ice caps will melt at a rate of 7.5 percent each decade, contributing to rising sea levels and higher temperatures.

△ **ANIMAL MIGRATION**
Tropical insects, birds, and mammals will migrate toward the poles as the climate and vegetation changes.

5°F (3°C) RISE

The probable scenario, given that humans cannot stop polluting immediately, is that the average global temperature will rise by 5°F (3°C).

△ **RISING SEA LEVEL**
Sea levels will rise by an average of 20 in (50 cm), severely disrupting weather systems and causing regular flooding in most coastal areas.

△ **ICE CAPS**
Ice caps will melt at an initial rate of 10 percent every decade, speeding up dramatically as their mass and self-cooling effect decrease.

△ **ANIMAL MIGRATION**
Mammals will follow insects and birds toward the poles in search of more temperate climates. Vulnerable species will be wiped out.

10°F (6°C) RISE

The worst-case scenario if humans continue to pollute at the current rate is that the temperature will rise by 10°F (6°C) by 2100. This would have disastrous consequences.

△ **RISING SEA LEVEL**
Sea levels will rise an average of 3 ft (90 cm), a catastrophic rise given that more than 100 million humans live within 3 ft (1 m) of the current sea level.

△ **ICE CAPS**
Ice sheets and ice caps will melt at an initial rate of 25 percent each decade, disappearing completely within a generation.

△ **ANIMAL EXTINCTION**
At least 30 percent of all animal species will become extinct through direct-heat effects or the destruction of their ecosystems.

Climate change is already underway. Temperatures are rising, the planet is changing, and it may be too late to stop it from happening—the question is, how hot will it get? Even a 5°F (3°C) rise will devastate the world. Humans can easily cope with temperature changes of a few degrees, the planet Earth cannot—here is a guide to what might happen.

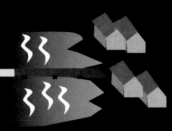

△ HUMAN DEATH TOLL
There will be increased deaths among the elderly and young in developed countries due to extreme temperatures, and in developing countries due to drought and famine.

△ COASTAL FLOODING
Flooding in low-lying coastal areas, including the South Sea islands, Florida, Louisiana, the Netherlands, and east England.

△ FOREST FIRES
There will be a 30 percent reduction in forest cover through drought and fires, releasing yet more greenhouse gases into the atmosphere.

△ HUMAN DEATH TOLL
There will be continuing deaths from regular high temperatures. Widespread drought and famine will start to affect the fit as well as the vulnerable.

△ COASTAL FLOODING
Regular severe flooding in most coastal areas. Coastlines will move up to 165 ft (50 m) inland.

△ FOREST FIRES
There will be a 50 percent reduction in forest cover through drought and widespread fires worldwide, adding to extinctions.

△ HUMAN DEATH TOLL
There will be global food shortages due to catastrophic drought. Crop failures will lead to famine in most areas, leading to a death toll of millions.

△ COASTAL FLOODING
Bangladesh submerged; eastern US seaboard cities swamped; half of Europe under water.

THE RULES OF DRINKING

You may think that drinking with humans would be a pleasant pastime free of any pitfalls. Everyone is relaxed, so who cares about etiquette? Wrong. When it comes to drinking there are all kinds of intricate rules—and the liberal consumption of intoxicating liquor makes a punch-up far more likely if you do the wrong thing. Here are some of the basic rules.

"You're not drunk if you can lie on the floor without holding on."
Dean Martin

MARTINI ETIQUETTE

1. A symbol of global sophistication, the martini has become *the* drink for hipsters from the late 19th century via 007 and the Rat Pack to expats everywhere and hip New Yorkers.

2. The most crucial etiquette question associated with the martini is not shaken or stirred; olive or no olive; but gin or vodka? Gin and vermouth is a match made in heaven, whereas vodka and vermouth was a match made by shrewd marketeers in the 1950s. Vodka is distilled to be virtually tasteless, so the vermouth's flavor runs through it effortlessly. That's one reason why fans of vodka-tinis often want theirs as dry as can be, more like a vodka straight-up than a mixed drink.

3. The original martini was made with sweet Italian vermouth, sugar syrup, and orange bitters, but today it can also be made with a dry French vermouth.

4. The method of making a martini may not be as important as the choice of liquor, but most thoughtful bartenders would agree that James Bond had it wrong when he insisted that his martinis be shaken. Not only does this make for a cloudy drink (which is less than ideal), but it will also be less cold or "pure."

HOW TO MIX A PERFECT DRY MARTINI

Using proportions of 8:1 or 4:1 gin or vodka to vermouth depending on taste.

* 2 fl oz (60 ml) gin (use best quality brands) ideally kept in freezer
* ½ fl oz (7.5–15 ml) vermouth (sweet or dry)
* ice cubes
* a twist of lemon peel or one green olive

1. Fill cocktail shaker with ice and add gin and vermouth. Stir clockwise (counterclockwise in the southern hemisphere) for several minutes, or shake vigorously. This cools the liquids and adds a dash of water.

2. Strain into cocktail glass.

3. Twist lemon peel over drink to release essential oils or add a green olive, and serve.

WHISKY ETIQUETTE

1. Most Japanese people drink whisky mizuwari style—with ice and mineral water. Expensive glacier ice, said to lend the most delicious taste to whisky, is a fad in Japan.

2. It's very important to know the difference between single malt and blended whisky; many whisky buffs keep at least two bottles at home—expensive single malts for close friends and connoisseurs and a cheaper, blended whisky for everyone else.

BEER ETIQUETTE— BUYING A ROUND.

1. Do not accept a drink from anyone if you don't intend to reciprocate and buy a round later that evening.

2. Even worse is accepting drinks and then just buying one for yourself when it is your turn. It will rebound on you later as you'll soon get a reputation as a cheapskate.

3. There is no hierarchy for buying rounds—everyone is equal in the barroom melée. Just remember "First shout" goes to whomever volunteers to buy the first round of drinks (but it will give you cred and get you into everyone's good books).

4. Changing drinks on people during a round is frowned upon—you shouldn't buy everyone a cheap house "special" and then ask for an expensive über-cool imported beer or triple single-malt on the return leg.

5. Taking a break—perhaps you don't want to get completely legless, in which case, wait until everyone's bought a round before abstaining. If you have to forego midround, ask for a soft drink (but remember, these can sometimes be more expensive than the hard stuff). Such a strategy also means that the next person buying a round won't feel like a cheapskate.

6. If you knock someone's drink over, you must insist on replacing it—at least that gives the aggrieved party the opportunity of saying yea or nay and avoids the possibility of a punch-up if proceedings are quite intoxicated. In some outback communities in Australia, the spilling of beer requires the guilty party to receive a punch in the arm from all the other members of the party, which could be over 50 people!

7. In friendly Japanese bars, customers often pour drinks for each other from bottles of beer as a gesture of companionship. If you are a fellow beer drinker, reciprocate with your own bottle. Don't begin to drink until everyone is served. Glasses are raised in the traditional salute as everyone shouts *Kampai*! (Cheers!).

8. Know your limits—and leave them (like the best stand-up comics) wanting more. If you follow these tips, your reputation as a sensible—but fun—professional will rise.

> ## "Beer makes you feel how you ought to feel without beer."
> ### Henry Lawson

RESTAURANT ETIQUETTE

1. Everything to your right you drink. Everything to your left you eat.

2. No more than four glasses are set on the table, used for (from left to right) champagne, water, red wine, and white wine.

3. How to hold a stemmed glass: if the drink is ambient or "warm," that is to say red wine or brandy, hold the glass at the base of the bowl. Cupping in one hand is acceptable to "warm" the glass and bring out the bouquet. A glass of white wine or cocktail like a martini is held by the stem—to preserve its chill.

VODKA ETIQUETTE

1. Boozing is a big part of social life and if you're not inclined to get drunk, say you're on antibiotics to save face. Alternatively, down the first shot of vodka in one, when everyone is watching you, but only sip from the glass during subsequent toasts.

2. Thankfully, no Russian drinks vodka without eating *zakuski* (snacks) after each shot or at least sniffing some black bread (surprisingly effective) to help soak up the alcohol. *Zakuski* usually consists of pickled vegetables with black bread.

3. Set your glass down on the table to be refilled; do not raise it to meet the bottle.

4. Toasts are a big deal in Moscow. It is well worth preparing a few well-chosen phrases (English is fine) if there is any chance that you will be socializing with Russians. Drink to international friendship, the success of their enterprise, or any other heart-warming goal. The second toast of the evening is usually *Za jenjin* ("to the women"). Russians will be delighted by your efforts.

FOOD AND DRINK

LOCAL DELICACIES

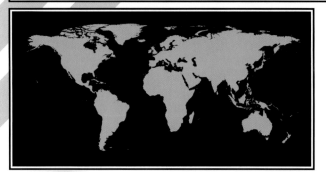

The proverb says when in Rome do as the Romans do, but let's hope that excludes eating—some of these dishes are definitely best left to the locals. According to another proverb, one man's meat is another man's poison and, while none of these delicacies will actually poison you, they could definitely put you off eating anything else for a while.

AUSTRALIA
Australian delicacies include kangaroo, ostrich, crocodile—and Vegemite, made from the yeast and malt by-products of beer-making. Nutritious witchetty grubs (left) are prized as "bush tucker."

SOUTH KOREA
Dog, dog, dog—in hot pot, soup, stir-fried, as chops, grilled, BBQ'd, or sweet & sour. Dog is also popular in China, Southeast Asia, and parts of Central/South America.

US
Look for bison, water buffalo, yak, squirrels' brains, and calves' testicles—known as prairie oysters, mountain oysters, or "swinging sirloin."

SPAIN & ITALY
Calves' testicles are *criadillas* in Spain and *granelli* in Italy. They are often peeled and boiled before being fried, grilled, or sliced into a pie.

CAMBODIA
Duck and chicken embryos make a popular dish prepared by boiling fertilized eggs in which the chicks or ducklings have started to form. Also eaten in China and other parts of Southeast Asia,

FRANCE
Famous for eating frogs' legs and snails, the French also eat donkey, mule, and horse, which can be used instead of beef in most recipes. A delicacy is horse/donkey sausage.

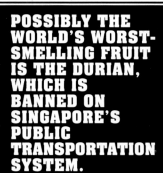

POSSIBLY THE WORLD'S WORST-SMELLING FRUIT IS THE DURIAN, WHICH IS BANNED ON SINGAPORE'S PUBLIC TRANSPORTATION SYSTEM.

MOST CONSUMED FOODS
ACCORDING TO UN FIGURES
1. WHEAT
2. STARCHY ROOTS
3. RICE
4. MEAT
5. SUGAR
6. CORN
7. TOMATOES
8. FISH & SEAFOOD
9. ORANGES & MANDARINS
10. BANANAS

INDONESIA
In Indonesia and much of Southeast Asia, fruit bats are eaten in soups, curries, and stir fries. They are also eaten in the Pacific islands, where the Samoans bake or fry them.

MYANMAR
A popular snack in Myanmar and other parts of Southeast Asia is chicken's feet, either in a soup or deep fried in batter, as here.

JAPAN
Boiled octopus. Also look for sushi and sashimi—raw fish dishes, including live lobster sashimi, known as *odori-gui* from "to dance" and "to eat" as it's still moving! A variant is *umasashi*—raw horse.

PERU
Fried, grilled, or stewed—guinea pigs are an important and widely eaten source of protein in Peru. The flavor is said to be similar to chicken.

UK
The British waste little of the animal: blood and fat go into black pudding, and offal such as tripe (below), heart, liver, lungs, spleen, and pancreas are fried with onions. Kidneys, liver, pigs' feet, tongue, and cows' udders are also consumed.

NORWAY
One Norwegian speciality is *smala hove*, a sheep's head, cut in half and grilled. The skull acts as a cooking pot for the brains, which are eaten with a spoon. Brains are also eaten as fritters and dumplings.

DEMOCRATIC REPUBLIC OF CONGO
In the Congo, monkeys are smoked over open fires to preserve the meat. The flesh of the mandrill, a type of baboon (below), is particularly valued.

LAOS
Deep-fried scorpion is a delicacy, often seasoned with vinegar. Another is tarantula, skewered and cooked over an open fire.

VENEZUELA
Tarantulas, which here can grow to the size of tennis balls with 10 in (25 cm) legs, are nutritious, being 60 percent protein. The flesh of the abdomen is said to taste of raw potato and lettuce, and that of the legs like prawns. The fangs are used afterward as toothpicks.

CHINA
Chinese delicacies include sheep's head, bull's penis, seahorse soup, bear's paw soup, shark's fin soup, and a parasitic fungus known as winter worm (right).

FIRST 10 EUROPEAN COUNTRIES TO HAVE MCDONALD'S
1971 GERMANY: MUNICH
1972 NETHERLANDS: VOORBURG
1973 SWEDEN: STOCKHOLM
1974 UK: WOOLWICH, LONDON
1975 SWITZERLAND: GENEVA
1977 IRELAND: DUBLIN
1977 AUSTRIA: VIENNA
1978 BELGIUM: BRUSSELS
1979 FRANCE: STRASBOURG
1981 SPAIN: MADRID

ORTOLAN
In France, it is illegal to hunt, buy, or eat ortolan, a tiny bird also known as a bunting, but it is so highly prized a delicacy that the law is often ignored. The birds are prepared by the traditional method of force-feeding them, drowning them in Cognac, and then roasting them. Traditionally, each person eats only one ortolan but on December 31, 1995, anticipating his imminent death from prostate cancer, French President François Mitterrand is said to have eaten two.

SPORTS AND LEISURE
BACKHANDERS

Every year thousands of men gather on beaches around the world to watch the superb ball skills displayed by female beach volleyball players. The game—which originated in California in the 1920s—has two people per team and the idea is to volley the ball back and forth over a net until the opposing side fails to return it. The key to success is the hand signal, executed behind the back out of sight of the opponents, usually by the nonserving partner just before the serve.

NO BLOCK/CROSS-COURT BLOCK
Player on the left will not block the ball, player on right will try to return the ball across the court.

LINE BLOCK/CROSS-COURT BLOCK
Player on the left will try to return the ball down the line, player on the right will try to return it across the court.

LINE BLOCK
Player on the right will try to return the ball down the line.

LINE BLOCK
Both players will try to return the ball down the line.

CROSS-COURT BLOCK
Player on the right will try to return the ball across the court.

LINE BLOCK/NO BLOCK
Player on the left will try to return the ball down the line, player on the right will not block the ball.

LINE BLOCK
Both players will try to return the ball down the line.

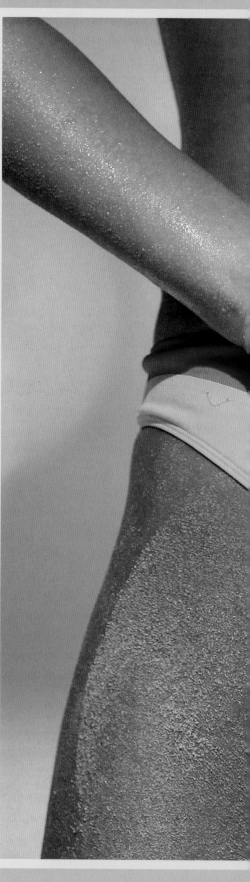

Horror Movies

JAMES BOND'S ARCH ENEMY GOLDFINGER SAYS:"ONCE IS HAPPENSTANCE.TWICE IS COINCIDENCE.THREE TIMES IS ENEMY ACTION." ON THE SAME BASIS, IF ONE CAST MEMBER DIES THAT'S UNFORTUNATE; IF TWO DIE THAT'S SINISTER; AND IF THREE OR MORE DIE THAT'S A CURSED MOVIE.

JAWS

So many things went wrong during the making of Steven Spielberg's 1975 movie *Jaws* that the crew nicknamed the film *Flaws*. The first producers, Richard Zanuck and David Brown, couldn't get the director they wanted and had to settle for the then little-known Steven Spielberg: one problem that proved to be for the best. Then they had to find another screenwriter because they didn't like any of the three drafts provided by Peter Benchley, who had written the novel on which the film was based.

When shooting did begin, one of the mechanical sharks sank straight to the bottom of the ocean, not having been tested in water. There were three model sharks (collectively nicknamed Bruce, after Spielberg's lawyer), all of which kept malfunctioning because the hydraulics controlling them became corroded in the saltwater. Various mishaps, such as sea-soaked cameras and other people's boats sailing into shot, might be expected on a marine shoot, but the crew really did begin to think the fates were against them when the shark-hunting boat *Orca* began to sink with the actors onboard. Naturally, the production went over budget but, for a Hollywood blockbuster, that seems a sign of normality rather than a cursed movie.

GONE WITH THE WIND

Three cast members have killed themselves since the movie was released in 1939 but, because they weren't the big stars, *Gone With the Wind* is often overlooked in the league tables of cursed movies. Actor Paul Hurst, who played the Yankee deserter killed by Scarlett O'Hara, committed suicide on February 27, 1953. Almost exactly two years later, actress Ona Munson, who played prostitute Belle Watling, committed suicide on February 11, 1955 at the age of 51. She took an overdose of barbiturates and left a note by her bed saying:"This is the only way I know to be free again… please don't follow me." Four years later, actor George Reeves (who also played Superman, *see above right*) died in disputed circumstances shortly before his wedding. There were rumors of foul play. Even before these three unfortunate events, violent deaths had touched two other people connected with the film. In 1940, Barton Bainbridge, first husband of Evelyn Keyes, the actress who played Scarlett's younger sister, Suellen O'Hara, committed suicide after threatening to kill Keyes. And then on August 16, 1949, Margaret Mitchell, who wrote the book upon which the film was based, died of her injuries five days after being hit by a car while crossing the street.

DREADED SUPERMAN

The story of the supposed "curse of *Superman*" began circulating widely after the tragic riding accident that paralyzed and ultimately killed actor Christopher Reeve. Believers in the curse think that *Superman*'s comic book creators, Jerry Siegel and Joe Shuster, may have cursed the character in revenge for being poorly paid by DC Comics. Supposed victims include the Fleischer brothers, whose business slumped shortly after producing the original *Superman* animated cartoon, forcing them to sell Fleischer Studios to Paramount in 1941. Actor George Reeves, who played Superman in the 1951 film *Superman and the Mole Men*, was found dead from a gunshot wound on June 16, 1959, just days before he was due to be married. The official verdict was suicide but many people close to Reeves refused to accept that could be true. Actress Margot Kidder, who played Lois Lane to Christopher Reeve's Superman, had a breakdown in 1996 as a result of bipolar disorder. And actor Lane Smith, who played Perry White (Clark Kent and Lois Lane's boss) in the 1990s televison series *Lois & Clark*, was diagnosed with Lou Gehrig's Disease in April 2005 and died two months later.

THE MISFITS

One critic described *The Misfits* as "more of a mausoleum than a movie" because it was the last film of both stars, Marilyn Monroe and Clark Gable; and their fellow actor, Montgomery Clift, died only four years after it was released. This bleak Western was written by playwright Arthur Miller, who created the role of Roslyn Taber especially for his wife, Marilyn Monroe, but author and actress argued constantly on set and divorced before the film was released. Clark Gable had a heart attack just three days after filming was completed and died 11 days later on November 16, 1960. The film was released in February 1961 and 18 months later, on August 5, 1962, Monroe was found dead in her bedroom with an empty bottle of sleeping pills beside her—theories that she was murdered have persisted ever since. Montgomery Clift, whom Monroe once described as "The only person I know who is in worse shape than I am," died on July 23, 1966, after what has been called Hollywood's longest suicide, due to his allegedly self-destructive substance abuse. *The Misfits* bombed on its release but achieved cult status after Monroe's death.

"THE FILM THAT KILLS"

A horror trilogy about poltergeists is prime material for rumors about supernatural curses. The fact that four cast members died soon after the *Poltergeist* trilogy was completed, some of them in unusual circumstances, has done nothing to squelch the rumors. *Poltergeist* was released on June 4, 1982, and five months later 22-year-old actress Dominique Dunne was strangled to death by a jealous ex-boyfriend. During the filming of *Poltergeist II*, 60-year-old actor Julian Beck died of stomach cancer (it had been diagnosed before auditioning for the role). The film was released in 1986 and, the following year, 53-year-old actor Will Sampson, who played the medicine man, died of postoperative kidney failure. During filming of *Poltergeist III*, 12-year-old actress Heather O'Rourke, who starred in all three movies, was diagnosed with Crohn's Disease and died on February 1, 1988 of toxic shock after an emergency operation arising from her condition. The ending was reshot using a body double and the film was released later that year.

Several other events have been attributed to "the Poltergeist Curse." In a *Poltergeist III* publicity photo of actress Zelda Rubenstein, her face was inexplicably obscured by a bright light: she later said her mother had died at the time of the photo session. While filming *Poltergeist III*, a set caught fire, injuring several crew members. An earthquake in 1994 damaged a house used in *Poltergeist I*. One suggested cause of the Poltergeist Curse is that human bones were supposedly used as props in *Poltergeist I*.

THE CURSE OF THE LEES

Chinese actor Bruce Lee was almost single-handedly responsible for transforming martial arts films from a minority art form into a mainstream film genre. Born at the hour of the dragon in the year of the dragon, Lee's last complete film was *Enter the Dragon*. On July 20, 1973, just a month before the film's première, Lee took a painkiller to ease a headache, fell asleep, and never woke up. The autopsy reported that he had died of a cerebral oedema (brain swelling) brought on by an allergic reaction to the painkiller. But conspiracy theories have thrived ever since—that he was murdered by the Chinese mafia for refusing to pay protection money; that a rival martial artist had given him *dim mak*, the touch of death; or that he had succumbed to evil spirits: "the curse of the dragon." His last film of all was the ironically titled *Game of Death*, which he had started filming in 1972. It was completed using body doubles wearing dark glasses.

The idea that Lee was cursed gained further currency in 1993 when his son Brandon also died an early death before completing his last film, *The Crow*, about a murder victim who is resurrected by a crow to wreak vengeance on his killers. On the night of March 30, 1993, Brandon was fatally shot by a stunt pistol fired by fellow actor Michael Massee. The official investigation concluded that the tip of a dummy bullet used in an earlier scene had been lodged in the chamber of the gun and was propelled out of the barrel by the blank round being used that night. (Dummy bullets look like real bullets for close-ups, while blanks make noise and flash for action shots.) Like his father's *Game of Death*, Brandon Lee's last film was completed using a stand-in.

ROSEMARY'S BABY

The curse of *Rosemary's Baby* has nothing to do with the film's production. Instead, the "curse" relates to its uncanny connections with two tragic events. Directed by Roman Polanski, the film tells the story of a woman (played by Mia Farrow) who is abused by a Satanic cult and forced to carry the Devil's baby. On August 9, 1969, a year after the film was released, Polanski's wife, Sharon Tate, was murdered by members of Charles Manson's cult the "Manson Family" while Polanski was in London working on his next film. Tate, eight and a half months pregnant, pleaded for the life of her unborn child before being stabbed 16 times by cult member Susan Atkins. Just over a decade later, John Lennon was murdered outside New York's Dakota Building, whose entrance appears several times in *Rosemary's Baby* as the exterior of the apartment building in which the film is set. A slim connection on its own, except that Lennon was a close friend of Mia Farrow. The Beatles song "Dear Prudence" is about Mia's sister, and appears on the *White Album* along with "Helter Skelter"—the song that Charles Manson cited as the main inspiration for his cult and its actions.

REBEL WITHOUT A CAUSE

Nicholas Ray's 1955 classic *Rebel Without a Cause* has certainly given cause for rumors about a curse—all three main stars died young in tragic circumstances. Most infamously, James Dean, who played Jim Stark, was killed in a car crash at the age of just 24 almost exactly four weeks before the film was released on October 27. On the afternoon of September 30, Dean left Los Angeles for a race meeting at Salinas Airport, California. He had intended to tow his Porsche Spyder to the race but, at the last minute, he decided to drive it there instead. Outside the small town of Cholame he collided head on with a Ford Tudor driven by student Donald Turnupseed, who had not seen the speeding silver Porsche in the twilight. Turnupseed escaped with minor injuries but Dean was pronounced dead on arrival in the hospital after being trapped in his car, which one witness described as looking "like a crumpled pack of cigarettes."

Twenty-one years later, on February 12, 1976, Dean's younger costar Sal Mineo was murdered at the age of 37. Returning home from a rehearsal of a stage play, Mineo was fatally stabbed as he walked through an alleyway close to his apartment in West Hollywood. Police initially suspected that the killing was a homophobic attack on the openly gay actor. But when Lionel Ray Williams was caught and convicted of the killing, it transpired that he had simply intended to mug Mineo and didn't even realize who he was. Five years later still, on November 29, 1981, Natalie Wood drowned at the age of 43 while spending time with on-off husband Robert Wagner on their yacht Splendor at Catalina Island, California. She was drunk at the time, and the verdict was accidental drowning. But inevitably rumors have persisted ever since that foul play was involved.

UNLUCKY BREAKS

When someone suggested that golfer Arnold Palmer had been lucky he retorted: "It's a funny thing, the more I practise the luckier I get." There's more to his quip than meets the eye, because it doesn't mean there's no luck in sport – it means that if you practise you can make the most of the lucky breaks. But wherever there are lucky breaks there are also unlucky ones...

▲ FORKED AGAIN

French cyclist Christophe was the favourite to win the 1913 Tour de France, having come second in 1912. But just as he took the lead a race vehicle hit his bike, snapping the front fork. It was illegal for cyclists to accept help but Christophe, a blacksmith, walked to the nearest village, found a forge, and made a new fork. In 1919, he led until the penultimate stage, when once again his fork snapped; again he forged a new one, and finished in third place. In 1922, he was lying third when his fork broke yet again – he was destined never to better his second place of a decade earlier.

FOURTH TIME LUCKY

Early in 1995, popular Italian cyclist Pantani was hit by a car but recovered to win two mountain stages in that year's Tour de France and a bronze medal in the world championships. That autumn, during the Milano-Turino race, a jeep drove into the pack and broke Pantani's leg in two places; he recovered in time for the 1997 Giro d'Italia but a black cat ran in front of him and put him out of the race again. Then, finally, in 1998, on his fourth attempt, his luck changed and he won both the Tour de France and the Giro d'Italia.

▲ FATHER AND SON

During the 400 metres semi-final at the 1992 Barcelona Olympics, disaster struck Britain's gold medal hopeful, Derek Redmond. His hamstring popped, as a result of which the official record states that he abandoned the race – but Derek was determined to finish. His father, Jim, jumped over a barrier to help, half-carrying Derek across the line to a standing ovation and the admiration of the world.

◄ MYSTERY COLLAPSE

In the 1956 Grand National, the Queen Mother's horse Devon Loch was heading for an unlikely victory after its two closest rivals fell at the first fence. Horse and jockey Dick Francis (later famous as a novelist) cleared the last fence but 50m (55 yards) from the line Devon Loch inexplicably collapsed, rose again but failed to finish. Theories are that the horse tried to jump a shadow, was distracted by the crowd, or had cramp. The Queen Mother's response was: "That's racing".

TRIPPING UP

At the Los Angeles Olympics, in 1984, South African-born Budd, running barefoot, was leading the 3000 metres with three laps to go when the American favourite, Mary Decker, tried to pass her. Decker caught Budd's heel and fell at the side of the track; Budd, cut by Decker's running spikes, kept her balance and finished seventh. Decker claimed Budd had deliberately tripped her (a difficult thing to do when the person you are tripping up is behind you) but the endless replays showed no evidence of this. It seems that it was an unfortunate accident that cost both women their chance of a medal.

◄ UNLUCKY 13

Miami Dolphins' quarterback Dan Marino is the best player never to have won a Super Bowl. Despite being widely regarded as one of the greatest quarterbacks in the history of American Football, his only Super Bowl appearance was a 1985 loss to the San Francisco 49ers. His shirt number was 13.

▼ MARATHON EFFORT

Italian Dorando Pietri finished first in the 1908 London Olympic marathon, but he didn't win. Some 275m (300 yards) from the finish his legs buckled and he fell to the track. He then struggled to his feet but fell several more times before finally stumbling across the line, held upright by a race official and still almost a minute ahead of second-placed Johnny Hayes (USA). Hayes contested the result and Pietri was disqualified for using "external support" but public support was such that the following afternoon Britain's Queen Alexandra presented Pietri with a special gold cup that she had donated at her own expense.

TEED OFF

In the 1999 Open, French golfer Jean van de Velde was three strokes in the lead at the final tee – and hoping to be the first Frenchman to win since 1907 – when he simply fell apart. His first shot landed on the fairway; the second hit a grandstand and went into the rough; the third went into the knee-deep water of Barry Burn; he took the drop and his fifth shot went into a bunker; his sixth found the green and his seventh the hole. Despite all this he still drew the match, but went on to finish third in a three-way play-off for the title.

▲ THAT KICK

In May 1968, British rugby league player Don Fox was having a dream Cup Final. He'd won the Man of the Match award and was about to put the icing on the cake by kicking the winning goal. With two minutes to go, he lined up a simple conversion to take Wakefield from 11–10 down to a glorious 12–11 victory. But it wasn't to be: he slipped on the waterlogged pitch and missed. Forty years later "That kick" still haunts him.

GOAAAAAAOWWWWWWWW!

In December 2004, the Swiss–Portuguese soccer player Paulo Diogo jumped onto a metal perimeter fence to celebrate setting up an 87th-minute goal for Servette FC against Schaffhausen in the Swiss first division. Recently married, he caught his new wedding ring on the barrier and tore off the top part of his finger as he jumped down. Stewards hunted for the missing part – and Diogo was booked for timewasting. Surgeons were unable to re-attach the missing joint and amputated the stump instead.

SUPERSIZE SCOTCH EGG

DIFFICULTY RATING:
›VERY EASY   ›EASYISH   ›MODERATE   ›A BIT TRICKY

Hard-boiled egg wrapped in sausage meat and coated in breadcrumbs—it's an odd delicacy. Popular in 19th-century Scotland (hence the name), Scotch eggs are normally smaller than a tennis ball, but much tastier. Here's how to make one the size of a football.

INGREDIENTS

12 large eggs
3 lb 8 oz (1.5 kg) sausage meat
1 bag breadcrumbs (8 oz/200 g)

METHOD

1 Separate the egg whites and yolks from the eggs and place into separate bowls. You will shortly combine this into one giant super egg.

2 This part is particularly tricky. You need to find two bowls, one smaller than the other. Pour half of the egg white into the larger bowl and suspend it in boiling water. Take the smaller bowl and use it to create an indentation in the egg white as it cooks. Do this twice so that you have two hemispherical pieces of cooked egg white.

3 Pour half the egg yolk into the smaller bowl and suspend in boiling water as before. Once this has cooked, you'll find it's the exact size of the indentation you created in the egg white earlier. Repeat to complete the other huge halfs of the mega egg.

4 Preheat an oven to 425°F/220°C. Mash the sausage meat into a flat base and use it to form a completely sealed casing. Wrap around the mega egg and coat with breadcrumbs.

5 Place Scotch egg on a baking tray and cook for 30 minutes, or until golden and crisp, like a normal-sized Scotch egg. Turn out onto a serving plate.

6 To serve, cut in half—but DO NOT eat all at once!

Super Scotch egg with standard-sized and mini versions for comparison.

HOW HEALTHY?
Estimated calories: 5,000
To burn this off you would need to skip at a fast pace for around 7 hours.

First white centerline

River Road in Trenton, Michigan, was the first road in the world to have what was called a "center line safety stripe." It was painted in the fall of 1911 at the instigation of Wayne County Road Commissioner Edward Norris Hines.

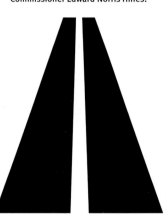

2 HOUR

PARKING 8:30AM – 5:30PM

First parking meter

American journalist Carlton Magee invented the parking meter in 1932, and the first 150 machines were installed in Oklahoma City on July 16, 1935. The following month Oklahoma churchman Reverend North became the first person in the world to be fined for overstaying a meter.

First car crash

The first collision between two motor vehicles occurred on Charing Cross Road, London, in 1897.

First auto fatality

In 1896, Mrs. Bridget Driscoll was run over in the grounds of the Crystal Palace, London, by Arthur Edsell, who was traveling at 4 mph (6 km/h). The first driver to be killed was Henry Lindfield in 1898: he died of shock after crashing his electric car en route from London to Brighton, England.

First drunk-driving conviction

At 12:45 p.m. on September 10, 1897, taxi driver George Smith crashed his electric cab into number 165 Bond Street, London. In court he admitted having drunk "two or three glasses of beer" and was fined 20 shillings.

First traffic light

The very first traffic light was a gas-lamp installed near Parliament Square in London, in 1868, to control horse-drawn traffic. The first electric traffic lights were invented by American Garrett Augustus Morgan and installed at the corner of Euclid Avenue and 105th Street in Cleveland, Ohio, in 1914.

HIT THE ROAD

When it comes to motor racing, "first" means "fastest." But on the ordinary roads, "first" means "earliest." As more humans hit the road, the number of road regulations has increased and ignoring them can have disastrous consequences.

First highway

The first high-speed d
carriageway with access
to motor vehicles only wa
Avus *autobahn* in Germa
urban highway that open
September 10, 1921. The
intercity highway was
Milano–Varese *autostr*
which opened on Septem
1924, in Italy.

First speeding conviction

On January 20, 1896, Walter Arnold of East Peckham, Kent, was arrested for exceeding the limit of 2 mph (3 km/h) in a built-up area. The policeman who arrested Arnold, who was estimated to be driving at 8 mph (13 km/h), caught him after giving chase on a bicycle.

First traffic warden

New York Mayor Robert Wagner introduced the world's first traffic wardens in June 1960. The London Borough of Westminster introduced Britain's first traffic

First wheel clamp

Wheel clamps first appeared in the 1900s and worked like a modern cycle lock, with two prongs that passed through the spokes for private security. As wheel designs changed, the early locks disappeared, only to reappear after WWII as a parking-enforcement device.

First speed camera

Dutch rally driver Maurice Gatsonides developed the first speed camera during the 1950s to test his performance. Speed cameras were introduced to British roads in 1992 for enforcing speed limits.

HIDE AND SEEK

James Bond, the world's best-known spy, had some incredible gadgets—think deadly briefcase, laser watch, underwater breather, and remotely controlled car— but even humans know they're fictional and that they work by film trickery. Real spies use some equally fantastic gadgets, and these ones truly do work.

► CONCEALED STORAGE

For anyone worried that their property may be searched, there are various forms of concealed storage available. They range from furniture and luggage with false compartments to hollowed-out hard-backed books and resealable canisters made to look like ordinary branded products, such as canned food, shaving cream, or spray paint.

▲ Concealed camera—pictures can be taken through the side by applying pressure to the cover

► CONCEALED UHF TRANSMITTERS

Short-range ultra-high frequency (UHF) transmitters can be concealed in any number of household objects, allowing spies to transmit their own conversations or listen in on others from up to 1,100 yd (1,000 m) away. Commonly used objects include calculators, pens, watches, telephone sockets, and electrical sockets, all of which can be made to operate normally despite their hidden extras.

▲ Pen with hidden transmitter

▲ Rectal tool kit—includes (from left to right) handle with pliers and wirecutters, file, drill bit, grinding tool, cutting blades, saw blade, and reamer

▲ RECTAL TOOL KIT

Escape tools and ingenious ways of hiding them are always useful. This CIA kit from the 1960s was designed for rectal concealment in case of a search. It contained nine separate tools, ranging from cutting blades to drill bits.

TELEPHONE VOICE CHANGER

Modern telephone voice transformers give users total control over the way their voices sound, allowing them to alter the timber, tone, formant (resonance of consonant and vowel sounds), reverberation, and pitch as they speak. The voice transformer will even remember the settings so that users can recreate the same voice for future calls.

WAVE DETECTORS AND WINDOW BOUNCERS

Wave detectors can "see" through walls by measuring electromagnetic radiation, showing people moving inside a building and even detecting people's breathing and heartbeats. Window bouncers mean that listeners no longer need to plant bugs to eavesdrop on conversations: a laser beam trained on a window can pick up the vibrations in the glass and re-create the original sound.

◀ POISON-TIPPED UMBRELLA

On September 12, 1978, a member of the Bulgarian secret service stabbed defector Georgi Markov in the leg with an umbrella as he stood at a bus stop in London. The umbrella was rigged to inject a tiny metal sphere containing ricin, which killed Markov three days later.

TRACKING DEVICES

GPS, the global positioning system, uses satellites communicating with computerized radio receivers to give the exact location, speed, and direction of the radio receiver. A tracker comprises a GPS receiver and a transmitter, and can be concealed in clothing, personal effects, or vehicles in order to track a person under surveillance.

▲ CONCEALED RECORDERS

Sometimes it's impossible to record at a distance and the agent must be able to get in close. Recorders can be concealed in a variety of objects, including hardback books, briefcases, and handbags. Microphones linked to hidden recorders can be concealed in belt buckles, buttons, pens, pins, and brooches, among other items.

▲ Miniature concealed camera with straps and remote control

▲ KGB umbrella

▶ LOCK-PICKING SET

Sets of up to 32 picks are available but an expert can pick most locks with a set of five. A set includes a torsion wrench for turning the bolt and several flat picks with variously shaped tips that can be inserted into the lock to operate the levers.

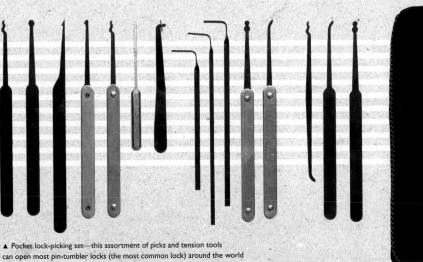

▲ Pocket lock-picking set—this assortment of picks and tension tools can open most pin-tumbler locks (the most common lock) around the world

MULTIPURPOSE PEN

The pen is one of the most versatile objects for concealing weapons or surveillance equipment because it can be carried and handled in most situations without suspicion. Items concealed in working pens include radio transmitters, microphones, bug detectors, cameras, miniature telescopes, poison pellets, and an electric stunning device.

▶ Concealed recording device in briefcase spine

◀ CONCEALED CAMERAS

Fixed CCTV cameras can be concealed in in any object that provides a good view of the room under surveillance, such as wall clocks, burglar-alarm sensors, or smoke alarms. User-operated still or video cameras can be concealed in portable objects, including cell phones, watches, briefcases, handbags, cigarette lighters, sunglasses, and brooches.

FLORA AND FAUNA

Bad hair day

According to St Matthew's gospel "the very hairs of your head are all numbered." Well, here are a few hairdos that would be better buried in the sand than left on display and numbered. All humans have the occasional bad hair day, but it looks as if, for these poor unfortunates, every day was a bad hair day.

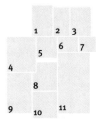

04. **70s-STYLE "FLICK"**
with tanktop to match.
05. **80s NEW ROMANTIC**
is parodied in a KFC ad
from 2000.
06. **SLICK KISS CURLS**
Max Hoggenheimer
(played by Sam
Bernard) in *The Girl
from Kays.*
07. **BEARD OLYMPICS**
Austria, 2005.
08. **60s PAGE BOY CUT**
in a magazine ad.
09. **80s BLEACHED PERM**
and earring
10. **HIS AND HERS WIGS**
in a magazine ad.
11. **HAIR, MOUSTACHE,**
and chest hair, too—
Douglas Bull, stuntman.

70S AFRO (main pic,
left) Don Brewer,
drummer for the band
Grand Funk Railroad.
01. **GREASY LOCKS**
Guy Pearce, actor.
02. **80s MULLET**
Pat Sharp, TV and
radio host.
03. **1910 WILD HAIR**
"Prof." W.H. McMillan,
one-man band in Texas.

**Douglas Bull
is an unsung hero...**

He's one of the unknown men
who perform dangerous
stunts in films, standing in for
the stars; and he's got the
scars to prove it. As a relaxation
from movie mayhem, he
buys his clothes from Hornes.
We've fitted his 46" chest
with this matching beach set.
The shirt costs £8.75 and
the shorts, £3.20. It's an easy
outfit for an active man...

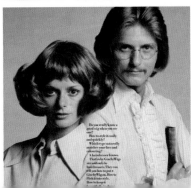

REAL NAMES

Real name	Celebrity name
Vincent Damon Furnier	ALICE COOPER
Alicia Augello Cook	ALICIA KEYS
Be'la Ferenc Dezso Blasko	BELA LUGOSI
Krishna Bhanji	BEN KINGSLEY
Eleanora Fagan Gough	BILLIE HOLIDAY
Lesley Charles	BILLY OCEAN
Robert Zimmerman	BOB DYLAN
Walden Robert Cassotto	BOBBY DARIN
William Michael Albert Broad	BILLY IDOL
Leslie Townes Hope	BOB HOPE
Paul Hewson	BONO
William Henry Pratt	BORIS KARLOFF
Archibald Alexander Leach	CARY GRANT
Carlos Irwin Estevez	CHARLIE SHEEN
John Charles Carter	CHARLTON HESTON
Cherylyn Sarkisian	CHER
David Robert Jones	DAVID BOWIE
David Seth Kotkin	DAVID COPPERFIELD
Dino Croceti	DEAN MARTIN
Derek van den Bogarde	DIRK BOGARDE
LaDonna Andrea Gaines	DONNA SUMMER
Doris Mary Ann Von Kappelhoff	DORIS DAY
Reginald Kenneth Dwight	ELTON JOHN
Declan Patrick Aloysius McManus	ELVIS COSTELLO
Marshal Mather III	EMINEM
Arnold Dorsey	ENGELBERT HUMPERDINCK
Eric Clapp	ERIC CLAPTON
Frederick Austerlitz	FRED ASTAIRE
Faroukh Bulsara	FREDDIE MERCURY
Jerome Silberman	GENE WILDER
Virginia Katherine McMath	GINGER ROGERS
Greta Lovisa Gustafsson	GRETA GARBO

MYTHS AND LEGENDS

SIX DEGREES OF CELEBRITY

THERE IS A THEORY THAT THE EARTH IS SUCH A SMALL PLACE THAT ANYONE CAN BE CONNECTED TO ANYONE ELSE BY A CHAIN OF NO MORE THAN SIX CONNECTIONS. IN 1994, INSPIRED BY THE PLAY *SIX DEGREES OF SEPARATION*, TWO AMERICAN STUDENTS INVENTED THE GAME "SIX DEGREES OF KEVIN BACON"—THE GOAL WAS TO LINK ANY HOLLYWOOD ACTOR TO BACON IN SIX STEPS. WELL, HERE ARE A FEW CONNECTIONS THAT MIGHT HELP YOU PLAY THE GAME.

LEFT HANDED

- ADOLF HITLER
- ALEXANDER THE GREAT
- BILL CLINTON
- BILL GATES
- BUZZ ALDRIN
- CHARLIE CHAPLIN
- DOUGLAS ADAMS
- FRIEDRICH NIETSZCHE
- GERMAINE GREER
- HENRY FORD
- JAMES BROWN
- JIMI HENDRIX (ambidextrous, but usually played guitar left-handed)
- JOAN OF ARC
- JOHANN SEBASTIAN BACH
- KEANU REEVES
- LEO TOLSTOY
- MARGARET THATCHER
- MATT GROENING (and many of the Simpsons)
- NAPOLEON BONAPARTE
- NICOLE KIDMAN
- OSAMA BIN LADEN
- PABLO PICASSO
- PAUL MCCARTNEY
- ROBERT DE NIRO
- SAMUEL BECKETT
- STEVE MCQUEEN
- URI GELLER

REAL NAMES CONTINUED...	Issur Danielovitch Demsky KIRK DOUGLAS	Sofia Villani Scicolone SOPHIA LOREN
Julius Henry Marx GROUCHO MARX	Brian Warner MARILYN MANSON	Arthur Jefferson STAN LAUREL
Ehrich Weiss HARRY HOUDINI	Norma Jean Mortenson MARILYN MONROE	Steveland Morris STEVIE WONDER
James Newell Osterberg Jr. IGGY POP	Ramón Estévez MARTIN SHEEN	Gordon Sumner STING
Henry John Deutschendorf Jr. JOHN DENVER	Marvin Lee Aday MEAT LOAF	Anna Mae Bullock TINA TURNER
Marion Michael Morrison JOHN WAYNE	Margaret Mary Emily Ann Hyra MEG RYAN	Bernard Schwartz TONY CURTIS
Roberta Joan Anderson JONI MITCHELL	Maurice Micklewhite MICHAEL CAINE	Allen Stewart Konigsberg WOODY ALLEN
Frances Gumm JUDY GARLAND	William Robinson ROCK HUDSON	

PILOTS

JOHN TRAVOLTA
▼
CLINT EASTWOOD
▼
MORGAN FREEMAN
▼
HARRISON FORD
▼
PATRICK SWAYZE
▼
EDDIE IZZARD
▼
MICHAEL CRAWFORD
▼

ANCESTORS

ABRAHAM LINCOLN * TOM HANKS

EDWARD III * RICHARD NIXON

HENRY I (POSSIBLY) * CLINT EASTWOOD

JOHANN SEBASTIAN BACH * KYLE MACLACHLAN

LOUIS BLÉRIOT * CATE BLANCHETT

ROBERT THE BRUCE * BARBARA CARTLAND

WILLIAM WORDSWORTH * MIKE MYERS

PARENTS-IN-LAW

ANDRÉ PREVIN IS WOODY ALLEN'S FATHER-IN-LAW

CECILLE B. DE MILLE WAS ANTHONY QUINN'S FATHER-IN-LAW

DON EVERLY WAS AXL ROSE'S FATHER-IN-LAW

EUGENE O'NEILL WAS CHARLIE CHAPLIN'S FATHER-IN-LAW

FRANZ LISZT WAS RICHARD WAGNER'S FATHER-IN-LAW

INGRID BERGMAN WAS MARTIN SCORSESE'S MOTHER-IN-LAW

RYAN O'NEAL WAS JOHN MCENROE'S FATHER-IN-LAW

VANESSA REDGRAVE IS LIAM NEESON'S MOTHER-IN-LAW

RIO FERDINAND
▼
DAVID COULTHARD
▼
GARY NUMAN
▼
ANGELINA JOLIE
▼
TOM CRUISE
▼
GEORGE H. BUSH
▼
GEORGE W. BUSH
▼
KURT RUSSELL
▼
KRIS KRISTOFFERSON

PALL BEARERS

* **1827** FRANZ SCHUBERT FOR LUDWIG VAN BEETHOVEN * **1928** J. M. BARRIE AND GEORGE BERNARD SHAW FOR THOMAS HARDY * **1959** PHIL EVERLY FOR BUDDY HOLLY * **1960** JAMES STEWART AND SPENCER TRACY FOR CLARK GABLE * **1981** ROCK HUDSON, FRANK SINATRA, GREGORY PECK, FRED ASTAIRE, LAURENCE OLIVIER, DAVID NIVEN, AND ELIA KAZAN FOR NATALIE WOOD * **1993** HUBERT GIVENCHY FOR AUDREY HEPBURN * **1994** EMERSON FITTIPALDI, RUBENS BARRICHELLO, DAMON HILL, DEREK WARWICK, JOHNNY HERBERT, GERHARD BERGER, ALAIN PROST, AND JACKIE STEWART FOR AYRTON SENNA * **1994** JOHN MCENROE, JIMMY CONNORS, AND BJORN BORG FOR VITAS GERULAITIS * **2000** SIR BOBBY CHARLTON, SIR TOM FINNEY, AND NAT LOFTHOUSE FOR SIR STANLEY MATTHEWS

CUSTOMS AND ETIQUETTE
NATIONAL TREASURES

Been there, done that, got the T-shirt. And if T-shirts aren't your bag, there are always plenty of finely crafted cultural artifacts to remind you of the highlights of your vacation—or not, as the case may be. Who buys the stuff? Surely there can't be that many doting grandparents and pestering children? But it's a global phenomenon, so there must be something about vacations that urges humans to take home local wares.

CANADA
Pack maple syrup if you dare: you could arrive home with a suitcase full of very sticky clothes.

THE US
If you're too far north for a Stetson, these Liberty shades are the perfect reminder of the Land of the Free.

HOLLAND
The clog keyring—cute or dreadful, depending on your point of view. Maybe they'd run out of windmill trinkets and wooden tulips.

PERU
When you get home you can buy a panpipes CD and pretend to play these yourself.

ENGLAND
A snow globe—the ideal souvenir of your visit to London, where the weather is always bad and the traffic is always stationary.

KENYA
When ivory poachers wipe out the last elephant this model will always remind you that they once existed.

SCOTLAND

Och aye. Scotland's national instrument was invented in Greece, but the kilt and sporran should keep you from confusing your vacations.

NORWAY

Worried about DVT? You'll be fine if you wear these reindeer hide slippers on the flight home.

ITALY
Why waste your time with D&G, Prada, Armani, or Versace when you can have this fashionable opera mask?

RUSSIA
Five Russian doll souvenirs for the price of one—or is that one for the price of five?

AUSTRALIA
Akubra is strine (Australian) for hat. Useful for keeping your "tinnies" (canned drinks) in the shade at the "barbie" (barbecue).

INDIA
If you can't find enough snakes to charm, any child will be thrilled with this supersized recorder.

BOLIVIA
A poncho probably seemed like a good idea at the time. Oh well, you could always use it for lining the dog's basket.

SWITZERLAND
What was it Orson Welles said in *The Third Man*? "Five hundred years of democracy and peace, and what did that produce? The cuckoo clock!"

IRELAND
Leprechaun: a creature with the magical power to make you fork out money that you could have spent on Guinness.

JAMAICA
Who wants a simple pencil and eraser when you can get one topped with a Rastafarian hat?

THAILAND
Some people bring back a wife, but a Buddha is much lower maintenance.

EGYPT
Egyptian souvenir merchants—they're all guilty of pyramid selling.

JAPAN
If you're (un)lucky, the sparklers in your cocktail will set fire to these quaint paper parasols.

FRANCE
It's the most visited monument in the world and 200 million people can't be wrong, so this may be the best souvenir of the bunch.

HAWAII
A floral lei is a traditional greeting or parting gift—and it's easier to pack than a ukelele or a grass skirt.

FLORA AND FAUNA

BIRD SCARER

This "mooning" scarecrow is enough to frighten the birds. A Kansas farmer, anxious to protect his crops, used two pumpkins for a novel effect.

KNIGHTS TEMPLAR

In 1118, nine French knights vowed to protect pilgrims traveling to the Holy Land, naming their order after the Temple of Solomon, which was close to their headquarters in Jerusalem. The order rapidly grew in numbers, power, and wealth until jealousy led to its suppression and, in 1312, to the dissolution of the order by Pope Clement V. The romance of the Templars' supposed connection with the Holy Grail has led to wild speculation that the order survives in secret to this day, exerting undue influence over international governments through control of organizations such as the UN.

CATHARS

Taking their name from the Greek *kathoroi* ("the pure"), the Cathars were a medieval sect of heretical Christians who believed that the human soul was essentially good and could be the route to salvation from the evils of the material world. The Cathars were suppressed during the 14th century by the Catholic Church's Inquisition. But conspiracists believe, as they do of the Templars, that the Cathars possessed treasures and mystical secrets that enabled the sect to survive in secret. Cathars are often named (along with the Knights Templar, Illuminati, and Freemasons, among others) in conspiracists' fantasy leagues of secret societies that are planning world domination.

MYTHS AND LEGENDS

JOIN THE CLUB

If there are any truly secret societies, by definition we don't know about them. But there are many secretive societies, both real and mythical. Secretiveness makes people suspicious, so many of these societies are the subject of rumors, accusations, and conspiracy theories—some of them well founded.

Though we have tried to be openminded and judicious while seeking out the best substantiated accounts of events, that still doesn't mean you should treat any of the [other] theories (or any of the "facts" related by us in our discussion of them) with anything other than complete disbelief.

ROSICRUCIANS

There are several so-called Rosicrucian societies, ranging from New Age astrological societies to philanthropic fraternities similar to Freemasony. All claim some connection to the mythical *Fraternatis Rosae Crucius* (Brotherhood of the Rosy Cross), which was first documented in an anonymous pamphlet published in 1614. The pamphlet described the foundation of the brotherhood in 1407 by a German monk, Christian Rosenkreutz, with the aim of promoting intellectual and spiritual self-improvement. Inverting the usual conspiracy theory that long-dead societies still exist, this fictional society has given rise to several real ones.

FREEMASONS

Freemasonry is a fraternal society whose members seek moral and spritual self-improvement by performing allegorical rituals based on stonemasonry. Because Freemasons (aka Masons) use private handshakes and passwords to identify themselves, conspiracists claim that Masonry is a secret society bent on world domination. There is no historical evidence of Freemasonry before the 17th century, and while most Masons trace their origins to the medieval stonemasons' guilds, some—and plenty of conspiracists—see Masonry as a continuation of the Knights Templar. But even government investigations have failed to uncover evidence of anything more than a philanthropic fraternal society.

ILLUMINATI

Founded in 1776 by Bavarian mystic Adam Weishaupt, the Illuminati (aka Order of Perfectibilists) was a small republican group of free thinkers, many of whom were also Freemasons. Fearing the influence of such antiestablishment groups, the ruler of Bavaria, Elector-Prince Karl-Theodor, banned all secret societies in 1784. However, as with the Knights Templar, conspiracists suspect that the order lived on. Since officially being disbanded, the Illuminati have been accused of conspiring to usurp the pope, controlling US politics, fomenting world communism, running the CIA, and plotting to take over the world by infiltrating international organizations.

MAFIA

Mafia means "hostility to the law," in the dialect of Sicily, where the first Mafia families came to power organizing criminal activities. During the 19th century, Mafia groups spread throughout Italy and then, through immigration, to the US—most prominently in New York and Chicago. The American Mafia became so powerful during the American Prohibition that the word "Mafia" came to be used as a generic term for any organized crime syndicate. The Mafia has been accused of involvement in countless internal killings, as well as the murders of such high-profile figures as trade-union leader Jimmy Hoffa, film star Marilyn Monroe, President John F. Kennedy, and his brother, Attorney-General Robert F. Kennedy.

YAKUZA

Often described as the "Japanese Mafia," the Yakuza is one of the world's largest and most active organized crime syndicates. Yakuza originated in roaming bands of "masterless Samurai," described by the Yakuza themselves as Robin Hood-style protectors of the people and by historians as ruthless vigilantes. The modern Yakuza operates not only in the traditional gangster areas of drugs, gambling, extortion, and prostitution, but also in property, banking, and shipping.

SKULL & BONES

Skull & Bones, a frat society at Yale University in the US, is accused by conspiracists of being a "secret establishment" leading to "hidden paths of power." However, despite US presidents Taft, Bush, and Bush Jr. being former Bonesmen, the list of known members fails to bear out the conspiracy theory that it's a moving staircase to power and influence.

OPUS DEI

Literally meaning "God's work," Opus Dei is an international Catholic organization founded in Spain in 1928 by José Maria Escriva de Balaguer, who died in 1975 and was canonized in 2002. The stated goal of Opus Dei is "to help people turn their work and daily activities into occasions for growing closer to God, for serving others, and for improving society." But many people are suspicious of the organization's "cultlike techniques" and fast-growing power, claiming that Opus Dei members controlled Franco's Fascist Spanish government, exert undue political influence in Italy and Latin America, and are attempting to influence US politics. One leading Spanish theologian described Opus Dei as being "like a Mafia shrouded in white."

THE BILDERBERG GROUP

Named after the Dutch hotel in which it first met in 1954, the Bilderberg Group is an unofficial, self-chosen international association of corporate, finance, media, and military power-brokers, top politicians, and members of various royal families. There is no membership as such, but many top figures are regularly invited to the annual conference. The group's original purpose was to foster international relations but—not surprisingly for an organization whose meetings are held at secret locations, minuted anonymously, and go unreported by the press—it has been accused of everything from exerting undue influence over US presidential elections to instigating wars and steering world politics and finance.

FLORA AND FAUNA

For girls, the curves and cleavage of the 50s and 60s were out and long legs were in, as demonstrated here by Jamie Lee Curtis, Brooke Shields, and Elle McPherson (long legs were here to stay but thankfully leg warmers and striped tights weren't). And for boys, military style was evidently The Right Stuff (although Mel Gibson seemed to prefer the rugged civilian look).

80 ICONS

01. **JAMIE LEE CURTIS**
the "Scream Queen"
shows off her
shapely legs.

Madonna (main photo,
left) a Material Girl.
01. **JAMIE LEE CURTIS**
the "Scream Queen"
shows off her
shapely legs.
02. **TOM CRUISE**
looking uniformly
good as "Maverick"
in *Top Gun* (1986).

03. **KIM BASINGER**
pouting as Elizabeth in
Nine 1/2 Weeks (1986).
04. **MEL GIBSON**
—blue-eyed charmer.
05. **WHITNEY HOUSTON**
model, actress,
and one of the most
successful pop singers
of all time.
06. **BROOKE SHIELDS**
nice legs, but too
bad about the stripes.
07. **ELLE MACPHERSON**
supermodel known
as "The Body."
08. **RICHARD GERE**
showing military
appeal as Zack Mayo
in *An Officer and
a Gentleman* (1982).

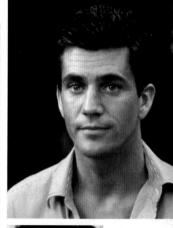

I like being a woman, even in a man's world. After all men can't wear dresses, but we can wear the pants.—Whitney Houston

NORTH POLE MARATHON

Cofounded by Richard Donovan in 2003, the North Pole Marathon is the world's coolest and northernmost marathon, and the only event of its kind to be run entirely on water—the frozen Arctic Ocean. After winning the first Antarctic Marathon (see below, opposite) in January 2002, Donovan ran a solo North Pole marathon that April to become the first person to run a marathon at both poles.

VENDÉE GLOBE

Founded by Frenchman Philippe Jeantot in 1989, the Vendée Globe is the world's only nonstop, single-handed, round-the-world yacht race. It starts and finishes in the town of Les Sables-d'Olonne in the Vendée *département* of western France. In 2000–01, 24-year-old English yachtswoman Ellen MacArthur, the youngest competitor ever to finish, came second in 94 days and 4.5 hours—the record time for a woman.

BEAST OF THE EAST

Billed as "America's Toughest Adventure Race," the six-day Beast of the East covers more than 300 miles (480 km) of mountain terrain and its tests of skill, stamina, and determination include whitewater canoeing, mountain biking, hiking, and climbing. Unlike many other extended endurance events, the race has no mandatory breaks, which means that competitors must judge for themselves when to rest, eat, and sleep.

WESTERN STATES TRAIL RIDE

Also known as the Tevis Cup, this 100-mile (160-km) endurance horse ride in California was first ridden in 1955 by Wendell Robie. Starting at 5:15 a.m. near Truckee, the trail passes over the Sierra Nevada and ends at 5:15 a.m. in Auburn. Vets check the horses at 30 miles (50 km) and 70 miles (115 km). The cup is awarded to the fastest finisher—if the horse is judged "fit to continue."

SELF-TRANSCENDENCE 3,100-MILE (5,000-KM) RACE

Founded in 1987 by Indian guru Sri Chinmoy, the annual Self-Transcendence Race is the world's longest footrace, held in New York State. Participants attempt to complete 5,649 laps of a 0.5488-mile (883-meter) course in no more than 51 days. The first person to win the race was Scotsman Al Howie, in 17 days and 9 hours.

LA RUTA DE LOS CONQUISTADORS

Billed as "the toughest mountain bike race on the planet," Costa Rica's La Ruta is a three-day, coast-to-coast race in tropical climates and through grueling terrain that rises to a height of 11,259 ft (3,432 m) up the Irazú Volcano.

◄ IDATROD DOG SLED RACE

Founded in 1973, this annual Alaskan race along the historic Idatrod (or Iditarod) Trail covers some 1,151 miles (1,853 km) in eight to fifteen days in subzero temperatures. Blizzards and gale force winds can take wind chill down to -100°F (-75°C).

BADWATER ULTRAMARATHON

This footrace covers 135 miles (217 km) in temperatures up to 130°F (55°C). The race starts 280 ft (85 m) below sea level at Badwater in Death Valley, California, and finishes 8,360 ft (2,533 m) above sea level at Mt. Whitney.

SPORTS AND LEISURE

EXTREME ENDURANCE

Endurance races are not just about speed, strength, and skill, they're also about grit, determination, and, in some cases, sheer survival. They are a test of the human spirit, because those crazy enough to take part are not only competing against each other, they're also competing against themselves. Here we have a selection of 14 of the Earth's ultimate races.

CROSS-CHANNEL SWIM

Until Englishman Captain Matthew Webb swam the English Channel in 1875, people thought it was impossible—and no one managed to repeat his feat for 36 years. Then they said it was impossible for a woman, until 1926, when American Gertrude Ederle became the sixth person and the first woman to do the swim. Since then some 800 people have achieved "the impossible."

TOUR DE FRANCE

The world's most famous cycle race, the Tour de France is a three-week stage race around France and, occasionally, neighboring countries. It was founded in 1903 by Henri Desgrange, editor of *L'Auto* newspaper, who introduced the race-leader's famous yellow jersey in 1919 to identify the leader and because the pages of *L'Auto* were yellow. In 2005, American Lance Armstrong won the Tour for a record 7th consecutive year.

EVEREST MARATHON

Held 11 times since 1987, the Everest Marathon is billed as the highest marathon in the world. The start line is at Gorak Shep, close to Everest Base Camp in Nepal, 17,000 ft (5,184 m) above sea level. The finish, after 26¼ miles (42.2 km) of rough mountain trails, is at Namche Bazaar, 11,300 ft (3,446 m) above sea level.

ANTARCTIC ICE MARATHON

The world's southernmost marathon, also known as the South Pole Marathon, takes place in the foothills of the Ellsworth Mountains at 80° south, in the interior of Antarctica. The race is run over permanent snow and ice, and runners face average temperatures of -4°F (-20°C). There is also an Antarctic Half Marathon and, for the really hardy, the Antarctic 60-mile (100-km) Ultra Race.

▲ IRONMAN AUSTRALIA

The Ironman Australia Triathlon has taken place annually since 1988 in Port Macquarie, comprising a 2½-mile (3.8-km) deep-water swim followed by a 112-mile (180.2-km) bike ride, and finally a 26¼-mile (42.2-km) run.

◄ MARATHON DES SABLES

Founded in 1986 by Frenchman Patrick Bauer, the Marathon des Sables ("Marathon of the Sands") is billed as the toughest footrace in the world. It covers approximately 150 miles (240 km) over six days through the Moroccan Sahara Desert, one of the world's most hostile environments. The entry fee includes a charge for "corpse repatriation."

SPORTS AND LEISURE

UNITED WE FALL

On 8 February 2006, skydivers from 31 countries got together over north-eastern Thailand to attempt a formation freefall world record by creating a 400-person snowflake in mid-air.

TECHNOLOGY
WORLD OF WAR

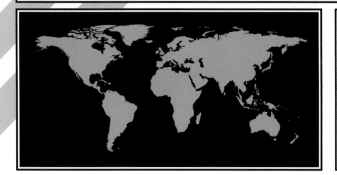

When it comes to armies, size matters. The soldiers below bear weapons scaled to represent their countries' military spend per person in 2005, according to CIA figures. This is the clearest way to look at military might, but there are others. Eritrea (96th by this measure) spends more of its GDP on armed forces than any other nation. And in total dollars the US (3rd by this measure) spends over six times as much as any other nation.

140. NICARAGUA
$4.76 PER PERSON

120. BENIN
$10.56 PER PERSON

100. PAKISTAN
$18.25 PER PERSON

80. MOROCCO
$42.78 PER PERSON

TOP 50 BIG GUNS IN TERMS OF SPEND PER PERSON
2005

1. ISRAEL $1,429.03 per person	**11. SAUDI ARABIA** $692.71 per person	**21. NETHERLANDS** $396.17 per person
2. SINGAPORE $1,009.94 per person	**12. NORWAY** $677.77 per person	**22. ITALY** $347.66 per person
3. UNITED STATES $935.64 per person	**13. UNITED ARAB EMIRATES** $624.27 per person	**23. FINLAND** $344.63 per person
4. NEW CALEDONIA $888.25 per person	**14. GREECE** $573.68 per person	**24. SWITZERLAND** $340.23 per person
5. BRUNEI $885.43 per person	**15. AUSTRALIA** $566.95 per person	**25. TAIWAN** $330.83 per person
6. KUWAIT $842.17 per person	**16. UNITED KINGDOM** $524.48 per person	**26. LUXEMBOURG** $315.43 per person
7. QATAR $837.73 per person	**17. CYPRUS** $492.22 per person	**27. JAPAN** $310.16 per person
8. OMAN $807.46 per person	**18. SWEDEN** $488.23 per person	**28. BELGIUM** $296.89 per person
9. FRANCE $766.62 per person	**19. GERMANY** $470.70 per person	**29. KOREA, SOUTH** $269.20 per person
10. BAHRAIN $764.44 per person	**20. DENMARK** $454.71 per person	**30. CANADA** $239.63 per person

GLOBAL MILITARY SPENDING WAS MORE THAN $1 TRILLION IN 2005—MORE THAN $160 FOR EVERY PERSON ON THE PLANET

60. MALAYSIA
$70.55 PER PERSON

40. NEW ZEALAND
$150.11 PER PERSON

20. DENMARK
$454.71 PER PERSON

1. ISRAEL
$1,429.03 PER PERSON

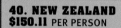

31. KOREA, NORTH $227.72 per person	**41. IRAN** $142.61 per person
32. LIBYA $225.46 per person	**42. LEBANON** $141.40 per person
33. SPAIN $213.18 per person	**43. JORDAN** $131.51 per person
34. SLOVENIA $183.99 per person	**44. BOTSWANA** $126.40 per person
35. AUSTRIA $182.90 per person	**45. PORTUGAL** $121.71 per person
36. IRELAND $174.30 per person	**46 = ESTONIA** $116.28 per person
37. SEYCHELLES $157.66 per person	**46 = TURKEY** $116.28 per person
38. CHILE $156.44 per person	**48. CZECH REPUBLIC** $116.22 per person
39. MALTA $150.55 per person	**49. CROATIA** $115.66 per person
40. NEW ZEALAND $150.11 per person	**50. ARGENTINA** $108.76 per person

DID YOU KNOW?

The nation with the least military spending in 2005 was Iceland, which spent nothing. It had no regular armed forces because, from 1951 to 2006, Iceland was defended by the US Icelandic Defense Force (IDF). The IDF withdrew in 2006 and an Icelandic Crisis Response Unit has since been established.

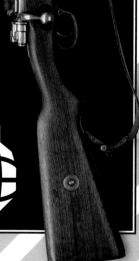

CUSTOMS AND ETIQUETTE
NATIONAL HEALTH

The previous page shows how much the countries of the world spend on war. Here we see how much they spend on health—the doctors pictured below are holding stethoscopes scaled to represent how much their governments spend on health per person. By contrast, the country whose citizens spend the greatest amount of their private money on health is the US.

140. INDONESIA
$40 PER PERSON

120. MONGOLIA
$90 PER PERSON

100. BELIZE
$142 PER PERSON

80. TONGA
$214 PER PERSON

TOP 50 SPENDERS

THESE WORLD HEALTH ORGANIZATION FIGURES FROM 2002 ARE FOR GOVERNMENT HEALTH SPENDING. IN ALL THE COUNTRIES HERE SOME PEOPLE PAY FOR THEIR OWN HEALTH CARE.

1. MONACO $3,388 per person	**11. CANADA** $2,048 per person	**21. FINLAND** $1,470 per person
2. NORWAY $2,845 per person	**12. SWITZERLAND** $1,995 per person	**22. NEW ZEALAND** $1,447 per person
3. LUXEMBOURG $2,620 per person	**13. AUSTRALIA** $1,832 per person	**23. ANDORRA** $1,345 per person
4. SAN MARINO $2,449 per person	**14. UNITED KINGDOM** $1,801 per person	**24. ISRAEL** $1,242 per person
5. UNITED STATES $2,368 per person	**15. BELGIUM** $1,790 per person	**25. PORTUGAL** $1,201 per person
6. ICELAND $2,353 per person	**16. IRELAND:** $1,779 per person	**26. NAURU** $1,184 per person
7. GERMANY $2,212 per person	**17. JAPAN** $1,742 per person	**27. SPAIN** $1,170 per person
8. SWEDEN $2,144 per person	**18. NETHERLANDS** $1,683 per person	**28. SLOVENIA** $1,158 per person
9. DENMARK $2,142 per person	**19. ITALY** $1,639 per person	**29. CZECH REPUBLIC** $1,022 per person
10. FRANCE $2,080 per person	**20. AUSTRIA** $1,551 per person	**30. GREECE** $960 per person

GLOBAL HEALTH SPENDING IN 2003 WAS MORE THAN $3.5 TRILLION, ABOUT $500 FOR EVERY PERSON ON THE PLANET. ALMOST HALF OF THAT TOTAL WAS SPENT IN THE US.

60. ROMANIA
$309 PER PERSON

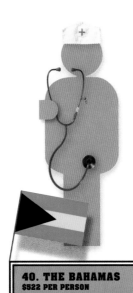

40. THE BAHAMAS
$522 PER PERSON

20. AUSTRIA
$1,551 PER PERSON

1. MONACO
$3,388 PER PERSON

31. HUNGARY
$757 per person

32. QATAR
$700 per person

33. BARBADOS
$696 per person

34. MALTA
$691 per person

35. PALAU
$664 per person

36. COOK ISLANDS
$648 per person

37. SLOVAKIA
$646 per person

38. BAHRAIN
$570 per person

39. UNITED ARAB EMIRATES
$551 per person

40. THE BAHAMAS
$522 per person

41. SOUTH KOREA
$519 per person

42. CROATIA
$513 per person

43. COSTA RICA
$486 per person

44. ARGENTINA
$480 per person

45. POLAND
$476 per person

46. ESTONIA
$461 per person

47. COLOMBIA
$444 per person

48. BELARUS
$430 per person

49. KUWAIT
$415 per person

50. ST KITTS AND NEVIS
$414 per person

Of those countries for which both health and military spending figures are available, Iceland has the greatest differential, having no military spending. San Marino is next, spending over 100 times more on health than armaments. At the other end of the scale, Iraq spent seven times as much on military as health.

THE CZECH REPUBLIC SPENDS THE GREATEST PERCENTAGE (91.4 PERCENT) OF PUBLIC, AS OPPOSED TO PRIVATE, MONEY ON HEALTH.

HUGH GLASS

In 1823, during an expedition up the Missouri River, fur trapper Glass was hunting for food when he stumbled upon a grizzly bear and her two cubs. The bear charged and Glass fought back, stabbing her with his hunting knife as she raked him with her claws. Finally, two of his companions shot the bear, but Glass was so badly mauled that the expedition leader thought he wouldn't survive 24 hours. He asked for volunteers to stay with Glass until he died and then bury him. The two men who had shot the bear volunteered to stay but abandoned Glass before he had expired, taking his rifle and hunting knife with them and later claiming that they'd been attacked by Arikaree Indians.

Glass found himself alone with a broken leg, wounds deep enough to expose the bone, and no equipment. Determined to survive, he set his broken leg, put maggots in his festering wounds to prevent gangrene, and began to crawl the 322km (200 miles) back to the nearest settlement, Fort Kiowa. Having learned from the Pawnee Indians how to live off the land, he survived on wild berries, roots, and the carcass of a bison killed by wolves. When he reached the Cheyenne River, he made a raft and floated downstream, arriving in Fort Kiowa six months after he had been abandoned.

Resuming life as a fur trapper, Glass swore to avenge himself on the men who had abandoned him. But when he did catch up with them, he spared one because he was so young and the other because he'd joined the army, and to kill a soldier would have meant the death penalty.

CHRIS RYAN

In January 1991, during the Gulf War, Chris Ryan (not his real name) was dropped into Iraq behind enemy lines. A soldier with Britain's elite Special Air Service, Ryan was a member of an eight-man reconnaissance patrol code-named Bravo Two Zero. Their job was to locate the launch site of the Scud missiles, which Iraqi dictator Saddam Hussein had begun firing into Israel in the hopes of provoking a retaliation that would destabilize the coalition fighting Iraq. But however well a military operation is planned and executed there is always an element of luck. In Bravo Two Zero's case luck went against them – their position was compromised when they were discovered by a young shepherd boy, and they were forced to flee to Saudi Arabia.

After surviving several firefights, the patrol split into two groups, both of which met with disaster. Four men were captured and tortured and two were killed, leaving Ryan and his last colleague hiding in the mountains. Desperately hungry, Ryan's colleague left their hideout to beg a shepherd for food. He didn't return and, when Ryan saw two Iraqi vehicles approaching, he realized his colleague must have been tortured into revealing his whereabouts. He tried to slip away but the vehicles were too close so he took drastic action, firing a rocket launcher at them. As the vehicles exploded he escaped, and so began a seven-day, 322-km (200-mile) survival hike through the desert extremes of heat and cold.

Several days into his flight, Ryan strayed into a guarded compound and triggered a search. Two guards spotted him, but he managed to knife them both silently, without attracting further attention, and once again managed to evade capture. He finally reached Saudi Arabia a few days later. Since leaving the SAS in 1993, Ryan has become a celebrity author, TV presenter, and survival expert.

OLD CHRISTIANS

On Friday 13 October 1972, a Uruguayan airforce plane, carrying the Old Christians rugby team from Uruguay to Chile with their friends and family, crashed in the Argentinian Andes. Twelve of the 45 passengers and crew were killed outright and six more died from injuries and exposure in the next few days as they awaited rescue. But rescue didn't come. The pilot had strayed off course, which meant the rescuers were searching the wrong area.

After ten days, the survivors were facing starvation, and resorted to attempting to eat strips of leather torn from the luggage. Then medical student Robert Canessa suggested the unthinkable: that their last resort was to eat the bodies of their dead comrades, which had been preserved in the cold. Reluctantly, they cut strips of flesh from the corpses of their friends, which provided them with the nutrition to survive. But six days later another catastrophe occurred: an avalanche hit the fuselage of the plane in which they were sheltering, killing eight more people.

Six weeks later, on Day 60, Canessa and Nando Parrado decided that their only hope of rescue was for the two of them to attempt the tortuous hike down from the mountains. After nine days, they managed to raise the alarm; rescuers reached the plane on 22 December, 72 days after the crash. In 2002, the 16 survivors, now in their 50s, finally played the fixture they had been flying to: they won 28–11.

STAYING ALIVE

Survival is the most primitive human instinct. So it's little wonder that humans are fascinated by the stories of people who've survived extreme situations. Not only that, but survival stories are structured like Hollywood movies: they start with something going horribly wrong, continue with a cocktail of adventure, suspense, ingenuity, and determination, and have a happy ending.

MAURO PROSPERI

During the 1994 Marathon des Sables – a gruelling 240-km (150-mile) footrace through the Moroccan Sahara Desert – a sandstorm separated Italian policeman Mauro Prosperi from his fellow competitors. Disoriented by the storm, he began running south instead of east, with 1,600km (1,000 miles) of empty desert ahead of him. On the second day, a rescue helicopter overflew Prosperi without seeing him. "That," he said later, "is when I realized I might die."

By the fourth day, Prosperi was reduced to drinking urine he'd saved in a bottle. His spirits soared when he thought he saw someone on the horizon — but the shape turned out to be a stone shrine. Prosperi slept in the shrine and the following morning he was awoken by the sound of a plane. Feverishly he set fire to his backpack as a signal flare, but again the pilot failed to see him. Prosperi was plunged into such despair that he cut his wrists with his penknife, but his blood was so thick from dehydration that it didn't flow. Instead of dying, he awoke the following morning with a new determination to survive.

First, he needed sustenance, which he found nesting in his shelter: "I saw these little bats huddled together in the corner of the tower, so I grabbed them with my bare hands. I crushed them and began to eat them." The next day, Prosperi ventured back into the desert, remembering the advice of the nomadic Tuareg people: "Go towards the clouds. It's easier to find water. It's easier to find life." Walking only in the mornings and late afternoons, Prosperi survived eating lizards and snakes. Then, on the seventh day, he found a pool of muddy water with footprints leading away from it. He was tempted to stay close to the water but knew he must find the owner of the footprints and continued to follow the clouds until he found a young shepherdess who raised the alarm. When he returned home the Italian press dubbed him "The Robinson Crusoe of the Sahara".

EDDIE RICKENBACKER

During World War I, American racing driver Eddie Rickenbacker took time out to become a fighter pilot, shooting down 26 enemy planes and winning the Congressional Medal of Honor. Rickenbacker didn't fight in World War II, but he worked tirelessly as a military adviser. On 21 October 1942, en route to review American air bases in the South Pacific and deliver a secret message to General MacArthur, the B-17 Flying Fortress bomber transporting him ditched into the Pacific close to Japanese-occupied territory.

Rickenbacker, his business partner, and the six crew found themselves adrift on the ocean with three life-rafts and scant supplies. Rickenbacker assumed the role of leader, tying the life-rafts together and eking out their water supply by collecting rainwater. The food ran out after three days but, on Day 8, after five days under the scorching sun with no food and little water, a seagull landed on Rickenbacker's head. He grabbed it, wrung its neck, and carefully divided it between the men, saving the entrails to use as bait for fishing.

On Day 13, one man died of exposure, and a week later Rickenbacker decided to separate the rafts to increase their chances of rescue. His desperate plan worked – four days afterwards, a US Navy search plane spotted one of the rafts, which led rescuers to the others. On 13 November 1942, after 24 days adrift, Rickenbacker was picked up. He was able to complete his assignment, successfully delivering his message to General MacArthur.

ERNEST SHACKLETON

In August 1914, Irish explorer Ernest Shackleton set out for Antarctica, hoping to become the first man to lead an expedition across the continent on foot. But the dream went awry before Shackleton had even reached his intended starting point – his ship Endurance was caught in the pack ice and frozen, in the words of the ship's storekeeper, "like an almond in a piece of toffee". Shackleton knew that eventually one of two things would happen – either spring would thaw the ice and free the ship, or the pressure of the constantly shifting ice would crush it like an eggshell. Unfortunately, it was the latter.

Expedition photographer Frank Hurley wrote: "The pressure develops an irresistible energy. The ship groans and quivers, windows splinter, whilst the deck timbers gape and twist." The following day, Shackleton gave the order to abandon ship. He and his crew set up camp on the ice and could only watch as the Endurance was broken to pieces. Six months later, the ice began to break up and they were able to launch three open lifeboats they had salvaged from the Endurance. After seven days and nights rowing through the freezing waters of the Antarctic, they finally made landfall on the uninhabited Elephant Island.

The only way for Shackleton to save his crew was to take the largest lifeboat and attempt to sail 1,287km (800 miles) across the South Atlantic to the whaling stations of South Georgia. Miraculously, he found that speck of land in thousands of miles of ocean. Five months after Shackleton's departure, the remaining crew were about to give up hope and launch another boat when a ship was sighted. It was Shackleton, on his fourth attempt to return to Elephant Island, his previous efforts having been thwarted by pack ice. Shackleton's navigator wrote: "By self sacrifice and throwing his own life into the balance he saved every one of his men."

JOE SIMPSON

In 1985, British mountaineer Joe Simpson and his climbing partner Simon Yates achieved a mountaineering dream, becoming the first people to reach the summit of Siula Grande in the Peruvian Andes. But on the way down the dream turned into a nightmare – Simpson slipped down an ice cliff, breaking his ankle and smashing his shin up through his knee joint. The only way to reach base camp 900m (3,000ft) below was for Yates to lower Simpson down the mountainside on a rope 90m (300ft) at a time.

Then disaster struck again. Unable to see what was below, Yates inadvertently lowered Simpson over a 30m (100ft) overhanging cliff above a crevasse. Simpson dangled in mid-air with Yates restraining his full weight, which was beginning to dislodge Yates from his collapsing snow hole. Yates held on for an hour and a half but, knowing that if Simpson's weight pulled him out of the hole they would both fall to almost certain death, he was faced with a gruesome decision – and he cut the rope.

Certain that Simpson was dead, Yates continued alone to base camp, which was a remarkable feat of mountaineering in itself. But Simpson hadn't died – an ice bridge within the crevasse had broken his fall. Realizing that he couldn't climb upwards, Simpson used his end of the severed rope to abseil lower into the crevasse. It could have been a fatal decision but, luckily, he reached the bottom before his rope ran out, and managed to crawl out of the ice through a side opening.

Still unable to walk, and in agonizing pain from his injuries, he spent four days crawling back to base camp with only melting ice to sustain him. He arrived at base camp the very night Yates was due to leave: had he been a few hours later, he really would have died.

TECHNOLOGY

Human spares

The first written record of an artificial limb concerns an ancient Greek criminal named Hegesistratus. He was condemned to death in 484 BCE, cut off his foot to escape his chains, and afterward made himself a wooden foot. (His efforts were in vain because he was recaptured and put to death.) Prosthetics have come a long way since then—the latest myoelectric limbs attach to nerve endings in the remaining limb stump and can be controlled by thoughts alone.

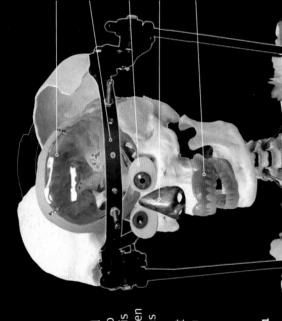

>> Key

01 **HEAD BRACE**
Stabilizes head and corrects posture

02 **CRANIAL IMPLANT**
Repairs skull and protects the brain

03 **PROSTHETIC EYES**
French surgeon Ambroise Paré made the first ones in the 16th century

04 **PLATED METAL ARTIFICIAL NOSE**
Common in the 17th century when many people lost their noses to syphilis

05 **DENTURES**
First made from bone in the 15th century

06 **PROSTHETIC HOOK HAND**

07 artificial electronic arm

08 **MYOELECTRIC HAND**
Responds to electrical brain impulses

09 **PROSTHETIC HAND**

10 **ARTIFICIAL IRON ARM**
Made for a knight in the 16th century

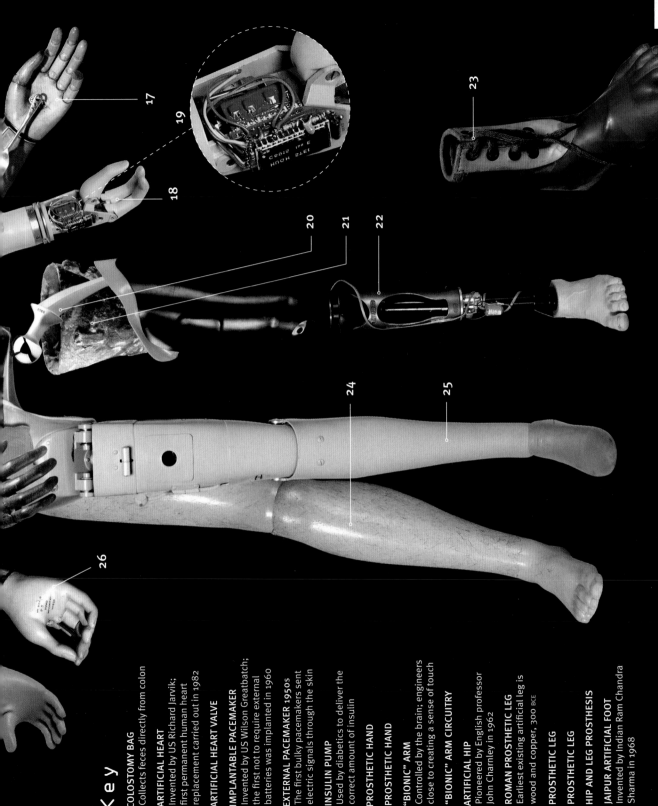

» Key

11 **COLOSTOMY BAG**
Collects feces directly from colon

12 **ARTIFICIAL HEART**
Invented by US Richard Jarvik; first permanent human heart replacement carried out in 1982

13 **ARTIFICIAL HEART VALVE**

14 **IMPLANTABLE PACEMAKER**
Invented by US Wilson Greatbatch; the first not to require external batteries was implanted in 1960

15 **EXTERNAL PACEMAKER 1950s**
The first bulky pacemakers sent electric signals through the skin

16 **INSULIN PUMP**
Used by diabetics to deliver the correct amount of insulin

17 **PROSTHETIC HAND**

18 **PROSTHETIC HAND**

19 **"BIONIC" ARM**
Controlled by the brain; engineers close to creating a sense of touch

20 **"BIONIC" ARM CIRCUITRY**

21 **ARTIFICIAL HIP**
Pioneered by English professor John Charnley in 1962

22 **ROMAN PROSTHETIC LEG**
Earliest existing artificial leg is wood and copper, 300 BCE

23 **PROSTHETIC LEG**

24 **PROSTHETIC LEG**

25 **HIP AND LEG PROSTHESIS**

26 **JAIPUR ARTIFICIAL FOOT**
Invented by Indian Ram Chandra Sharma in 1968

COMMUNICATION
SWEET NOTHINGS

L ove is blind. And it can strike any time, any place, anywhere, so it's best to be prepared. It's often difficult enough to say those three little life-changing words in your own language, so here's some help finding the right phrase if you happen to stumble blindly across Mr. or Ms. Right anywhere on Earth. It sounds so romantic in a foreign language, especially whispered huskily in an endearingly/ excruciatingly broken accent.

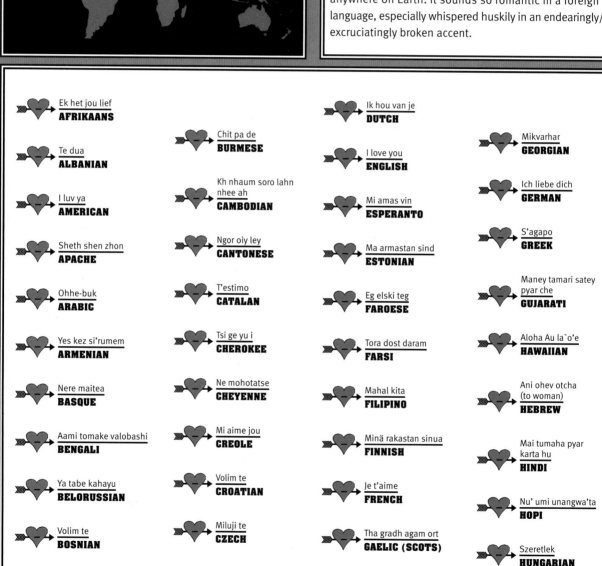

Ek het jou lief
AFRIKAANS

Te dua
ALBANIAN

I luv ya
AMERICAN

Sheth shen zhon
APACHE

Ohhe-buk
ARABIC

Yes kez si'rumem
ARMENIAN

Nere maitea
BASQUE

Aami tomake valobashi
BENGALI

Ya tabe kahayu
BELORUSSIAN

Volim te
BOSNIAN

Obicham te
BULGARIAN

Chit pa de
BURMESE

Kh nhaum soro lahn nhee ah
CAMBODIAN

Ngor oiy ley
CANTONESE

T'estimo
CATALAN

Tsi ge yu i
CHEROKEE

Ne mohotatse
CHEYENNE

Mi aime jou
CREOLE

Volim te
CROATIAN

Miluji te
CZECH

Jeg elsker dig
DANISH

Ik hou van je
DUTCH

I love you
ENGLISH

Mi amas vin
ESPERANTO

Ma armastan sind
ESTONIAN

Eg elski teg
FAROESE

Tora dost daram
FARSI

Mahal kita
FILIPINO

Minä rakastan sinua
FINNISH

Je t'aime
FRENCH

Tha gradh agam ort
GAELIC (SCOTS)

Tá grá agam ort
GAELIC (IRISH)

Mikvarhar
GEORGIAN

Ich liebe dich
GERMAN

S'agapo
GREEK

Maney tamari satey pyar che
GUJARATI

Aloha Au la`o'e
HAWAIIAN

Ani ohev otcha (to woman)
HEBREW

Mai tumaha pyar karta hu
HINDI

Nu' umi unangwa'ta
HOPI

Szeretlek
HUNGARIAN

Eg elska thig
ICELANDIC

Saya cinta padamu
INDONESIAN

Negligevapse
INUIT

Ti amo
ITALIAN

Aishite imasu
JAPANESE

Norul sarang hae
KOREAN

Khoshim awée
KURDISH

Te amo
LATIN

Es tevi miilu
LATVIAN

Bahibak
LEBANESE

As tave myliu
LITHUANIAN

Ech hun dech gär
LUXEMBOURGEOIS

Te sakam
MACEDONIAN

Saya cintakan kamu
MALAY

Njan ninne premikunnu
MALAYALAM

Inhobbok
MALTESE

Wo ai ni
MANDARIN

Me tula prem karto
MARATHI

Ni mits neki
NAHUATL

Ayor anosh'ni
NAVAHO

Jeg elsker deg
NORWEGIAN

Mujhe tumse muhabbat hai
PAKISTANI

Mi ta stimabo
PAPIAMENTO

Mahn dousett daram
PERSIAN

Kocham cie
POLISH

Eu te amo
PORTUGUESE

Main tainu pyar karna
PUNJABI

Te iubesc
ROMANIAN

Ya tebya lyublyu
RUSSIAN

Ou te alofa outou
SAMOAN

Volim te
SERBIAN

Ke a go rata
SETSWANA

Ndinoluda
SHONA

Maa tokhe pyar kendo ahyan
SINDHI

Techihhila
SIOUX

Lu`bim ta
SLOVAK

Ljubim te
SLOVENIAN

Waan ku gealahay
SOMALI

Te amo
SPANISH

Mama oyata arderyi
SRI LANKAN

Ninapenda wewe
SWAHILI

Jag älskar dig
SWEDISH

I chaa di gärn
SWISS-GERMAN

Mi lobi joe
SURINAM

Mahal kita
TAGALOG

Ua here vau la oe
TAHITIAN

Wa ga ei li
TAIWANESE

Nan unnai kathalikaraen
TAMIL

Nenu ninnu premistunnanu
TELUGU

Rak te
THAI

Keyagorata
TSWANA

Ha eh bak
TUNISIAN

Seni seviyorum
TURKISH

Ya tebe kahayu
UKRAINIAN

Mi-an aap say piyar karta hun
URDU

Anh ye^u em (to woman)
VIETNAMESE

'Rwy'n dy garu di
WELSH

Ikh hob dikh lib
YIDDISH

Ngiya kuthanda
ZULU

9

Santa's 9 reindeer are Dasher, Dancer, Prancer, Vixen, Comet, Cupid, Donner, Blitzen, and, of course, Rudolph ◆ In Tarot, no. 9 is the Hermit ◆ Cats are supposed to have 9 lives. The origin of this belief is thought to stem from ancient Egypt, where cats were revered as deities ◆ Some sects in ancient Egypt, as well as cultures such as Baha'I, and some Celts and ancient Greeks, worshipped a group of 9 gods known as the Ennead. This ancient and sacred symbol is a 9-pointed star ◆ 9 is considered to be a mystical number by many religions, being a trinity of trinities ◆ In ancient Greek mythology, the Hydra was a 9-headed water snake ◆ The Magic Square is a grid of 9 squares in which the first 9 numbers are arranged such that all horizontal, vertical, and diagonal lines add up to 15. This square is considered sacred in Islamic, Tibetan, Buddhist, Celtic, Indian, and Jewish traditions ◆ In Judaism, 9 symbolizes intelligence and truth. A chanukiyah is a 9-headed candleholder used during Hannukah ◆ Some orders of Buddhism recognize 9 heavens, believing 9 to have spiritual power; many Buddhist rituals require 9 monks ◆ In baseball, there

are 9 players on each team and a game lasts 9 innings ◆ Before the advent of squad numbers, 9 was the number of the main striker in soccer (aka "the leader of the line"), the hooker in rugby league, and the scrum-half in rugby union ◆ Composers Beethoven, Schubert, Bruckner, and Mahler all died having completed 9 symphonies ◆ 9 knots tied in black wool are supposedly a charm to cure a sprained ankle ◆ 9 is lucky in China because it sounds like the Chinese for "longlasting" ◆ 9 is unlucky in Japan because it sounds like the word for "pain" ◆ To test if a number is divisible by 9, add up its digits; if the answer has more than one digit, add them up until you're left with one digit; if (and only if) that digit is 9, the original number is divisible by 9. For example, to test 228,114 add 2 + 2 + 8 + 1 + 1 + 4 = 18 then add 1 + 8 = 9, so the original number is divisible by 9 ◆ A human pregnancy lasts 9 months ◆ The solar system was considered to have 9 planets: Mercury, Venus, Earth, Mars, Jupiter, Saturn, Uranus, Neptune, and Pluto. But in 2006, the International Astronomical Union redefined a planet: Pluto was relegated to "dwarf planet" ◆ On average, right-handed people live 9 years longer than left-handers.

REMOTE CONTROL

In 2001, French surgeons in New York performed an operation on a patient in France by robot. Clever stuff, but it couldn't have been done without computers. Or cameras. Or asepsis. Or anaesthesia. Or a basic understanding of anatomy. In fact, it took about 2,600 years for humans to develop the expertise necessary to perform this groundbreaking transatlantic operation.

DA VINCI SURGICAL ROBOT SYSTEM IN ACTION

COMPUTER-ASSISTED SURGERY

Professor Marescaux said that he believed his pioneering Lindbergh Operation "ushers in the third revolution we've seen in the field of surgery in the past ten years". The second revolution, without which the Lindbergh Operation would not have been possible, was the development of computer-assisted surgery in the late 1990s. It enhanced the safety of the surgeon's movements while introducing the concept of distance between surgeon and patient. According to Marescaux, it was "a natural extrapolation to imagine that this distance – [then] several metres in the operating room – could potentially be... several thousand kilometres".

START HERE
TO GO BACK THROUGH HISTORY

KEYHOLE SURGERY

The first revolution described by Marescaux took place in the 1980s with the introduction of a camera small enough to be inserted into the body via a small incision. This meant that surgeons could perform Minimally Invasive Surgery (MIS, popularly known as keyhole surgery) without having to open up the abdomen and thorax. The advantages were manifold: less time in the operating theatre for patient and surgical team; a clearer view of the afflicted area for the surgeon; less pain and blood loss; a vastly reduced risk of infection; and shorter recovery times.

OPERATION LINDBERGH

On 7 September 2001, a French surgical team working in New York made history when they successfully removed a gall bladder from a patient 4,830km (3,000 miles) away in Strasbourg, France. The transatlantic operation was named after the first person to fly solo across the Atlantic. The development of a high-speed fibre-optic link provided by France Telecom ensured that there was no time delay as Professor Jacques Marescaux controlled the ZEUS Robotic Surgical System in New York and watched a robot in Strasbourg replicate his every move during the 54-minute operation.

▲ REMOVAL OF A GALL BLADDER BY REMOTE CONTROL SURGERY

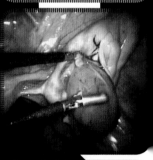

▲ REMOVING AN OVARIAN CYST BY KEYHOLE SURGERY

ASEPSIS

Sterilizing equipment is vital to prevent infection. At one time, medics and surgeons treated patients without even washing their hands — sometimes after performing post-mortems. In 1847, Hungarian obstetrician Ignaz Semmelweiss pioneered the use of antiseptics in hospitals after a fellow surgeon died from an infected cut. Semmelweiss was ridiculed for his ideas, but he inspired English surgeon Joseph Lister to introduce antiseptics to surgery in the form of carbolic acid spray in 1865.

▲ LISTER OPERATES IN A MIST OF CARBOLIC ACID (1865)

OPTICAL INSTRUMENTS

Modern keyhole surgery is performed using an endoscope — a video camera connected to a fibre-optic cable, which is known as a laparoscope (abdomen) or a thoracoscope (thorax). Primitive endoscopes didn't have fibre optics but used simple telescopic rod and lens systems. In 1901, they were successfully used on dogs by the German physician Georg Kelling. In 1910, Swedish surgeon Hans Christian Jacobaeus pioneered the use of laparoscopy in humans for diagnostic purposes.

▲ MODERN FLEXIBLE ENDOSCOPE WITH A FIBRE-OPTIC CABLE

ANAESTHESIA

Early attempts at painkilling included the use of hypnotism, opium, and nitrous oxide ("laughing gas"). The first true anaesthetic was ether, used in the US by Dr Crawford Long in 1842. Long performed ten operations using ether but gave up when the local community threatened to lynch him for sorcery. Four years later, ether was used at Massachusetts General Hospital for the first public demonstration of surgery under anaesthesia. "The patient declared that he felt no pain... Knowledge of this discovery spread from this room throughout the civilized world and a new era for surgery began".

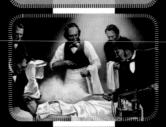

► DOCTOR CRAWFORD LONG (1815–78)

AMBROISE PARÉ

Ambroise Paré started off as an army surgeon in 1537 before going on to become royal surgeon to four French kings. He is often referred to as "the father of modern surgery" in tribute to the surgical advances he pioneered, particularly the use of ligatures after amputation instead of cauterization with boiling oil or red hot irons. He was also a pioneer of obstetrics and the first physician to use prosthetic limbs (see page 202). He designed hands with jointed fingers and the first artificial legs with moveable ankle and knee joints. One of his sayings was: "Cure occasionally, relieve often, console always".

▼ AMBROISE PARÉ (1510–90) AT WORK

ANDREAS VESALIUS

Surgery could not take place without an understanding of anatomy, and the 16th-century Belgian physician Andreas Vesalius is considered the Father of modern anatomy. As Professor of Surgery at Padua University, Vesalius was one of the first people to dissect a human cadaver, allowing him to challenge accepted anatomical thinking and provide a clearer and more accurate understanding. In 1543, he published his seminal work *On the Structure of the Human Body*. He went on to become court physician to two Holy Roman Emperors.

SUSHRUTA

The Indian surgeon Sushruta, who worked in northern India during the 6th century bce, is the earliest known practitioner of surgery. He published his pioneering techniques in a book called *Sushruta Samhita (Sushruta's Compendium)*, which includes descriptions of more than 100 surgical instruments and 300 surgical procedures. These included plastic surgery, which Sushruta taught himself while reconstructing the faces of people who had had their noses amputated as a punishment. Modern rhinoplasty techniques are essentially the same as those pioneered by Sushruta 2,600 years ago.

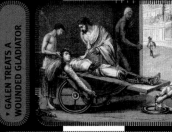

► GALEN TREATS A WOUNDED GLADIATOR

GALEN

Before Vesalius, the accepted understanding of human anatomy prevailed unchallenged for over 1,300 years, having been formulated during the 2nd century ce by the Greek physician Claudius Galenus (129–216). Galen, as he became known, learned his skills as physician to the gladiators, asserting that combat wounds were "windows into the body". He later became physician to several Roman emperors and published widely on philosophy and medicine. He performed many operations on humans that would not be repeated for 2,000 years, such as the removal of cataracts.

► ILLUSTRATION OF MALE INTERNAL ORGANS

FLORA AND FAUNA

SELF-IMPROVEMENT 1

Humans have been tattooing each other since the Stone Age—and not always for decoration. In addition to being worn proudly throughout history as status symbols and tribal marks of belonging, tattoos have also been used to mark outcasts, slaves, convicts, and concentration camp inmates. In the 21st century, tattoos remain popular across the board, from gang identification to celebrity fashion statements.

1 2
3 4 5
6 9
8
7

SPIDER TATTOO (main photo, left) on the back of a bald man's head.

01. DRAGON, 1882
Tattoo of Duke of York (later King George V).

02. 19TH-CENTURY FRENCH
Human skin tattooed with different figures.

03. "ICEMAN" HAND
From a 5,200-year-old mummy.

04. HENNA TATTOO
Melindi tribal decoration.

05. MYANMAR
Chinese tribal woman with facial tattoos.

06. SAMOA
Traditional body tattoos.

07. BLACK LIGHT INK
The "Lets Rock" tattoo is invisible except under black (UV) light.

08. BELLY TATTOO
Pregnant woman with tattoos on her belly and hands.

09. YAKUZA
Japanese gangster tattoos—now fashion items intended to shock.

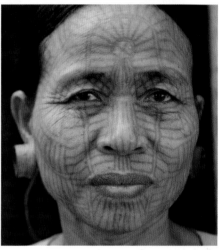

Painted lady

Londoner Isobel Varley is proud to be the world's most tattooed senior citizen. She had her first tattoo—a small bird on her shoulder—in 1986 at the age of 49. By 2000, she was completely covered to the wrists, ankles, and neck. Since then, the tattoos have spread to her hands, feet, and face. If you're thinking of following her lead, it'll cost you about $40,000 and a great deal of pain: Isobel also has 16 genital piercings.

SPORTS SUPERSTITIONS

One of the great things about sports is that there's always an element of luck in addition to the skill required. And where there's luck, there's superstition. Some people believe they can influence their luck by going through certain rituals, and sports stars are no exception—in fact, judging from some of their rituals, sports stars are considerably more superstitious than anyone else.

Detroit Tigers pitcher Mark "The Bird" Fidrych became a national celebrity for his strange on-field behavior. His repertoire included talking to himself, talking to the ball, taking aim with the ball as if it were a dart, strutting around the pitcher's mound like a bird, and preparing the mound so carefully that his ritual was known as "manicuring the mound."

One of ice hockey's greatest-ever goalkeepers, Canadian Patrick Roy, would talk to his goalposts during the game, explaining: "They're my friends." He made a point of never stepping on the red or blue lines, and before a game he would skate out to the blue line and stare at the net, visualizing it shrinking.

Several African nations are said to employ *marabouts* (healers or witch doctors) to influence their luck. The Confederation of African Football says: "We are no more willing to see witch doctors on the pitch (field) than cannibals at the concession stands." In 2000, Senegal was beating Nigeria until an official removed a "charm" from the back of the Senegal net. Nigeria then scored twice to win. Two years later, a marabout was reported to have smeared a potion on the Senegal posts.

Wade Boggs of the Boston Red Sox was as famous for his superstitions as for his hitting. He practiced the same way at the same time every day, hitting the same number of balls; and he always wrote the word *chai* (Hebrew for "life") in the dirt before batting.

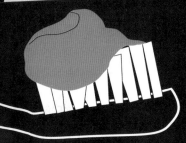

Former Atlanta Braves, Chicago Cubs, NY Mets, and Philadelphia Phillies pitcher Steven "Turk" Wendell always leaped over the baseline on entering or leaving the field. He brushed his teeth and chewed liquorice between innings, and drew three crosses in the dirt at the start of an inning.

The rituals of Sweden and Philadelphia Flyers former goalkeeper Pelle Lindbergh included always wearing the same Swedish-made orange T-shirt under his gear, and only ever drinking a Swedish drink called Pripps between periods—and even then, only if there were two ice cubes in the cup.

Before the start of each half of every game he plays, Blackburn Rovers goalkeeper Jason Brown goes through the same ritual. He rests his head against first one goalpost and then the other, keeping his eyes closed and his hands together as though praying.

Croatian tennis player Goran Ivanišević—who once said, "The trouble with me is that every match I play against five opponents: umpire, crowd, ball boys, court, and myself"—has a number of superstitions. He always rises from his chair after his opponent; never steps on the lines of the court; and if he wins, he repeats the day's events as closely as possible the following day.

Yugoslav tennis star Jelena Dokic never steps on the white court markings, bounces the ball five times on her first serve and twice on the second, blows on her right hand while waiting for her opponent to serve, and insists that ball boys and girls throw the ball to her underhand.

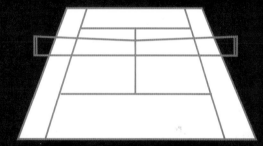

Michael "Air" Jordan, widely rated as one of the greatest basketball players of all time, graduated from the University of North Carolina. To maintain his luck, he always wore his blue North Carolina shorts under his Chicago Bulls uniform.

Former Wales goalkeeper Leigh Richmond Roose, winner of 24 caps between 1900 and 1911, was said to wear a lucky shirt (from his first club) beneath his jersey. This was reputedly never washed. The press noted: "He apparently is a trifle superstitious about his football garments, for he seldom seems to trouble the charwoman with them."

LA Dodgers shortstop Anthony "Nomar" Garciaparra is famous for his strange combination of glove adjustments and toe taps while batting. His less obvious superstitions are getting dressed exactly the same way every game day and stepping on each dugout step with both feet.

AT A STRETCH

Performing a vertical version of the splits, a man loosens up for the day with some early morning stretching exercises on the shore of West Lake in Hangzhou, China.

TROUBLE AHEAD

Roadsigns the world over are designed to be easily read and easily understood. And anyone who's read their Highway Code should know that signs giving orders are circular and those giving warnings are triangular or diamond-shaped. But some of these have been customized by the locals to give their very own meaning.

04. **CYCLISTS BEWARE**
    New Zealand
05. **DUCK CROSSING**
    With egg addition
06. **NO DOG POOPING**
    The Netherlands
07. **BEWARE MOOSE**
    On the loose
08. **ROAD BENDS**
    Smiley face added
09. **PEDESTRIAN
    CROSSING**
    New Mexico
10. **CROSSWALK**
    Customized riders

1 2
3 4 5
6
7 8 9
10

CASSOWARY (main
photo, left) Customized
cassowary crossing,
Queensland, Australia
01. **PEDESTRIAN
    CROSSING**
    Customized for naturists
02. **SNOW HAZARD**
    Beware snowfalls
03. **NO PEDESTRIANS**
    Customized
    target practice

FOREVER YOUNG

A lot of child stars go on to become adult stars but what becomes of those who don't? It's often hard to separate the character from the actor, so it's surprising to find that Oliver Twist grew up to be an osteopath and Prairie girl Jenny Wilder posed for *Playboy*.

❖ DARLENE GILLESPIE

From the ages of 14 to 17, Darlene Gillespie was one of the original Mouseketeers, singing and dancing on the *Mickey Mouse Club* television show (1955–58). She also recorded several albums for Disney. Since then, she has served time in prison for aiding and abetting her third husband to commit fraud.

❖ JUDY GARLAND

The most famous child star of all signed for MGM at the age of 12. Four years later, Judy Garland won global fame playing Dorothy in *The Wizard of Oz* (1939). Driven hard by the studio, her film and television career was distinguished, if troubled. She was also a popular singer. Her personal life was troubled, too: married five times, she died of a drug overdose, aged 47.

❖ DANNY LLOYD

As a six-year-old, Danny Lloyd played Danny "Doc" Torrance in the 1980 film *The Shining*. He was unaware until years later of the nature of the film or the significance of his famous line, "Redrum! Redrum!" He is now a biology teacher in Illinois.

❖ LUKE HALPIN

Luke Halpin began acting at the age of eight and appeared in numerous television series before playing Sandy Ricks in the film *Flipper* (1963). He is now a marine technician and pilot for TV and film productions.

❖ JOSH SAVIANO

There is an urban myth that Josh Saviano, who played Kevin Arnold's best friend Paul Pfeiffer in the long-running TV show *The Wonder Years* (1988–93), is the real identity behind provocative singer Marilyn Manson. Far from it—he graduated from Yale and became a corporate lawyer.

❖ TODD BRIDGES

From the age of 13, Todd Bridges played Willis Jackson in the long-running television series *Diff'rent Strokes* (1978–86). After the show ended, he continued acting and was arrested several times for violent and drug-related crimes. He now works as a motivational speaker warning against the dangers of drug abuse.

❖ SHANNON DOHERTY

Shannon Doherty, who played Jenny Wilder in *Little House on the Prairie* (1982–84), is still an actress and posed for *Playboy* in 1994 and 2003.

❖ THE WALTONS

Most of the cast of *The Waltons* have pursued successful acting careers since the series. Among those who chose other routes, Earl Hamner (narrator) is a television writer and producer, Kami Cotler (Elizabeth) is a teacher, and Judy Norton (Mary Ellen) has modeled for *Playboy*.

❖ THE OSMONDS

Donny Osmond is a singer, actor, talk and game show host, and record producer. Wayne, Jay, Merrill, and Jimmy still perform as The Osmond Brothers, and Marie is a radio host and doll-maker. Alan Osmond rarely performs due to multiple sclerosis.

JORDY (LEMOINE)

As the youngest singer (age four and a half) to have a number one single, Jordy's "*Dur dur d'être un bébé*" ("It's really tough being a baby") sold two million copies in France and was a hit across Europe and Japan in 1992. In 1994, the French government banned Jordy from TV and radio out of concern that he was being exploited by his parents. In 2006, he released his first single in 12 years.

INGER NILSSON

Swedish-born Inger Nilsson, who played Pippi Longstocking in the hugely popular *Pippi Langstrump* films (1969–70) and TV series (1969–73), was so closely associated with her role that she was unable to build on her early success. In 1978, she released a disco single, *Keep on Dancing*, and now works as a medical secretary, although she still takes on small stage roles.

THE BRADY BUNCH

Mike Lookinland, who played youngest brother Bobby Brady in *The Brady Bunch* (1969–74), took several film and television roles before becoming a camera operator. Eve Plum, who played middle sister Jan Brady, also had a successful acting career and now works as an artist.

ANNETTE FUNICELLO

The only one of the original *Mickey Mouse Club* Mouseketeers to be personally chosen by Walt Disney, Annette Funicello went on to have a successful acting and singing career. She later founded the Annette Funicello Fund for Neurological Disorders and launched her own line of teddy bears.

JONATHAN GILBERT

Jonathan Gilbert played Willie Orelson from 1974–83 in *Little House on the Prairie*. Unlike his award-winning sisters, Melissa (who also appeared in the same show) and Sara, he chose not to pursue an acting career and now works as a Wall Street stockbroker.

LINDA BLAIR

Before accepting the obscenity-spewing, head-spinning role in *The Exorcist* (1973) at the age of 14 to fund her expensive hobby of horseback riding, Linda Blair wanted to be a vet. Since then, she has continued acting and showjumping, suffered drug problems, and established her own animal charity, the Linda Blair World Heart Foundation.

MARY BADHAM

At the age of 10, Mary Badham played Jean Louise "Scout" Finch in *To Kill a Mockingbird* (1962) and was nominated for an Academy Award for best supporting actress. She is now an art restorer.

MARK LESTER

At the age of nine, Mark Lester, a stage-school veteran, played the title role in the multiple Academy Award-winning musical *Oliver!* (1968). He continued acting until he reached the age of 18, then dabbled in drugs and alcohol before training as an osteopath.

PETER OSTRUM

As a 14-year-old, Peter Ostrum starred as Charlie Bucket in *Charlie and the Chocolate Factory* (1971). He turned down several more film roles and now works as a vet.

CHARLIE KORSMO

At the age of 12, Charlie Korsmo played "The Kid" in the 1990 hit *Dick Tracy*. He has since worked for the American federal government, the Environmental Protection Agency, and the Republican Party.

ROAD TRIP

A crash causes havoc during the one-day 160-mile (259-km) Paris–Roubaix cycle race in northern France. The race is nicknamed L'Enfer du Nord ("The Hell of the North") and La Pascale ("the Easter race").

In the 90s, breasts were back—in a big way. This was thanks in no small part to Pamela Anderson in *Baywatch* (the world's most watched television show) and Eva Herzigova's ads for Wonderbra. When someone compared Herzigova with 50s' pin-up Marilyn Monroe, Eva replied: "curves aside, we have very little in common." For men, Brad Pitt and Johnny Depp made cheekbones chic.

Booty

```
    2   3
  1
4   6
5   7
```

03. DAVID HASSELHOFF
baring his chest as
Mitch Buchannon
in *Baywatch*.

04. HALLE BERRY
first African-American
woman to win a Best
Actress Oscar.

05. JOHNNY DEPP
all chiseled features
as Wade Walker
in *Cry Baby* (1990).

06. JENNIFER LOPEZ
actress, singer,
and fashion designer,
aka J-Lo.

07. UMA THURMAN
as director Quentin
Tarantino said,
she's "up there with
Garbo and Dietrich
in goddess territory."

EVA HERZIGOVA (main
photo, left) "Hello boys"—
Eva's ad for Wonderbra.

01. BRAD PITT
chic cheekbones.

02. PAMELA ANDERSON
wearing *that* red
swimsuit as C. J.
Parker in *Baywatch*.

Beauty is only skin deep. I think what's really important is finding a balance of mind—Jennifer Lopez

THE BEAUTIFUL GAME

THE GOOD

The world's most popular type of football, soccer is probably the world's most popular sport period. It's had its full share of great moments but, as with most things, there's also a dark side. Take a look at the good, the bad, and the ugly sides of soccer.

GREAT GAMES

MAGICAL MAGYARS 1953

England had never been beaten at home by any team from outside the UK. But at Wembley Stadium on November 25, 1953, the "Magical Magyars" demolished England 6–3. England's Gil Merrick was gracious in defeat, saying, "… it was a privilege to play against them, to see football like that."

EUROPEAN CUP FINAL 1960

The highest-scoring final, often called the best game ever. A record 135,000 people at Hampden Park, Glasgow, saw Real Madrid beat Eintracht Frankfurt 7–3 for the fifth consecutive title. The *Glasgow Herald* summed up Real's performance: "Thank you, gentlemen, for the magic memory."

EUROPEAN CUP FINAL 1999

On 90 minutes, the UEFA president left the stand to present the cup to Bayern Munich, who led Manchester United 1–0. But United scored twice in a minute from injury-time corners to win 2–1. When the president emerged from the tunnel, he thought: "It cannot be. The winners are crying and the losers are dancing."

N. KOREA V PORTUGAL 1966 ⋯⟩

In the 1966 World Cup quarter final, North Korea shocked Portugal by going 3–0 up after 25 minutes. But half an hour later, Portugal was level, and went on to win 5–3 in one of the greatest ever comebacks.

GREAT WORLD CUP GOALS

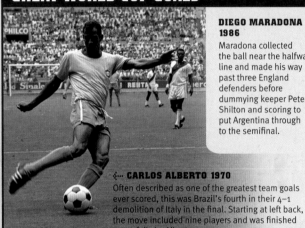

DIEGO MARADONA 1986

Maradona collected the ball near the halfway line and made his way past three England defenders before dummying keeper Peter Shilton and scoring to put Argentina through to the semifinal.

PELE 1958

Pele was only 17 when he scored a sublime goal in Brazil's 5–2 final defeat of Sweden. Chesting down a cross, he used his thigh to flip the ball over one Swedish defender before volleying it low past the keeper.

GEOFF HURST 1966

A legendary goal for England. Hurst gathered the ball on the halfway line as commentator Kenneth Wolstenholme said: "Some people are on the pitch. They think it's all over… " As Hurst blasted the ball into the German net, Wolstenholme finished: "… It is now."

⋯⟩ CARLOS ALBERTO 1970

Often described as one of the greatest team goals ever scored, this was Brazil's fourth in their 4–1 demolition of Italy in the final. Starting at left back, the move included nine players and was finished powerfully by Alberto.

ARCHIE GEMMILL 1978

Scotland v Netherlands in the group stages. Gemmill drew one defender, jumped another's tackle, then pushed the ball through the legs of a third before lifting it over the advancing keeper.

GREAT GOAL CELEBRATIONS

MARCO TARDELLI 1982 ⋯⟩

After scoring Italy's second goal in the 1982 World Cup final against Germany, Tardelli sprinted toward the Italian bench with his fists clenched in front of him and tears pouring down his face, yelling wildly.

ROGER MILLA 1990

Cameroon forward Roger Milla scored four goals in the 1990 World Cup finals, and celebrated each with his legendary dance around the corner flag. Two of his goals were against Romania and two against Colombia.

JULIUS AGHAHOWA 2002

After scoring the opening goal for Nigeria v Sweden in the 2002 World Cup, Aghahowa performed seven back flips and a backward somersault. His most extravagant celebration ever was 12 backflips.

DENNIS BERGKAMP 1998

After scoring a last-minute winner for the Netherlands against Argentina in the quarter-final of Euro 98 in France, Bergkamp looked up to the heavens with his arms in the air and fell flat on his back with his arms still pointing to the sky.

LIVERPOOL V ARSENAL 1989

Arsenal needed to win by two goals. Michael Thomas scored their second in injury time to win the league championship with the very last kick of the season.

← DENNIS BERGKAMP 1998

In the closing minutes of the Netherlands v Argentina quarter-final, Bergkamp controlled a long pass from de Boer in the box, passed the ball between the legs of the defender with his second touch, and hit the back of the net with his third to win the game.

← JURGEN KLINSMANN 1994

Notorious for trying to milk penalties by diving, Klinsmann celebrated his first goal for Tottenham Hotspur (in a 4–3 away victory at Sheffield Wednesday) with a dive, which was copied by other members of the Spurs team.

THE BAD

MATCH-FIXING

↓ ITALIAN BRIBES AND RELEGATION

At the end of the 1979/80 season, A. C. Milan and S. S. Lazio were relegated to Serie B for match-fixing, and six years later Roma was barred from UEFA after the club's manager tried to bribe a referee. In 2006, Juventus, Fiorentina, and Lazio were relegated to Serie B for match-fixing.

↓ MARSEILLES CORRUPTION

Marseilles enjoyed extraordinary success from 1989–93. Then, in 1994, club President Bernard Tapie was charged with corruption and match-fixing. Marseilles was stripped of the 92/93 Division 1 title and relegated to Division 2 for trying to bribe players from Valenciennes to throw a game.

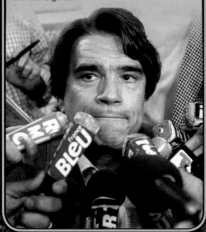

THE UGLY

MISSES, WHISTLES, AND MURDER

ROB RENSENBRINK 1978

With the score at 1–1 in the last minute of the 1978 World Cup Final against Argentina, Dutchman Rob Rensenbrink missed an open goal. The Netherlands lost 3–1 in extra time.

↑ ERIC CANTONA 1995

On January 25, 1995, Manchester United's French star Cantona was sent off for kicking a Crystal Palace player. As he left the field, Palace fan Matthew Simmons abused him and Cantona delivered a flying kick to the fan's chest. He received a nine-month ban and narrowly avoided jail.

VINNIE JONES 1988

Vinnie Jones cemented his reputation as a soccer hardman when he was photographed grabbing Paul Gascoigne's testicles while playing for Wimbledon against Newcastle United.

ANDRES ESCOBAR
1967 - 1994

← ANDRÉS ESCOBAR 1994

Colombian defender Escobar, "The Gentleman of Soccer," scored an own goal during a 1994 World Cup match against the US on June 22. Ten days later, he was killed outside a bar in Medellín by a gunman who reportedly shouted: "Goooooooooooooal!"

DENNIS EVANS 1953

When Evans heard the final whistle, he kicked the ball into the back of his own net to celebrate Arsenal beating Blackpool 4–0. Except the whistle had been blown by a spectator and Evans's own goal made it 4–1.

VITAL STATISTICS

All humans have a body, but most people know very little about it. The closer you look, the weirder it gets. There are all sorts of fascinating facts about the human body that most of the species have never even thought about—despite having more neurons in their brains than the number of people who have ever walked on the planet since *Homo sapiens* first stood upright.

SNEEZING

expels air and mucus from the nose at speeds of up to 100 mph (160 km/h). **COUGHING** expels air from the throat at speeds of up to 60 mph (96.5 kmph). People with **RED HAIR** are more susceptible to pain than those with dark or blonde hair, and need 20 percent more anesthesia during operations

The **HUMAN LIVER** will grow back to its original size even if up to 80 percent of it is removed. The water in a young coconut can be used as substitute **BLOOD PLASMA**

The average person grows 6½ ft (2 m) of **NASAL HAIR** during a lifetime

The average human produces 2.3 pt (1.1 liters) of **SALIVA** every day—12,000 gallons (45,460 liters) in a lifetime

During **PREGNANCY**, the average woman's uterus expands up to 500 times its normal size. **BABIES** are born with about 300 bones, one-third of which fuse during childhood

The average human has more than 60,000 miles (100,000 km) of **BLOOD VESSELS**—that's a quarter of the way round the Earth at the equator

HUMAN SNORING can reach 69 decibels—almost as loud as a pneumatic drill, which ranges from 70–90 decibels

The average human body contains enough **FAT** to make eight standard-size bars of soap.

The average human body contains enough **CARBON** to make 900 pencils, enough **PHOSPHORUS** to make 2,200 match heads, and enough **IRON** to make a 3 in (7.5 cm) nail

69
decibels

A human has the same number of **VERTEBRAE** in the neck as a **GIRAFFE** (seven)

The average person releases almost 1 pt (500 ml) of intestinal **GAS** every day

Humans share 96 percent of their **DNA** with chimpanzees. The number of genetic differences between chimps and humans is 10 times less than between rats and mice

THE SPAN of a person's outstretched arms, from fingertip to fingertip, is the same as their height

In a lifetime, the average **MAN** ejaculates over 5 gallons (20 litres) of semen

There is approximately 0.2 mg of **GOLD** in every person

A person is more likely to catch cold by **SHAKING HANDS** than by kissing someone

There are nearly twice as many bacteria in one person's **MOUTH** as there are people in the whole world

Humans can **SURVIVE** longer without food (several weeks) than without sleep (a few days)

We have **52 BONES** in our feet—almost a quarter of the body's total of 206 bones (approximately; the total number of bones varies from person to person)

People who suffer from **GUM DISEASE** are much more likely to have a stroke or heart attack than those who don't

MONEY, MONEY, MONEY

Judging by the number of sayings, proverbs, songs, and books about it, people are obsessed with money. But really it's wealth, not money, that "makes the world go round." Money is just a name for the tokens that represent wealth. Around the world some pretty odd things have been used as tokens of wealth.

A

A STONE DISKS The Yap Islands (part of the Pacific state of Micronesia) are famous for their stone money, known as Fé. These carved stone disks can be up to 13 ft (4 m) in diameter. While you wouldn't get many in your wallet, they do have the advantage of being difficult to steal.

B CHECKS A check is an instruction to your bank to pay money, and technically you don't need a checkbook to write one. There's a story of a city council writing a check for $580,000 to a building contractor on a 2 x 4 ft (60 x 120 cm) slab of concrete, and another of a man writing a check with paint on the side of a cow.

C SALT Roman soldiers and civil servants were paid a salt ration known as a *salarium*. When coins later came to be paid instead of salt, the allowance kept the same name, which is the origin of the word for wages in many European languages, including "salary" in English.

D FEATHER ROLL In the Santa Cruz Islands, traditional ceremonial money was made by gluing red feathers to a strip of fiber and attaching shells and beads before wrapping it in palm leaves.

E HUMAN SKULLS Sumatra takes its name from the Sanskrit Swarna Dwipa, meaning "Isle of Gold," because gold was once mined there. But 15th-century Sumatrans didn't use that gold as money—they used human skulls.

F PEPPERCORNS Peppercorns were once highly priced enough to be used as money. King Alaric I of the Visigoths, instrumental in the downfall of the Roman Empire, is said to have demanded 3,000 lb (1,360 kg) of pepper in 408ce as part of a ransom for the city of Rome. In England, a symbolic minimal rent is still known as a "peppercorn rent."

G LIBERIAN KISSI PENNIES The intricate shape indicates the quality of the iron because it can be worked in four ways—hammered, twisted, drawn to points, and sharpened to a blade.

H CURRENCY FROM HELL One of the traditions of the Chinese New Year is to burn ceremonial paper currency from the "Bank of Hell" in honor of the dead. Tradition has kept up with the times—20th-century innovations included Bank of Hell checkbooks and bills depicting world leaders in place of the King of Hell.

I ORNAMENTAL TOOLS Archeologists have unearthed arrowheads made from semiprecious stones, copper ax heads, mother-of-pearl fishhooks, and other such impractical tools that were once valuable as a means of exchange.

J COWRIES Cowrie shells were widely used as money from ancient times well into the 20th century. They were convenient because of their size and durability—and they looked valuable.

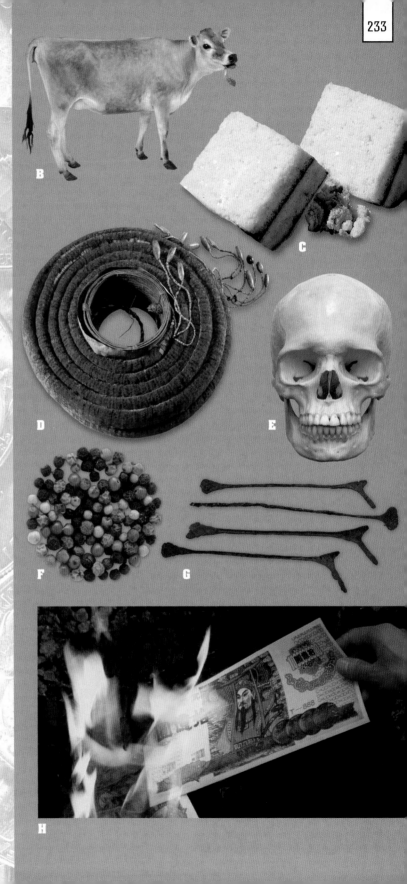

B

C

D

E

F

G

H

Paper planes

For people, folding their first paper plane that will fly properly is an important milestone. Historically, it was a skill passed down from father to son but, in more enlightened times, the skill is shared between the genders. It is now equally important for both boys and girls to learn plane-folding and to pass the skill on to their sons and daughters.

DART

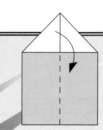

1 Take a letter-size piece of paper. Fold it down the center line along the longest edge to make a crisp crease. Unfold it.

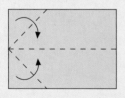

Hold at the tip, throw hard, and the Dart will fly through the air

2 Take the top left-hand corner and fold it down to meet the center line, then do the same with the top right-hand corner.

3 You now have a large triangle at the top. Fold this down along its baseline.

4 Take each of the top corners and fold them down to meet the center line, but leave a flat section at the top.

5 You will have a small triangle at the bottom of the folded area. Fold this upward to secure the flaps.

6 Now fold in half along the center line. Fold down the wings as shown so that the nose aligns with the top.

7 Your Dart will look like this. Fold along the dotted line and tuck the nose inside. You are ready to fly.

GLIDER

1 As for the Dart (above), fold a letter-size sheet of paper down the center line along the longest edge to make a crisp crease. Unfold it.

2 Take the top left-hand corner and fold it down to meet the center line, then do the same with the top right-hand corner.

3 Fold the triangle down.

4 Fold the tip of the triangle back on itself.

5 Fold two triangles to the center line.

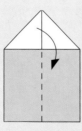

BOOMERANG

Thrown sideways, the Boomerang should circle back to you

1 Crease the paper down the center line. Bring two triangles to the center to make crease marks. Unfold.

2 Tuck a flap down, taking the points of the triangle creases as your baseline.

3 Fold back the two triangles along the crease marks.

  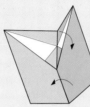

4 Fold back triangles of the top layer of paper...

5 ... so that your model looks like this. Now get ready for a slightly tricky dual maneuver.

6 Push the center of the triangle with a finger on the fold. At the same time, fold from the center line to the outside edges.

7 This is the shape you want to achieve. Turn your plane upside down if its nose seems to slope the wrong way.

8 Fold back the wings.

9 Fold the central triangle down and tuck it to one side, so it no longer sticks up above the wings.

10 Crimp the wingtips as shown. Lift the wings up so they are angled slightly upward.

Some throwing tips: keep the Dart smooth and level; point the Glider's nose slightly downward; hold the Boomerang underneath and tilt sideways.

Gently release the Glider and it will soar gracefully through the air

  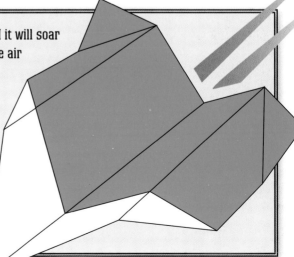

6 Fold two triangles back, tucking them neatly under.

7 Your Glider now looks like this. Recrease the center fold to make it crisp.

8 Make creases for the wings and fold them up. Tuck triangles up at the wingtips.

PLANE SPOTTING

Yes, it's definitely a plane, but what kind? With this spotter's guide you'll be able to identify every kind of plane that's ever flown, from the Wright Flyer to the new Airbus. Well, nearly every kind of plane.

Maxim Multiplane
British
First flight: Kent, 31 July 1894

Lilienthal No 11 Hang-glider
German
First flight: Berlin, 1894

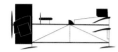

Fabre Hydravion
French
First flight: March 28, 1910

Paulhan-Tatin Aero-Torpille
French
First flight: 1911

Sikorski Bolshoi
Russian
First flight: May 10, 1912

Rumpler Taube
Austrian
First flight: 1913

Vickers Vimy
British
First flight: November 30, 1917

Tarrant Tabor
British
First flight: November 30, 1917

Fokker D.VIII
German
First flight: December 1917

Handley Page V/1500
British
First flight: May 22, 1918

Caproni Ca.60 Transaero
Italian
First flight: March 4, 1921

Caproni Ca.90
Italian
First flight: October 13, 1929

Junkers-Ju 52/3m
German
First flight: October 13, 1930

Handley Page H.P.42
British
First flight: November 17, 1930

Macchi MC.72
Italian
First flight: 1931

Messerschmitt Bf 109
German
First flight: September 1935

Junkers Ju 87 Stuka
German
First flight: September 17, 1935

Hawker Hurricane
British
First flight: November 6, 1935

Bristol Type 138A
British
First flight: May 11, 1936

Supermarine Spitfire
British
First flight: March 5, 1936

Bristol Beaufighter
British
First flight: July 17, 1939

Heinkel He 178
German
First flight: August 27, 1939

Ilyushin Il-2 Shturmovik
Soviet
First flight: October 1939

North American P-51 Mustang
British/US
First flight: October 25, 1940

Messerschmitt Me 163 Komet
German
First flight: August 13, 1941

The Concorde
British/French
First flight: Toulouse, March 2, 1969

Rockwell International Space Shuttle
US
First flight: April 12, 1981

Lockheed F-117A Nighthawk
US
First flight: June 18, 1981

Boeing 767
US
First flight: September 26, 1981

6 Line a second bucket with plastic wrap, grease, and dust with confectionary sugar. Pour mixture into this bucket.

 7 Allow to set for 24–48 hours and turn out. Dust with confectionary sugar to taste.

8 Find a pitchfork and a giant bonfire to toast this massive monster. Don't burn it!

The massive marshmallow in all its glory, with three standard-sized marshmallows for comparison.

THE SHARPEST TOOL IN THE BOX

Humans and their penknives have moved on from sharpening quill pens—now their gadgetry includes memory sticks and MP3 players.

➡ **18th century** The USA might not have existed but for a penknife. In 1743 George Washington's mother gave him a penknife, saying, "Always obey your superiors." In 1777, Washington nearly resigned his army command during the Revolutionary War. An officer pointed to the penknife and his duty. Washington tore up his resignation and led his country to independence.

➡ **19th century** The Swiss Army knife was born in 1891, when a manufacturer started making "Soldier's knives" for the Swiss Army. A rival followed suit and the government split the contract: Victorinox uses the slogan "the Original Swiss Army Knife" and Wenger "the Genuine Swiss Army Knife."

➡ **20th century** Swiss Army knives became standard gear for NASA's astronauts, and were featured in New York's MOMA as an example of outstanding functional design.

1891 VICTORINOX "SOLDIER'S KNIFE"
The very first Swiss Army knife, which was issued to all new recruits.

Live by the penknife

INDIAN AIRLINES FLIGHT 524 1976
"Is there a doctor on board?" came the call over the PA system—fortunately there was. A child was choking on a piece of candy. The doctor decided a tracheotomy would be needed but there was no scalpel in the first-aid kit. "Does anybody have a penknife?" came the second call. Another passenger handed the doctor a Victorinox Swiss Officer's knife, with which he performed the tracheotomy and saved the young child's life.

THE FOAL AT LAKE CONSTANCE
Friends ridiculed a German optician who bought himself a Swiss Survival knife for a cycle tour, but he had the last laugh. One afternoon, at Lake Constance in southern Germany, he saved a newborn foal, whose umbilical cord had failed to detach, by cutting it with his new knife.

Die by the penknife

WILLIAM COWPER 1763
Anxious before a law exam, English poet William Cowper attempted four times to kill himself in December 1763. First he bought laudanum. Unable to bring himself to swallow the poison, he decided to drown but couldn't face that either. He tried to stab himself with his penknife but the blade broke. Finally he hanged himself with a garter but it snapped just as he lost consciousness. He lived another 37 years.

HANS STANLEY 1780
This 18th-century British politician killed himself with a penknife in the grounds of Althorp House, ancestral home of the late Diana, Princess of Wales. On the morning of January 12, during a visit to Earl Spencer, Stanley cut his throat in the woods and died before help could be summoned.

2005, THE WENGER GIANT

The latest Wenger Swiss Army knife offers 141 functions, weighs 2 lb (900 g) and costs nearly $1,000. Known as the Giant, it features every blade ever incorporated into the Swiss Army knives made by Wenger.

1897 THE "OFFICER'S KNIFE"
The first Swiss Army knife to have the distinctive red handle.

2005 SWISS MEMORY
Victorinox penknife incorporating LED flashlight and removable 256-2GB MB USB memory stick.

1. Integrated swivelling compass with sight line/ruler (cm and in)
2. 2 x key rings
3. Toothpick
4. Tweezers
5. Screwing bit
6. Screwing bit PH 1
7. Nail clipper
8. Blade with Scout mark
9. Large blade
10. Nail file/nail cleaner/screwdriver for small cross head screws
11. Corkscrew
12. Flat screwdriver with safety lock system/cap lifter/wire bender
13. Flat Phillips screwdriver
14. Can opener
15. Reamer
16. Wood saw
17. Graduated saw
18. Metal file/metal cutting saw
19. Fish scaler/fish disgorger/lineguide
20. Magnifying glass/precision screwdriver
21. Phillips screwdriver with safety lock system
22. Flat Phillips screwdriver
23. All-purpose wrench
24. Small blade
25. 3 x bit holder
26. Semi-round nose pliers
27. Combination pliers
28. Serrated edge scissors and lever
29. Multipurpose pliers/tag clamp/inside and outside wire cutters
30. Multifunctions detachable tool
31. Junior blade
32. Laser pointer
33. Diode light
34. Integrated holder
35. 2 x integrated Pocketgrip holder with screwing bits
36. Detachable hexagonal wrench/screwdriver/spoke key openings/extension lever
37. Chain rivet setter/detachable curved hexagonal male key
38. Blade for case opener
39. Round needle file
40. Graduated rule/magnifying glass/spring bars tool
41. Toolbox
42. Reamer
43. Pin-punch bit 0.8
44. Pin-punch bit 1.2
45. Fine fork for spring bars tool
46. Screwdriver blade 0.8
47. Screwdriver blade 1.2
48. Round needle file
49. Phillips screwdriver bit 1.5
50. Tool holder Minathor
51. Bevelled blade
52. Cigar cutter
53. Combination tool
54. Hexagonal key
55. Curved key
56. Detachable 10mm hexagonal key
57. Military knife blade
58. Special military screwdriver
59. Fix screwdriver
60. Reamer for gun
61. Screwdriver for gun
62. Stud key golfer
63. Golf reamer
64. Snap hook
65. Green repairer
66. Graduated tread depth gauge (mm/in) detachable sliding bit holder
67. Detachable sliding bit holder
68. Blade for grafting knife
69. Blade for grafting knife
70. Blade for grafting knife
71. Blade for grafting knife
72. Blade for grafting knife
73. Retractor blade for grafting knives
74. Small blade
75. Scissors
76. Nail file/nail cleaner/screwdriver for small cross head screws
77. Green repairer
78. Screwdriver/can opener/cap lifter
79. Screwdriver
80. Reamer
81. Blade
82. Combined tool: screwdriver/can opener/cap lifter
83. ½ serrated blade

Cultural references

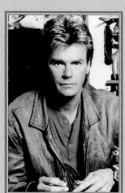

The Swiss Army knife is now part of popular culture, notably as the signature element of the American TV show *MacGyver*. This secret agent hero escaped from any predicament using a roll of duct tape and his trusty Swiss Army knife. The show even spawned its own Swiss cutlery set. The Swiss Army knife has also been spoofed with inventions like the Swiss Army shoe in the film *Naked Gun*.

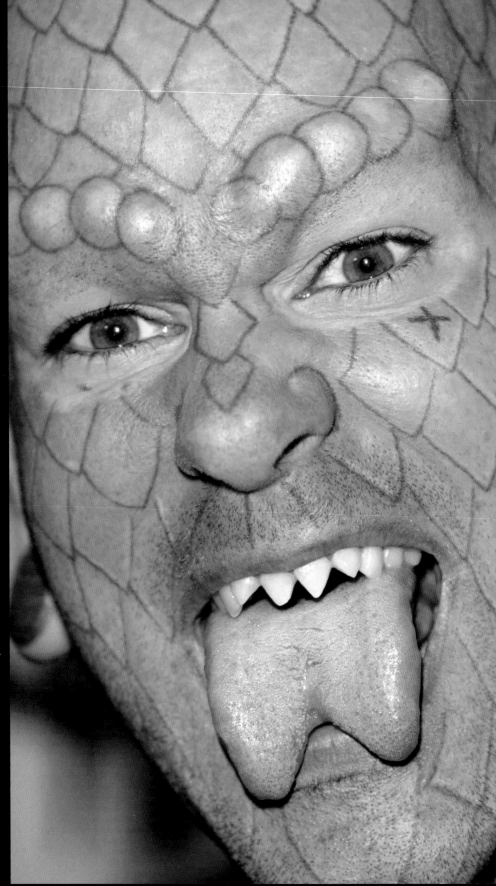

FLORA AND FAUNA

SELF-IMPROVEMENT 2

M any humans are unhappy with who they are, or how they look, or both. A particular taboo in one part of Western society is growing old, so those who are rich enough spend vast amounts of money paying surgeons to suck out some bits, insert others, and stretch their skin in order to make them look younger, or otherwise change their appearance.

03. **JODIE MARSH**
Glamour model shows off the tools of her trade.

04. **KERRY ELIA**
Her breast implants exploded—twice.

05. **LOLO FERRARI**
The world's largest breasts have their uses.

06. **MICHAEL JACKSON**
The skin gets paler and the nose ever narrower.

07. **AMANDA LEPORE**
Transsexual icon with enlarged lips and more.

08. **CHER**
Singer puts the sex into sexagenarian.

09. **PETE BURNS**
Singer-songwriter calls himself Freak Unique.

```
        2
     1
   4    5
3
            8
            9
  6
    7
```

ERIK SPRAGUE (main photo left) Also known as the Lizard Man.

01. **JOCELYNE WILDENSTEIN**
Socialite dubbed Cat Woman and Bride of Wildenstein by tabloids.

02. **DONATELLA VERSACE**
Designer's designer lips.

>URBAN MYTHS 2

From punk beards to kidney harvesting, humanity's urban myths—also known as urban legends—are apocryphyal stories that tend to disturb even as they raise an uneasy laugh. Often starting with a distorted version of a true event, extra details and embellishments are added as the story passes from person to person.

>GOOD LUCK, MR. GORSKY

In July 1969, one-fifth of the world's population watched on television as Neil Armstrong became the first human to walk on the Moon. His famous utterance "That's one small step for [a] man, one giant leap for mankind" was interrupted by static and there has been argument ever since about whether he said "man" or "a man"—without the "a" his famous statement is meaningless.

Everyone then became so absorbed in watching him walk on the surface of the Moon that *FEW PEOPLE THOUGHT ABOUT WHAT HE SAID NEXT.* Footage of the moonwalk reveals that as he took his second step he said: "Good luck, Mr. Gorsky." Mission Control thought he was referring to a Soviet cosmonaut, but checks revealed that there was no cosmonaut by that name.

For years, the famously reticent Armstrong refused to divulge who he was referring to. But in July 1995, during a rare press conference in Florida, a reporter brought up the question again and Armstrong came clean. Saying that *HE HOPED HE WOULDN'T CAUSE ANYONE EMBARRASSMENT* now that his childhood neighbors Mr. and Mrs. Gorsky had passed on, Armstrong explained that one summer as a child he had been playing baseball with his brother, who had hit the ball into the Gorskys' yard. When Neil went to collect the ball *HE HAD DISTINCTLY HEARD MRS. GORSKY*, through an open window, *SAYING TO HER HUSBAND*: "Lobster thermidor? You'll get a lobster thermidor the day the kid next door walks on the Moon."

>CRUISE CONTROL

In fall 2000, Merv Grazinski, a recently retired American from Oklahoma City, spent his retirement bonus on the brand new Winnebago motorhome that he had always dreamed of. A few weeks later, he and his wife, Lillian, set off on their first long-distance trip, having stocked up the cupboards and fridge in the back of the motorhome.

After making their way slowly through the suburban traffic to the freeway, Mr. and Mrs. Grazinsky decided to relax with a cup of coffee. Lillian went into the back to make the coffee while Merv checked the map to see that they wouldn't have to leave the freeway in the next half hour. He set the Winnebago in cruise control and then *LEFT THE DRIVER'S SEAT AND WENT INTO THE BACK TO JOIN LIL FOR A RELAXING COFFEE.* Before he had even sat down, the motorhome had left the road, rolled down an embankment, and overturned. Miraculously, the Grazinskys weren't seriously injured, having been cushioned by the soft furnishings in the back. But the motorhome was a write-off.

Fortunately, the story has a happy ending: *MERV SUCCESSFULLY SUED* Winnebago for failing to instruct him to remain in the driver's seat while in cruise control. *HE WAS AWARDED $1.75M,* plus a new motorhome.

>MOWING THE LAWN

Punk rock had its heyday in the late 1970s. Torn T-shirts, safety-pinned jeans, studded facial piercings, and multicolored Mohawks started out as rebellious antiestablishment behavior but soon became just another fashion statement.

During this brief golden age, a *YOUNG PUNK ROCKER WITH A VIBRANT GREEN MOHAWK AND MATCHING GREEN BEARD WAS BROUGHT INTO THE HOSPITAL UNCONSCIOUS, WITH SEVERE NECK INJURIES AND A BROKEN JAW FROM A FIGHT.* Divested of his studded leather jacket he began to look a bit more human, but it took the nurses a while to prep him to have his jaw wired because they had to remove so many facial piercings. They also had to shave off his beard in order to fit a brace to support his head and neck. As they shaved his beard, the nurses *NOTICED A TATTOO ACROSS HIS THROAT SAYING "KEEP OFF THE GRASS."* Apparently the technician fitting the brace was as amused as the nurses because when the young punk came around he noticed that a new message had appeared on his neck—in surgical marker someone had written: "Sorry, had to mow the lawn."

>DISTRESS SIGNAL

The world's first cash machine was installed in 1967 at Barclays Bank in Enfield, north London, England. It was a huge convenience for customers, who no longer had to line up at the counter to withdraw money, although the maximum withdrawal was just £10 ($15).

But, as the maximum withdrawal limit increased and cash machines became a common feature of cities around the globe, *THEY ALSO BECAME A HUGE CONVENIENCE TO MUGGERS*, who only had to walk up to people as they stood in the line and force them to withdraw money and hand it over. As the problem became worse during the 1990s, banks tried to find ways of combating the muggers. Some banks moved their cash machines into brightly lit foyers rather than holes in the wall, but this proved expensive and difficult to keep secure.

Then, in 2006, one enterprising software engineer came up with the perfect solution. He was able to program the machine so that *IF SOMEONE WAS FORCED TO WITHDRAW CASH THEY COULD KEY IN THEIR PIN IN REVERSE*—the machine would then say that the account was overdrawn and refuse to dispense cash.

At the same time, the program would contact the police with the location of the machine and a message that an attempted mugging was taking place, thus increasing the chances of *CATCHING THE CULPRITS WITHOUT PUTTING THE VICTIM AT RISK BY DOING ANYTHING TO ANGER THE MUGGER*.

>BABYSITTER'S INTRUDER NIGHTMARE

During the 1960s, a teenage girl in Perth, Western Australia, was babysitting for neighbors who habitually phoned to check that the children had settled down for the night.

But when the phone rang as expected and the babysitter answered it, *ALL SHE HEARD WAS HEAVY BREATHING*. The phone rang again five minutes later, and this time she was reluctant to pick it up. However, thinking that it might be the neighbors wanting reassurance about the children, she did—and this time the crank caller said "I'm watching you," and *BEGAN TO DESCRIBE WHAT SHE WAS WEARING*. Scared stiff, the girl broke the connection and immediately dialed the police, who told her that if the crank called again she should keep him talking while they traced the call. Sure enough, as soon as she hung up the phone it rang again, and this time the caller said, "*I THINK YOU'D BETTER CHECK THE CHILDREN*," laughed maniacally, and quickly slammed the phone down as though he was aware that the call might be traced.

The terrified girl locked all the doors and windows and ran upstairs to check on the children, ignoring the phone when it rang yet again. But the missed phone call was the police calling to tell her to get out of the house because the call had been traced to an upstairs extension. Coming down the staircase as she ran up it to the children was a *MASKED MAN, COVERED IN BLOOD AND CARRYING A MEAT CLEAVER*.

>KIDNEY HARVESTING

In 1996, a student at the University of Texas went to a party where he had a few beers and picked up a girl, who seemed surprisingly open to his advances. He was amazed and delighted when she suggested leaving the party and going to a bar where they could have a few more drinks in privacy, and even more staggered when she suggested going back to her hotel room.

But he didn't remember anything else until the next morning, when *HE AWOKE NAKED IN A BATH OF ICE*. He had a terrible headache and there was a dull ache in his lower back. He rubbed his eyes and looked around, trying to work out where he was, when he saw a note written on the wall in lipstick. It read: "*CALL 911 OR YOU WILL DIE.*"

Still feeling groggy—which he assumed was a hangover from the alcohol he'd consumed—he picked up a telephone that had been left on a cabinet next to the bathtub. He called 911 and told the operator about the weird situation he was in. The operator told him not to make any sudden movements. *WAS THERE A SMALL TUBE PROTRUDING FROM HIS LOWER BACK?* To his horror, the student found that there was. The operator told him not to move from the bathtub of ice and to wait for an ambulance, which was being sent as a top priority—he was the latest victim of a gang that was targeting students and removing their kidneys for sale on the black market.

When this story was reported in student newspapers, the gangs found that students became more wary, and so began targeting lone business travelers instead. In the late 1990s and early 2000s, reports emerged of similar horrors happening to business travelers in cities across the US, and later Europe. *MOST OF THE VICTIMS WERE MEN SITTING ALONE HAVING A NIGHTCAP AT THE HOTEL BAR.* A fellow businessman or attractive woman would offer to buy the victim a drink, and the next thing the hapless person would remember was waking up minus a kidney.

1 EMPIRE STATE BUILDING
NEW YORK, COMPLETED 1931

6,500 WINDOWS

At 485 yd (443 m) high, it was the world's tallest building for 40 years, until the World Trade Center surpassed it in 1971; it is now the ninth tallest, although it still has the second highest number of storys after the Sears Tower in Chicago.

2 CHANNEL TUNNEL
BRITAIN TO FRANCE, OPEN 1994

The first plans for a Channel Tunnel were drawn up in 1802, but were abandoned because war broke out between Great Britain and France the following year. It is 31 miles (50 km) in length and carries 6.8 million passengers a year.

THE SEVEN WONDERS OF THE ANCIENT WORLD

▲▲ The Great Pyramids, Egypt
▲ The Hanging Gardens of Babylon, Iraq
▲▲ The Statue of Zeus, Olympia
▲ The Temple of Artemis at Ephesus, Turkey
▲ The Mausoleum at Halicarnassus, Turkey
▲▲ The Colossus of Rhodes, Greece
▲ The Lighthouse of Alexandria, Egypt

7 WONDERS OF THE WORLD

AS CHOSEN BY THE AMERICAN SOCIETY OF CIVIL ENGINEERS

Why 7? Because the ancient Greeks considered seven to be a magical number. The seven wonders of the ancient world were selected by the 2nd-century Greek writer Antipater of Sidon but only one—the Great Pyramids of Egypt—survives today. So, in 1995 the AMERICAN SOCIETY OF CIVIL ENGINEERS joined a growing trend and voted for the new set of seven wonders featured here.

3 GOLDEN GATE BRIDGE
SAN FRANCISCO, COMPLETED 1937

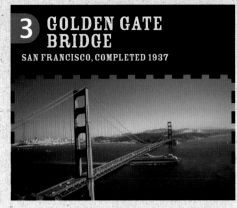

A safety net underneath the bridge during construction saved the lives of 19 workers, who thereby became members of the Halfway to Hell Club.

 **1¼ MILES LONG**

73 YARDS ABOVE WATER

4 CN TOWER
TORONTO, ONTARIO, OPEN 1976

Currently the world's tallest freestanding structure, in 2008 or 2009 Canada's CN Tower will be overtaken by the Jakarta Tower in Indonesia, which will be 16 ft (5 m) taller. It has 181 storys.

 **605 YARDS**

5 ITAIPÚ DAM
BRAZIL AND PARAGUAY, OPEN 1991

Damming the Paraná River, the Itaipú Dam will continue to hold the record for the world's highest power capacity until the Three Gorges Dam, China, begins to generate power in 2009.

SEVEN WONDERS ACCORDING TO:

JAMES BOND FANS
1 URSULA ANDRESS
2 HONOR BLACKMAN
3 DIANA RIGG
4 JILL ST. JOHN
5 CATHERINE SCHELL
6 JANE SEYMOUR
7 BRITT EKLAND

THE BEER DRINKERS' SOCIETY
1 MOORTGAT DUVEL (BELGIUM)
2 WESTMALLE DUBBEL (BELGIUM)
3 CANTILLON SAINT LAMVINUS (BELGIUM)
4 RODENBACH GRAND CRU (BELGIUM)
5 AYINGER CELEBRATOR (GERMANY)
6 SCHNEIDER AVENTINUS (GERMANY)
7 SAMUEL SMITH IMPERIAL STOUT (UK)

MOUNTAINEERS
1 EVEREST, ASIA
2 ACONCAGUA, SOUTH AMERICA
3 MCKINLEY, US
4 KILIMANJARO, AFRICA
5 ELBRUS, EUROPE
6 VINSON MASSIF, ANTARCTICA
7 KOSCIUSKO, AUSTRALIA

INTERNATIONAL ART THIEVES
1 PICASSO (551 PAINTINGS STOLEN)
2 MIRO
3 CHAGALL
4 DALI
5 RENOIR
6 DURER
7 REMBRANDT

WWW.URINAL.NET
1 AMUNDSEN-SCOTT SOUTH POLE STATION, ANTARCTICA
2 TAJ MAHAL, INDIA
3 NATURE'S CALL BY CLARK SORENSEN, SAN FRANCISCO
4 ROTHESAY'S PUBLIC TOILETS, ISLE OF BUTE
5 MYSTIQUE NIGHT CLUB, BANGKOK
6 WOMEN'S URINAL AT DAIRY QUEEN, PORT CHARLOTTE, FLORIDA
7 THE FELIX, HONG KONG

6 PANAMA CANAL
PANAMA, COMPLETED 1914

The lowest toll ever paid was 36 cents, by the American explorer Richard Haliburton, who swam the 50 mile (80 km) canal in 1928. He registered as a ship and the toll was based on his weight.

7 NORTH SEA PROTECTION WORKS
THE NETHERLANDS, COMPLETED 1932

Pictured is the Eastern Scheldt River storm surge barrier, the largest of 13 dams comprising the North Sea Protection Works. A plaque at one end reads: "Here the tide is ruled by the wind, the Moon, and us."

FOOD AND DRINK

BIG BIRD

Many people traditionally eat turkey for celebrations such as Thanksgiving and Christmas. In 1966, to avoid the embarrassing problems caused by unexpected guests arriving for dinner, breeders in California produced this 60-lb (27-kg) bird—seen here standing with 35-lb (16-kg) Donny Bigfeather.

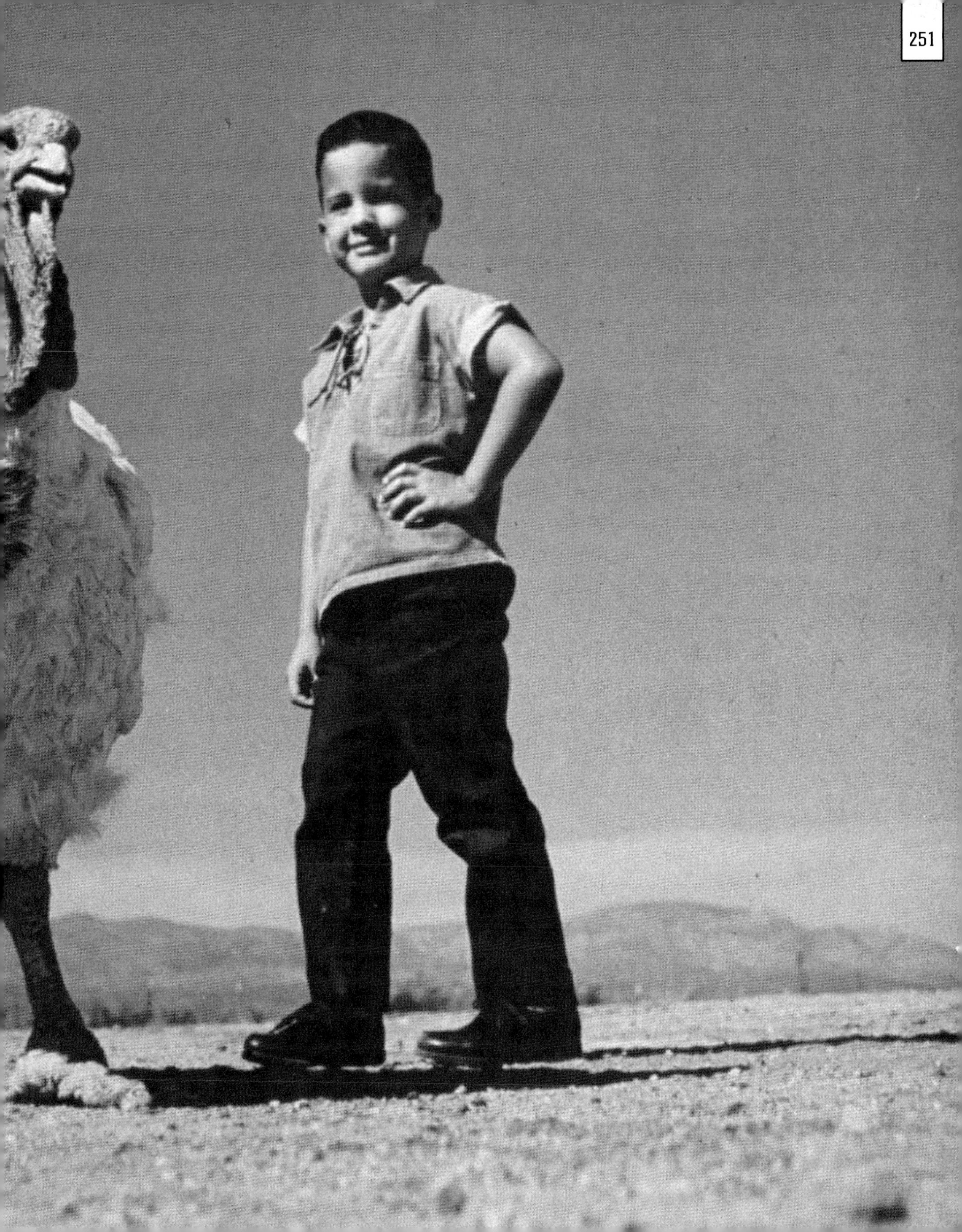

WHAT TO DO
WITH A SPOON

Forgotten your Swiss Army knife? Don't worry—if you find yourself having to land a lunar module or start an engine, there are other tools to use. In fact, they're all around you on Earth. With the right outlook, anything from a spoon to a pair of panty hose can get you out of a tight spot.

BANANA PEEL IS AN EXCELLENT ALTERNATIVE SHOULD YOU FIND YOURSELF OUT OF SHOE POLISH.

ALLIED PRISONERS IN COLDITZ MADE A GLIDER OUT OF **FLOORBOARDS** AND **SLEEPING BAGS.**

IN MAY 1995, A WOMAN FLYING FROM HONG KONG TO BRITAIN SUFFERED A LIFE-THREATENING TENSION PNEUMOTHORAX. TWO DOCTORS ON THE FLIGHT USED A **COAT HANGER** AND A BOTTLE OF MINERAL WATER TO PERFORM EMERGENCY SURGERY TO RELEASE AIR FROM HER PLEURAL CAVITY.

FOR MANY YEARS, RESOURCEFUL AFRICANS HAVE MADE EXTREMELY RESILIENT SHOES FROM **USED TIRES** AND **STRING.** SINCE THE RUBBER IS VULCANIZED, IT IS ROBUST—IT IS DESIGNED TO LAST FOR 15,000–30,000 MILES (24,000–48,000 KM) OF DRIVING.

A LOS ANGELES DOCTOR USES **PAPER CLIPS** TO DISLODGE FOREIGN BODIES THAT HAVE GOTTEN STUCK IN TODDLERS' NOSES. HE STRAIGHTENS THE CLIP, BENDS A SMALL TRIANGLE IN ONE END TO HIDE THE SHARP TIP, THEN MAKES A HOOK BY BENDING THE TRIANGLE AT AN ANGLE TO THE SHAFT.

AMERICAN ASTRONAUT BUZZ ALDRIN USED A **BALLPOINT PEN** TO OPERATE A SWITCH IN THE LUNAR MODULE AFTER THE LEVER SNAPPED OFF.

A HEATED **PAPER CLIP** CAN BE USED TO RELIEVE PRESSURE AFTER HITTING A FINGER AND BLACKENING THE NAIL; THE HOT PAPER CLIP WILL BURN THROUGH THE NAIL AND ALLOW BLOOD TO FLOW THROUGH THE HOLE.

BARNES WALLIS, INVENTOR OF THE BOUNCING BOMB, USED A RUBBER **BAND** TO FIRE **PING PONG** BALLS ACROSS AN INDOOR SWIMMING POOL TO SIMULATE HOW A BOUNCING BOMB MIGHT WORK.

ON 9/11, MINUTES BEFORE WTC1 COLLAPSED, WINDOW-CLEANER JAN DEMCZUR USED A **SQUEEGEE** TO PRISE OPEN ELEVATOR DOORS AND BREAK THROUGH FIVE LAYERS OF DRY WALL, SAVING HIMSELF AND FIVE OTHERS.

WHEN A CHILD WAS HIT BY A CAR ON THE ROAD OUTSIDE A YORKSHIRE, ENGLAND, DOCTOR'S HOUSE, THE INVENTIVE DOCTOR USED A **BREAD KNIFE** FROM HIS KITCHEN TO PERFORM AN EMERGENCY TRACHEOTOMY.

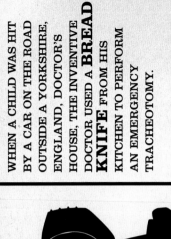

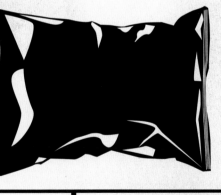

IN 2004, BRITAIN'S FAMILY PLANNING ASSOCIATION REPORTED THAT CASH-STRAPPED TEENS WERE USING **POTATO CHIP BAGS AND PLASTIC WRAP** AS CONDOMS.

WOMEN'S **PANTY HOSE** ARE IDEAL FOR REPLACING BROKEN FAN BELTS IN CAR ENGINES.

AN EMERGENCY TRACHEOTOMY CAN BE PERFORMED WITH A **RAZOR BLADE** AND A **BALLPOINT PEN.**

CHRISTOPHER COCKERELL, INVENTOR OF THE HOVERCRAFT, MADE HIS PROTOTYPE BY PUTTING A **CAT-FOOD CAN** INSIDE A **COFFEE CAN** AND USING A VACUUM CLEANER WITH THE MOTOR REVERSED TO BLOW AIR THROUGH THE GAP BETWEEN THE WALLS OF THE CANS.

A STAGE MANAGER USED A 6-IN (15-CM) **NAIL** TO REPLACE A 32-AMP FUSE JUST BEFORE A SHOW.

FRANK MORRIS, CLARENCE ANGLIN, AND JOHN ANGLIN USED **NAIL CLIPPERS, SPOONS,** AND A DRILL MADE FROM A **FAN** TO CHIP AWAY AT THE CONCRETE AROUND THE AIR SHAFTS IN THEIR CELLS AND SO ESCAPE FROM ALCATRAZ PRISON IN SAN FRANCISCO BAY.

England's Alan Knott and Australia's Alan Turner look on as Lord's first streaker hurdles the stumps.

LORD'S STREAKER 1975

One of the first sports-event streakers in Britain was merchant-navy cook Michael Angelow, who ran naked onto the field at Lord's cricket ground during the 4th Test of the England–Australia Ashes series. Journalists had a field day with puns about ball tampering, googlies, and seamen.

EMPEROR NERO 67 BCE

At the Olympic Games in 67BCE, the Emperor Nero "won" the chariot race despite not finishing. He arrived drunk and crashed his chariot—but because no one dared race against the violent, tyrannical emperor, he was nonetheless crowned Olympic Champion.

JAMAICAN BOBSLEIGH 1998

Jamaica has never experienced snow or ice but, in 1998, the sun-drenched nation entered the Winter Olympic bobsleigh competition in Calgary, Canada. With several sprinters on the team, they made a strong start but crashed and finished last, inspiring the feature film *Cool Runnings*.

SPORTS AND LEISURE

WINNERS AND

The excitement of human sports lies not only in the skill and athleticism of the sportsmen but also in the thrills and spills of the sports they play—for instance, it may be exciting to watch the fastest humans on Earth run the 100 meters, but it's far more memorable if someone falls over. Here are some of sports' spectacular winners and losers.

SYLVESTER CARMOUCHE 1990

One foggy afternoon in January 1990 at the Delta Downs Racetrack in Louisiana, jockey Sylvester Carmouche stopped while hidden in the fog. He waited for the other riders to come around again and then set off ahead of them, winning the race by 24 lengths—such a large margin that suspicions were immediately raised.

FRED LORZ 1904

At the 1904 Olympics in St. Louis, US, runner Fred Lorz celebrated winning the marathon with such gusto that officials investigated. They discovered Lorz had collapsed with cramps and taken a 11 mile (17.75 km) lift by car back to the stadium before crossing the line in first place.

GOLF ON THE MOON 1971

In 1971, US astronaut Alan Shepard played two golf strokes on the Moon using an improvised club. The Royal & Ancient Golf Club later sent him a telegram reading: "Warmest congratulations to all of you on your great achievement and safe return. Please refer to the Rules of Golf section on etiquette, paragraph 6, quote—before leaving a bunker a player should carefully fill up all holes made by him therein, unquote."

JACK BRABHAM 1959

When Stirling Moss dropped out of the 1959 US Grand Prix at Sebring, Florida, Jack Brabham only needed to finish the race to win the Drivers' Championship. He ran out of fuel on the last lap but pushed his car over the line in fourth place to claim the title.

LLOYD SCOTT 2002

In 2002, Lloyd Scott raised $150,000 for charity by "running" the London marathon in a deep-sea diving suit. At 130 lb (59 kg), it was so heavy he had to rest every 1,300 ft (400 m). He finished in the slowest time to that date: 5 days, 8 hours, 29 minutes, and 46 seconds.

BORIS ONISHENKO 1976

At the 1976 Olympics in Montreal, Soviet pentathlete Boris Onischenko managed to score hits during the fencing event without actually touching his opponents. It turned out that he'd rigged his épée to register hits when he squeezed the handgrip— he was disqualified and the press dubbed him "Disonishenko."

SOCCER IN THE TRENCHES 1914

During World War I, a truce was called over Christmas 1914, and troops from both sides played a number of informal soccer matches. On January 1, 1915, *The Times* published a letter from a British Army Major stating that troops in his sector had lost 3–2 to Germans from the opposing trenches.

LOSERS

BJØRGE LILLELIEN 1981

When Norway beat England 2–1 in a 1981 FIFA World Cup qualifier, commentator Bjørge Lillelien yelled: "Lord Nelson, Lord Beaverbrook, Sir Winston Churchill, Sir Anthony Eden, Clement Attlee, Henry Cooper, Lady Diana—we have beaten them all. We have beaten them all. Maggie Thatcher, can you hear me? Maggie Thatcher, I have a message to you during your election campaign. I have a message to you: we have knocked England out of the World Cup of football. Maggie Thatcher, as they say in your language in boxing bars around Madison Square Garden in New York: your boys took a hell of a beating! Your boys took a hell of a beating!"

Norwegian commentator Bjørge Lillelien

CHAPTER 12

12 mph was the average speed of traffic in London in 1900 and in 2000 ✹ Most calendar systems have 12 months. The Roman calendar had 10 until Julius and Augustus Caesar inserted months named after them (July and August), which is why the 9th, 10th, 11th, and 12th months (September, October, November, and December) are named after the Latin words for the numbers 7, 8, 9, and 10 ✹ The basic units of time—60 seconds in a minute, 60 minutes in an hour, and 24 hours in a day—are all divisible by 12 because the ancient Babylonians, who originated the system, counted in base 12 ✹ In those countries whose legal system follows the Anglo-Saxon model, there are 12 people on a jury ✹ The 12 signs of the zodiac (whose cycle traditionally began in spring) are Aries, Taurus, Gemini, Cancer, Leo, Virgo, Libra, Scorpio, Sagittarius, Capricorn, Aquarius, Pisces ✹ The 12 signs of the Chinese zodiac are Rat, Ox, Tiger, Rabbit, Dragon, Snake, Horse, Sheep, Monkey, Rooster, Dog, Boar ✹ In Tarot, no. 12 is the Hanged Man ✹ In the Christian New Testament, there are 12 apostles: Simon (Peter), Andrew, James, John, Philip, Bartholomew, Thomas, Matthew, James, Thaddeus, Simon the Zealot, Judas Iscariot ✹ The 12 tribes of Israel were those of Reuben, Simeon, Judah, Issachar, Zebulun, Dan, Naphtali, Gad, Asher, Benjamin, Ephraim, Manasseh ✹ Shi'a Islam recognizes 12 original Imams: Ali, Hasan, Husayn, and 9 of Husayn's descendants ✹ The equation $12^2 = 144$ is also true if the digits are reversed: $441 = 21^2$ ✹ 12 is the smallest number with 6 divisors (1, 2, 3, 4, 6, and 12) ✹ 12 is commonly used as a sales unit, called a dozen. 12 dozen is 1 gross ✹ The highest wind force on the Beaufort Scale is Force 12: Hurricane. The 13 points on the scale (numbered 0–12) are: 0 calm, 1 light air, 2 light breeze, 3 gentle breeze, 4 moderate breeze, 5 fresh breeze, 6 strong breeze, 7 near gale, 8 gale, 9 strong gale, 10 storm, 11 violent storm, 12 hurricane ✹ A human being has 12 pairs of ribs ✹ 12 men have walked on the Moon.

60 SECONDS TO SAVE THE WORLD

Earth is a rapidly overheating planet, and most humans now agree that it is due to our own activities, particularly pollution and burning fossil fuels. Given the overheating you might choose not to go and live on Earth, but if you do, here are some ways that you and the humans already living there can reduce the damage you do.

WEAR MORE INDOORS

During the winter months wear more clothes indoors and set the thermostat at no more than 61°F (16°C). Come on, pashminas and Ugg boots can look cool indoors, too.

BUY ENERGY-SAVING MACHINES

Energy-saving "white goods," such as washing machines and dishwashers, use a third less energy than normal models since they are just as effective at lower temperatures. Using a 104°F (40°C) wash cycle rather than a 130°F (60°C) cycle means you use a third less electricity. Reduce the wash to a 86°F (30°C) cycle and the amount saved is even higher. The energy-saving logo is your guarantee that the product will save energy, cost less to run, and help not to destroy the environment.

RECYCLE

Paper, plastic, glass, aluminum cans, foil, cardboard, batteries, and textiles—you know the score. Just remember, 88 percent of all Sunday newspapers are not recycled—that's 440,000 trees—and "Americans throw away enough aluminum to rebuild their commercial aircraft fleet every three months."

PUT FOIL BEHIND YOUR RADIATORS

This may sound like primitive home repair, but installing aluminum foil behind any radiators that are on outside walls will help to reflect the heat into the room, rather than out of it, saving heat and money.

INFLATE YOUR TIRES: SAVE GAS

If you have to drive, keep your vehicle tires correctly inflated: you can easily do it at the local gas station. Someone somewhere has calculated that if we drove around at the correct pressure, it would save 9.3 million gallons (35 million liters) of fuel per DAY and reduce the mountains of tires from the scrap heap every year.

REPLACE YOUR LIGHTBULBS

Here's a bright idea: use only low-energy fluorescent bulbs. They produce the same amount of light as an ordinary bulb BUT emit 70 percent less CO2. They also last 12 times longer because they don't waste as much energy by turning it into heat and thus save money. Replacing 10 bulbs could save 1 ton of carbon.

TURN OFF STANDBY

Switching an electrical device off rather than leaving it on standby can save a household $70 (£37) per year; just unplugging chargers across the UK could save enough electricity to power 180,000 homes and reduce carbon by ¼ million tons every year. A hi-fi/stereo, TV, video recorder, DVD player, digital TV top box, computer and peripherals, computer monitor, laptop computer, broadband modem, answering machine, battery charger, and cell phone charger together would use 83 watts in 24 hours if left on standby. So what does 83 watts for 24 hours a day, (727 kW-units of electricity in a year) actually mean in nonscientific-speak? Well, it's about the same amount of pollution as is produced by driving 870 miles (1,400 km) in a typical car, or about 10 percent of the pollution from the average person's annual electricity and gas use.

SAY "NO" TO PLASTIC BAGS

Take your own recyclable or canvas bag when shopping; if you feel you must use those nasty plastic bags make sure you return them for recycling.

FLUSH LESS: SAVE WATER

Several gallons of drinkable water go down the drain every time a toilet is flushed. Placing an empty 1-quart (1-liter) plastic bottle in the cistern of each toilet tank will save that amount of water in each flush. Water is precious—ask the 2.6 billion people who do not have clean water to drink or somewhere safe to go to the bathroom.

ONLY BOIL AS MUCH WATER AS YOU NEED

Every day the UK drinks 229 million cups of tea or coffee or 9.5 million every hour, which is enough to fill 22 Olympic swimming pools. So if humans boil just what they need to drink that would save enough electric power to keep 374,000 homes going.

DRIVE LESS

Walk, cycle, or take public transportation for shorter journeys: or at least ditch the SUV, which, if you can afford that kind of vehicle, makes you eligible to buy a hybrid car at the very least. Perhaps you should also consider if you really need an off-road 4WD quasi-military vehicle to drive around a city?

OWNEY THE DOG

In 1888, a stray mongrel named Owney began traveling on mail trains and became a familiar sight at post offices across North America. Postal clerks began attaching mail tags to Owney's collar until it was so weighed down that the Postmaster General had a special jacket made. In 1895, clerks sent Owney on a world cruise. Riding on mail trains and steamships, he sailed from Tacoma, Washington, to Japan and China, through the Suez Canal to North Africa and Europe, and then home via the Azores. Owney is now preserved in the Smithsonian in Washington, D.C., wearing some of his 1,017 tags, representing some 150,000 miles (240,000 km) of travel.

ARCTIC TERN

Six species of bird migrate more than 10,000 miles (16,000 km) annually. The most amazing journey is that of the arctic tern, which sees more daylight than any other animal. Arctic terns breed in arctic or subarctic regions during the near 24-hour daylight of the northern summer, then migrate south to enjoy the near 24-hour daylight of the antarctic summer. But they don't rest—while in the south, they remain at sea, just north of the polar ice. They're rarely seen migrating because the journey takes place almost entirely over water.

NEPTUNE THE DOG

Newfoundland dogs are renowned for their swimming abilities, and the aptly named Neptune was no exception. A pet on board a boat being towed up the Mississippi River, Neptune fell overboard when the boat listed in bad weather. Three days and 50 miles (80 km) later, after the boat had docked in New Orleans, Neptune swam alongside and jumped back on board.

SUGAR THE CAT

Stacy Wood lived in Anderson, California, and when he retired in 1952 he and his wife decided to move to Oklahoma. Thinking that it was unfair to take their cat, Sugar, on the long road trip, and that she would be happier in familiar surroundings, they left her with a neighbor. But two weeks later, Sugar disappeared from the neighbor's house—and 14 months after that she trotted into the grounds of the Woods' new home in Oklahoma. She had traveled 1,500 miles (2,400 km) at an average of 25 miles (40 km) a week— including crossing the Rocky Mountains— to reach a place she had never been before.

MONARCH BUTTERFLY

On their annual migration, Monarch butterflies fly up to 3,000 miles (4,800 km) from northwestern US and Canada to California and Central Mexico. Traveling on air currents to speed their journey, they cover an average of 50 miles (80 km) a day. But the distance is not the only notable fact—the complete round trip takes two or even three generations of butterflies, each of which must travel by instinct rather than by navigation. Some 300 million Monarch butterflies make the journey south. More than half never complete the trip, but their offspring, born en route, continue the journey back to where their parents or grandparents set out from.

FLORA AND FAUNA

ANIMAL MILES

All humans know that birds migrate because they see them line up on the telephone wires in the fall, fly off, and reappear in the spring. But it's more surprising to discover that butterflies and turtles migrate thousands of miles. Or that some birds commute daily by ferry. Or that two toadfish traveled nearly 3 million miles (5 million kilometers) on a space shuttle.

TURNSTONES FRED AND FREDA

In 2007, the St. Mawes Ferry Company in Cornwall, England, reported that, instead of flying the 1½ miles (2.4 km) across the Fal River, a pair of turnstones was using the ferry to commute from Falmouth to feed in the rock pools at St. Mawes. Ferry captain John Brown said: "They arrive for a breakfast of breadcrumbs at 8:15 a.m. before we set out, and never miss the last ferry back. We aren't sure why they don't fly. Maybe they're a bit lazy or like the company." The crew named the pair Fred and Freda.

CHESTER THE TORTOISE

In 1960, eight-year-old Malcolm Edwards was given a tortoise as a pet and named it Chester. Malcolm's father painted a white cross on Chester's shell so that he wouldn't get lost in the grass but Chester nonetheless managed to escape. In 1978, someone saw Chester 450 yd (410 m) from Malcolm's house but he wasn't caught. Then, in 1995, long after the 43-year-old Malcolm had resigned himself to the loss of Chester, a neighbor found him just 100 yd (91 m) from the house. Chester had traveled a tortastic 750 yd (685 m)— 450 yd (410 m) in the first 18 years before doubling back and covering a further 300 yd (275 m) between 1978 and 1995.

LOGGERHEAD TURTLE

In July 1994, American researchers tracked Rosita, a female loggerhead, as she crossed the Pacific from Baja California to Kyushu, Japan, where she arrived in November 1995. Research has since shown that loggerheads hatch in Japan, migrate to Baja California to mature, and return to Japan to nest— a round trip of 13,000 miles (21,000 km). Sadly, Rosita's welcome to Japan after her 6,500 mile (10,500 km) journey was to be trapped in a fisherman's net and killed.

TOADFISH

Toadfish are so called not just because they look like toads but also because the male of some species can inflate their swim bladders to make their mating call, as toads do with their throats. The longest journey ever made by any fish was more than 3 million miles (4.8 million km). In 1998, two oyster toadfish were taken on board the space shuttle Discovery to research the effects of weightlessness on balance. The aural canal of the oyster toadfish is similar to that of vertebrates, including humans, which enabled Mission Specialist Scott Parazynski to make observations that may help treat equilibrium disorders, including motion sickness, on Earth.

GREAT WHITE SHARK

Scientists always thought that Great Whites stay relatively close to shore. Then, in 2005, a team led by South African Dr. Ramón Bonfil decided to find out for sure by tagging the dorsal fin of a female and releasing her at Gansbaii on the South African coast. They were amazed when they tracked the shark 6,879 miles (11,000 km) to Exmouth Gulf in Australia—and back again. It is the longest shark journey ever recorded, covering over 12,400 miles (20,000 km) in just nine months, which scientists noted was "the fastest return migration of any swimming marine organism known." Bonfil's team named their shark Nicole, after shark-loving Australian actress Nicole Kidman.

WHISKY THE DOG

In October 1973, Australian truckdriver Geoff Hancock pulled into a truckstop on the outskirts of Darwin. He wasn't intending to stop for long, so he left his fox terrier, Whisky, in the cab—or so he thought. When he returned he found that Whisky had gone. After searching the grounds of the truckstop Geoff sadly began the long drive home thinking that he would never see Whisky again. Incredibly, eight and a half months later, in June 1974, Whisky arrived at Geoff's home in Melbourne after a record journey of some 1,800 miles (2,900 km).

Natural ✚ REMEDIES

In Western society, any form of medicine that doesn't conform to certain narrowly defined norms is referred to as "alternative" medicine. That includes some well-respected disciplines that have been tried and tested over centuries in Eastern cultures. It also includes some medical practices that are plain weird.

HEAT CUPPING

Cupping has been used for centuries in many cultures, starting with the use of hollow animal horns to drain toxins out of snakebites and evolving through bamboo cups to glass. Modern cupping therapy uses suction and negative pressure to relax soft tissue, drain toxins and excess fluids, and increase blood flow to the skin and muscles.

LEECHES

COW-DUNG POULTICES

RHINO HORN

URINE THERAPY

CHINESE GALLNUTS

APITHERAPY

DONG CHONG TSIA TSIAO

MAGGOTS

LEECHES

After attaching themselves to the skin, leeches inject anesthetic and anticoagulants (to keep blood flowing), then suck blood from the host. In medieval times, they were used medically to "bleed" patients and so "balance the humors." In modern medicine, they're used after operations to reduce clotting, relieve pressure, and stimulate circulation.

COW-DUNG POULTICES

Once used widely in the West, cow dung was a traditional cure for acute skin conditions such as ulcers, inflammation, abscesses, and boils.

RHINO HORN

Rhinoceros horn is best known in the West as a supposed aphrodisiac. It is used in Chinese medicine to treat conditions such as fever, convulsion, delirium, headache, toothache, and snake bites.

URINE THERAPY

Traditional in many Eastern cultures, urine therapy is now becoming more prevalent in the West. This therapy includes drinking one's own urine as well as massaging it into the skin.

CHINESE GALLNUTS (WUBEIZI)

Chinese gallnuts are secreted by trees, such as the Chinese sumac, when stimulated by the larvae of certain aphids. The tannin-rich gall hardens into a "nut" used for treating a wide range of ailments.

APITHERAPY

This ancient treatment uses bee products (*apis* is the Latin for bee). Honey and royal jelly are common enough—but apitherapy also includes the use of bees' venom, either by live stings or by injection. Venom therapy is said to be effective for arthritis, bursitis, tendonitis, and shingles, among other conditions.

DONG CHONG TSIA TSIAO

Literally translated as "winter caterpillar summer grass," this is a very expensive Chinese medicine made from butterfly larvae infected with a special fungus, and is said to have properties similar to ginseng.

MAGGOTS

Used to treat wounds since antiquity, maggots made a comeback in the 1990s as part of the battle against antibiotic-resistant bacteria. They speed up wound recovery by consuming dead tissue and killing bacteria, thus preventing the wound from festering, and by stimulating the body's own self-healing functions.

THE RULES OF BUSINESS

Human business is about one side communicating what they want the other side to know—which may or may not include the truth. Truth or lies, there are certain rules that have to be obeyed, and those rules differ from country to country. Here are some of the finer points of business etiquette from around the globe.

MEETINGS

SAUDI ARABIA/ARAB COUNTRIES

• Make appointments several weeks in advance. Try to schedule meetings in the morning—many Arabs take a siesta in the afternoon. Do not attempt to arrange appointments on Fridays (the Muslim day of prayer and rest).

• It is not uncommon to have a meeting canceled once you arrive, and it is accepted custom to keep foreigners waiting.

• In many Muslim countries, feet are perceived as dirty—any display of the sole of the foot is considered insulting. Don't cross legs in front of a figure of authority.

• When negotiating price, remember that haggling is expected. Saudis will often make an initial offer that is extremely low or high, depending on whether they are buying or selling.

INDIA

• Use a light handshake when greeting a male at the start of the meeting. Only shake an Indian woman's hand if she offers it—otherwise try the alternative peace greeting: hold the palms of both hands together under the chin, smile, bow, and say "Namaste."

• Try not to stand with your hands on your hips, as this is considered an aggressive posture.

JAPAN

• Don't blow your nose into a handkerchief even if you have a terrible cold. The Japanese think that using a cotton hankie and storing it in your pocket is the height of bad manners (which is surprising to foreigners, given that it's acceptable for Japanese men to cough loudly and spit out phlegm in public). Use paper tissues instead, and do it discreetly.

• Always have a *meishi* (business card) with you, ready to give out. To be without a *meishi* at a meeting is a disaster—if you are given a *meishi* and you do not return the gesture, you are effectively saying that you're not interested in pursuing this relationship.

• Always keep the card in front of you; putting it away is a signal that the meeting is over.

CHINA/HONG KONG

• Business cards are always exchanged after the initial introduction, using both hands. Have one side of your card translated into Mandarin or Cantonese with the characters printed in gold—an auspicious color.

• Ask a Chinese friend to select a good name for your business card – if you try to spell out your name phonetically you will look silly.

• Do not underestimate the importance of keeping face. If you are late, allude to a mistake, cause embarrassment, or are confrontational, the loss of face may ruin a business relationship.

FRANCE

• When negotiating, remember that a refusal does not necessarily mean the discussion is over—sometimes it is just beginning.

• Good debating skills that demonstrate an intellectual grasp of the situation and all its ramifications will impress; discussions may be heated and intense.

• Because of their love of *grands projets* (large plans), the French often go for the bigger picture instead of looking at the details.

ITALY

• Italians prefer to do business with people they know and trust; a third-party introduction goes a long way to providing an initial work platform.

• The concept of *bella figura* (beautiful figure) is extremely important and refers to the ability to present yourself well. Do everything you can

to show how your proposal enhances their *bella figura*—whether you are worth knowing and doing business with may be more important than the details of your proposal.

• Meetings can last a long time because everyone must express an opinion, even if only one person can make the decision.

• Don't be surprised when heated debates and arguments erupt in meetings—they are simply a function of the free-flow of ideas and of Italians' typically passionate way of expressing themselves. Expect a lot of hands to be waved around.

GERMANY

• Appointments are mandatory and should be made 1–2 weeks in advance; meetings stick to strict agendas, including starting and ending times; punctuality is taken extremely seriously.

• There is a strict protocol to follow when entering a room: the eldest or highest-ranking person goes in first; men enter before women, if their age and status are roughly equivalent.

• Be patient—Germans are detail oriented and may want to discuss and understand every subclause before coming to an agreement.

• At the end of a meeting, some Germans like to signal their approval by rapping their knuckles on the tabletop.

ENTERTAINING

FRANCE

• French culture values *savoir vivre* (knowing how to live), and the French love to socialize over long meals with plenty of wine.

• Business lunches are usually sit-down affairs and conversation over food is rarely work related.

• Whatever you do, don't suggest grabbing a sandwich for lunch to eat at your desk—this will make your Gallic colleagues think that you are dull and boring.

• While refusing wine at lunch is acceptable, albeit unusual, refusing wine at a dinner would be considered rude.

ITALY

• Networking is a full-time occupation in Italy; personal contacts allow people to get ahead, so it is important to spend time developing a social relationship.

• Your business colleagues will be eager to know about your personal life before conducting business with you. In turn, take the time to ask questions about their family and personal interests, as this helps build the relationship.

JAPAN

• So you've impressed your new colleagues with your karaoke skills and cried into your Japanese whisky. Now you're on the way back to your hotel in a taxi. Just remember not to open or close a taxi door—the driver will take care of that—and when you get into a taxi, the most important person sits in the middle. Okay?

RUSSIA

• Always hand in your coat at the coat check when visiting a restaurant or theater—draping it over the back of your chair is frowned upon. This Russian custom has its roots in the weather: in winter, the snow dripping off coats would quickly turn a restaurant into a river. If your coat lacks a collar hook, the attendant may charge you for the use of a hanger.

CHINA/HONG KONG

• Table manners are generally relaxed when eating out, though there are certain rules: never start before the host; try everything but never eat the last piece; always return chopsticks to the rest when you want to drink; always refuse a second helping at least once, unless you want to appear greedy; and leave some food in your bowl when you have finished.

• Remember—burping is considered a compliment.

SAUDI ARABIA

• When eating a meal on the floor, you may sit cross-legged or kneel on one knee.

• Eat only with the right hand as the left is considered unclean.

• Part of Saudi hospitality is to shower guests with more food than they can possibly eat. Try a bit of everything that is served—honored guests are often offered the most prized item, such as a sheep's head, so be prepared.

• There is little conversation during meals so that diners may relish the food.

COMMUNICATION

JAPAN

• Japanese communication stresses harmony. The word "yes" can lead to confusion. Yes (*hai*) does not mean "Yes, I agree with you" (or "That is what I am going to do."). More often, it means "Yes, I hear what you are saying." The word "no" (*iie*) is deemed overly blunt in certain contexts.

• Expect silences—pauses in conversation are an important part of communication.

• Don't be put off if someone falls asleep during a conference. If you are giving a speech, keep the audience alert by saying that questions will be accepted afterward.

• Many Japanese businesspeople now shake hands rather than bow. If someone does bow to you, respond by bowing back slightly lower than the level of their bow.

INDIA

• It is considered rude not to attempt to give a person what they ask for—rather than disappoint with a negative answer, Indians will give you the response they think you want to hear.

• An affirmative answer may be deliberately vague, so look for nonverbal or other cues, such as a reluctance to commit to a time for a meeting.

CHINA/HONG KONG

• As with many Asian cultures, silence is a form of communication; try to resist the urge to jump into the conversation if your Chinese counterpart remains silent for a minute.

• When you first meet, expect questions considered extremely personal in your country.

• Hong Kong Chinese are generally nonconfrontational and will never overtly say "no" for fear of embarrassing the other person.

• If someone sucks air through their teeth while you are speaking, it means that they are unhappy with what you have just said. Try to restate your position or modify your request.

ANIMAL HOUSE

Since time immemorial people have kept pets. Dogs were the first animals to be domesticated and kept as companions and, with cats, they remain by far the most popular choice of pet. But some people just have to be different. Forget dogs and cats, fish and birds, hamsters and guinea pigs, here are some of the weirder pets that have been kept by presidents, kings, and other assorted oddballs.

WILD ANIMALS

NEW YORKER Antoine Yates was arrested for keeping Ming, a Bengal tiger, and Al, a 3-ft (90-cm) Caiman alligator, in his Harlem apartment.

KING JAMES I kept 11 lions, two leopards, three eagles, two owls, two mountain cats, and a jackal at the Tower of London.

FORMER HEAVYWEIGHT Boxing Champion Mike yson owned a pet tiger.

CHECHEN LEADER Ramzan Kadyrov, a friend of Mike Tyson, was pictured with a pet tiger in 2006. Kadyrov said he also had a lion and had once owned a wolf and a bear.

WHEN A BABY HIPPO washed up in Tony and Shirley Joubert's river-front garden in South Africa they adopted her. "Jessica" shares the home and swims with the children.

PIGS

US POP singer and actress Jessica Simpson has a pot-bellied pig named Brutus.

AFTER BREAKING UP with girlfriend Kelly Preston in 1988, US actor and director George Clooney took custody of their 300 lb (300 lb) pot-bellied pig, Max. Max died in 2006 after sharing Clooney's home for 18 years, sometimes sleeping on the actor's bed. Asked whether he would get another pig, Clooney said, "No. I think Max covered all my pig needs."

MAMMALS, BIRDS, AND REPTILES

THEODORE "TEDDY" ROOSEVELT loved hunting, but once reputedly refused to shoot a bear cub, prompting "Teddy" bears to be named after him. Among other things he owned a zebra, a coyote, and a hyena.

JOHN QUINCY ADAMS was given a pet alligator by the Marquis de Lafayette that he kept at the White House.

CALVIN COOLIDGE had two lion cubs, an antelope, a pygmy hippo, a wallaby, a donkey, a goose, and several raccoons, as well as other more conventional pets.

MONKEYS

KING ALEXANDER of Greece died in 1920 after being bitten by his pet monkey.

ELVIS PRESLEY kept dogs, horses, and a chimpanzee named Scatter, who is said to have wrought havoc in movie mogul Sam Goldwyn's office.

OVER THE YEARS, pop star Michael Jackson has kept numerous exotic pets at his Neverland ranch, the most famous of them being his chimp, Bubbles.

PLAYBOY SUPREMO Hugh Hefner has a zoo license, and keeps peacocks and spider monkeys as pets.

RATS

SOCIALITE PARIS HILTON once had a pet rat and has also owned a tiger. Her honey bear was confiscated since it is illegal to keep one as a pet in the state of California.

ACTOR ANGELINA JOLIE had a female rat called Harry, who would bathe with her.

ENGLISH ACTOR Rupert Grint, Ron Weasley in the Harry Potter films, adopted the two rats used to play Ron's fictional pet, Scabbers.

OTHER CELEBRITY rat owners include Clint Eastwood, John Cleese, Grace Slick, and Pink (whose rats are called Thelma and Louise).

CRUSTACEANS

FRENCH POET Gérard de Nerval had a pet lobster named Thibault, which he took for walks in Paris. He said that lobsters were "peaceful, serious creatures, who know the secrets of the sea, and don't bark."

ACTOR KIM BASINGER lists hermit crabs among her 21 pets.

SNAKES

IN DECEMBER 2006, American Ted Dres [sic] was choked to death by his 13-ft (4-m) pet boa constrictor at his home in Cincinnati. A spokesman for the Cincinnati Society for the Prevention of Cruelty to Animals said: "People who keep these types of animals as pets should know exactly what they're doing and what they're capable of. They don't realize they could be a few seconds away from death."

SEATTLE SUPERSONICS basketball player Mikki Moore keeps three albino pythons and three American alligators at his home in Atlanta, Georgia.

Cloud spotting part I

CLOUD TYPES

Clouds not only form in different shapes, they also form at different altitudes. At one extreme, stratus clouds can form at ground level, while at the other, nacreous clouds can form in the stratosphere, right on the edge of space.

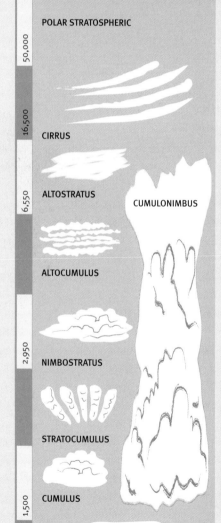

POLAR STRATOSPHERIC

50,000

16,500

CIRRUS

ALTOSTRATUS

6,550

CUMULONIMBUS

ALTOCUMULUS

2,950

NIMBOSTRATUS

STRATOCUMULUS

1,500

CUMULUS

HEIGHT (FT)

STRATUS

POLAR STRATOSPHERIC CLOUD (50,000–82,000 ft/ 15,000–25,000 m) Also known as nacreous clouds, they form in the stratosphere where they glow brightly in vivid colors.

CONTRAILS (16,500–45,000 ft/5,000–13,700 m) Contrails, also known as vapor trails, are artificial cirrus clouds. They are formed by water vapor condensation triggered by jet exhaust particles or low pressure vortices caused by jet aircraft wings.

PILEUS (1,500–45,000 ft/460–13,700 m) Deriving from the Latin for "cap," these small, flat clouds appear above cumulonimbus or cumulus clouds. Formed by updrafts in the parent cloud, they often indicate severe weather to come.

CUMULONIMBUS (1,500–45,000 ft/460–13,700 m) These dense, heaped clouds often build into immensely tall anvil-shaped towers, indicating rain and often thunder.

STRATOCUMULUS UNDULATUS (1,500–6,550 ft/ 460–2,000 m) Undulatus is the name given to clouds that the wind has shaped into a wavy, undulating pattern. These include cirrocumulus, cirrostratus, altocumulus, stratus, and stratocumulus.

STRATOCUMULUS (1,500–6,550 ft/460–2,000 m) These layered rolls of cloud, larger than those in altocumuli, commonly form above subtropical and polar oceans. They are usually associated with dry but dull weather.

*E*arth is often referred to as the "blue planet," but the main colors when you look at it from space are blue and white, from the 70 percent ocean cover and the clouds that are always visible over some part of the globe. Aside from playing a vital role in distributing water, clouds are also a useful predictor of weather changes.

CIRROSTRATUS (16,500–45,000 ft/ 5,000–13,700 m)
More of a sheet than the layered curl that the name suggests, high milky strands of cirrostratus are often a sign of rain to come.

CIRROCUMULUS (16,500–45,000 ft/5,000–13,700 m)
These curled heaps of high-altitude cloud, also known as "mackerel sky," are a sign of unsettled weather and are usually short-lived.

CIRRUS (16,500–45,000 ft/5,000–13,700 m)
Cirrus means "curl," and these delicate curly wisps of cloud, made up of ice crystals high in the atmosphere, are often a sign of imminent bad weather.

NIMBOSTRATUS (2,950–9,850 ft/ 900–3,000 m)
Nimbus means "rain" and a solid mass of these gray layered rainclouds overhead can only mean one thing: you're going to get wet.

ALTOCUMULUS (6,550–23,000 ft/ 2,000–7,000 m)
Starting at the height that cumulus ends, these midlevel patches of cloud, characterized by globular masses or rolls, usually indicate imminent sunshine.

ALTOSTRATUS (6,550–23,000 ft/2,000–7,000 m)
These midlevel, thin blue or gray sheets often make the Sun or Moon look indistinct and may develop into rain clouds.

CUMULUS (1,500–6,550 ft/460–2,000 m)
Cumulus means "heap," which will help you remember the name of these heaped fluffy clouds. Bright white with gray bases, they are associated with sunny spells.

OROGRAPHIC (0–33,000 ft/0–10,000 m)
Deriving from the Greek for "mountain," these clouds are formed when a mass of air is forced to rise by the presence of a mountain, often resulting in rain on the windward side.

STRATUS (0–1,500 ft/0–460 m)
Stratus means "layer." These foggy gray layers are often so low that you find yourself walking through them in a miserable clinging drizzle.

Cloud spotting **part II**

MAMMATUS (1,500–6,550 ft/460–2,000 m)
Caused by convection currents, these cloud
pouches, here over Denver, Colorado, form beneath
cumulonimbus in thundery conditions. The name
derives from "mammary," after their breastlike shape.

There are hundreds of "facts" that humans accept as true without ever really checking them for accuracy. Some can be explained in terms of their historical context, but others have no scientific basis. For example, nervous fliers are told that they're more likely to be killed by a donkey than a plane crash—but which organization records the number of donkey-related deaths?

MODERN MYTHS

Can a human get stuck on a **VACUUM TOILET** in an **AIRPLANE?** No: in 2001, a tabloid newspaper reported that an obese woman had got stuck to a vacuum toilet by trying to flush it while sitting on it. This is not possible, since the suction only lasts a few seconds, and only reaches 3 psi.

Will a **TOOTH** left in cola **DISSOLVE OVERNIGHT?** No: in 1950, an expert witness testified that a tooth would begin to dissolve after two days. The defense countered that the same is true of fruit juice. But who's going to hold a mouthful of juice or cola for two days?

Everyone believed the world was **FLAT** until **COLUMBUS** sailed around it. No, and no. A small minority thought it was flat (and some still do) but, since ancient times, mainstream science and religion have held it to be spherical. And it was Magellan's expedition that proved it by sailing all the way around, although Magellan died en route.

Humans use **10 PERCENT** of their **BRAINS**. PET and MRI scans show this to be untrue, yet the myth persists—maybe because at one time neurologists only understood how 10 percent of the brain functioned.

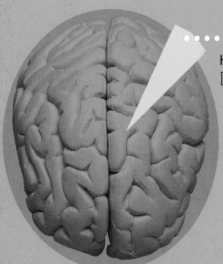

A myth persists that putting something as small as a **COIN** on a railroad track will derail a **TRAIN**. Errant teenagers who've tried to derail a train will know that this doesn't happen—the train just flattens the coins. (But DON'T try this for yourself.)

Next time someone tells you you have the memory of a **GOLDFISH** you can take it as a COMPLIMENT (kind of). Far from the myth that they can only remember anything for three seconds, goldfish can be trained to recognize color patterns and to complete an obstacle course. And they can remember them up to three months later.

EDISON didn't invent the lightbulb or ELECTRICITY. Joseph Swan demonstrated a working lightbulb nine months before Edison, but Edison got his patent in first. And although Edison pioneered direct current electricity, it was Nikola Tesla, funded by George Westinghouse, who created alternating current.

WATER does not **SPIRAL** down drains COUNTERCLOCKWISE in the northern hemisphere, clockwise in the southern, and straight down at the equator—it spirals whichever way you swirl it. The Coriolis force affects the direction of wind patterns and cyclones but nothing as insignificant as bathwater.

HAIR AND NAILS do not continue growing after DEATH. Biological functions cease at death, and it is a myth that hair and nails continue growing. They appear to do so because, as the body dehydrates, the skin shrinks back, making hair (particularly facial hair) and nails appear longer by comparison.

In 2002, the news media reported that **BLONDES** will be EXTINCT by 2202 because too few people carry the gene. Not only is this untrue, but it's not even news—bogus reports of blonde extinction have been circulating since 1865.

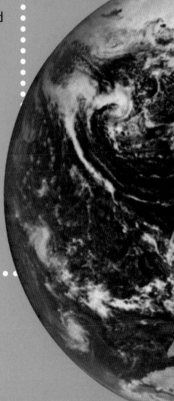

In 1938, long before humans ventured into space, American explorer Richard Halliburton wrote: "Astronomers say that **THE GREAT WALL** of China is the only man-made object visible FROM THE MOON." The myth continues, despite the fact that Apollo astronauts have since stated that no man-made objects are visible from the Moon.

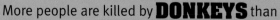

More people are killed by **DONKEYS** than AIRPLANE CRASHES. So The Times newspaper in the UK reported an expert saying in 1987. The expert is not named and the estimate cannot be verified because no one keeps a global record of donkey deaths.

O n the catwalk, the 2000s ushered in the "size 0" debate. Are stick-thin fashion models bad role models? Meanwhile, on stage and screen, the gossip has been all about artificial enhancement—who's had what done out of the dizzying array of "improvements" available, from nips, tucks, and augmentations to reductions, injections, and implants.

00s

IDOLS

Latin-American pop singer to make No. 1 in the US, UK, and Australia.

03. GEORGE CLOONEY from ER to "A" list.

04. SCARLETT JOHANSSON frequently voted the sexiest woman alive.

05. GISELE BUNDCHEN Brazilian supermodel, said to be the world's highest-paid model.

06. KYLIE MINOGUE from Aussie soapstar to global sex symbol.

07. BEYONCE KNOWLES singer, actress, dancer, and model.

08. TYSON BECKFORD Bronx-born model and actor, one of the world's richest male supermodels.

ANGELINA JOLIE (main photo, left) Looking fetishistic at a photography exhibition launch party in Tokyo in 2005.

01. PENELOPE CRUZ the Spanish siren pouts for the camera.

02. SHAKIRA Colombian singer, dancer, and actress, the first

I DO HAVE TATTOOS AND I DO WEAR LEATHER, BUT THERE ARE OTHER SIDES OF ME— ANGELINA JOLIE

the panel on which the Mona Lisa is painted has the 1:1.618 golden ratio

bodice to hands is in golden ratio to width of body

Mona Lisa

eye to top of face: width of eyes

the eye itself fits the golden ratio

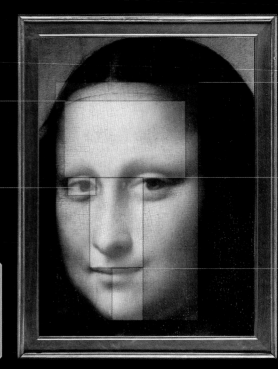

the whole face conforms to perfect mathematical proportions

width of mouth: eyes to mouth

half width of mouth: chin to mouth

Critics still argue about whether or not Leonardo da Vinci applied the golden ratio to the Mona Lisa consciously or unconsciously. Did he construct her face according to mathematical principles or does her face happen to fit the golden proportions because our instinctive idea of beauty does so? The rectangles placed over her face are in the 1:1.618 proportions of the golden ratio.

CUSTOM AND ETIQUETTE

RULES OF ATTRACTION

DIVINE PROPORTIONS

Next time you tell someone they look divine you'll be able to explain the science behind it. Ancient Greek mathematicians were fascinated by a ratio that kept cropping up in their geometry: 1:1.618, which they called phi. In 1509, Italian mathematician Luca Pacioli explained in his book *De Divina Proportione* how objects

We all know an ideal face when we see one but what makes it perfect? Is beauty really in the eye of the beholder, as the proverb suggests, or is there a science behind it? Well, yes. Symmetry is important but there's more to it than that—the ancient Greeks recognized a mathematical "golden ratio." Its proportions are most pleasing to the eye, and the most beautiful faces fit that ratio.

Italian sculptor Michelangelo applied the golden ratio to his sculpture David—the Renaissance ideal of male beauty—both in the proportions of the body and of the face. The width of David's mouth is the same as the distance between his eyes and correlates to the eye-to-mouth measurement.

David

• Ingrid Bergman •

▲ The shape and size of her head corresponds to the golden proportion.

► Chin-to-eye length and width of mouth fit ratio

► The width of her chin is in proportion to the distance to her eyes and from one pupil to the other.

• Audrey Hepburn •

► Width of mouth fits with length from mouth to eyebrows.

▼ Eye-to-nose length corresponds to the width of her eyes.

• Lucy Liu •

▼ Ear-to-ear distance is in ratio to ear-to-chin distance.

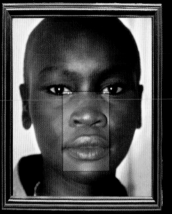

• Alek Wek •

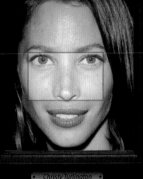

• Christy Turlington •

• Queen Nefertiti •

with proportions in the ratio of 1:1.618 were aesthetically most pleasing. The book was illustrated by Leonardo da Vinci, who is thought to have used these proportions—later known as the golden ratio—in the Mona Lisa. Together, Pacioli and da Vinci brought phi to the attention of artists and architects, who began to use it in their work. More recently, physiognomists have noted that phi appears in faces consistently seen as beautiful, in the ratio of eye-to-mouth width, pupil-to-nose width, eye-to-nose height, and so on.

phi = 1.618034

5 ASPECTS OF OUTER BEAUTY

1 SYMMETRY
2 PROPORTION
3 COMPLEXION
4 YOUTHFULNESS
5 HEALTH

5 ASPECTS OF INNER BEAUTY

1 INTELLIGENCE
2 GENEROSITY
3 HUMOR
4 EXUBERANCE
5 SYMPATHY

5 WAYS MAGAZINES MODIFY FACES

1 IMPROVING SKIN TONE
2 AIRBRUSHING WRINKLES
3 AIRBRUSHING FRECKLES AND BLEMISHES
4 BRIGHTENING EYES
5 WHITENING TEETH

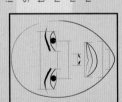

• James Dean •

▲ Width of eyes fits with eyes-to-nose length.

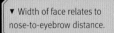

▼ Width of face relates to nose-to-eyebrow distance.

◄ The jaw width is in proportion to the length from chin to nose.

► Width of eyes corresponds to distance from eyes to mouth.

• Rudolph Valentino •

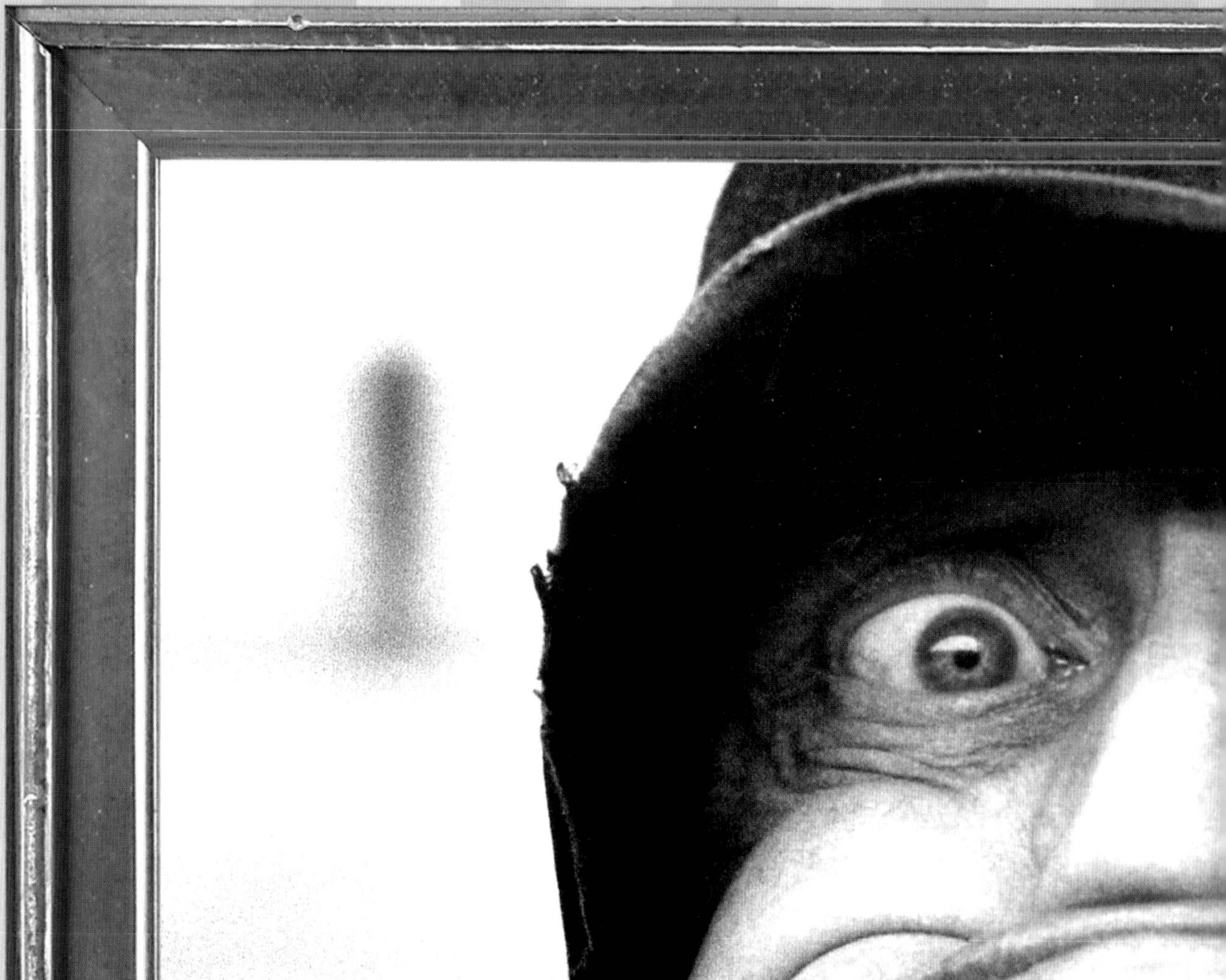

Some humans strive for beauty, others for ugliness. Gurning – named after an ugly fish called a gurnard – is the art of pulling ugly faces: no golden ratio here. World Gurning Championships are held annually in Cumbria, England.

OUT OF PLACE

Ever wondered who makes up the names humans use for everyday objects? Quite often they come from Latin or Greek, but far more interesting are the ones named after places. This handy map shows you the location of 25 places in the world that are better known for the objects named after them.

(1) NOKIA The small town of Nokia, on the banks of the Nokianvirta River in western Finland, is home to one of the biggest telecommunications companies in the world. Nokia started life as the local paper mill.

(2) MAGENTA As a marketing ploy for the recently discovered dye, the color magenta was named after the Battle of Magenta, which took place on June 4, 1859, near the Italian town of Magenta.

(3) MARATHON This long-distance footrace commemorates the feat of the ancient Greek messenger Pheidippedes, who died after running about 22 miles (35 km) from Marathon to Athens with news of the Athenian victory at the Battle of Marathon in 490BCE.

(4) NEANDERTHAL The name for Stone Age humans derives from the place where the first remains were found: the Neander Valley (*Thal*) in Germany, itself named after theologian Joachim Neander.

(5) COACH/KOCS The various vehicles described as coaches, from horse-drawn to railroad carriages, all take their name from the Hungarian town of Kocs, where particularly fine examples were made during the 15th century.

(6) MOTOWN The Motown (aka Tamla-Motown) record label is named after its city of origin: Detroit, Michigan, also known as Motor City.

(7) RUGBY Rugby football is named after the private school in Rugby, England, where the rules were codified in 1846 by senior pupils.

(8) MANILA The fiber used for manila rope and manila paper (often for envelopes) is named after Manila, capital city of the Philippines.

(9) HAVANA Havana cigars are named after the city of Havana, capital of Cuba, where they are made. The name may come from a native chief.

(10) OLYMPIC GAMES/ OLYMPIA/MOUNT OLYMPUS The modern Olympic Games were inspired by an ancient Greek festival in honor of the god Zeus, who held court on Mount Olympus. The valley where the festival took place was named Olympia.

(11) BIKINI In 1946, French designer Jacques Heim unveiled a tiny two-piece swimsuit that he said would be as explosive as the atomic bomb, tested four days earlier on the Bikini Atoll in the Pacific.

(12) JEANS/GENOA Jeans are named after their original fabric: a heavy twilled cotton called gene fustian, first made in Genoa, Italy (*Gênes* in French).

(13) DENIM/NÎMES Denim is the name of fabric first made in Nîmes, France, where it is called *serge de Nîmes*.

(14) ANGORA This fine wool comes from Angora rabbits. It is similar to mohair, the hair of Angora goats. The animals are named after an earlier name for Ankara, the capital of Turkey.

(15) BALACLAVA This hat-mask, designed to protect British soldiers in the Crimean War from the cold, was named after the town where the Battle of Balaclava was fought in 1854.

(16) TUXEDO The first dinner jacket was worn by American Griswold Lorillard to the Autumn Ball of the Tuxedo Park Country Club in New York in 1886.

(17) CADILLAC The car company was named after 17th-century French explorer Antoine Laumet de La Mothe, sieur de Cadillac, who in 1701 founded Detroit, Michigan, where Cadillacs were first built. Cadillac is an area of the Gironde, France.

(18) PARMESAN/PARMA Parmesan cheese and Parma ham both take their name from the Italian province of Parma where they originate.

(19) SKID ROW Skid row means a run-down neighborhood. To be "on skid row" means to be down on your luck. The original Skid Row was in Seattle, Washington.

(20) PORT/OPORTO Port is named after the Portuguese district of Oporto, where wine merchants first began fortifying wine with brandy in the 18th century.

(21) BUDWEISER/BUDWEIS This trademark used by two brewers, one American and one Czech, derives from Budweis, the German name for the Czech town of Budejovice.

FEZ This red felt hat, aka a *checheya* or *tarboosh*, is named after the Moroccan city of Fez, where it originated.

22

23

CHAMPAGNE Sparkling wine is only Champagne if it was made in the northeast French region of Champagne.

24

LESBIAN/LESBOS The Greek poet Sappho, who wrote love poems about other women, was born on the island of Lesbos, hence the name "lesbian" for a woman who loves another woman.

25

HAMBURGER/HAMBURG German immigrants brought the Hamburg steak to the US in the late 1800s, where it was later served on a bun and called a hamburger. Similarly, frankfurter is a sausage originating in the Germany city of Frankfurt.

1 2 3 4 5 6 7 8 9 10 11 12 13 14 15 16 17 18 19 20 21 22 23 24 25

SIGN LANGUAGE

Don't know the local language? Hand signs can be a useful way to get your message across. But beware—they don't all mean the same thing everywhere. Some may be friendly enough at home, but could get you into serious trouble in other parts of the world.

RISK FACTOR: ✴ **DANGEROUS** ✴ **MEDIUM** ✴ **HARMLESS**

TIME OUT

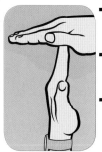

- US: time out (most sports) or technical foul (basketball)
- UK: tea break (cultural equivalent of time out)
- Japan: check please!

✴ ✴ ✴ ✴ ✴

BECKON

- General meaning: come here (impolite)
- Possible sexual invitation depending on circumstance

✴ ✴ ✴ ✴ ✴ UNIVERSAL

THE FINGER

- Universal meaning: "f**k you"; aka "middle finger salute"; "flipping the bird"
- Ancient Romans called this gesture *digitus impudicus*

✴ ✴ ✴ ✴ ✴ UNIVERSAL

POINT

- Universal way of indicating a particular object or direction
- Most cultures consider it rude to point at a person
- The ability to follow a pointing finger is said to be the origin of language

✴ ✴ ✴ ✴ ✴ UNIVERSAL

VICTORY/PEACE

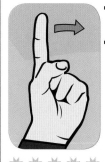

- Meaning: often "Victory" (from WWII); since the 1960s "Peace"
- Italy, Spain, Portugal (if done behind someone's head): "cuckold" (offensive)

✴ ✴ ✴ ✴ ✴
✴ ✴ ✴ ✴ ✴

REVERSE VICTORY

- UK/Aus: "f**k off"—a slightly less offensive version of the finger, *above*
- UK: known as "V" sign
- US: synonymous with Victory/Peace sign (harmless)

✴ ✴ ✴ ✴ ✴

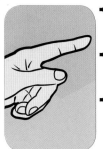

THUMBS UP

→ US and Western Europe: sign of approval
→ Middle East, West Africa, South America, Russia: "Up yours" (offensive)
→ Origin: Roman gladiatorial games

INDEX FINGER

→ US and Western Europe: one, "wait", or "one moment"
→ Middle East, Turkey, Greece: "f**k you"

HORNS

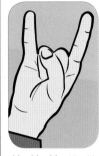

→ Occult: to give or ward off the evil eye
→ For Pagans: the horned god
→ For Satanists: the devil
→ Italy, Brazil: "your wife is messing around"
→ Rock music: heavy metal salute

HAND WAVE

→ Universal meaning: hello or goodbye
→ China: if palm down means come here

VULCAN SALUTE

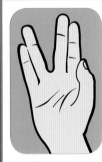

→ TV culture: "Live long and prosper"—used in the TV series *Star Trek* by the character Spock, a member of the fictional species of pointy-eared Vulcans
→ Origin: benedictory gesture in Judaism

UNIVERSAL

OK

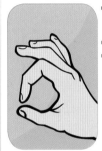

→ US/Europe (except Germany): OK
→ Japan: money
→ Brazil, Germany: in these countries this gesture means "a***hole" (extremely offensive)

CLENCHED FIST

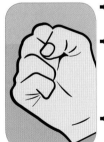

→ Used at head height: sign of aggression
→ When raised high by nationalist, revolutionary, and oppressed groups: defiance (as in Black Power salute)
→ Military: request for heavy weapons

UNIVERSAL

BLAH BLAH

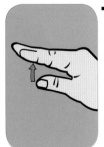

→ Meaning: too much talk/boring/I'm not listening (contemptuous)

UNIVERSAL

BANG BANG

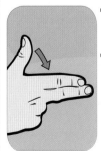

→ This can be used menacingly to mean "I am going to kill you"
→ US: It is also sometimes used as a greeting

UNIVERSAL

ODD JOBS

The saying goes that there are known knowns, known unknowns, and unknown unknowns. So it is with jobs. There are the traditional jobs that a human knows to be normal and there are the jobs that a human knows to be odd. Then there are the jobs that are so odd no one even knew they existed.

GROOM OF THE STOOL

In the courts of Britain's Tudor monarchs, the Groom of the Stool was responsible for the king's lavatorial needs, including wiping the royal bottom. One 15th-century text instructs: "Look there be blanket, cotton, or linen to wipe the nether end… "

WRINKLE CHASER

Ever wondered how shoe leather is so smooth when cows are not? That's thanks to the wrinkle chasers of this world, who iron out the wrinkles as the shoes are being made.

BODY PART DOUBLE

Humans all know that actors have stunt doubles for good reasons. But some actors aren't happy with their attributes, so they hire in other people's backsides, breasts, and so on for the close-ups.

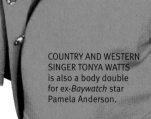

COUNTRY AND WESTERN SINGER TONYA WATTS is also a body double for ex-*Baywatch* star Pamela Anderson.

BULLET-PROOF VEST TESTER

These days, they use highly calibrated equipment but, at one time, they just took a guy outside and shot him. From 1919 until the 1950s, NYPD marksmen shot at Leo Krouse, who wore the latest bullet-proof vests made by the Spooner Armor Co.

CASTRATO

A castrato was a male singer with a high vocal range achieved through castration before puberty, usually by placing the victim in a bath so hot that he lost consciousness and then crushing the testicles manually. Popular in 17th- and 18th-century Italy, the last castrato died in 1922.

BIRD'S NEST COLLECTOR

Bird's nest soup is a prized delicacy in China and South-East Asia. It's made from the nests of cave swiftlets, and someone has to collect them. It's a dangerous job, involving clambering over vertiginous fragile bamboo scaffolding in dark underground caves.

HOT WALKER

The people who walk racehorses around after a race are known as hot walkers, and it's an important job: if a horse doesn't cool down properly before returning to the stall, the overheating can cause kidney damage.

TEAM MASCOT

Many sports fans might not think of this as a job, but it's hard work. One professional said it's like wearing a fur coat in a sauna while doing aerobics.

FLUFFER

Want a job in porn but not ready to strut your stuff in front of the cameras? Fluffers work off-camera making sure the male stars are ready to perform.

SANDWICH DESIGNER

It's not as simple as deciding between squares or triangles—it's about coming up with the new flavor combinations and thinking ahead to the Sandwich Designer of the Year Awards. (Yes, really.)

CHICKEN SEXER

Commercial breeders need to know the gender of chicks early, but it's hard to tell before six weeks. So they employ specially trained chicken sexers, who can tell by looking inside the rectum.

CHIMNEY SWEEP

A notoriously unpleasant and dangerous job in Victorian times, chimney sweeping improved with telescopic brushes and vacuum devices. Chimney sweeps currently command high wages because there are so few of them left.

PIG/BULL MASTURBATOR

The last thing livestock breeders want is for animals to have sex with each other. They collect semen to artificially inseminate the females—and for that they need someone to masturbate the males.

FURNITURE TESTER

Here's one for those who prefer their work horizontal (the salesmen above demonstrate how *not* to test a bed). Furniture companies need someone to test their sofas, reclining chairs, and beds.

JOB FOR LIFE

Many humans worry about what will happen to them if their job becomes redundant. No such worries for Michael Scott—as soon as he finishes painting San Francisco's Golden Gate Bridge it's time to start again at the other end.

Come fly with me

airline meals

1909 German Count Ferdinand von Zeppelin forms Deutsche Luftschiffahrt Aktiengesellschaft (Delag), the first commercial airline. Silver-service meals are served aboard his airships.

1914 The first full meal to be served on an airplane (as opposed to airship) is served on the giant biplane *Ilya Mourometz I* over Russia.

1919 The first regular airline meals are prepacked lunchboxes sold on Handley Page Transport's London–Brussels service, for 15 pence (75 cents) each.

1925 French airline Air Union claims to be the first to serve hot meals, comprising a five-course hot lunch with wine.

1952 The first airline meals to be served aboard a jet are served on BOAC's inaugural jet service between London and Johannesburg, marking the start of the modern era.

✈ 1950s MAGAZINE AD FOR AIR FRANCE HIGHLIGHTING THE IN-FLIGHT DINING EXPERIENCE.

Present Day
Modern airline meals are generally cooked, frozen, and then reheated on the ground before takeoff. They are usually bland in order to appeal to as many passengers as possible and to avoid flatulence and bad breath in the confined cabin. Special diets are catered to on request. Pilot and copilot eat completely different meals to minimize the risk of both contracting food poisoning.

✈ MODERN AIRLINE MEALS, KEPT WARM BY A METALLIC WRAP, USUALLY COME WITH A STARTER AND DESSERT.

airline safety

safest airlines
There are no official rankings for airline safety but according to www.askcaptainlim.com, the following airlines have the lowest accident rates (measured per 100,000 takeoffs):

1	AMERICA WEST (US)	0.00
	SOUTHWEST (US)	
	QANTAS (AUSTRALIA)	
4	ALL NIPPON (JAPAN)	0.22
5	DELTA (US)	0.23
6	BRITISH AIRWAYS (UK)	0.27
7	LUFTHANSA (GERMANY)	0.30
8	NORTHWEST (US)	0.35
9	CONTINENTAL AIRLINES (US)	0.40
10	UNITED AIRLINES (US)	0.43

black box
The flight data recorder, or "black box" (so called despite being bright orange or red), was invented by Australian David Warren in 1953 while investigating the crash of the world's first jet airliner, the de Havilland Comet. In 1960, Australia was the first country to make black boxes compulsory.

✈ FLIGHT DATA RECORDER, AKA THE "BLACK BOX."

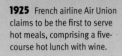

flying facts

1783 The Parisian suburb of Gonesse has connections with flight, long before Le Bourget and Charles de Gaulle airports are built nearby. In 1783, an unmanned hydrogen balloon, which has been launched in Paris, lands in Gonesse and is attacked by locals, who think it is a monster.

1853 The first heavier-than-air craft to carry a human in free flight is a glider manned by inventor George Cayley's coachman, who afterward said: "Please, Sir George, I wish to give notice. I was hired to drive, not to fly."

1890 Steam plays a part in the pioneering of flight. The first heavier-than-air craft to take off under its own power is a steam-powered monoplane built by Frenchman Clément Ader. The last steam-powered flight is in 1894.

1903 At 10:35 a.m. on December 17, the Wright Brothers make what is generally accepted to be the first sustained, controlled, and manned airplane flight. This famous flight covers less distance than the wingspan of a Jumbo Jet.

in-flight entertainment

worst airlines

The 10 airline accidents (excluding terrorist acts) with the greatest number of fatalities are:

1	PAN AM/KLM	Canary Islands. Runway collision. 583 killed.
2	JAPAN AIRLINES	Japan. Aircraft hit mountain. 520 killed.
3	SAUDIA AIRLINES/ KAZAKH AIRLINES	India. Midair collision. 349 killed.
4	TURKISH AIRLINES	France. Crash immediately after takeoff due to open cargo door. 346 killed.
5	SAUDIA AIRLINES	Saudi Arabia. Onboard fire. 301 killed.
6	IRAN AIR	Persian Gulf. Shot down when *USS Vincennes* mistook it for enemy plane. 290 killed.
7	AMERICAN AIRLINES	US. Engine fell off. 273 killed.
8	KOREAN AIR	USSR. Shot down after straying into Soviet airspace. 269 killed.
9	AMERICAN AIRLINES	New York. Disintegrated in midair. 265 killed.
10	CHINA AIRLINES	Japan. Aircraft stalled at 300m (984ft). 264 killed.

1922 The first airline steward to serve on an airplane (as opposed to an airship) is Jack Sanderson of Daimler Airways.

1930 Lieutenant Ellen Church becomes the first stewardess, working for Boeing Air Transport (later part of United Airlines).

→ IN 1930, ELLEN CHURCH, A NURSE, BECAME THE FIRST STEWARDESS.

1925 The first in-flight movie is *The Lost World*, shown during an Imperial Airways flight.

→ *THE LOST WORLD* WAS THE FIRST IN-FLIGHT MOVIE AND ONE OF THE FIRST DINOSAUR MOVIES.

1947 Pan Am's *Clipper* magazine becomes the first in-flight magazine.

1961 The first regular in-flight movies are inaugurated on July 19 by TWA, with *By Love Possessed* on a flight from New York to Los Angeles.

comfort

Skytrax World Airline Star Ranking has awarded five stars to just four airlines for service and comfort: Cathay Pacific Airways, Malaysia Airlines, Qatar Airways, and Singapore Airlines.

survivors

The following have all survived plane crashes: politician Yasser Arafat; race car driver David Coulthard; actor and director Clint Eastwood; opera singer Luciano Pavarotti; rock star Sting; actor Patrick Swayze; actor Dame Elizabeth Taylor; and aviation pioneers the Wright brothers.

→ ELIZABETH TAYLOR AND MIKE TODD AND THEIR PLANE *THE LIZ*, 1958.

nonsurvivors

The following all died in aviation crashes: aerospace pioneers John Alcock, Amelia Earhart, Amy Johnson, and Yuri Gagarin; musicians Glenn Miller, Buddy Holly, the Big Bopper, Ritchie Valens, Otis Redding, and John Denver; boxer Rocky Marciano; and car manufacturer Charles Rolls.

→ BUDDY HOLLY (1936–59) WAS AN AMERICAN ROCK'N'ROLL PIONEER.

→ MAJOR GLENN MILLER (1904–44) WAS AN AMERICAN BANDLEADER.

1909 If he'd had an alarm clock, Hubert Latham might have been a household name. On July 25, Latham is due to make his second attempt at flying the English Channel—but he is woken by an aircraft engine as Louis Blériot takes off to achieve the historic first.

1919 When John Alcock and Arthur Brown make their famous first nonstop crossing of the Atlantic in June, they fly for 16.5 hours through fog and sleet in an open cockpit, with coffee, beer, sandwiches, and chocolate to sustain them. They end their historic journey by crashing nose-first in an Irish

1976 Concord means "agreement" or "peace and harmony." It is an apt name for the world's first supersonic airliner, which is a collaboration between Britain and France. The biggest argument is whether to spell the name with the final "e," as in French, or without, as in English.

→ THE AEROSPATIALE-BAE CONCORDE COULD FLY FROM LONDON TO NEW YORK

QUOTE UNQUOTE

They say a picture is worth a thousand words, but some people paint with words, creating striking visual images with their phrases. French writer André Breton thought that people who don't use their imagination visually are idiots—so, for any wordsmiths out there, here are a few choice phrases that conjure up graphic images.

" THE MAN WHO CAN'T VISUALIZE A HORSE GALLOPING ON A TOMATO IS AN IDIOT."

French writer and surrealist **André Breton**

A woman needs a man like a fish needs a bicycle.
Australian educator **Irina Dunn** *(often erroneously credited to Gloria Steinem)*

To see a world in a grain of sand
And heaven in a wild flower
Hold infinity in the palm of your hand
And eternity in an hour.
English poet, painter, and mystic **William Blake**

Every ceiling, when reached, becomes a floor upon which one walks as a matter of course and prescriptive right.
English writer **Aldous Huxley**

The true way leads along a tightrope, which is not stretched aloft but just above the ground. It seems more designed to trip than to be walked along.
Bohemian author **Franz Kafka**

" SPACE ISN'T REMOTE AT ALL. IT'S ONLY AN HOUR'S DRIVE AWAY IF YOUR CAR COULD GO STRAIGHT UPWARD."

English astronomer and mathematician
Sir Fred Hoyle

Imagine a number of men in chains, all under sentence of death, some of whom are each day butchered in sight of the others; those remaining see their own condition in that of their fellows, and looking at each other with grief and despair await their turn. This is an image of the human condition.
French philosopher **Blaise Pascal**

The great nations have always acted like gangsters, and the small nations like prostitutes.

US film director **Stanley Kubrick**

Air pollution is turning Mother Nature prematurely gray.

US newspaper columnist **Irv Kupcinet**

Age imprints more wrinkles in the mind than it does on the face.

French Renaissance writer
Michel de Montaigne

The epitome of love is a door without a handle.

English singer-songwriter **Tony Peek**

EVERYTHING IS A MIRACLE. IT'S A MIRACLE THAT ONE DOES NOT DISSOLVE IN ONE'S BATH LIKE A LUMP OF SUGAR."

Spanish artist **Pablo Picasso**

I like to drive with my knees; otherwise, how can I put on my lipstick and talk on the phone?

American actress **Sharon Stone**

Writing a book of poetry is like dropping a rose petal down the Grand Canyon and waiting for the echo.

US novelist, playwright, and poet **Don Marquis**

Youth leaks from you. It doesn't leave a note or slam the door. You're just left there older, with dead spiders for eyes and fire-retardant hair.

Irish comedian **Dylan Moran**

WHEN A DOG BITES A MAN THAT IS NOT NEWS, BUT WHEN A MAN BITES A DOG THAT IS NEWS."

Disputed: variously attributed to New York Sun editor **John B. Bogart**,
US journalist **Charles Anderson Dana**, *and US architect*
Charles Amos Cummings

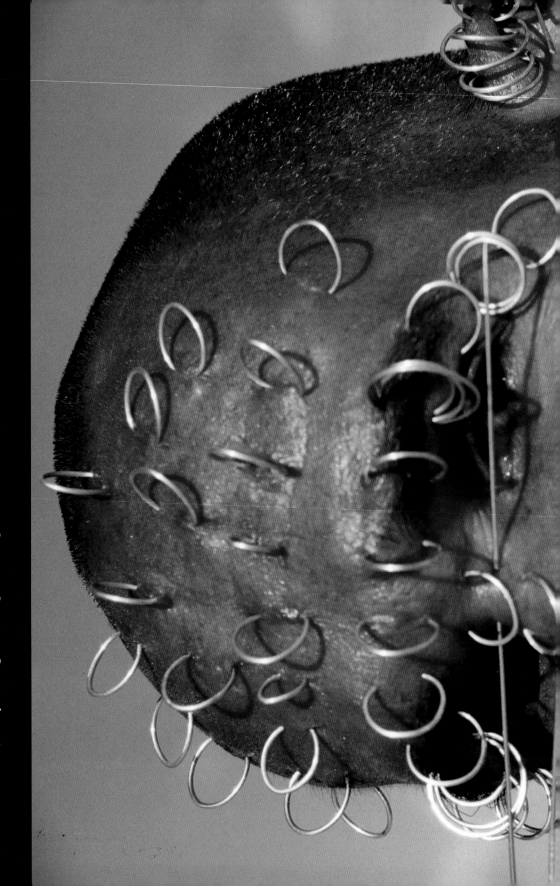

LORD OF THE RINGS

Body piercing is popular with humans of many cultures, although this man is likely to have a problem getting through airport metal detectors, to say nothing of shaving or blowing his nose.

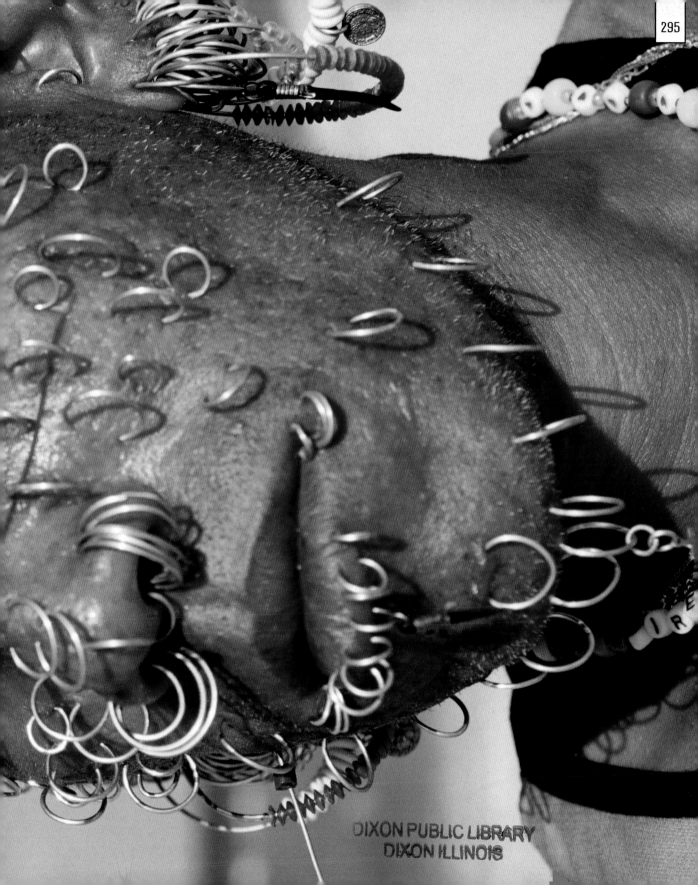

TECHNOLOGY
HUMAN TRANSPORTERS

Most humans are quite happy to travel around in ordinary planes, trains, automobiles, and boats—the kind that are available to everyone. But there's always someone striving to be different. The result is some weird and wonderful vehicles, such as boats modeled on dolphins and tanks modeled on legs.

TRANSFORMER MONSTER TRUCK

Based on the children's line of toys that transform from motor vehicles and planes into awesome robots, this Transformer Monster Truck shoots flames during a 1996 show in Denver, Colorado.

SPACESHIPONE

On October 4, 2004, SpaceShipOne, air-launched from on top of an airplane, won the $10 million Ansari X Prize as the first privately built reusable manned spacecraft to go into space twice within two weeks.

DOLPHIN WATERCRAFT

The Innespace Dolphin is a submersible personal watercraft. The "downward lift" of its wings enables it to dive, jump, and barrel roll just like a dolphin.

LAND WALKER

The camouflage and guns on the side of this "bipedal exoskeleton"—or "walking tank" to the rest of us—suggests it will have a military application. At 11 ft (3.4 m) tall and weighing 2,205 lb (1,000 kg), it's an imposing figure, but it only moves at 0.93 mph (1.5 km/h).

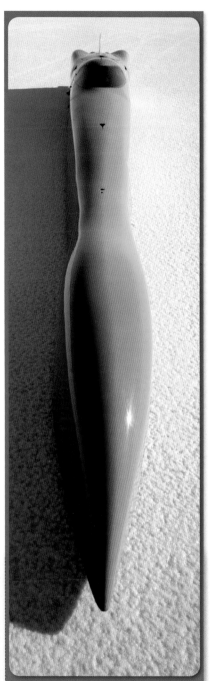

THRUST SSC

SSC stands for Supersonic Car, and on October 15, 1997, *Thrust SSC* lived up to its name when RAF pilot Andy Green drove it across Black Rock Desert, Nevada, at 763.035 mph (1,227.952 km/h).

STREAMLINED RACE CAR

Many modern vehicles are aerodynamically designed for speed and fuel efficiency. This racing car, seen at Bonneville Salt Flats, Utah, takes streamlining to the extreme.

LITTLE SOCCER
HORRORS

With most sports your chances of injury are pretty low unless you're actually playing. Sadly, that's not true of soccer, which has seen a number of notorious incidents where crowd trouble or poor crowd control has led to large numbers of spectators being injured or killed.

OLYMPIC MAYHEM One of the worst death tolls resulting directly from crowd rioting occurred during the qualifying rounds for the 1964 Olympic Games. The Games themselves were held in Tokyo during October but the qualifying match between Latin American rivals Argentina and Peru was played on May 24, 1964, at the National Stadium in Lima, Peru. With Argentina a goal ahead, the referee disallowed a Peruvian equalizer two minutes from time. Two fans stormed the field and attacked the referee, and when he consequently stopped the game all hell broke loose. **Fans tore up the stadium and then went on the rampage through Lima** —318 people were killed, another 500–1,000 injured, and martial law was declared in order to quell the rioting. At the Games that October Hungary won gold, Czechoslovakia silver, and Germany bronze.

SOCCER WAR During the late 1960s, large-scale emigration from El Salvador to neighboring Honduras led to political tension, which erupted into a war. It has been **dubbed the Soccer War, because it followed escalating crowd trouble** at three qualifying matches for the 1970 FIFA World Cup. There were minor disturbances at the first game on June 6, 1969, when Honduras beat El Salvador 1–0 in Honduras. A week later, on June 15, El Salvador beat Honduras 3–0 in El Salvador and there was violence against the Honduran fans. It led to border closure and recriminations against Salvadorians living in Honduras. There was full-scale rioting at the playoff in Mexico on June 27—in which El Salvador beat Honduras 3–2 to qualify—and Honduras broke off diplomatic relations with El Salvador. Eighteen days later, on July 14, the Salvadorian army and air force attacked Honduras, making some headway across the border before stalling due to fuel and ammunition shortages. The main fighting lasted four days— the Soccer War is also known as the 100 Hours War—and there was a ceasefire on July 20 after six days. Losses were c. 2,000 on each side.

SOVIET UNDERSTATEMENT In 1982 Dutch club HFC Haarlem qualified for the UEFA Cup for the first (and so far only) time. Having beaten AA Ghent 5–4 on aggregate, on October 20 that year they traveled to Spartak Moscow's Luzhniki Stadium for the first leg of the second round— **a match that was to prove memorable for the wrong reasons.** Gess scored for Spartak after 17 minutes, and with the score still at 1–0 with only a few minutes remaining, many fans began to leave early through the only exit that had been left open. Then, on 90 minutes, Shvetsov scored Spartak's second goal and many of the leaving fans tried to return to the stand, colliding with others who were on their way out. Police allegedly prevented anyone from returning by **pushing fans down the narrow icy staircase, resulting in a stampede that killed an estimated 340 people, the worst spectator disaster on record.** The official death toll was 66, and the only mention in the Soviet media was two sentences at the end of the match report, stating: "Yesterday in Luzhniki after the soccer match an accident occurred. There are some injured among the spectators." The full story did not emerge until an independent inquiry was held in 1989. In 2007, the 25th anniversary of the tragedy, Spartak and Haarlem played a memorial game.

Not surprisingly, this caused a stampede...

HEYSEL HOOLIGANS

Football hooliganism reached its lowest point on May 29, 1985, at the European Cup Final between the holders, Liverpool, and the Cup Winner's Cup holders, Juventus, in Heysel Stadium, Brussels. Opposing fans in adjacent sections of the aging stadium began throwing missiles at each other. About an hour before kickoff, Liverpool fans broke through an inadequate security fence separating them from the Juventus fans. After a running battle on the terraces, a mass of British supporters charged toward Italian fans, who pressed back against a wall. It collapsed, crushing many of them to death. Despite the deaths, the fighting continued for two hours, with Juventus fans attempting to charge the Liverpool fans in retaliation for the initial attack; both sides threw bottles, cans, and even pieces of concrete from the collapsed wall. **With the authorities fearing further trouble if the game was abandoned, it kicked off with riot police still fighting the Juventus fans.** Juventus won 1–0. Thirty-nine people had been killed and some 600 injured in what Time magazine called "Soccer's Day of Shame" and a subsequent UEFA chief called "the darkest hour in the history of the UEFA competitions." British Prime Minister Margaret Thatcher and the Queen both issued formal apologies to the people of Belgium and Italy, and British clubs were banned indefinitely from playing in Europe. The ban was eventually lifted in 1990.

Soccer's day of shame... the darkest hour

GATE OF FIRE

Matches between the Argentinian clubs Boca Juniors and River Plate are known as El Superclásico—the superderby. Their rivalry is so renowned that one British newspaper listed watching them play in Buenos Aires as one of the "50 sporting things you must do before you die." Unfortunately, that is just what 74 people did on June 23, 1968, when **Boca fans dropped burning torches onto River fans** from a balcony above the lower terraces. In the panic, many River fans tried to escape through Gate 12, which was locked, causing a crush that killed 74 fans and injured more than 150 others.

HILLSBOROUGH

Britain's worst sports disaster occurred before the scheduled FA Cup semifinal between Nottingham Forest and Liverpool, which was to be played on April 15, 1989, at Sheffield Wednesday's Hillsborough Stadium. Thousands of Liverpool fans arrived late and, as the 3 o'clock kickoff drew closer, a bottleneck of c. 5,000 people developed outside the turnstiles at the Leppings Lane end of the stadium. Fearing violence, and in a misguided attempt to relieve the crush, police made a fatal decision. They opened a gate without turnstiles, causing a sudden rush of people onto the already crowded terraces. People at the front were crushed against the high-security fencing, an antihooligan feature of most soccer stadia at the time. (Such fencing was removed from all grounds after the inquiry into the Hillsborough disaster.) **At first the authorities were unaware there was anything wrong** and Forest fans at the other end of the stadium jeered, thinking Liverpool fans were causing trouble. But when police ran onto the field and ordered the referee to stop the game, and as bodies were passed over the fencing and laid out on the field, the scale became clear—96 Liverpool fans had been killed and another 200 injured. A memorial to the 96 who died stands outside Hillsborough, bearing the title of the Liverpool club song: "You'll Never Walk Alone."

"You'll Never Walk Alone"

MAFIA ITALY/US

Also known as the Cosa Nostra ("our thing") and the Mob, the Mafia originated in 19th-century Sicily and spread to Italy and the US. Unlike street gangs, the Mafia has no obvious hand signals, tattoos, or symbols. Nor do they have a distinctive dress code, preferring expensive suits to baseball caps or jackets emblazoned with logos. Initiates take a vow of *omertà*, or silence, forbidding them from cooperating with the authorities.

YARDIES JAMAICA/UK/US

The name refers to the back streets ("backyards") of Trenchtown, Jamaica, where crime and gang violence became the norm in the 1950s, and it is now used to describe gangs of Jamaican descent in the UK and the US. In contrast with their impoverished roots, Yardies flaunt their wealth with expensive cars, designer gold jewelry, and automatic weapons.

AL CAPONE, head of the Chicago Mafia, on his way to Atlanta Federal Penitentiary after conviction for Federal Income Tax Evasion in 1932.

BIKER GANGS US/WORLD

American gangs include the Bandidos (founded in 1966 in Texas), Outlaws (founded in Illinois in 1935), Pagans (founded in 1959 in Maryland) and, most famous of all, Hells Angels, which was formed in 1948 in Fontana, California, and now has an estimated 2,500 members in 30 countries. Distinguishing features are denim vests emblazoned with the club name, colors, and chapter location.

HELLS ANGELS at 4th July weekend event.

GANG CULTURE

Throughout history humans have gathered together in groups for safety, comradeship, or mutual well-being. On the streets of cities around the world this tribal instinct can be seen in the way that people form gangs, many of which can be identitifed by their own signs, symbols, hand signals, and dress codes.

YAKUZA JAPAN

Also known as the "Japanese Mafia," the Yakuza is one of the world's largest organized crime syndicates, originating in roaming bands of "masterless Samurai." The name reflects these humble origins, deriving from Ya-Ku-Sa, or 8-9-3, the weakest hand in the Japanese card game *Oichu-Kabu*, which is said to indicate the organization's ability to overcome the worst odds. Distinguishing features include full-body tattoos and missing fingers, due to the practice of *yubitsume*—cutting off your finger as an apology for transgressions.

PEOPLE NATION & FOLK NATION US

Most street gangs in the US are broadly affiliated to one of two "unions": the People Nation and the Folk Nation. Gang symbols appear as graffiti on their home turf and are often embroidered on jackets or baseball caps. People Nation symbols are based around the number five (for example, a hand, five-pointed crown, or five-pointed star) and the left, or sinister, side. Folk Nation symbols are themed around the number six (for example, a six-pointed star or die showing 6) and aspects of the devil, such as horns or tail.

TRIADS CHINA

Triad is a collective term for various underground gangs and criminal organizations operating in China, Hong Kong, Taiwan, and Western countries with large Chinese populations. Triads originated in an 18th-century resistance movement whose goal was to restore the Han dynasty: one of its names was *Sanhehui* ("Three Harmonies Society") and it used triangles in its imagery, hence the name Triad. During the 20th century, Triads metamorphosed from a patriotic organization into a criminal one. Like the Mafia, members have no obvious distinguishing characteristics.

TRIAD SOCIETY is portayed in the bloody film *A Better Tomorrow II*.

NORTEÑOS/SUREÑOS US

Two groups of California Latino gangs unrelated to the People Nation or Folk Nation, see below, are the Norteños ("northerners," from north of Delano, California) and Sureños ("southerners"). Norteño emblems are based on the color red, the letter "N" (for prison gang Nuestra Familia), and the number 14 or 4, "N" being the 14th letter of the alphabet. Sureño emblems are based on the color blue, the letter "M" (for prison gang Mexican Mafia), and the number 13 or 3.

BNG PHILIPPINES/EUROPE/AMERICAS

The infamous Bahala Na Gang ("Come What May Gang") originated during the 1940s as a Filipino prison gang. During the 1990s, the BNG rose to prominence in the Philippines as a perpetrator of high-profile crimes such as murder, drug trafficking, car-jacking, and kidnapping, and has since extended operations into Europe and the Americas. Identifying symbols include a question-mark tattoo on any part of the body.

LA-BASED BLOODS wearing distinctive red bandanas. Members tend to align themselves with the People Nation.

NOT IN REAL LIFE

All humans know that movies aren't real. But films should be believable, and to do that they have to obey the laws of physics. Otherwise, instead of escaping into the fantasy world, a human tends to sit there nudging the person in the next seat, saying: "It wouldn't happen like that."

Star Wars: Return of the Jedi (1983)

SPACE
- Large asteroids are thousands of miles apart, which means that spaceships would not have to dodge continuously to avoid them.
- Sound does not travel through the near-vacuum of space, so any explosion would be silent, as in early episodes of *Star Trek*. If sound did travel through space, it would travel more slowly than light, so the sound would come after the flash, like thunder after lightning.
- Spaceships need thrust to change direction: they don't bank like airplanes, as occurs in *Star Wars* and countless other space-combat scenes.

GUNS
- Fired one-handed, a .44 caliber Magnum, as used in *Dirty Harry,* would be uncontrollable, the recoil lifting the barrel, possibly breaking the firer's wrist, and sending the bullet into the air.
- Real bullets don't flash when they hit an object, even a metal one. They're made of lead and sometimes clad with copper, neither of which sparks even when impacting on steel.
- A real machine gun would need to be reloaded after 1.8 seconds of rapid fire. And if it could be fired continuously, as in *Terminator*, *Matrix* etc, it would overheat to the point of the barrel melting.
- Real bullets do not pack enough punch to hurl a victim backward through the air.

Dirty Harry (1971)

The Dukes of Hazzard (2005)

TRANSPORTATION
- Real helicopters are flown from the right-hand seat, but in Batman Forever, Die Another Day, and Rambo, the pilot sits on the left. M:I2 and X-Men got it right.
- Real cars don't explode as soon as they hit something. Even if the car does catch fire, explosions are rare and delayed.
- A real vehicle can only jump a gap with a steep launching ramp, but movie vehicles often do so from a shallow incline or, as in *Speed*, with no incline at all.

ACTION
- A real person trying to jump through a safety-glass window would knock themselves out; if they jumped through a plate-glass window, they would tear themselves to shreds. In films, they escape unhurt through a shower of broken glass.
- Real terrorists do not plant bombs with large, bright-red LED countdown timers, as in *Broken Arrow, The Fifth Element,* etc.
- Real laser beams are not visible unless they're passing through a medium that scatters the light, such as smoke; security beams don't show up in the air so that people can conveniently step over them.
- A real person cannot outrun an explosion and dive for cover before the blast reaches them—explosions occur at more than 135,000 mph (217,260 kmph) and the current 100 m record is less than 23 mph (37 kmph).
- A real cigarette cannot ignite a pool of gasoline.

X-Men: The Last Stand (2006)

WESTERNS
- A real six gun can only fire six rounds before being reloaded.
- Two wranglers are often seen driving massive herds of cattle that would require at least three times that number of wranglers to control them.
- Cowboys are often portrayed eating cans of beans by the fire but, according to Western author Owen Wister, who witnessed the Wild West first hand, their staple diet was canned sardines, potted chicken, and canned devilled ham.

SUPERHEROES
- You know that superheroes don't exist, but they're portrayed as existing in the real world and operating in cities populated by real humans. If a superhero were able to catch a falling heroine, the chances are that the sudden deceleration would break her neck.

Superman: The Movie (1978)

Cowboy (1958)

HISTORICAL
- Dinosaurs and cavemen existed in different eras of history. They didn't coexist, as in films like D. W. Griffiths' *One Million BC* and the 1966 remake *One Million Years BC.*
- Victorian London smogs were a dirty greenish-yellow (hence the name "pea souper"), not white, as in films like *From Hell.*
- In the US and Britain, witches were hanged or pressed, not burned at the stake as in *Witchcraft* and *Love at the Stake*. *The Crucible* got it right.

One Million BC (1940)

CHAPTER

1

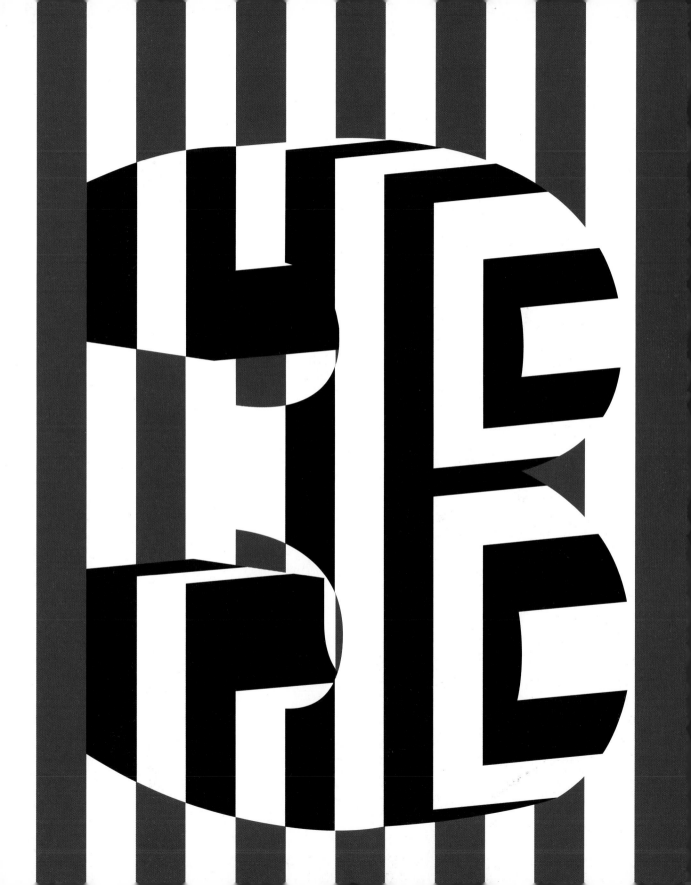

13

The US flag, the *Stars & Stripes*, has 13 stripes, representing the original 13 states that secured independence from Britain ❋ The US dollar bill carries references to the 13 states: a pyramid with 13 levels, a shield with 13 bars, and an eagle with 13 stars over its head, 13 arrows in its left talon, and in its right an olive branch with 13 leaves and 13 olives. Two Latin phrases on the bill each have 13 letters ❋ Fear of number 13 is termed triskaidekaphobia ❋ A deck of cards has 13 cards in each suit ❋ In Tarot, card no. 13 is Death ❋ A defining feature of rugby league is that there are 13 players on a team—in France it is known as Rugby à Treize or Jeu à Treize (Game of 13) ❋ 13 steps lead up to a gallows where condemned criminals are hanged ❋ 13 is considered unlucky in many cultures, so many American buildings do not have a 13th floor. The superstition was strengthened when the US Apollo 13 Moon mission suffered a near-fatal explosion ❋ The 1980 slasher film *Friday the 13th* and its many sequels took their titles from the fact that Friday is considered the unluckiest day of the week and the 13th the unluckiest date of the month, so the combination is doubly unlucky ❋ If the first of a month is a Sunday, the 13th will be a Friday ❋ Ancient Egyptians believed that

13 stages of learning were required to attain wisdom ✲ The superstition that it is unlucky to seat 13 people at a dinner table originates in Norse myth, which says that Loki intruded at a banquet in Valhalla, becoming the 13th guest, and Balder was killed as a result. The superstition was reinforced by Christ's Last Supper with his 12 disciples, after which both he and Judas Iscariot met their demise. In France, people called *quatorzièmes* used to be paid to attend a meal if a 14th person was required at the table ✲ 13 is the age at which Jewish boys are considered responsible for their actions, and become Bar Mitzvah, or "one to whom the commandments apply" ✲ For Sikhs, 13 is lucky because the Punjabi word for 13 also means "yours," which resonates with "I am yours, O Lord" ✲ The Aztec week had 13 days ✲ The Kabbalah names 13 spirits of evil ✲ There are 13 lunar months in the year, which led various civilizations, including the Maya and Jews, to consider 13 an auspicious number ✲ The equation $13^2=169$ is also true if the digits are reversed: $961=31^2$.

REACH FOR THE SKY

How long does it take humans to build a skyscraper? The foundations of the world's tallest building were laid in 1999 and it opened five years later in 2004. But it would take a lot longer than that if they were working from scratch —to learn how to make safety elevators, steel, reinforced concrete, and curtain walls would take about 3,500 years.

START HERE
TO GO BACK
THROUGH HISTORY

◄ 2004: TAIPEI 101 IN TAIPEI CITY, TAIWAN

THE WORLD'S TALLEST BUILDINGS

At one time, nations showed off their wealth by building temples, cathedrals, and palaces. Now it's skyscrapers. For over a century, the US boasted the world's tallest buildings but, in 1996, Asia took over with Malaysia's Petronas Twin Towers. In 2004, Taipei 101 in Taipei City, Taiwan, became the world's tallest habitable building at 101 stories and a roof height of 1,474 ft (449.2 m), incorporating a special pendulum to prevent it from moving too much in the wind. But it won't remain the tallest for long—two super-skyscrapers are under construction in Dubai, both of which are expected to be over 2,300 ft (700 m) tall.

RISING LAND PRICES

It wasn't just advancing technology that prompted the rise of the skyscraper—it was also about economics. Companies wanted their head-quarters near the financial districts of fast-growing cities like Chicago and New York, but space was running out and land prices were rising. The American solution, as Scottish critic William Archer put it, was to "tilt a street on end and call it a skyscraper." When Chicago passed laws limiting buildings to 40 stories, New York became the skyscraper capital of the world. The crème de la crème was the 1,453 ft (443 m), 102-story Empire State Building, which opened in 1932 and remained the world's tallest building for 40 years.

◄ 1932: EMPIRE STATE BUILDING, NEW YORK CITY

GLASS CURTAIN WALLS

One of the most striking features of modern skyscrapers is that they appear to be made out of glass. This is possible because the glass walls don't carry any of the structural load—they hang from a central load-bearing frame and are, therefore, known as curtain walls. The world's first building to feature a glass curtain wall was the Hallidie Building, completed in 1918 in San Francisco and named after Andrew Smith Hallidie, the man who invented San Francisco's cable-car system. Appropriately, it is now the home of the San Francisco branch of the American Institute of Architects.

▲ 1918: SAN FRANCISCO'S HALLIDIE BUILDING

BESSEMER PROCESS

Steel for skyscrapers and reinforcing rods could not have come about without an ingenious technique named after its inventor, English metallurgist Henry Bessemer. Bessemer invented a new artillery shell for use in the Crimean War, but it proved too powerful for the cast-iron cannon in use at the time. So in 1855, he found a way of improving the strength of cast iron by blasting cold air into molten iron in a Bessemer Converter. This reduced the impurities in the iron, making a stronger, more versatile product known as mild steel, which was used for railroad lines, shipbuilding, armaments, and, later, skyscrapers.

▲ 1855: BESSEMER CONVERTER

IRON AGE

None of the preceding would have been possible without iron, which occurs naturally in the form of iron ore. During the second millennium BCE, people in the Middle East, notably the Hittites, invented furnaces that enabled them to heat the ore-bearing rocks sufficiently to melt the iron ore. The iron ore was then beaten to remove the impurities and produce wrought (meaning "worked") iron. This in turn was used to make tools and weapons that were harder and superior to the earlier bronze ones. The idea of iron smelting took a long time to spread, and the Iron Age is usually dated from c. 1,500BCE.

▲ IRON AGE: MAKING WROUGHT IRON

REINFORCED CONCRETE

The invention of steel wasn't enough on its own to build the modern skyscrapers that followed. Those required another versatile building material, which began to supersede steel during the 20th century: reinforced concrete, aka ferroconcrete. This is concrete that has been strengthened by setting it around steel-reinforcing rods, a technique pioneered by Frenchman Joseph-Louis Lambot in 1848. It was later adapted and improved by others, including Frenchman Joseph Monier, who patented reinforced concrete beams in 1868. Reinforced concrete is fireproof and, with a strength to weight ratio of between 1:300 and 1:500, is much stronger than steel alone.

▲ 1854: ELISHA GRAVES OTIS PROVES THE ELEVATOR IS SAFE

SAFETY ELEVATOR

Even with the building techniques in place, no building over a few stories high would have been practicable without the invention of the safety elevator by American Elisha Graves Otis in 1852. Elevators had existed for many years but, in 1854, Otis gave a dramatic demonstration of the invention that made them safe enough for common use. He stood in an elevator high above the crowd at New York's Crystal Palace and called for the rope to be cut with an ax. The rope was cut—and nothing happened, thanks to his invention of ratchets that locked into the guide frame in the event of any sudden downward movement.

◄ 1832: JAMES NASMYTH'S STEAM HAMMER

INDUSTRIAL REVOLUTION

At about the same time as cotton-spinner-turned-architect William Strutt was designing the revolutionary iron-framed Flax Mill, the Industrial Revolution was gaining momentum in Britain, Europe, and North America. Triggered by the invention of the rotary steam engine by Scottish engineer James Watt in 1781, inventions such as James Nasmyth's steam hammer made it easier and cheaper to forge wrought iron and steel. But before steel came the mass production of improved cast iron, lighter and stronger than brick construction, which was used for railroads, bridges, and the first iron-framed building.

◄ 1885: HOME INSURANCE BUILDING, CHICAGO

SKELETON FRAMES

Before curtain walls, buildings were supported either by columns or by the walls, both of which restricted height. The curtain wall was made possible by the development of "skeleton frame" construction. Pioneered by American engineer William le Baron Jenney, this technique involved supporting the weight of the building not with load-bearing walls but with an internal skeleton of iron and steel: the walls simply hung from the frame. The first building erected using this technique was the Home Insurance Building in Chicago, often cited as the first skyscraper, despite being only 10 stories high when it opened in 1885 (two stories were later added).

IRON FRAMES

William le Baron Jenney may have built the first steel-framed skyscraper, but American inventor and architect James Bogardus is often regarded as the "father of the skyscraper." He used cast-iron columns and girders in his five-story Cast Iron Building in New York City (1848). But even Bogardus had antecedents: the world's first iron-framed building, often referred to as "the grandfather of skyscrapers," was Benyon Marshall & Bage's Flax Mill, designed by William Strutt and built in 1797 in Shrewsbury, Shropshire, England. One of the hazards of flax was the flammable fibers, and the mill was built from cast-iron columns and beams to reduce the risk of fire damage.

▲ 1797: FLAX MILL IN SHREWSBURY, ENGLAND

14 MINUTES AND 14 STITCHES

On August 22, 1965, San Francisco Giants batter Marichal hit LA Dodgers catcher Johnny Roseboro twice over the head with his bat, opening a 2 in (5 cm) gap that required 14 stitches. The two teams brawled for 14 minutes on the field before peace was restored.

EAR-BITING

In November 1994, Evander Holyfield took the world heavyweight title from Mike Tyson. In the rematch on June 28, 1997, Holyfield comprehensively outboxed Tyson, whose frustration boiled over in the third round: spitting out his mouthguard he held Holyfield in a clinch and bit off part of his ear. Immediately after the restart, Tyson did it again and the fight was stopped, resulting in a near riot.

HEAD-BUTTING THE REFEREE

Already a controversial basketball player, Chicago Bulls Dennis Rodman sealed his reputation on 16 March 1996 in a game against the New Jersey Nets – he was sent off by ref Ted Bernhardt and reacted by head-butting Bernhardt over the left eye.

SPORTS AND LEISURE

BAD SPORTS

Sports are a fraught business, especially for men. As if keeping a lid on their egos and pride weren't enough, there's all that testosterone and adrenaline to deal with. When things go wrong in front of thousands of people, half of whom are cheering their opponent and jeering their every mistake, some sportsmen get very angry.

TENNIS SUPERBRAT

John McEnroe is rated as one of the greatest tennis players of all time, but he is almost as famous for his temper as for his tennis. Dubbed the Superbrat by the British press, he regularly abused rackets, opponents, and umpires—his most famous outburst was at Wimbledon in 1981, when he yelled at one umpire the immortal phrase: "You cannot be serious!"

FINAL

In the 110th minute of the 2006 World Cup Final, France's Zinedine Zidane was walking away from an argument with Italy's Marco Materazzi when he suddenly turned, ran at Materazzi, and head-butted him in the chest. "Zizou" was sent off in the last game of his career.

KNOCKED OUT COLD

On February 21, 2000, Vancouver Canucks ice hockey forward Donald Brashear upset the fourth most penalized player in NHL history, Boston Bruins defender Marty McSorley. With less than three seconds of the match remaining, McSorley swung his stick two-handed into the side of Brashear's head, leaving him unconscious on the ice. McSorley later said: "I got too carried away."

GRAND PRIX BRAWL

Eliseo Salazar failed to move over as race leader when Nelson Piquet lapped him in the 1982 German Grand Prix, forcing Piquet's car off the track and leaving Salazar's wrecked. Piquet got out of his car and began punching and kicking Salazar.

GLITZY BENZ

This Mercedes Benz in Key West, Florida, is encrusted with marbles, dripping with beads, and is sporting a selection of sunglasses. A mannequin's head adorns the radiator.

ALL LIT UP

Californian Jim Rattan on his Vespa scooter, pimped with 27 lights and 20 mirrors.

PEDAL PIMPING

Proud young owner on a pimped bicycle at Kearny Park, Fresno, California.

HARLEM COWBOY

The owner of this motorcycle has customized it with fancy metalwork similar to that seen on Mexican saddles.

Many people in the developed world are in love with their cars. For some, that means obsessively polishing their cherished vehicles every weekend; for others (like Queen and the Rolling Stones) it means writing songs about them. But the ultimate expression of car love is extreme customization—otherwise known as pimping your ride.

THE "MAD CAD"
Larry Fuente took four years to customize his 1960 Cadillac Sedan de Ville with over a million beads and baubles. bangles.

HAPPY ACCIDENTS

PLAY-DOH®

In the 1950s, Americans Noah and Joseph McVicker invented a flour, water, and kerosene-based wallpaper cleaner. It wasn't much good at cleaning wallpaper, but it's been a highly popular modeling material for children since 1956.

They say that necessity is the mother of invention but sometimes serendipity is the father. Serendipity is the name for happy results arising from complete accidents, and it seems to be an important characteristic for inventors. While some struggle for years to achieve a specific goal, others make their name from things that many inventors would have overlooked.

KEVLAR®

In 1963, chemist Stephanie Kwolek of Du Pont was researching an improved means of joining simple molecules into long chains, but the experiment went wrong. Rather than ditching the cloudy liquid she'd created, Kwolek tried spinning it into fibers and found that she had produced a revolutionary synthetic material five times as strong as steel of the same weight. Kevlar® absorbs energy like a spider's web, by spreading the force from the point of impact, and it is used in everything from bullet-proof vests and suspension bridge cables to racing cars and fishing lines.

COR D

Correction fluid was invented in 1951 by bank secretary Bette Nesmith Graham (mother of the Monkees' Michael Nesmith). She noticed that the bank's signwriters simply painted over any mistakes they made, and realized the possibilities of masking errors.

BUBBLE GUM

Legend has it that bubble gum was invented in 1928 when American Walter Diemer of the Frank H. Fleer Company brewed up a batch of chewing gum that went wrong, being less sticky and more stretchy than standard gum. But the name on the patent is Gilbert Mustin, and Fleer had developed an earlier bubble gum in 1906 that was not marketed.

SAFETY PIN

In 1849, the Richardson brothers agreed to cancel New Yorker Walter Hunt's debt if he could invent something using a single piece of wire. After three hours' twisting he came up with the safety pin.

BLACK & DECKER® WORKMATE®

In 1961, South African Ron Hickman damaged a kitchen chair while using it as a sawhorse. This annoying error made him a multimillionaire because it prompted him to invent a folding workbench. Rejected by eight companies, including Black & Decker®, he began producing it himself. It sold so well that, in 1972, Black & Decker® bought the manufacturing rights.

LIQUORICE ALLSORTS

In 1899, Charlie Thompson, a salesman for Bassett's candies, spilled his tray of samples over the store counter of a prospective customer in Leicester, England. The customer hadn't been interested in any of the individual candies but, when he saw the colorful assortment, he placed an order for a mixed bag: the first ever Liquorice Allsorts.

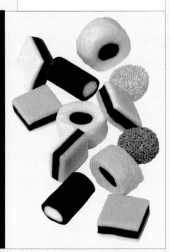

POST-IT® NOTE

In 1969, American Spencer Silver of 3M technology company invented a glue that wouldn't stick. No one could find a use for it until five years later when Silver's colleague, Art Fry, a member of the church choir, used the "unglue" to stop page markers from falling out of his hymn book. The Post-it® note was born.

MICROWAVE OVEN

When scientist Percy LeBaron Spencer walked past a piece of radar equipment called a magnetron it melted a chocolate bar in his pocket. So he created the world's first microwave oven by cutting a hole in the side of a kettle and directing the microwave beam from the magnetron through the hole.

CATSEYES® ROADSTUDS

One night in 1933, Englishman Percy Shaw was driving home when he saw his headlights reflected in the eyes of a cat, alerting him to the fact that he was veering off the road. He immediately thought that reflectors embedded in the road surface would make night driving much safer and named his invention Catseyes®.

ROLL-ON DEODORANT

Deodorant used to come in cans and was applied with the fingers. Then a product developer for a deodorant company looked at his ballpoint pen in an idle moment and realized that the method used to deliver ink could also be used to deliver deodorant— a roll-on is effectively a giant ballpoint.

VELCRO®

Instead of just picking off the troublesome cockleburs that attached themselves to his dog's fur during a walk in 1941, Swiss George de Mestral looked at them under a microscope and reproduced nature's clever hook-and-loop system. He took the name of his invention from the French *velours croché*, meaning "hooked velvet."

SLINKY®

The Slinky® was conceived in 1943, when American Navy engineer Richard James saw an engine spring slide off a table on a rolling ship. He thought that a lightweight version would make a good toy.

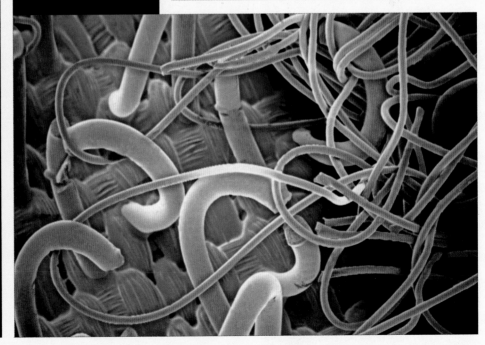

EMERGENCY ROOM

They say that pain is relative. What is excruciating to some people may be no more than a minor irritation to others. But there can be little doubt that the painful experiences featured here—ranging from a pencil stuck in the bladder to having one's entire face and scalp ripped off—are pretty extreme by anyone's standards.

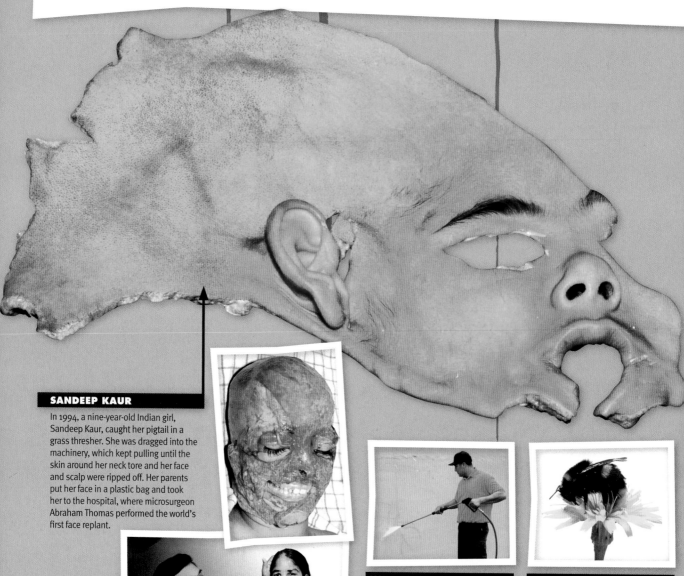

SANDEEP KAUR

In 1994, a nine-year-old Indian girl, Sandeep Kaur, caught her pigtail in a grass thresher. She was dragged into the machinery, which kept pulling until the skin around her neck tore and her face and scalp were ripped off. Her parents put her face in a plastic bag and took her to the hospital, where microsurgeon Abraham Thomas performed the world's first face replant.

MUTHUVATTI ABDUL

In November 2006, Indian construction worker Muthuvatti Abdul was hospitalized with a burst intestine after a friend on a Bahrain building site inflated him with a high-pressure air-hose up his rectum.

JOHANNES RELLEKE

In January 1962, Dutchman Johannes Relleke was attacked by a swarm of bees in Rhodesia (now Zimbabwe). He jumped into the Gwaii River but the bees continued to attack until rain drove them off. A record 2,443 bee stings were removed from Relleke's body.

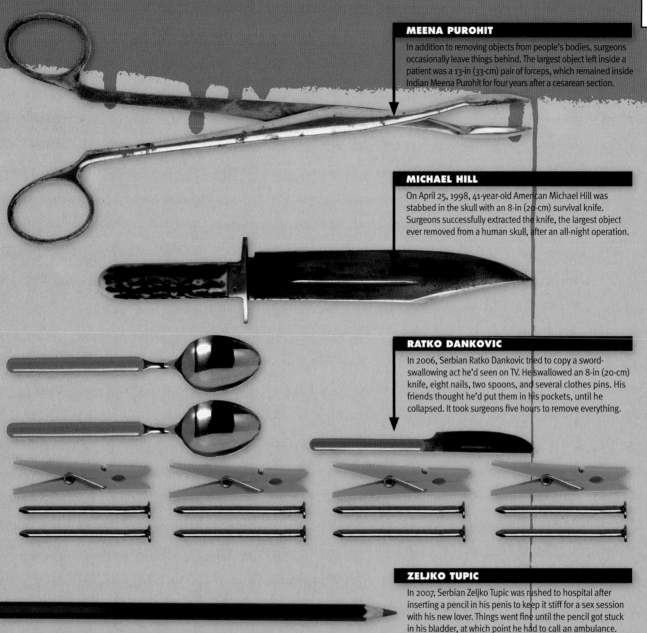

MEENA PUROHIT

In addition to removing objects from people's bodies, surgeons occasionally leave things behind. The largest object left inside a patient was a 13-in (33-cm) pair of forceps, which remained inside Indian Meena Purohit for four years after a cesarean section.

MICHAEL HILL

On April 25, 1998, 41-year-old American Michael Hill was stabbed in the skull with an 8-in (20-cm) survival knife. Surgeons successfully extracted the knife, the largest object ever removed from a human skull, after an all-night operation.

RATKO DANKOVIC

In 2006, Serbian Ratko Dankovic tried to copy a sword-swallowing act he'd seen on TV. He swallowed an 8-in (20-cm) knife, eight nails, two spoons, and several clothes pins. His friends thought he'd put them in his pockets, until he collapsed. It took surgeons five hours to remove everything.

ZELJKO TUPIC

In 2007, Serbian Zeljko Tupic was rushed to hospital after inserting a pencil in his penis to keep it stiff for a sex session with his new lover. Things went fine until the pencil got stuck in his bladder, at which point he had to call an ambulance.

JOHN WAYNE BOBBIT

On June 23, 1993, John Wayne Bobbit woke up to find that his wife Lorena had cut off his penis with a kitchen knife. She threw the severed organ out of the car window as she drove away, but police found it and surgeons managed to reattach Bobbit's missing part.

ALLAN RAY

Basketball player Allan Ray—then with Villanova University, now with the Boston Celtics—had to be treated in 2006 after apparently having his eyeball poked out of its socket. Video footage appeared to show the eye springing out of the socket but, in fact, his eyelid had been pushed behind his eye, causing *only* soft tissue damage—still pretty painful!

EXCESS

MR. MOJO RISIN'

In the mid-6os, LA-based rock band The Doors was banned from the Whiskey-A-Go-Go for playing its "Oedipal melodrama" The End, and in March 1969 lead singer **JIM MORRISON** was arrested (and later convicted) by the Florida authorities for indecent exposure and profanity during a gig in Miami. One of Morrison's more famous nicknames, "Mr. Mojo Risin"—an anagram of "Jim Morrison"—made an appearance in the song LA Woman. After finishing

ALL

SCRUBBER FOR LIFE

On October 7, 2005, the 45-year-old English DJ and singer **BOY GEORGE**, real name George O'Dowd, was arrested by New York police for possessing cocaine, which he denied was his, and was given a five-day community service sentence, sweeping garbage off the streets of New York. The former Culture Club frontman made light of the punishment by saying that he'd "always been a scrubber."

AREAS

ROCK RIDERS

Once promoters have negotiated the contract to hire a band, there's still the rider to contend with— that's the detailed spec for sound and lighting requirements and, of course, the all-important artists' dressing room demands. These range from provision of clean underwear (US rockers Jane's Addiction) to the color of the walls (J-Lo), and usually include a very detailed breakdown of what range of liquor is required. And the more famous the band, the more picky the demands. Las Vegas rockers The Killers used to make do with cheddar cheese but now that they've made it big they insist on camembert and brie—and they have a novel way of telling what day it is: their rider specifies a plentiful supply of Jack Daniel's whiskey and Absolut vodka for gigs on Mondays, Wednesdays, and Fridays; Maker's Mark whiskey and gin on Tuesdays, Thursdays, and Saturdays; and Jameson's Irish whiskey and tequila on Sundays. The Killers cite Bruce Springsteen as one

Rockers are getting old. Bruce Springsteen's rider now demands green tea and soy milk, while the Rolling Stones request a snooker table backstage. But it wasn't always so—rock'n'roll is built on legends of excess. Rock stars take behavior to extremes, from driving cars into swimming pools to

what became the band's last album, the bearded and overweight Morrison moved to Paris, having let himself go on an excess of drugs and booze. On July 3, 1970, he was found dead in his bathtub. The official report listed cause of death as heart failure but there was no autopsy, leaving the way open for all kinds of speculation, ranging from accidental drug overdose to suicide. His grave at Père-Lachaise cemetery, marked by the words "Faithful to his spirit," is one of Paris's most popular tourist attractions. In 1978 the remaining band members reunited to record *An American Prayer*, setting music to poems recorded by Morrison in 1970.

THEATRE OF PAIN

In 1982 English drummer Nicholas Dingley, better known as Razzle, joined Finnish glam-rock band Hanoi Rocks. Two years later, during the band's first US tour, Razzle visited his friend Vince Neil, singer of rock band Mötley Crüe. After spending the day at Redondo Beach in California, Neil drove them both to a liquor store—speeding and drunk, Neil lost control of the car and 24-year-old Razzle died of his injuries before reaching the hospital. Neil, who was convicted and served time for manslaughter, dedicated Mötley Crüe's 1985 album, *Theatre of Pain*, to his late friend.

DRUMMIN', RIDIN', AND FISHIN'

Led Zeppelin's hotel-trashing excesses became the stuff of legend, drummer John "Bonzo" Bonham leading the way by riding his motorcycle along the corridors of the Continental Hyatt House hotel in Los Angeles. On July 28, 1968, the band was staying at the Edgewater Inn in Seattle, Washington, right on the edge of the sea, and Bonham and tour manager Richard Cole landed several mud sharks and a red snapper from their hotel-room window. The ensuing practical jokes, in an adjoining room where the band Vanilla Fudge was staying, passed into legend when Frank Zappa wrote a song about it.

SHOOTING GALLERY

Ex-*Sex Pistol* SID VICIOUS (John Ritchie) was arrested and charged with the murder of his girlfriend, Nancy Spungen, on October 12, 1978. He allegedly awoke from a drugged stupor to find Spungen crumpled up, dead on the bathroom floor of their Chelsea, London, hotel room. She had received a single stab wound to her abdomen and bled to death. He was arrested and charged with her murder, although he said he had no memory of having done so. Some theories suggested that Spungen was murdered by drug dealers. Vicious died of a heroin overdose just four months later on February 22, 1979.

THE GREAT SURVIVOR

Rolling Stones guitarist KEITH RICHARDS appears to be so immune to most conventional abuse that his excesses have passed into folklore. One legend has it that during the Stones' 1973 European tour, when Richards needed to kick a heroin addiction quickly, he underwent a complete blood transfusion in Switzerland. Actually, Keith had undergone a kidney dialysis-type process, which had filtered out the toxic (heroin) substances that had built up in his bloodstream. It was also claimed that Richards needed to provide a clean blood sample to get a US visa. Fast forward 30 years and the 62-year-old

defied death once more after falling out of a cococut tree and suffering a mild concussion, delaying the "Bigger Bang" tour by a few months.

FLOWERPOT MAN

Baby-faced Beatle SIR PAUL McCARTNEY is not quite as innocent as he appears, despite penning the chart-topping *Rupert and the Frog Song* (1984). He has been arrested four times for either smuggling or possessing cannabis—in 1972 (Sweden), 1973 (Scotland), 1980 (Japan, where he spent 10 days in jail), and 1984 (Barbados).

of their influences but that clearly doesn't extend to sobriety: Springsteen now contents himself with soy milk, green tea, and cinnamon raisin bagels, while his saxophonist Cal Clemens survives on green Gatorade, Coca-Cola, caviar, and roast chicken. When it comes to drink, Jennifer Lopez is more concerned with what she doesn't want, specifying "no tomato, apple or grape juice"—but she does insist that her dressing room, furniture, and fixtures are all white.

HEARTS OF DARKNESS

It's hard to imagine that reformed alcoholic and Country Club celebrity golfer ALICE COOPER was once the same man who allegedly bit the head off a chicken and staged his own guillotine execution live on stage. According to Cooper, aka Vincent Furnier, someone threw some poultry at him while he was playing a gig in Toronto in September 1969, with John Lennon, Yoko Ono, and The Doors. When

he threw the chicken back, blood and feathers went everywhere and the shock rock legend was born.

In 1982, OZZY OSBOURNE (pictured left) staged a repeat of Cooper's animal abuse by biting the head off a bat that had been thrown onto the stage during a gig in Des Moines, Iowa. Ever the showman, Osbourne picked up what he thought was a rubber toy (it was dead!) and bit into it. But it wasn't, and Ozzy was rushed to a nearby hospital for rabies shots.

"DON'T WORRY, IT'S NOT LOADED"

These were the last words of guitarist Terry Kath from jazz-rock band Chicago on January 23, 1978. Kath was putting away some guns at a roadie's home after a party, when thinking that the gun wasn't loaded, he put the barrel to his head, pulled the trigger and killed himself instantly.

BROWN AT NIGHT = VAN HALEN FRIGHT

Rock bands demands for tour "freebies," known as riders, are notorious. Van Halen's standard contract, containing a clause demanding a bowl of M&Ms with all the brown ones removed, was more demanding than most. In fact, it was a cunning safety clause to ensure that each venue had fully read the contract for setting up their gear. If the band spotted a brown M&M in the bowl backstage, it meant there was likely to be a far more serious health and safety problem onstage. It also gave the management a fail-safe opt-out clause.

THE STUFFING OF LEGENDS

In 1976, Elvis "The King" Presley flew a couple of cops 1,000 miles (1,600 km) from Memphis to Denver in the middle of the night, to demonstrate his favorite sandwich (a supersized monster stuffed with peanut butter, jam, and a pound of bacon) from the Colorado Gold Mine Company restaurant. After calling the restaurant for the ultimate "takeout," all hell broke loose. The restaurateur, his wife, and a waiter sped off to the airport with 22

"Fool's Gold" sandwiches, a bucket of Perrier, a case of champagne, and a large icebox. Elvis's plane touched down at 1:40 a.m. and taxied to a private hangar where the restaurateur personally brought Elvis's order on silver trays.
During his career, Elvis's weight veered from 165 lb (75 kg) to 260 lb (118 kg) at his death.
There is a whole subgenre of Elvis cookbooks, including: *Are You Hungry Tonight?: Elvis' Favorite Recipes* by Brenda Butler; *Fit For A King: The Elvis

Presley Cookbook by Elizabeth McKeon; *The Presley Family & Friends Cookbook: A Cookbook from Those Who Knew Elvis Best* by Edie Hand; and *Graceland's Table: Recipes and Meal Memories Fit for the King of Rock and Roll* by Ellen Rolfes.

Balloon sculpture

Practice a witty banter to entertain your audience while you twist

One of the most useful skills known to humanity is the ability to make animals and swords out of balloons. It can keep humans amused for hours so, if you want to ingratiate yourself with anyone from a room full of children to bigwigs at a luncheon, follow these simple instructions.

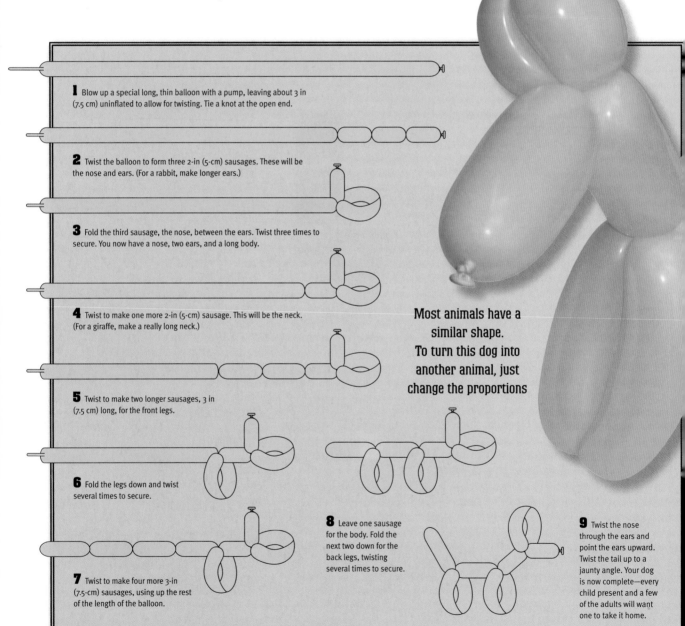

1 Blow up a special long, thin balloon with a pump, leaving about 3 in (7.5 cm) uninflated to allow for twisting. Tie a knot at the open end.

2 Twist the balloon to form three 2-in (5-cm) sausages. These will be the nose and ears. (For a rabbit, make longer ears.)

3 Fold the third sausage, the nose, between the ears. Twist three times to secure. You now have a nose, two ears, and a long body.

4 Twist to make one more 2-in (5-cm) sausage. This will be the neck. (For a giraffe, make a really long neck.)

5 Twist to make two longer sausages, 3 in (7.5 cm) long, for the front legs.

6 Fold the legs down and twist several times to secure.

7 Twist to make four more 3-in (7.5-cm) sausages, using up the rest of the length of the balloon.

8 Leave one sausage for the body. Fold the next two down for the back legs, twisting several times to secure.

9 Twist the nose through the ears and point the ears upward. Twist the tail up to a jaunty angle. Your dog is now complete—every child present and a few of the adults will want one to take it home.

Most animals have a similar shape. To turn this dog into another animal, just change the proportions

Always leave the end of the balloon uninflated so it doesn't pop when you twist it. If a balloon does pop, have a joke ready to make it look intentional

SWAN

You need a very long white balloon to do justice to the graceful curves of a swan.

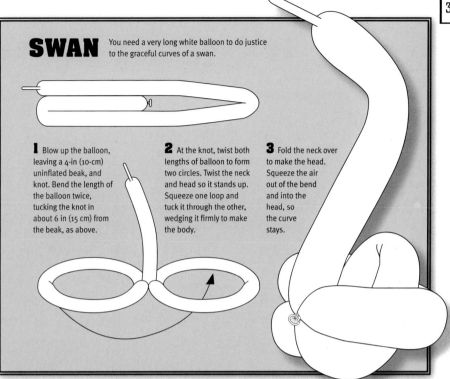

1 Blow up the balloon, leaving a 4-in (10-cm) uninflated beak, and knot. Bend the length of the balloon twice, tucking the knot in about 6 in (15 cm) from the beak, as above.

2 At the knot, twist both lengths of balloon to form two circles. Twist the neck and head so it stands up. Squeeze one loop and tuck it through the other, wedging it firmly to make the body.

3 Fold the neck over to make the head. Squeeze the air out of the bend and into the head, so the curve stays.

SWORD

This is the ideal way to have a safe sword fight, where no one gets hurt.

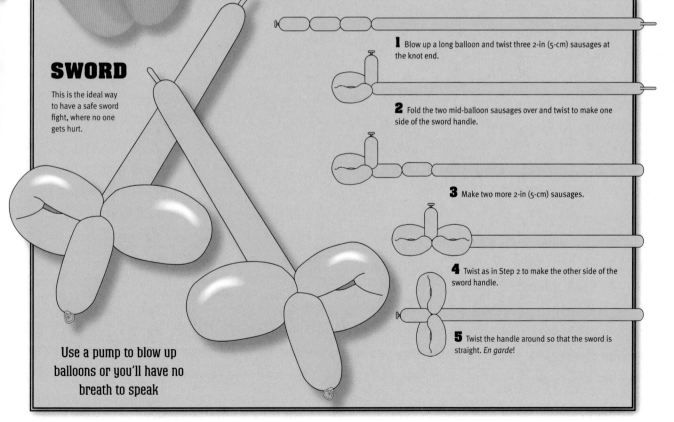

1 Blow up a long balloon and twist three 2-in (5-cm) sausages at the knot end.

2 Fold the two mid-balloon sausages over and twist to make one side of the sword handle.

3 Make two more 2-in (5-cm) sausages.

4 Twist as in Step 2 to make the other side of the sword handle.

5 Twist the handle around so that the sword is straight. *En garde!*

Use a pump to blow up balloons or you'll have no breath to speak

SPORTS AND LEISURE

EXTREME SPORTS

There's no official dividing line between mainstream and weird sports, although inclusion in the Olympic Games is often a sign that humans are taking a fringe sport seriously. Among the more unusual sports, some, such as cheese rolling, are traditional; others, like elephant polo and bed racing, are variations on mainstream sports; and yet others, like zorbing and extreme ironing, are simply peculiar sports invented by adrenalin-crazed thrill-seekers.

CHEESE ROLLING

The Cooper's Hill Cheese Rolling and Wake, a tradition going back hundreds of years, takes place every May in Gloucestershire, UK. Competitors pursue a large Double Gloucester cheese down the steep slopes of Cooper's Hill, and the first person to the bottom wins the cheese. The ambulances waiting at the foot of the hill are always busy.

OCTOPUSH

Octopush, aka underwater hockey, is an international sport in which two teams wearing snorkels and flippers use short sticks known as "pushers" to slide a puck across the bottom of a swimming pool and into the opposing team's goal. It was invented in 1954 by four divers from Southsea, UK.

DWARF THROWING

Also known as dwarf tossing, this sport—which involves throwing dwarves across a bar room onto a mattress or crash mat—is so offensive that it is banned in parts of Canada, France, and the US. The first World Dwarf-throwing Championships were held in Australia in 1986.

ZORBING

Have you ever wondered what it's like to be a hamster running around a wheel in a cage? Try zorbing—rolling down a hill in a giant inflatable sphere. Zorbing originated in Rotorua, New Zealand, where there's a 220-yd (200-m) course on which zorbers can reach 30 mph (50 kph).

BED RACING

One team member has a nap while the others push the bed as fast as possible around the course. Here, Kelly Siska looks none too relaxed as her brothers push the "Hawaiian Clipper" in the 5th Annual Delray Beach Bed Race in Florida.

TOE WRESTLING

Invented in Ye Olde Royal Oak Inn in Staffordshire, UK, during the 1970s. The World Toe-wrestling Organization (WTWO) failed to gain Olympic status but it has organized a World Championship since 1993. In 2005, Paul and Heather Beech, aka Mr. and Mrs. Toeminator, won the men's and women's events.

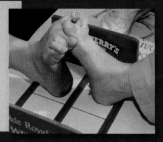

ELEPHANT POLO

Each elephant has two riders: a mahout who controls it and a player whose mallet can be anything from 5 to 12 ft (152 to 366 cm) long, depending on the size of the elephant. The sport orginated in India in the early 20th century, and the World Elephant Polo Association (WEPA) was formed in 1982.

REDNECK GAMES

Founded by Mac Davis in 1996 as an antidote to the Atlanta Olympics, the annual Redneck Games takes place in Georgia, and includes Mudpit Belly Flop, Hubcap Hurl, Seed Spitting Contest, Armpit Serenade, Bobbin' For Pigs' Feet (left), and Redneck Horseshoe—toilet seat throwing.

BOG SNORKELLING
The World Bog Snorkeling Championships have taken place annually since 1985 in the Waen Rhydd peat bog, near Llanwrtyd Wells in Wales. Participants swim two lengths of a 60-yd (55-m) smelly mud trench without using conventional strokes. In 2006, there was a "bog off" for first place after a tie on 1 minute 42 seconds.

BOARD SPORTS

Extreme ironing is described on its official website as "the latest danger sport that combines the thrills of an extreme outdoor activity with the satisfaction of a well-pressed shirt." Devotees of the sport take their ironing boards anywhere from the highest heights to the greatest depths.

COMMUNICATION
I WANT TO BE LEFT ALONE...

I f you're traveling the world, you'll need to talk to the locals. On pages 30–31 you can discover how to make friends by meeting and drinking, and on pages 204–205 you can find out how to take things a step further with sweet nothings. Now you can discover how to extricate yourself from the results of any drunken liaisons by saying "Leave me alone" in 54 languages.

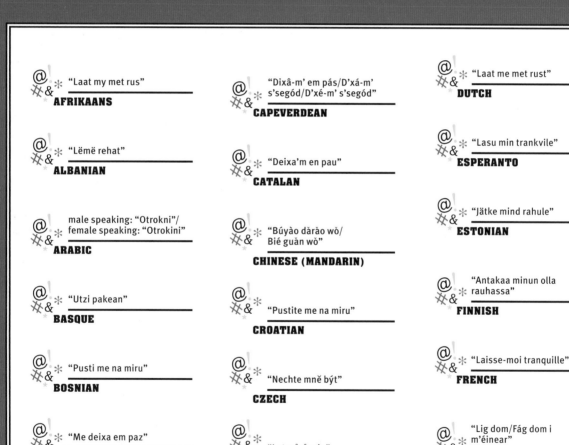

"Laat my met rus"
AFRIKAANS

"Lëmë rehat"
ALBANIAN

male speaking: "Otrokni"/
female speaking: "Otrokini"
ARABIC

"Utzi pakean"
BASQUE

"Pusti me na miru"
BOSNIAN

"Me deixa em paz"
BRAZILIAN PORTUGUESE

"Ostavete me namira"
BULGARIAN

"Dixâ-m' em pás/D'xá-m'
s'segód/D'xé-m' s'segód"
CAPEVERDEAN

"Deixa'm en pau"
CATALAN

"Búyào dǎrǎo wǒ/
Bié guǎn wǒ"
CHINESE (MANDARIN)

"Pustite me na miru"
CROATIAN

"Nechte mně být"
CZECH

"Lat wårå mig"
DALECARLIAN

"Lad mig være i fred"
DANISH

"Laat me met rust"
DUTCH

"Lasu min trankvile"
ESPERANTO

"Jätke mind rahule"
ESTONIAN

"Antakaa minun olla
rauhassa"
FINNISH

"Laisse-moi tranquille"
FRENCH

"Lig dom/Fág dom i
m'éinear"
GAELIC (IRISH)

"Lhig yn raad dou"
GAELIC (MANX)

Translations courtesy of Simon Ager at www.omniglot.com

@#&* "Laß mich in Ruhe"
GERMAN

@#&* male speaking: "Áse me ísiho"/female speaking: "Áse me ísihi "
GREEK

@#&* "Mujhe akela chod do"
HINDI

@#&* "Hagyjon engem békén"
HUNGARIAN

@#&* "Jangan ganggu saya"
INDONESIAN

@#&* "Lasciami in pace/Vattene"
ITALIAN

@#&* "Hottoite"
JAPANESE

@#&* "Honja naebeoryeo dushipshio"
KOREAN

@#&* "Atstājiet mani mierā "
LATVIAN

@#&* "Atstokite/Palikite mane ramybėje"
LITHUANIAN

@#&* "Viknete policija"
MACEDONIAN

@#&* "Jangan ganggu saya"
MALAY

@#&* "Teinii ttiisa"
MOROCCAN

@#&* "La meg være alene"
NORWEGIAN

@#&* "Velam kon"
PERSIAN

@#&* "Lot me toch"
PLAUTDIETSCH

@#&* "Zostaw mnie w spokoju/ Zostaw mnie"
POLISH

@#&* "Deixa-me em paz"
PORTUGUESE

@#&* "Lăsa-mă în pace"
ROMANIAN

@#&* "Ostav'te menja v pokoe"
RUSSIAN

@#&* "Ndisiyawo ndiri ndega"
SHONA

@#&* "Pustite me na miru"
SLOVENIAN

@#&* "Déjeme en paz"
SPANISH

@#&* "Usinisumbue"
SWAHILI

@#&* "Lämna mig ifred"
SWEDISH

@#&* "Lubayan mo ako/Lumayas ka sa harapan ko/Huwag mo akong pakialamanan"
TAGALOG

@#&* male speaking: "Yaa yung kap phom"/female speaking: "Yaa yung kap chan"
THAI

@#&* "Larim mi"
TOK PISIN

@#&* "Ntlogele"
TSWANA

@#&* "Beni rahat bırak"
TURKISH

@#&* "Zalyšte mene u spokoji"
UKRAINIAN

@#&* "Đừng làm phiền tôi"
VIETNAMESE

@#&* "Gad lonydd i fi"
WELSH

SUPERSIZE FISH STICK

DIFFICULTY RATING:
>VERY EASY   >EASYISH   >MODERATE   >A BIT TRICKY

Fish sticks and peas is one of those meals that has humans reliving their childhoods. For those whose appetites have developed with adulthood, here's how to make a grown-up version: more of a fish leg than a fish stick, with giant peas to match.

INGREDIENTS

4½ lb (2 kg) white fish fillets
1 loaf of white bread
large bag of frozen peas

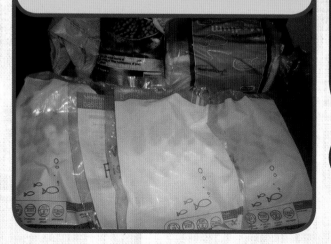

METHOD

1 Remove fillets from packaging and grill for 20–30 minutes under a high heat, or until cooked through. Remove from grill, tip into a large bowl, and mash mercilessly with a fork, removing any stray bones.

2 Break up the loaf of bread into small pieces and place in a hot oven until golden brown (but not burned). Remove, and allow to cool.

3 Use a blunt object such as a rolling pin to beat the toasted bread into breadcrumbs. You might want to put the breadcrumbs in a bag first to stop them from flying everywhere, but it's entirely up to you.

329

4 Retrieve the mashed fish and mold into a fish-stick shape. Cover completely with toasted breadcrumbs until it bears some resemblance to the original.

5 Cook the peas, strain off the water, and allow to cool before mashing them into bits and reforming them into giant pea shapes.

6 Arrange neatly on a baking tray and put back into the oven on a low heat until crispy. All you need now are some gigantic fries and you'll have yourself a great meal!

WARNING
Fish is very good for you (although not this much at once), but please make sure you cook it well, and watch out for bones.

The fabulous fish stick and prodigious peas hot from the oven, with standard-sized versions for comparison.

VAN GOGH

Dutch painter Vincent van Gogh had difficulty selling any paintings during his lifetime, but three Van Goghs are now among the world's top 10 most expensive paintings. Van Gogh shot himself on July 27, 1890, at or near the scene of his last painting, and died of his wounds two days later.

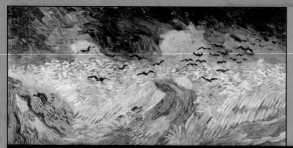

VAN GOGH'S LAST PAINTING, "WHEAT FIELD UNDER THREATENING SKIES WITH CROWS" (1890)

FRANZ KAFKA

Kafka's novels were unpublished during his lifetime and his last request was that all of his papers be burned. Fortunately, his request was ignored. His three novels, *The Trial*, *The Castle*, and *America*, were all published posthumously.

GEORGE ARMSTRONG CUSTER, 1839–76

KURT COBAIN

Cobain, pioneer of grunge and lynchpin of rock band Nirvana, died on April 5, 1994, an apparent suicide. Death made him a legend, and since then his records have sold faster: in 2006, he was the top-earning dead celebrity, grossing an estimated $50 million from October 2005 to October 2006.

COBAIN DURING THE MTV UNPLUGGED SESSIONS AT SONY STUDIOS NYC, 18 NOVEMBER 1993

GENERAL CUSTER

Custer has been described both as an American cavalry hero and as a vain fool for trying to attack 2,000 Native Americans without waiting for reinforcements. There is little doubt that he is more famous for dying during his infamous and suicidal Last Stand than he would have been had he lived.

JFK

Since his assassination on November 22, 1963, John F. Kennedy's memory has been kept alive by conspiracy theories. It's impossible to know what he might have achieved had he lived, but he could hardly have been remembered more vividly than he is for the manner of his death.

MYTHS AND LEGENDS

BETTER OFF DEAD

Philosophers, priests, and Bob Dylan have all said that death is not the end, it's a new beginning. For all of the people and objects featured here, that has proved true in the sense that since their deaths they have all become more famous or more successful than they were in life.

MARILYN MONROE

Hollywood legend Marilyn Monroe's last film *The Misfits* bombed when it was released but became a success after her sudden and controversial death in 1962. Since then Marilyn has been ever-present in Forbes Magazine's list of top-earning dead celebrities.

MARILYN MONROE IN 1959, THREE YEARS BEFORE HER CONTROVERSIAL DEATH

ELVIS PRESLEY

"The King" died on August 16, 1977, after consuming quantities of at least 14 prescription drugs. Several rereleases topped the charts early this 21st century, and Elvis topped Forbes Magazine's list of top dollar-earning dead celebrities from 2001–05, the first five years of the list's existence.

THE TITANIC

Yes, it was the world's largest and most luxurious oceanliner, but others would have come along and the Titanic would have been just a past glory. Except that by hitting an iceberg and sinking on its maiden voyage in 1912, the Titanic was recalled passionately enough to spawn a Hollywood blockbuster nearly 90 years later.

THE HINDENBERG

The world's largest airship is more famous for bursting into flames on May 6, 1937, than for flight. Airships were rendered obsolete largely because of the disaster: German chancellor Adolf Hitler banned all further commercial flights, and the rapid development of the rival airplane ended the era of the flying hotel.

JAMES DEAN

Dean died in a car crash on September 30, 1955, after completing his third and last film, *Giant*, released posthumously in 1956. Paul Newman took the next part Dean was scheduled to play. Newman's career, though successful, never brought him the legendary status held by Dean thanks to his early death.

PRESLEY PERFORMING AT ONE OF HIS LAST CONCERTS ON JUNE 20, 1977

CRIME *Lasts*

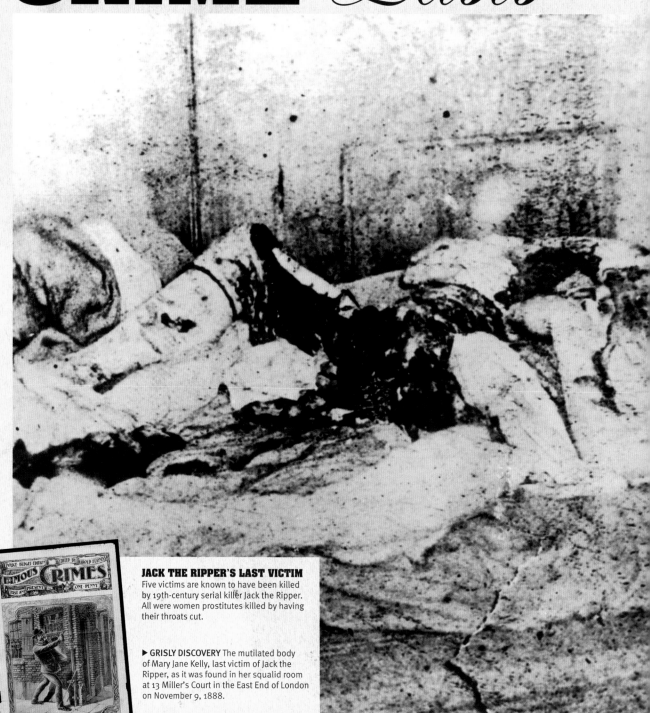

JACK THE RIPPER'S LAST VICTIM
Five victims are known to have been killed by 19th-century serial killer Jack the Ripper. All were women prostitutes killed by having their throats cut.

▶ **GRISLY DISCOVERY** The mutilated body of Mary Jane Kelly, last victim of Jack the Ripper, as it was found in her squalid room at 13 Miller's Court in the East End of London on November 9, 1888.

Humans are always recording firsts but lasts often pass unnoticed, usually because no one is aware at the time that a particular event won't happen again. Crime and execution lasts are different because they're often the result of a change in the law, so everyone knows in advance that they will be lasts.

LAST MAN EXECUTED BY THE AX

For his part in the 1745 Jacobite Rebellion, 80-year-old Simon Fraser, Lord Lovat, was executed at Tower Hill, London. The blow was so hard that Lovat's head flew from his body and the ax was embedded in the block.

LAST WOMAN BOILED ALIVE IN ENGLAND

Multiple poisoner Margaret Davy was executed in March 1547 by being chained to a gantry above a cauldron of boiling water and repeatedly plunged in and out "until life was extinct."

LAST AMERICAN PIRATE EXECUTED BY HANGING

A crowd of 10,000 watched Albert E. Hicks hang at Bedloe's Island, New York, on Friday July 13, 1860.

LAST PUBLIC EXECUTION BY GUILLOTINE

In June 1939, Eugene Weidmann was guillotined for six murders. Executioner Henri Desfourneaux was so slow in setting up the guillotine that the execution took place in broad daylight instead of at dawn. The delay allowed photographers to take such shocking pictures that a new law was passed shortly afterward, stating that all future executions would be carried out in private.

LAST STAGECOACH ROBBERY BY A WOMAN

In the Wild West in May 1899, Pearl Hart and accomplice Joe Boot robbed passengers of $431 on Arizona's Benson-Globe stagecoach. They were arrested three days later and Hart was sentenced to five years; she served just two before being paroled and later appearing in Wild West shows as The Arizona Bandit.

LAST BRITISH CONVICTS TRANSPORTED

Britain transported convicts to penal colonies in North America from 1597 until 1776, and in Australia from 1787. The last convict ships arrived in Fremantle, Western Australia, on January 10, 1868.

LAST WITCH EXECUTED IN EUROPE

When Bavarian servant Anna Maria Schwagel was abandoned by her lover, she had a breakdown and was taken into a mental asylum. The matron heard her constantly murmuring, "It was the Devil in the form of the coachman who betrayed me." As a result, Schwagel was beheaded for witchcraft on April 11, 1775.

LAST WOMAN EXECUTED BY DECAPITATION IN JAPAN

Prostitute O-Den Takahashi was executed on January 31, 1879, for slitting the throat of a sleeping customer. After failing twice to cut off her head cleanly, the executioner hacked through her neck while she was still conscious.

LAST PRISONER OF ALCATRAZ

On March 21, 1963, the last 27 inmates were removed from Alcatraz Island, San Francisco Bay, which for 29 years had been a notorious prison. The last imate to be incarcerated was also the last to board the boat—he was Frank C. Weatherman, prisoner no #AZ-1576.

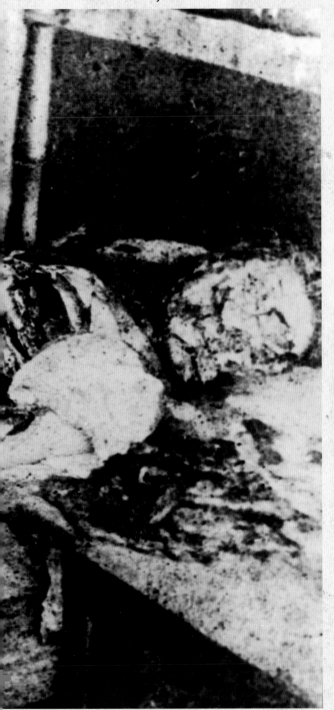

WAYS TO GO

One thing about all animals on Earth is certain—they're all going to die. Some humans hope to die quietly in their beds; others want to go out in a blaze of glory. But very few will make their exit in the bizarre manner of the people here.

RULERS

KINGS OF BURMA (NOW MYANMAR)

King Theinkho of Burma (now Myanmar) was killed by a farmer whose cucumbers he ate without permission.

King Minrekyawswa was crushed by one of his own elephants.

King Nandabayin laughed to death upon being told that Venice was a free state without a king.

KING OF NORWAY

Haakon VII died after slipping on the soap and smashing his head on the bathtub faucets.

ATTILA THE HUN

He died of a nosebleed on his wedding night.

KING OF FRANCE

Charles VIII died while playing tennis. He bowed to his wife to allow her to serve first. As he raised his head he smashed it into a wooden beam, fracturing his skull, which killed him.

ROMAN EMPEROR

Claudius choked to death on a feather put down his throat by his doctor to make him vomit.

PEOPLE OF ACTION

ISADORA DUNCAN

American dancer Isadora Duncan died when her shawl got caught in the spokes of the rear wheel of her open-topped car, breaking her neck as she waved to friends and pulled away after calling "Adieu, my friends, I am going to glory."

HOUDINI

Hungarian escapologist Harry Houdini died after claiming that he could withstand any punch to the stomach. He was taken by surprise and died of a ruptured appendix brought on by the challenger.

AMY JOHNSON

English pioneer aviatrix Amy Johnson died after crash-landing in the Thames Estuary and being sucked underneath the boat that went to her rescue.

JIM FIXX

The man famous for making jogging popular died of a heart attack—while out jogging.

WRITERS

AESCHYLUS

Ancient Greek playwright Aeschylus died when an eagle dropped a tortoise on his head, mistaking his bald pate for a rock. (Eagles do this to break the tortoise shell and get at the meat.)

SOPHOCLES

Little is known about the death of Sophocles, another ancient Greek playwright, but according to various legends he either choked on a grape; killed himself trying to deliver a long sentence without drawing breath; or died of joy at the success of his play *Antigone*.

DYLAN THOMAS

Welsh poet Dylan Thomas died doing what he loved best—drinking. He collapsed in 1953 at the White Horse tavern in Greenwich Village, Manhattan, New York.

MUSICIANS

GLENN MILLER

The US jazz musician and band leader disappeared in a plane over the English Channel during World War II. He may have been hit by bombs dumped by the RAF returning from an air raid.

SONNY BONO

The US pop star died after skiing into a tree.

CHET BAKER

The US jazz trumpeter fell to his death from a second-floor hotel window, hitting his head on a concrete post. Murder was ruled out as the door was locked from the inside.

MAMA CASS

Legend has it that the singer with the Mamas and Papas pop group choked to death on a ham sandwich. In fact, she died of a heart attack brought on by being overweight.

RICHIE VALENS

The 1950s rock star died in a plane crash with singer Buddy Holly, after tossing a coin with Holly's guitarist Tommy Allsup for a seat on board. Later, Allsup opened the Heads-Up Saloon bar, in memory of the lucky coin.

THINKERS AND SCIENTISTS

FRANCIS BACON

The 16th-century English philosopher Francis Bacon died of pneumonia after pioneering the concept of frozen food by stuffing snow into a chicken.

TYCHO BRAHE

By tradition, Danish astronomer Tycho Brahe died of a burst bladder, feeling it was bad manners to get up from a banquet to relieve himself. Recent evidence suggests mercury poisoning, leading to rumors that he might have been murdered by rival astronomer Johannes Kepler.

Chaucer wrote "murder will out" and Shakespeare wrote "murder cannot be hid long." But murderers are not always caught, however terrible their crimes may be. Regrettably, there are all too many unsolved murders—and, given that the first few hours are vital to an investigation, the longer ago a crime was committed, the more likely it is to remain unsolved.

JACK THE RIPPER 1888

As many as 14 murders have been attributed to 19th-century serial killer Jack the Ripper. It is generally accepted that he murdered at least five women, all of them prostitutes, in the Whitechapel area of east London between August and November 1888. The first of the five was Mary Anne Nichols, aka Polly Nichols, whose mutilated body was found on August 31, 1888, in Buck's Row (now Durward Street) with the throat cut. On September 8, the body of Annie Chapman was discovered in Hanbury Street in a similar condition, and shortly afterward police received a taunting letter signed "Jack the Ripper." The letter may have been a hoax but the nickname stuck, and more than a century later still provokes speculation as to the identity it hides. On September 30, there were two murders: those of Elizabeth Stride in Berner Street (now Henriques Street), whose body was not mutilated—implying that the Ripper had been interrupted—and Catherine Eddowes in Mitre Square later the same night. On November 9, the disembowelled and partially dismembered body of the Ripper's last victim, Mary Jane Kelly (aka Marie Jeanette Kelly), was discovered by her rent collector. The Ripper was never caught. He possibly lived as late as the 1950s. Among suggested suspects are: the Duke of Clarence (eldest son of King Edward VII); artist Walter Sickert, who appeared obsessed with the murders; Dr. Pedachenko, a Russian surgeon allegedly sent to Britain by the Czarist secret police to test the British police system; and a lawyer named Druitt, whose body was found floating in the Thames River shortly after the last murder. It has even been suggested that "Jack" was a woman.

THE BLACK DAHLIA 1947

Elizabeth Short was determined to be an actress, so in 1946, at the age of 22, she moved to Hollywood where she worked intermittently as a waitress. On January 14, 1947, she left the Biltmore Hotel in downtown Los Angeles, apparently after meeting a man there, and was never again seen alive. The following morning, housewife Betty Bersinger saw what she thought was a broken store mannequin lying in a vacant lot in Crenshaw, near Hollywood—it turned out to be the two halves of Elizabeth's naked and bruised body. There were rope marks on her ankles and wrists and gashes, 3 in (7.5 cm) wide, carved at each side of her mouth. Because of her striking black hair the press dubbed her the "Black Dahlia." When news of her particularly gruesome murder was made public, several people immediately made false confessions—one researcher puts the number as high as 50. Since the killer has never been caught, and, therefore, nothing is known about how or why she was killed and cut in half, Elizabeth's murder has fascinated people ever since. James Ellroy wrote *Black Dahlia*, a fictional account based on the known facts, which was made into a feature film in 2006.

ASSASSINATION OF A PRIME MINISTER 1986

The unsolved assassination of Sweden's Prime Minister Olof Palme in 1986 shocked Sweden almost as much as the Kennedy assassination shocked the US 23 years earlier. Palme became Prime Minister in 1969 and proved to be a controversial leader, criticizing the US for its involvement in Vietnam, the USSR for putting down the Czechoslovakian rising known as the Prague Spring, General Franco for his right-wing regime in Spain, and South Africa for its apartheid regime. At home, he pushed through major constitutional reforms but lost power in 1976 over proposals to fund the welfare system through higher taxes. He returned to power in 1982 and was reelected in 1985. His premiership and his life ended on the night of February 28, 1986, as he was walking home in central Stockholm after a visit to the movies with his wife, Lisbet. Since Palme often refused protection, the couple was not accompanied by bodyguards. A lone gunman ran up behind them and shot Palme in the back, fatally wounding him. A second shot hit Lisbet and the gunman ran off before the police could be called. Husband and wife were both rushed to the hospital where Lisbet recovered, but Palme was pronounced dead on arrival. A plaque now marks the spot where Palme was assassinated, and streets and squares have been named after him in Stockholm and other major cities in Sweden, and in countries as far afield as Nicaragua, Russia, Namibia, and Iraq. Palme has even been commemorated by a hip-hop group, *The Latin Kings*, who set one of his speeches to music. The identity of the assassin has never been established, and no organization has ever claimed responsibility.

KILLER ON THE LOOSE

MOST HYPED MURDER 1994

On June 17, 1994, television programs were interrupted by news footage of a bizarre low-speed police car chase involving film star and former American football player O. J. Simpson, who was eventually arrested for the murder of his ex-wife, Nicole, and her friend Ronald Goldman. One of the most hyped trials in history began in January 1995 and ended on October 3 with O. J. being found not guilty, despite seemingly overwhelming forensic evidence. As far as the American criminal justice system is concerned, this means that the murders remain unsolved, although in February 1997 Simpson was found guilty in a civil suit and ordered to pay $8.5 million in damages.

THE BOY IN THE BOX 1957

On February 25, 1957, police found the naked, battered body of a young boy, aged 4–6 years, in a cardboard box in Philadelphia. Despite pictures of the child being sent to every Philadelphia household, and subsequent features on the television shows *America's Most Wanted* and *Cold Case*, neither the victim nor the murderer has ever been identified. In 2002, a woman claimed that her violent mother had bought the boy in 1954 and systematically abused him before killing him in a fit of temper. However, the woman had a history of mental illness and there was no evidence to back up her story.

LAKE BODOM MURDERS 1960

Finnish heavy metal band Children of Bodom is named after the victims of this multiple murder and has written several songs about it. In the early hours of June 5, 1960, four teenagers camping on the shore of Lake Bodom, just west of Helsinki, were attacked with a knife. Maila Irmeli Björklund and Anja Tuulikki Mäki, both 15, and Seppo Antero Boisman, 18, were all killed. Nils Wilhelm Gustafsson, also 18, survived. The killer (or killers) was never identified but in June 1972, almost 12 years later, the case seemed to have been solved—a man who worked on the lakeside committed suicide, leaving a note confessing to the murders. Police discovered that he had indeed been working there that day, but had left the lake by the time the killings took place. No further leads appeared until March 2004, almost 44 years after the murders, when investigations using DNA profiling of blood stains implicated the survivor, Nils Gustafsson. It was claimed that Gustafsson had murdered his girlfriend, Björklund, in a jealous rage before attacking the others. The trial lasted over a year; Gustafsson was acquitted on October 7, 2005.

ZODIAC KILLER 1968–69

The self-styled "Zodiac" killer boasted of 37 murders but it is thought that he actually killed five people. In his first attack, on December 28, 1968, he shot two young lovers in their car. In July 1969, he attacked another couple in similar circumstances, one of whom survived. That August he sent the first of many taunting letters to newspapers, claiming responsibility for the three murders and calling himself "the Zodiac." In September 1969, he stabbed a third couple in their car, and again one of them survived; and in October 1969, he shot cab driver Paul Stine. Several of the letters contained cryptograms, which, if deciphered, may one day reveal the Zodiac's identity.

CHURCH SHOOTING 1980

In 1977, Monseñor Óscar Romero became the fourth Archbishop of San Salvador, the capital of El Salvador. He had been chosen because of his conservatism but soon ruffled feathers by becoming an outspoken critic of human rights abuse, poverty, and El Salvador's civil war. On March 24, 1980, he was shot while celebrating Mass at a chapel near his cathedral, his blood spattering the altar. A quarter of a million people attended his funeral, which was marred by an explosion and gunfire, causing a panic in which between 30 and 50 people were killed. The timing of the assassination, the day after Romero had called for soldiers to obey God rather than the corrupt government and to stop abusing human rights, left little doubt that the assassination was carried out by Salvadoran death squads, almost certainly on the orders of republican military leader and politician Major Roberto D'Aubuisson. D'Aubuisson died in 1992 without being brought to trial and the truth behind Romero's murder has still not been resolved. In 1997, Pope John Paul II bestowed on Romero the title of Servant of God, the first step toward canonization.

CONTACT SPORT

A karate master breaks a stack of wooden blocks with his head. Scientists say that accomplishing this trick is a question of physics, as well as skill, and has nothing to do with supernatural strength.

Famous last words 1

It's surprising how eloquent famous people manage to be when death is upon them. Either that, or history records the last clever thing they said rather than their actual final croaky request for water or painkillers. But while some of the last words that follow may be apocryphal, others, such as Donald Campbell's, are hauntingly genuine.

MEHER BABA

Indian Guru Meher Baba spoke his last words in 1925, 44 years before his death. The last thing he said before taking a vow of silence was:

❝Don't worry, be happy.❞

DIED 1969

RENÉ DESCARTES

The French philosopher's last words were:

❝ My soul, thou hast long been held captive. The hour has now come for thee to quit thy prison, to leave the trammels of this body. Then to this separation with joy and courage. ❞

DIED 1650

MIGUEL DE CERVANTES

The last words of Spanish writer Cervantes, author of the comic epic *Don Quixote*, were written in a letter to his patron:

❝ Already my foot is in the stirrup. Already, great Lord and master, the agonies are upon me as I send these lines. Yesterday they administered to me the last rites. Today I am writing this. Time is short. Agony grows. Hope lessens. Only the will to live keeps me alive. Would that life might last until I might kiss the feet of your excellency. Seeing your excellency back in Spain, hale and hearty, might restore me to life. But if it be decreed that I must die, heaven's will be done. May your excellency know at least what my wish was and know also that he had in me a servant so faithful as to have wished to have served your excellency even after death. ❞

DIED 1616

JULIUS CAESAR

Roman emperor Julius Caesar (left) was assassinated by a conspiracy led by his former confidant Marcus Junius Brutus. His last three words, as Brutus stabbed him, were:

❝ Et tu, Brute? ❞
– And you, Brutus?

DIED 44 BCE

PAUL GAUGUIN

French Post-Impressionist painter Paul Gauguin (above) died on the Marquesas Islands. His last words were a note to a missionary:

❝ Would it be too much to ask you to come and see me? My eyesight seems to be going and I cannot walk. I am very ill. ❞

DIED 1903

HENRIK IBSEN

When the Norwegian playwright's nurse assured visitors to his sickbed that Ibsen's health was improving, his last words were:

❝ On the contrary. ❞

DIED 1906

EMPEROR NERO

Modesty was not the strong point of the Roman emperor Nero. Having nurtured ambitions as a poet, philosopher, actor, and musician, his last words were:

❝ Qualis artifex pereo. ❞
– How great an artist dies in me.

DIED 68 CE

PLATO

The ancient Greek philosopher's last words were a tribute to another great philosopher:

❝ I thank the guiding providence and fortune of my life: first, that I was born a man and a Greek, not a barbarian nor a brute; and next, that I happened to live in the age of Socrates. ❞

DIED C. 348 BCE

DONALD CAMPBELL

English car and speedboat racer Donald Campbell died trying to set a new water speed record in his turbo-jet hydroplane Bluebird. A recording of his last radio transmission was released in 1997:

❝ Roger, Paul. I am starting the return run now. Nose is up. Pitching a bit down here as I drive over my own wash… Tramping like mad, full power, tramping like hell here. I can't see much. The water's very dark… green… I can't see anything… Hello, the bow's up. I have gone… ❞

DIED 1967

ANNA PAVLOVA

The last words of the Russian prima ballerina (right), most famous for creating the role of the Dying Swan, were:

> " Get my Swan costume ready. "

DIED 1931

JAMES CROLL

Scottish physicist and geologist James Croll was a lifelong teetotaller, but he decided on his deathbed to try some whisky:

> " I'll take a wee drop of that. I don't think there's much fear of me turning to drink now. "

DIED 1890

LEONARDO DA VINCI

The last words of this Italian genius were:

> " I have offended God and mankind because my work did not reach the quality it should have. "

DIED 1519

ETHEL WATERS

Shortly before her death the American blues singer told an interviewer:

> " I'm not afraid to die, honey. In fact, I'm kind of looking forward to it. I know that the Lorod has his arms wrapped around this big, fat sparrow. "

DIED 1977

NICCOLÒ MACHIAVELLI

Italian statesman and political philosopher Niccolò Machiavelli gave the world the word "machiavellian," from his assertion that political ends justify any means necessary. His contempt for the existing order was revealed in his last words:

> " I desire to go to hell and not to heaven. In the former place I shall enjoy the company of popes, kings, and princes, while in the latter are only beggars, monks, and apostles. "

DIED 1527

MARK TWAIN

The American novelist left a written memo by his deathbed:

> " Death, the only immortal, who treats us all alike, whose peace and refuge are for all. The soiled and the pure, the rich and the poor, the loved and the unloved. "

DIED 1910

EUGENE O'NEILL

The American playwright's last words were:

> " I knew it. I knew it. Born in a hotel room and, God damn it, died in a hotel room. "

DIED 1953

CARL PANZRAM

When asked on the gallows whether he had anything to say, the American mass-murderer replied:

> " Yes. Hurry it up, you Hoosier b*****d. I could hang a dozen men while you're fooling around. "

DIED 1930

SOCRATES

Sentenced to death for impiety, the ancient Greek philosopher's last words were:

> " Crito, I owe a cock to Asclepius. Will you remember the debt? "

DIED 399 BCE

KARL MARX

When the housekeeper of Karl Marx (right) asked if he had a last message to give to the world, he replied:

> " Go on, get out! Last words are for fools who haven't said enough. "

DIED 1883

VOLTAIRE

French Enlightenment writer Voltaire's public rejection of religion explains the nature of his last words, spoken to a priest who visited his deathbed hoping that he might repent:

> " In God's name, let me die in peace! "

Then, looking at the lamp burning at his bedside, he said:

> " The flames already? "

DIED 1778

GOING,

| POPULATION 500,000 | POPULATION 3,500 | POPULATION 2,500 | POPULATION 500 | POPULATION 500 | POPULATION 450 |

VULNERABLE   **ENDANGERED**   **CRITICALLY ENDANGERED**

AFRICAN ELEPHANT

POPULATION
c. 500,000
HABITAT
Sub-Saharan Africa

REASONS ENDANGERED
Poaching for bushmeat
and ivory: despite the
ivory trade being made
illegal, some 10,000
elephants are killed
every year for ivory.

BENGAL TIGER

POPULATION
3,000–4,500
HABITAT
Mainly India. Some
in Bangladesh, Bhutan,
China, Nepal, and
Myanmar

REASONS ENDANGERED
Poaching for medicines,
aphrodisiacs, and fur.
Widespread destruction
of habitat for human
settlement and decline
of prey species.

EASTERN LOWLAND GORILLA

POPULATION
2,000–3,000
HABITAT
Eastern DR Congo

REASONS ENDANGERED
Hunting, and
destruction of habitat
by commercial mining
for tin and tantalum,
which is used in
capacitors of electronic
equipment such
as cell phones.

PYGMY HOG

POPULATION
500
HABITAT
Assam, India

REASONS ENDANGERED
Destruction of grassland
habitat through burning
for clearance, and
hunting. The pygmy hog
is the world's smallest
pig: adults are just 27½
in (70 cm) long, 12 in
(30 cm) tall, and weigh
about 22 lb (10 kg).

GRAY NURSE SHARK

POPULATION
500
HABITAT
Coastal waters of
Atlantic, Indian, and
West Pacific Oceans

REASONS ENDANGERED
At one time killed in
the mistaken belief that
they were dangerous
to humans; in fact,
they are harmless.
Continued danger from
illegal fishing and shark
finning for soup.

MEDITERRANEAN MONK SEAL

POPULATION
400–500
HABITAT
Atlantic and East and
South Mediterranean

REASONS ENDANGERED:
Hunted by fishermen
competing for fish;
food scarcity due to
overfishing by humans;
entanglement in
fishing nets; pollution;
and human activity,
including tourism near
breeding grounds.

GOING, GONE

POPULATION
120

POPULATION
35

POPULATION
1

When something's dead, it's dead. But when it's extinct, it's as dead as a dodo. Portuguese sailors named this flightless bird the *doudo*—Portuguese for silly—not just because it looked silly (which it did), but also because it behaved in a fatally silly way. Having no natural predators, dodos had no sense of danger and just stood around while sailors hunted them to extinction. Now that humans are supposedly more enlightened, there's no excuse for sending more animals the way of the dodo.

EXTINCT IN WILD

EXTINCT

GRAND CAYMAN BLUE IGUANA

POPULATION
120 in protected areas
HABITAT
Grand Cayman, Cayman Islands

REASONS ENDANGERED
Human settlement, leading to loss of habitat and deaths on roads; predation by dogs and feral cats. Population up from 25 in 2002 thanks to conservation.

AMUR LEOPARD

POPULATION
35 in wild
HABITAT
Eastern Russia

REASONS ENDANGERED
Poaching, destruction of habitat by forest fires and commercial development, and decline of prey species.

PINTA ISLAND GALAPAGOS GIANT TORTOISE

POPULATION
1
HABITAT
Pinta Island, Galapagos archipelago

REASONS ENDANGERED
Hunted for food in 19th century; goats destroyed remaining habitat. The last one, Lonesome George, is kept at the Charles Darwin Foundation research station and may live another 100 years.

TASMANIAN TIGER

EXTINCT
1936
HABITAT
Tasmania, Australia, and New Guinea

REASONS FOR EXTINCTION
Hunted as a threat to sheep. The last known example died in Hobart Zoo on September 7, 1936. The species was officially declared extinct in 1986.

PYRENEAN IBEX

EXTINCT
2000
HABITAT
Spanish and French Pyrenees

REASONS FOR EXTINCTION
Uncertain: possibly competition with other species. Some poaching. A small population survived in the Ordesa National Park but the last one, named Celia, was hit by a falling tree and found dead on January 6, 2000.

YANGTZE RIVER DOLPHIN (BAIJI)

EXTINCT
2006
HABITAT
Yangtze River, China

REASONS FOR EXTINCTION
Chinese industrialization leading to pollution and use of river for fishing, transportation, and hydroelectricity. Known as the Goddess of the Yangtze, the species was declared extinct on December 13, 2006.

LAST MEALS

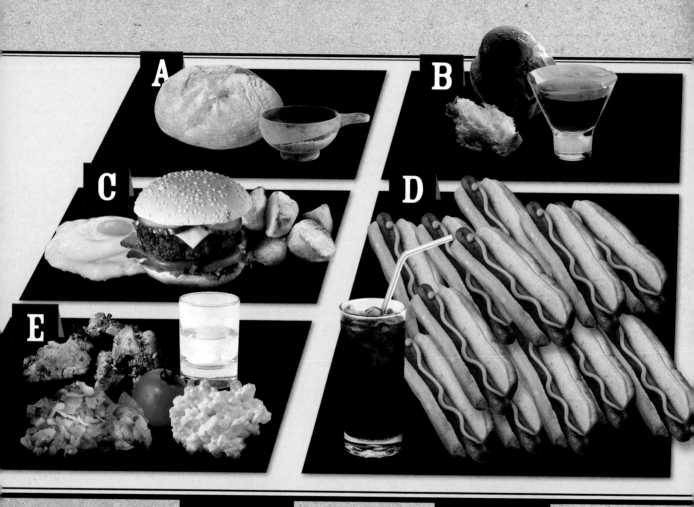

A. LAST SUPPER

According to the Christian gospels, Christ's last meal was a Passover supper of bread and wine that he shared with his disciples. Holy Communion is a symbolic reenactment of this Last Supper.

B. KING CHARLES I

On January 30, 1649, English monarch Charles I was beheaded after being sentenced to death for treason by Oliver Cromwell's parliament. His last meal was bread and a red wine. He reputedly wore two shirts to his execution to prevent him from shivering, lest the people watching mistake coldness for fear.

C. GARY GILMORE

Gary Gilmore was accused of committing two murders while carrying out armed robberies, but was only tried for one. Offered the choice of hanging or firing squad he said: "I'd prefer to be shot." He was executed on January 17, 1977, after a last meal of hamburger, eggs, and potatoes. His last words were "Let's do it."

D. JOHN ROOK

John William Rook was executed by lethal injection on September 19, 1986, for the rape and murder of a nurse. His last meal was a dozen hot dogs with mustard and a can of cola.

E. LARRY WHITE

Larry Wayne White was executed on May 22, 1997, for the murder of a 72-year-old woman. His last meal was liver and fried onions, tomatoes, cottage cheese, and a glass of water. The state refused him a last cigarette on health grounds.

"Dead man walking" is the call that goes up in US prisons when a condemned man is led to the death cell—or, less often, "dead woman walking." Part of the pre-execution ritual, equivalent to a last cigarette, is the prisoner's last meal, eaten in the knowledge that it will not be digested. Here are 10 meals consumed by "dead men eating."

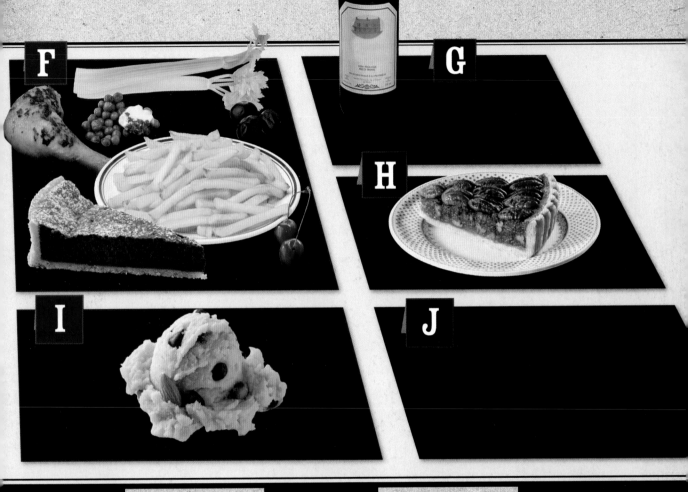

F. BRUNO HAUPTMANN

Bruno Hauptmann was executed on April 3, 1936, for the abduction and murder of the 20-month-old son of American pioneer aviator Charles Lindbergh. Despite paying a $50,000 ransom, Lindbergh's baby was found dead two months later. Hauptmann's last meal was celery, olives, chicken, french fries, buttered peas, cherries, and a slice of cake.

G. ADOLF EICHMANN

Nazi war criminal Adolf Eichmann once boasted: "I will leap to my grave laughing because the feeling that I have five million human beings on my conscience is for me a source of extraordinary satisfaction." The only person to be judicially executed in Israel, his last meal was half a bottle of Carmel (a dry red wine).

H. RICKEY RECTOR

Rickey Ray Rector was executed by lethal injection on January 24, 1992, after killing a civilian and a police officer while robbing a convenience store. His mental fitness to be executed was called into question when he left part of his last meal saying that he wanted to keep his pecan pie "for later."

I. TIMOTHY McVEIGH

Timothy McVeigh, aka "the Oklahoma Bomber," was executed on June 11, 2001, for his part in killing 168 people in the 1995 Oklahoma City bombing. His last meal was two pints of mint chocolate chip ice cream.

J. LARRY HUTCHERSON

Larry Eugene Hutcherson was executed on October 25, 2006, for the murder of an 89-year-old woman. He didn't request a final meal, choosing instead to eat from a prison vending machine with members of his family.

famous LAST WORDS 2

> People who are prepared to express strong opinions often go a long way. But if you live by the sword, you die by the sword—those strong opinions can prove spectacularly wrong, severely embarrassing the person who expressed them and, in some cases, costing their companies millions of dollars.

tony blair

"**S**addam Hussein's… weapons of mass destruction program is active, detailed, and growing. The policy of containment is not working. The WMD program is not shut down, it is up and running now. The intelligence picture is extensive, detailed, and authoritative."

British Prime Minister Tony Blair on September 25, 2002

margaret thatcher

"**N**o woman in my time will be Prime Minister or Chancellor or Foreign Secretary—not the top jobs. Anyway, I wouldn't want to be prime minister; you have to give yourself 100 percent."

Britain's Margaret Thatcher, who in 1979 became the first female Prime Minister in Europe

"**F**orget it, Louis. No Civil War picture ever made a nickel." *irving thalberg*

Irving Thalberg, head of production at MGM, advising Louis B. Mayer not to bother bidding for the film rights to *Gone With the Wind*

"**W**ho the hell wants to hear actors talk?" *harry warner* of Warner Brothers, 1927

irving fisher

"**S**tocks have reached what looks like a permanently high plateau."

Irving Fisher, Economics Professor at Yale University, in 1929, just before the Wall Street Crash

jono coleman

"**S**he's a great little actress, but I don't think she'll be giving up the day job any time soon."

Australian disc jockey Jono Coleman after playing Kylie Minogue's first single

"**T**his "telephone" has too many shortcomings to be seriously considered as a means of communication. The device is inherently of no value to us."

Western Union internal memo, 1876 *western union*

"**N**o flying machine will ever fly from New York to Paris." *orville wright*

American aviation pioneer Orville Wright

"**Y**ou care for nothing but shooting, dogs, and rat catching, and you will be a disgrace to yourself and your family."

robert darwin

Robert Darwin to his young son, Charles, who would go on to formulate the Theory of Evolution by Natural Selection

dionysius lardner

"**N**o steamship could be built large enough to carry sufficient coals for a voyage across the Atlantic."

Irish professor and science writer Dionysius Lardner, early 19th century

"**T**he wireless music box has no imaginable commercial value. Who would pay for a message sent to nobody in particular?"

rca

Associates of David Sarnoff, head of the Radio Corporation of America (RCA), responding to his requests for investment during the 1920s

"**A**irplanes are interesting toys but have no military value."

French Marshal Ferdinand Foch, Allied Commander-in-Chief at the end of World War I

ferdinand foch

William Thomson, Lord Kelvin, President of the Royal Society, in the 1890s

lord kelvin

"**H**eavier-than-air flying machines are impossible."

"**T**elevision? The word is half Greek and half Latin. No good will come of it."

Editor of the UK's *Manchester Guardian* (attributed), 1928

charles prestwich scott

"**W**e don't like their sound. Groups with guitars are on their way out."

dick rowe

Dick Rowe, A&R man at Decca, turning down the Beatles in 1962

"**E**verything that can be invented has been invented."

Charles H. Duell, Commissioner, US Office of Patents, 1899 (widely attributed, possibly apocryphal)

charles b. duell

"**A** guitar's all right, John, but you'll never earn your living by it."

John Lennon's Aunt Mimi

aunt mimi.

"**T**he abdomen, the chest, and the brain will forever be shut from the intrusion of the wise and humane surgeon."

Sir John Eric Ericksen, Surgeon-Extraordinary to Queen Victoria

eric ericksen

"**H**is ears are too big. He looks like an ape."

American film producer Darryl F. Zanuck, refusing to sign Cary Grant to Warner Brothers

darryl f. zanuck

"**I** believe it is peace for our time... peace with honor." *neville chamberlain*

British Prime Minister Neville Chamberlain on September 29, 1938, less than a year before the outbreak of World War II

WHERE
THERE'S A WILL...

Humans love an oddball. Eccentrics make life more interesting, and some of them also make death more interesting with their strange bequests. Most people leave their fortune to their families, some to charity, and a few to fund museums and prizes. But some eccentrics use their will as a way to have the last laugh.

FAT REWARDS

An anonymous Scotsman found an intriguing way of rewarding his daughters for eating well: in his will he bequeathed to each of them her weight in one pound notes. The elder daughter, who was slightly slimmer, inherited £51,200. The younger one reaped the rewards of a bigger appetite by inheriting £57,433.

CURSED INHERITANCE

Oliver Winchester made his fortune producing rifles, and when he died in 1880 his last bequest was not unusual: he left the entire fortune to his son, William. But William died the following year, aged only 41. He left everything to his wife, Sarah, to whom it proved more of a curse than a blessing. Sarah inherited more than $20 million, plus just under 50 percent of the Winchester Repeating Arms Company: the company that built what Confederate soldiers called "the damned Yankee rifle you could load on Sunday and shoot all week."

Grieving for her husband, Sarah consulted a medium who told her that the ghosts of the thousands killed by Winchester rifles were seeking vengeance, and that the only way to appease these restless spirits was to continuously build a house for them. Legend has it that the medium told her:

"You can never stop building the house. If you continue building, you will live.
Stop and you will die." Sarah moved to Santa Clara, California, and began building in 1884, continuing until her death on September 5, 1922. In those 38 years,

SHE SPENT $5.5 MILLION

extending the house to some 160 rooms covering an area of 4 acres (1.6 hectares), making it one of the US's largest homes.

Now known as the Winchester Mystery House, this bizarre creation has 1,257 windows, 950 doors, and 367 stairs in 40 staircases, some of which lead nowhere.

USE MY SKULL

In 1955, Argentinian Juan Potomachi left the equivalent of some $85,000 to his local theater, Teatro Dramatico, on the condition that they used his skull when performing one of the most misquoted scenes in Shakespeare's play *Hamlet*. Hamlet, who finds Yorick's skull in a graveyard, is often misquoted as saying: "Alas, poor Yorick. I knew him well." The correct quote is... actually...

... "ALAS, POOR YORICK. I KNEW HIM, HORATIO."

THE LURE OF MONEY

When Canadian lawyer and financier Charles Millar died in 1928, he left more than half a million dollars-worth of cash and shares in a series of bizarre posthumous social experiments.

To discover how far people would go in betraying their principles for wealth he left shares in a race track to a preacher and a judge whom he knew to be against gambling (both accepted), shares in a brewery to a group of churchmen whom he knew to be opposed to alcohol (only one said no), and a vacation home to three people who hated each other, on the condition that they share it (they did).

Strangest of all, he left $500,000 (sometimes recorded as $750,000) to whichever woman from Toronto, Canada, "has given birth to the greatest number of children at the expiration of 10 years from my death." The subsequent race to give birth became known as the Stork Derby. It was tied by four women, each of whom gave birth to nine children in those 10 years: Annie Smith, Isabel MacLean, Kathleen Nagle, and Lucy Timleck. A fifth woman, called Pauline Clarke,

GAVE BIRTH TO TEN CHILDREN, BUT WAS DISQUALIFIED

because five of them were born out of wedlock. A sixth woman, Lillian Kenney, was disqualified because several of her 12 children had died and she could not prove that they were not stillborn.

Clarke and Kenney were each given a $12,500 consolation prize and the remainder of the prize money was divided among the other four.

STORK DERBY

ALL IN A NAME

London stationer John Nicholson was so proud of his family name that he left most of his estate for the benefit of poor people named Nicholson. Part of his will, dated April 28, 1717, specified that £100 a year should be divided among poor boys or girls who wanted to learn a trade—if they were named Nicholson. Another £100 a year was to fund the weddings of impoverished couples who could not afford to marry—but only if both their names were Nicholson. Nicholson appointed five executors of his will, all of them called... Nicholson.

MAY THE NAME OF NICHOLSON LIVE FOREVER

MARITAL STRIFE

In 1940, the German Romantic poet Heinrich Heine was challenged to a duel by the husband of a woman Heine had publicly accused of adultery with another writer. Fearing he might be killed in the duel, he quickly married his girlfriend, Mirat, so that she would not be left destitute.

HE LEFT HER HIS ENTIRE ESTATE ON ONE CONDITION...

In any event, he survived the duel and, when he eventually died 16 years later, he left his entire estate to Mirat on one condition—that she remarried. Clearly their relationship had gone downhill because the reason Heine gave for this strange condition was "so that there will be at least one man to regret my death."

CRIME WRITER'S LAST WORK

English crime novelist Dame Agatha Christie bequeathed an unpublished novel to her fans. During World War II, Christie wrote and deposited for safe-keeping the last case of her fictional detective, Miss Marple. Called *Sleeping Murder*, it was published after her death as her...

... LAST BEQUEST TO HER MILLIONS OF FAITHFUL FANS.

THE END IS NIGH

The end is nigh! All human talk is of global warming but they'll probably all be dead long before that happens. Humans are under constant threat of imminent catastrophe from asteroids, solar flares, biotech disasters, and much, much more. Earth and any surviving animals would actually be better off without humans around—but if they're sucked into a black hole they'll all go together.

ASTEROID IMPACT

An asteroid impact wiped out the dinosaurs and it could happen again. In December 2004, astronomers estimated that asteroid 2004 MN4 had a 1-in-38 chance of hitting Earth in 2029. Scientists now say it's no longer on a collision course—but there will be others.

GAMMA-RAY BURST

There's no way of predicting these unfathomably powerful energy blasts from exploding stars (supernovae). The result of a supernova occurring within 1,000 light-years could either burn off the ozone layer, creating an oxygen-less inferno, or cause another ice age.

BLACK HOLE

When stars collapse, they create a gravity field so strong that not even light can escape. If a black hole approached the solar system, we wouldn't see it until it was too late. Even if Earth weren't sucked in and crushed, its orbit would be altered, taking us out of the zone crucial for life to continue.

MAGNETIC-FIELD REVERSAL

This happens every 100,000 years or so. And it's been 780,000 years since the last one, so it could happen again soon. The magnetic field dwindles, reverses, and regains strength, but, in the meantime, Earth has no protection from particle storms and cosmic rays. The field is currently decreasing.

MEGA VOLCANIC ERUPTION

So-called "super volcanos" occur every 50,000 years or so, filling the atmosphere with ash and sulfur that veils the Earth in darkness for several years, lowers global temperatures, and alters climate. Scientists estimate such an eruption is 12 times more likely than an asteroid impact.

GLOBAL PANDEMIC

Pandemics kill more people than any other man-made or natural disaster. The black death killed c. 75 million and the world is a much more crowded place now. The flu killed 20 million between 1918 and 1920, and AIDS has already killed nearly 30 million. Watch out for H5 avian flu, SARS, and MRSA.

GLOBAL WARMING

This is already happening. Rising temperatures will mean less oxygen in the air, melting ice caps, higher sea levels causing widespread flooding, extreme weather conditions, crop failures and food shortages, animal extinctions—and a vicious circle, meaning it doesn't just get steadily worse, it will accelerate.

BIOTECHNOLOGY DISASTER

Genetic modification (GM) of plants or animals supposedly creates improved genetic strains for food or medicine. But nature isn't controllable, and GM can cause harm as well as do good. Modified genes leaking into weeds and pests could cause eco-havoc; and GM diseases would make very nasty bio-weapons.

PARTICLE ACCELERATOR MISHAP

In the 1990s, concerns were raised that a Relativistic Heavy Ion Collider in New York might create a subatomic black hole that would swallow the material around it, growing ever bigger and eventually consuming the Earth. (Scientists have given assurances that such a scenario is impossible.)

NANOTECHNOLOGY DISASTER

Technology is getting smaller all the time. Scientists have developed robots so small they can be sent into the body to carry out medical procedures; and self-replicating robots are on the way. So how long before self-replication gets out of control, or terrorists get hold of microscopic robots developed as weapons?

NUCLEAR DESTRUCTION

MAD or "Mutually Assured Destruction" (the fact that the superpowers would destroy each other if nuclear war broke out) is what kept the Cold War chilled. But that balance of power doesn't apply to the Middle East, North Korea, India, or Pakistan, all of which have been developing nuclear weapons.

TELOMERE EROSION

Chromosomes are kept stable by "caps" called telomeres. As humans age, the telomeres get shorter, leading to age-related diseases. One theory is that they get shorter from one generation to the next, and as the human race ages, diseases will strike earlier, potentially causing a population crash and extinction.

CUSTOMS AND ETIQUETTE

THAT'S ALL, FOLKS

When humans die, their friends and family put the body in a box and then generally either burn it or bury it. In most parts of the world, funerals are somber affairs, but in Ghana they add a touch of pizzazz by building coffins that reflect the character of the deceased—here, a fisherman is taken on his funeral procession in a coffin made in the image of a tsile fish.

GLOSSARY OF USEFUL WORDS

Would you rather be a martyr to pentheraphobia or medomalacophobia? Do you know your double eagle from your eagle, your knot from your serif? And what do MACHO and PDS stand for? Humans don't know the meaning of half their own words, so read on and stun them with your superior knowledge of this miscellany of special terms.

AAM
In aviation, acronym for an Air-to-Air Missile: a radar- or heat-guided missile fired at an enemy aircraft or missile fired from another aircraft.

Accommodation
Not just somewhere to live; in human biology, the process by which the eyes adjust to focus on nearby or distant objects.

Aga
Acronym for a range-style stove, taken from the initial letters of the Swedish *Aktienbolager Gas Akumulator* company.

Aileron
In aviation, a movable control surface on an aircraft wing's far trailing edge.

Alan (Whickers)
Cockney rhyming slang for "knickers" (British word for underpants).

Alektorophobia
An exaggerated and persistent fear of chickens.

Anticline
In geology, an archlike upward fold of rock due to horizontal compression.

Apogee
In astronomy, the point on a body's orbit at which it is at its greatest distance from the Earth.

Architrave
In architecture, a decorative molding used around a wall recess or opening, such as a doorway.

Arctophile
A person who collects teddy bears.

Aristotle
Cockney rhyming slang for "bottle."

Arithomania
An abnormal, uncontrollable, or obsessive urge to count objects.

Avicide
The act of deliberately killing, or a person who deliberately kills, birds.

Baculum
A bone found in the penis of some mammals.

Bad bishop
Chess term meaning a bishop that is unable to move because it is blocked by its pawns. It has nothing to do with ecclesiastics who deserve to be defrocked. *See also* Episcopicide.

Baguazhang
Martial art whose name means "eight shapes palms."

Boreal
In geography, referring to the colder parts—snowy winter, short summer—of the northern hemisphere between the Arctic and temperate zones.

Bouquet
Collective noun referring to a group of pheasants.

Bowrit
Nautical term for a spar extending forward from the bow of a ship, to which the foremast is fastened.

Bruxomania
An abnormal, uncontrollable, or obsessive urge to grind one's teeth.

Cadmean victory
A military victory that places the victor at a disadvantage, named after the ancient Phoenician Prince Cadmus, who slew a monster and cast its teeth across the ground, only to find that the teeth became soldiers.

Caryatid
In architecture, a column carved as a female figure.

Casque
A bony growth on the head of an animal.

Catadromous
In biology, describes freshwater fish, such as eels, that migrate to the sea to breed.

Ceticide
The act of deliberately killing, or a person who deliberately kills, whales.

Chaff
Radar-reflective particulate matter released by an aircraft to confuse radar detection sytems; also, the husks of corn separated by threshing; also, to tease someone.

Chiromania
An abnormal, uncontrollable, or obsessive urge to masturbate.

Chitin
In biology, the horny substance that forms the shell of arthropods (crustaceans, insects, spiders).

Clinker
Nautical term used to describe a wooden ship built with overlapping planks.

Clowder
Collective noun referring to a group of cats.

Commensal
In biology, living in close association with, but not interdependent on, an organism of another species.

Conchologist
A person who collects or studies shells.

Coping stone
In architecture, an overhanging stone laid on top of a wall to protect it from the elements.

Copoclephile
A person who collects key rings.

Coprolalomania
An abnormal, uncontrollable, or obsessive urge to use foul language.

CRBT
Internet chatroom acronym meaning "Crying real big tears."

Cremnomania
An abnormal, uncontrollable, or obsessive interest in cliffs.

Cruck
Building term for a pair of large beams used as a frame to support a roof.

Cryptic
In biology, describes the plumage pattern and colors that disguise a bird in its favored habitat.

Cryptocrystalline
Geological term meaning made from crystals too small to be seen with the human eye.

Curse of Scotland
Card-players' nickname for the nine of diamonds.

Cut a voluntary
Fox-hunting term for falling off one's horse.

Dancing queen
Bingo-calling term for the number 17.

Deltiologist
A person who collects or studies postcards.

Devil, The
Poker players' nickname for a hand of three sixes, after 666, "the number of the beast."

Diesel
Named after its inventor, 19th-century German engineer Rudolf Diesel, an internal combustion engine (and its fuel).

Doldrums
A region of very light winds close to the equator.

Double Eagle
Golfing term for a score of three shots under par on a given hole. Rarer than an eagle (two under par) or a birdie (one under par)—and soaring above a bogey/double bogey (one/two over par).

Double top
Darts term for the number double 20.

Drapetomania
An abnormal, uncontrollable, or obsessive urge to run away.

Duck
Cricketing term for being out without scoring a run, derived from the duck's-egg shape of "O."

Episcopicide
The act of deliberately killing, or a person who deliberately kills, a bishop.

Eversible
Usually with reference to a bodily part such as the intestines, capable of being turned inside out.

Exaltation
Collective noun for a group of larks.

Forest
Poker players' nickname for a hand of four threes (four "trees").

Fumarole
In volcanology, a vent in or near a volcano through which hot gases can escape.

Futtock
Boat-building term for a curved piece of wood that forms part of the rib or frame of a ship.

Gegenschein
A faint patch of light in the sky that can be seen opposite the Sun on a moonless night.

Gephyromania
An abnormal, uncontrollable, or obsessive urge to cross bridges. The opposite of gephyrophobia/gephydrophobia—an exaggerated and persistent fear of crossing bridges.

Gestapo
Acronym for the Nazi secret police, from the initial letters of *GEheime STAats POlizei*.

Gondola
The passenger compartment that hangs from a balloon or airship.

Guillotine
Device for beheading, named after the 18th-century French physician Joseph-Ignace Guillotin's proposal for a more humane method of execution.

Hadley cell
In geography, the large-scale circulation of air in warmer regions, caused by warmed air rising near the equator, traveling to mid-latitudes, cooling and descending, and returning to the equator as the trade winds.

Hank (Marvin)
Cockney rhyming slang for "starving."

Horsemen, The
Poker players' nickname for a hand of four kings (from the Four Horsemen of the Apocalypse).

HOTAS
Aeronautical acronym for Hands-On Throttle And Stick—a flying system with all the switches on the throttle and control stick.

Ichthyophobia
An exaggerated and persistent fear of fish.

Inclusion
In geology, a crystal or fragment of another substance enclosed in a crystal or rock.

Ithyphallic
In sculpture, showing an erect penis.

Jeet Kune Do
Martial art whose name means "way of the intercepting fist."

Kakorrhaphiophobia
An exaggerated and persistent fear of failure or defeat.

Karate
Martial art whose name means "way of the empty hand."

Knot
Collective noun referring to a group of toads.

Laser
Acronym for Light Amplification by Stimulated Emission of Radiation—a device producing an extremely powerful, narrow beam of light.

Lek
A gathering of birds at which males put on displays of mock fighting, while females look on and choose which to mate with.

Leotard
One-piece, tight-fitting garment worn for dance and exercise, named after 19th-century French trapeze artist Jules Léotard.

Linonophobia
An exaggerated and persistent fear of string.

Littoral
In geology, refers to the shoreline, expecially the area between the high- and low-water marks.

Logophobia
An exaggerated and persistent fear of words.

Lord Nelson
Darts and cricketing term for a score of 111 (one eye, one arm, one testicle).

Machicolation
In medieval castles, a projecting parapet with floor openings through which molten lead or stones could be dropped on attackers.

MACHO
Astronomical acronym for MAssive Compact Halo Object—a very low-luminosity object, such as a planet or black hole, that exists in the halo of a galaxy but is usually too faint to be seen directly.

Macropocide
The act of deliberately killing, or a person who deliberately kills, kangaroos.

Medomalacophobia
An exaggerated and persistent fear of losing erection during sexual intercourse.

Melba
The 19th–20th century Australian opera singer Dame Nellie Melba gave her name to two delicacies: thin, crispy Melba toast and the fruit sundae dessert Peach Melba.

Meninges
In human biology, three membranes that surround and protect the brain and spinal cord.

MODEM
Acronym for a device used to connect a computer to a telephone line, from the initial letters of MOdulator-DEModulator.

Motown
Poker players' nickname for a hand of two jacks and two fives (jacks on fives sounds like Jackson Five).

Murder
Collective noun referring to a group of crows.

Nicotine
The addictive alkaloid found in tobacco, named after Jean Nicot, the 16th-century French diplomat said to have introduced tobacco to France.

Nogging
Building term for a short piece of wood set between two studs, joists, or rafters to strengthen stud walls, floors, and roofs.

Numinous
Divine; anything regarded as mysterious or "the wholly other" leading to belief in the sacred or supernatural. Not to be confused with luminous—radiating or reflecting light.

Numismatist
A person who collects coins.

Nunatak
In geography, a mountaintop rising above an ice sheet that is otherwise covering the land.

Oenophilia
A love of wine.

Ossicles
In human biology, the three tiny bones in the middle ear that convey vibrations from the eardrum to the inner ear.

Pair of dogs
Poker players' nickname for a hand of two kings and two nines (two K9s).

Pantophobia
An exaggerated and persistent fear of everything.

Parliament
Collective noun referring to a group of owls.

Glossary continued

PDS
Internet chatroom acronym meaning "Please don't shout" (or, rather, "Please DON'T USE CAPITALS").

Peep
Collective noun referring to a group of chickens.

Pentheraphobia
An exaggerated and persistent fear of one's mother-in-law.

Philemaphobia
An exaggerated and persistent fear of kissing—not to be confused with philophobia, a fear of love.

Photophore
In zoology, a light-producing organ, especially in some fish.

Phreatic eruption
A type of volcanic eruption where groundwater is turned into steam by contact with hot rocks near the Earth's surface.

Pixel
Acronym for a single element of a digital image, from the initial letters of PICture (PIX) and ELement.

Pogonophobia
An exaggerated and persistent fear of beards.

Polyandry
Marriage of a woman to more than one husband at once.

Poop deck
In nautical terms, the highest deck on a ship, fitted above the quarter-deck.

Praline
Confection of nuts in caramelized sugar, named after the 17th-century French soldier with a sweet tooth, Field Marshal César de Choiseul, Count du Plessis-Praslin.

Pyrrhic victory
A victory achieved at almost as great a cost as defeat, named after King Pyrrhus of Epirus.

Radar
Acronym for a radio detection system, from the initial letters of RAdio, Detecting, And Ranging.

Richard (the Third)
Cockney rhyming slang for "turd."

RTBM
Internet chat room acronym meaning "Read the bloody manual."

Sandwich
Named after 18th-century English aristocrat John Montagu, the 4th Earl of Sandwich, who reputedly called for his meat between two slices of bread so he wouldn't have to leave the gambling table to eat.

Sans serif
Typographical term for the absence of decorative lines on the ends of printed letters (like this typeface; compare with this serif typeface).

Schistosity
In geology, foliation (leaf-life layers) that occurs in coarse-grained metamorphic rocks, generally the result of flaky mineral grains.

Screed
In building, a layer of mortar laid over a concrete floor pad for a smooth finish.

Scute
In zoology, any of the horny plates that form the outer covering of turtle shells or other similar protective structures.

Sessile
In biology, fastened to a solid surface and unable to move freely. It usually relates to invertebrates such as barnacles that live in the water. In plants, sessile describes flowers or leaves that have no stalk and grow straight from the stem.

Se-tenant
Philatelic (stamp-collecting) term for two or more stamps that are issued together on a sheet even though they are of different values or designs, often forming part of a composite design.

Shrapnel
A term for either a shell filled with metal fragments or the flying fragments of the shell casing, named after English army officer Henry Shrapnel, who invented the pellet-filled shell.

Shrewdness
Collective noun referring to a group of apes.

Skewer
In chess, forcing a player to move one piece thereby exposing another to capture.

Skulk
Collective noun referring to a group of foxes.

Slaty cleavage
In geology, the tendency of a rock, such as slate, to break along very flat planes into thin sheets.

Sophist
In philosophy, someone who seeks to win an argument rather than to find the truth. (In ancient Greece, a sophist was a teacher who taught the arts of oratory.)

Space-time
The intimate combination of space with a fourth dimension of time, first proposed in 1908.

Spandrel
In architecture, the triangular area between the sides of two adjacent arches and the line across their tops.

Speculum
In zoology, a colorful patch on a duck's hindwing formed by secondary feathers.

Supernova
In astronomy, a catastrophic event that destroys a star and temporarily causes its brightness to increase massively.

SWIM
Internet chatroom acronym meaning "See what I mean?"

Tantivy
A fox-hunting term for riding at full gallop.

Tegestologist
A person who collects or studies beer mats.

Tête-bêche
A philatelic term for a pair of stamps that are joined together but with one upside down.

Timbromania
An abnormal, uncontrollable, or obsessive interest in postage stamps.

Trichotillomania
An abnormal, uncontrollable, or obsessive urge to pull out one's hair.

Twilight zone
In biology, a vertical zone of water ranging from 660–3,300 ft (200–1,000 m) deep, where too little light penetrates to support photosynthesis.

Unkindness
Collective noun referring to a group of ravens.

Village People
Poker players' nickname for a hand of four queens.

Voussoirs
In architecture, the wedge-shaped blocks used in the construction of an arch or vault.

Wernicke's area
In human biology, part of the temporal lobe that plays a key role in speech; damage to this area causes fluent nonsense.

WIMP
Astronomical acronym for Weakly Interacting Massive Particle, a large part of the dark-matter content of the universe not yet detected.

WTGP?
Internet chatroom acronym meaning "Want to go private?"

Xylophagous
Of certain insects (best kept out of wooden houses and furniture), wood-eating.

Yardang
In geology, a wind-sculpted ridge of rock in a desert.

Zugzwang
Chess term meaning a situation in which any move a player can make is disadvantageous.

A

Abagnale, Frank 106
AC/DC 57
accidents 15, 78-9, 102-3, 124-5, 140-1, 156-7, 224-5, 238-9, 291, 298-9, 316-17
Adams, John Quincy 268
Aeschylus 335
AIDS 74, 91
aircraft 39, 78, 234-5, 236-7, 238-9, 290-1
Alberto, Carlos 228
album titles 56-7
Alcatraz 34, 253, 333
Alcock, John 291
alcohol 30-1, 84-5
Aldrin, Buzz 82, 253
alien abduction 131
alligators 25, 268-9
Ambrose, St 48
American Society of Civil Engineers 248-9
Anderson, Pamela 226, 227
Andress, Ursula 73, 249
anesthesia 211, 230
Anglin, John & Clarence 34, 253
angling 102
animals see Flora & Fauna
Apple, Fiona 57
Argyll and Sutherland Highlanders 142-3
Aristophanes 19
armed forces 196-7
Armstrong, Neil 82, 90, 246
asepsis 211
assassinations 55
Astaire, Fred 149
asteroids 350
athletics 172-3
atomic bomb 79, 351
9/11 attacks 50
Attila the Hun 334
Auschwitz 35
avalanches 75

B

Bacon, Roger 335
Bahala Na Gang (BNG) 301
Bailey, Robert Francis 68
baked beans 95
Baker, Chet 335
balloon sculpture 320-1
balls 88-9
barcodes 58, 94
Bardot, Brigitte 33
Barzun, Jacques 115
BASE jumping 102
baseball 114-15, 216, 310
Basinger, Kim 191, 269
basketball 217, 310
Bates, Paddy 146
beach volleyball 168-9
bears 16, 128, 268
The Beatles 51, 148, 319, 347
beauty 278-9
Beck 57
Beckford, Tyson 277
Beckham, David 148, 153
bed racing 318
beer 30-1, 165, 249
bees 96-7, 265, 316
Bentley, Dr. John Irving 68

Bergkamp, Denis 228-9
Bergman, Ingrid 279
Berlin Wall 35
Berry, Halle 227
Bessemer process 309
Bigfoot 50
Biker gangs 300
The Bilderberg Group 189
Billy the Kid 34
biometric ID cards 59
birds 262-3
black box 290
Black Dahlia 336
black holes 350
Blair, Tony 346
Blake, George 35
Blake, William 292
Blériot, Louis 291
Blondin, Charles 38
blood transfusions 101
BMX, freestyle 103
Bobbit, John Wayne 317
bobsled 254
body language 116-17
body piercing 294-5
bog snorkeling 323
Bogataj, Vinko 124
Bono, Sonny 335
bouncing bomb 253
boxing 26-9, 310
Brabham, Jack 255
The Brady Bunch 223
Brahe, Tycho 335
Brando, Marlon 12-13, 32-3
breakfast cereals 95
Breton, André 292
Brown, Arthur 291
Brown, Henry "Box" 35
bull-riding 104-5
Bundchen, Gisele 277
Burma, Kings of 334
Burns, Pete 245
Burton, Jake 53
business etiquette 266-7
Busst, Dave 125
butterflies 153, 262
The Byrds 56

C

Caesar, Julius 259, 340
cameras, concealed 178-9
Campbell, Donald 340
cancer 91
cannons 83
Cantona, Eric 229
Capone, Al 300-1
Carmouche, Sylvester 254
cars 89, 130-1, 297, 312-13
Cartwright Jr., Alexander 114
Casanova, Giacomo 34
cashpoints 247
Cass, Mama 335
Cathars 188
cats 120-1, 262
celebrities 32-3, 72-3, 132-3, 182-3, 190-1, 226-7, 268-9, 276-7
cell phones 58
Cervantes, Miguel de 340
Chamberlain, Neville 347
Channel Tunnel 248
Charles I, King 344
Charles VIII, King 334
cheerleading 102

cheese rolling 318
Cher 245
Chernobyl 79
chimpanzees 269
Christie, Agatha 349
Christie, Julie 73
civil unrest 131
cleats, soccer 88
climate change 162-3, 260-1, 351
climbing, mountain 103, 249
cloning 101
Clooney, George 268, 277, 279
clothing 64-7, 112
clouds 270-3
CN Tower 249
Cobain, Kurt 330
Cockerell, Christopher 253
coffee, instant 94
Cold War 82, 351
Columbus, Christopher 274
Communication
    Attract a mate 116-17
    Famous last words 340-1, 346-7
    Gang culture 300-1
    I want to be left alone 326
    Meet and drink 30-1
    Out of place 282-3
    Quote unquote 292-3
    Sign language 284-5
    Sweet nothings 204-5
    Trouble ahead 220-1
    Where there's a will... 348-9
    World karaoke 144-5
Concorde, The 291
concrete, reinforced 309
Connery, Sean 72, 73
conservation 260-1
conspiracies 90-1, 188-9
Coolidge, Calvin 268
Cooper, Alice 319
cosmetic surgery 244-5
cost of living 112-13
Cowper, William 242
Crass, Derrick 124
credit cards 58
cricket 254
crime 14-15, 54-5, 247, 332-3, 336-7, 344-5
Crippen, Dr. Hawley 55
crocodiles 128
Croll, James 341
Cruise, Tom 191
crustaceans 269
Cruz, Penelope 277
Culture 57
Curtis, Jamie Lee 191
Custer, General George 330
Customs & Etiquette
    Gurning 280-1
    It's still illegal... 134-5
    It's still legal... 16-17
    Job for life 288-9
    Men of the world 64-5
    Million-dollar humans 148-9
    National health 198-9
    National treasures 184-5
    Odd jobs 286-7
    Rules of attraction 278-9
    Rules of business 266-7
    Rules of dating 126-7
    Rules of drinking 164-5
    Rules of the road 46-7
    That's all, folks 352-3
    When in Rome 48-9
    Women of the world 66-7

    Work-life balance 112-13
    World party 40-1
    Worth its weight in gold 150-1
cycling 154-5, 172, 193, 224-5
cyclones 75

D

Darwin, Charles 347
dating 126-7, 204-5
Daytona 500 125
Dean, James 24, 32-3, 171, 279, 331
death 334-5, 340-1, 344-5, 348-9, 352-3
Dempsey, Jack 26
Depp, Johnny 226, 227
Derek, Bo 132
Descartes, René 340
desert survival 128
Devil's Island 34
Dickens, Charles 62, 69
Dingley, Nicholas 319
disasters 74-5, 78-9, 350-1
disease 15, 74, 91, 350
diving, free 102
DNA 55, 59, 101, 231
dodos 343
dogs 20-1, 101, 262-3
donkeys 275
doors, breaking down 131
driving 46-7, 176-7
drugs 16, 86-7, 318-19
Duncan, Isadora 334
Dunn, Irina 292
durian fruit 166
dwarf throwing 318
Dylan, Bob 57, 180, 330

E

Earth see Planet Earth
earthquakes 75, 131
ebola 91
Edison 275
Eichmann, Adolf 345
Eiffel Tower 107, 185
Ekberg, Anita 73
Ekland, Britt 133
electric chair 54-5
Electric Light Orchestra 56
electricity, saving 261
elephant polo 318
elevators 309
Elia, Kerry 245
emergencies, medical 316-17
Empire State Building 248, 308
end of the world 350-1
endangered species 342-3
endurance races 192-3
energy, saving 260-1
entertaining, business 267
environment, care of 260-1
epidemics 74, 91, 350
Escobar, Andrés 229
etiquette see Customs & Etiquette
Evans, Dennis 229
Everest, Mount 38-9, 193, 249
evolution 83
executions 55, 333, 344-5
expenditure, national 196-9
extinction 162, 342-3, 351

F

Faulkner, William 85
Fawcett, Farrah 133
Ferrari, Lolo 245
festivals 40-1
films 170-1, 222-3, 302-3
fingerprinting 55, 59
fire 25, 68-9, 83, 129, 131, 163
fish 95, 263, 275
Fixx, Jim 334
flirting 116-17
floods 131, 163
Flora & Fauna
    00s idols 276-7
    50s pin-ups 32-3
    60s sex symbols 72-3
    70s stars 132-3
    80s icons 190-1
    90s booty 226-7
    Animal house 268-9
    Animal miles 262-3
    At a stretch 218-19
    Bad hair day 180-1
    Bird scarer 186-7
    Breaking rank 142-3
    Comfort stop 136-7
    A narcotic web 86-7
    Going, going, gone 342-3
    Lord of the rings 294-5
    Man v beast 70-1
    "Man's best friend" 20-1
    Most deadly 44-5
    Paint that cat 120-1
    Painted lady 214-15
    Pet projects 100-1
    Queen bee 96-7
    Self-improvement 212-13, 244-5
    Superhuman 42-3
    Unwanted guests 92-3
    Vital statistics 230-1
    Wild sex 118-19
Foch, Marshal Ferdinand 347
Folk Nation gang 300
Food & Drink
    Come fly with me 290
    Big bird 250-1
    Dying for a drink 84-5
    Everyone loves a sausage 18-19
    Food firsts 94-5
    Last meals 344-5
    Local delicacies 166-7
    Supersize cookie 80-1
    Supersize fish stick 328-9
    Supersize maki 36-7
    Supersize marshmallow 240-1
    Supersize Scotch egg 174-5
football 124, 125, 173
forest fires 25, 129, 163
Frazier, Joe 27
Freemasons 188
frozen food 95
Fullmer, Gene 28-9
funerals 352-3

G

Gable, Clarke 347
gadgets, spies' 178-9
Gagarin, Yuri 82, 291
Gainsbourg, Serge 57
Galen 211
gang culture 300-1
Gardner, Ava 33
Garland, Judy 222
Gauguin, Paul 340
Gemmill, Archie 228
genetic modification 351
George V, King 341
Gérard, Balthasar 55
Gere, Richard 191
Gibson, Mel 191
gifts 48-9
Glass, Charles 35
Glass, Hugh 200
global warming 162-3, 260-1, 351
gold 150, 231
Golden Gate Bridge 249, 288-9
golf 88, 172-3, 255
Gone With the Wind 170, 346
Great Pyramids of Egypt 248
Great Wall of China 275
greetings 48
Grint, Rupert 269
gunpowder 83
gurning 280-1

H

Haakon VII, King 334
hairstyles 180-1
Hallidie, Andrew Smith 308
hand signs 168-9, 284-5
Harry, Debbie 133
Hanoi Rocks 319
Hasselhoff, David 227
health 198-9, 210-11, 264-5, 316-17
Hefner, Hugh 269
Heine, Heinrich 349
helicopters, firefighting 25
Hell's Angels 25, 300
Hepburn, Audrey 33, 279
Herbert, A. P. 18
Herzigova, Eva 226
Heysel Stadium 299
highways 177
Hillsborough Stadium 299
Hilton, Paris 269
The Hindenberg 331
hippos 268
Hitler, Adolf 51, 331
Holly, Buddy 291, 335
home-brewing 84-5
hooch 84-5
hooliganism, soccer 298-9
horse racing 173, 254, 286
hostage situations 130
Houdini 179
Houston, Whitney 191
hovercraft 253
Hoyle, Sir Fred 292
humans
  attraction between 116-17, 126-7, 278-9
  body facts & figures 230-1
  characteristics of 6
  and climate change 163

clothing 64-7
  and conformity 142-3
  evolution of 83
  insurance of body-parts 148-9
  Man v beast 70-1
  parasites 92-3
  phobias 152-3
  physical extremes 42-3
  spare parts 202-3
Hunt, Marsha 133
Hurst, Geoff 228
Huxley, Aldous 292
Hyneman, Jamie 140-1

I

Ibsen, Henrik 340
ice, thin 129
ice caps, polar 162
ice hockey 216, 311
ice pops 94
Identikit 55
Illuminati 189
industrial accidents 79, 351
Industrial Revolution 83, 309
injuries 102-5, 124-5, 156-7
insects 70-1, 76-7, 118-19, 152-3
insurance, body-parts 148-9
internet 58-9, 107, 127
inventions 122-3, 314-15, 346-7
invitations 48
Iron Age 83, 309
ironing, extreme 324-5
islands, artificial 146-7
Itaipú Dam 249

J

Jack the Ripper 332, 336
Jackson, Michael 245, 269
James I, King 268
Jaws 170
Jenney, William le Baron 309
jobs, unusual 286-7
Johansson, Scarlet 277
Johnson, Amy 291, 334
Johnson, Jack 26
Johnson, Samuel 31
Jolie, Angelina 269, 276, 277
Jones, Vinnie 229
jungle survival 129

K

Kafka, Franz 292, 330
karaoke 144-5
karate 338-9
Kath, Terry 319
Kennedy, John F. 82, 91, 330
keyhole surgery 210-11
Kidman, Nicole 153, 263
kidney harvesting 247
Killers, The 318
kite-flying 102
Klinsman, Jurgen 229
Knievel, Robert "Evel" 124
Knights Templar 188

Knowles, Beyonce 277
Kraftwerk 57
Krupa, Michael 35
Kubrick, Stanley 293
Kupcinet, Irv 293

L

Lake Bodom murders 337
Lambot, Joseph-Louis 309
landslides 74
Last Supper 306-7, 344
Lauda, Niki 125
lavatories 136-7, 274
law 16-17, 46-7, 134-5
Lawson, Henry 165
Led Zeppelin 319
Lee, Bruce 171
leeches 265
left handers 182, 209
Lennon, John 347
Leonardo da Vinci 38, 122, 278-9
Lepore, Amanda 245
Liebnitz, Gottfried 62
lightning 129
Lillelien, Bjorge 255
limbs, artificial 202-3
lions 268
Liu, Lucy 279
lobsters 269
lock-picking 179
Long, Dr. Crawford 211
Lopez, Jennifer 227, 319
Loren, Sophia 73
Lorz, Fred 254
Louis, Joe 26
love, language of 204-5
Lustig, Victor 107
luxury goods 150-1

M

McCartney, Paul 51, 319
McDonald's 167
McEnroe, John 311
MacGregor, Gregor 106
MacGyver 243
Machiavelli, Niccolò 341
MacPherson, Elle 191
McSorley, Marty 311
McVeigh, Timothy 345
Madonna 190
Mafia 189, 300
Magellan, Ferdinand 274
maggots 269
Malarchuck, Clint 124
malaria 15, 44
Mansfield, Jayne 33
Manson, Charles 171
Maradona, Diego 228
marathons 192-3, 201, 254-5, 282
Marciano, Rocky 27
Marescaux, Jacques 210
margarine 95
Marquis, Don 293
marriage 16-17
Martians 50-1
Martin, Anna 68
Martin, Dean 164

martini 30, 165
Marx, Karl 341
match-fixing 229
medicine, alternative 264-5
meetings, business 266-7
Meher Baba 340
Michelangelo 278
microchips 58
microwaves 315
migrations 262-3
military spending 196-7
Milla, Roger 228
Miller, Glenn 291, 335
minefields 130
Minogue, Kylie 277, 346
The Misfits 170
Mona Lisa 278
money 232-3
monkeys 269
Monroe, Marilyn 32, 170, 331
Montaigne, Michel Eyquem de 293
Montgolfier brothers 101
moon landings 82, 90, 255, 275
Moore, Mikki 269
Morales, Erik "El Terrible" 27
Moran, Dylan 293
Morris, Frank 34, 253
Morrison, Jim 318-19
Moto-X, freestyle 154
motor racing 89, 124-5, 255, 311
motorcycles, customized 312
muggers 247
mugging 131
Muhammad Ali 27, 73
murder 14, 24-5, 78, 336-7, 344-5
music 56-7, 144-5
Myths & Legends
  Better off dead 330-1
  Conspiracy theories 90-1
  Crime firsts 54-5
  Crime lasts 332-3
  Fact or fiction 140-1
  Forever young 222-3
  Great balls of fire 68-9
  Great escapes 34-5
  Hit the road 176-7
  Hoaxing Times 50-1
  Join the club 188-9
  Killers on the loose 336-7
  Modern myths 274-5
  Six degrees of celebrity 182-3
  Staying alive 200-1
  Urban myths 24-5, 246-7
  Ways to go 334-5
  Ways to make money 106-7
  Who's afraid of...? 152-3

N

names 56-7, 182-3, 282-3
Nefertiti, Queen 279
Neil, Vince 319
Nero, Emperor 254, 340
Nerval, Gérard de 269
Newman, Paul 72, 73
Newton, Sir Isaac 83
Niagara Falls 38, 101
Nixon, Richard M. 91
Norteños/Sureños gangs 301

North Sea Protection Works 249
nuclear technology 79, 351
numbers, the meaning of
  one 12-13
  two 62-3
  three 110-11
  seven 160-1, 248
  nine 208-9
  twelve 258-9
  thirteen 306-7

O

Oasis 57
octopush 318
oil spills 78
Old Christians rugby team 200
Olympic Games 254-5, 282, 298
O'Neill, Eugene 341
Onishenko, Boris 255
optical instruments 211
Opus Dei 189
organs, artificial 202-3
origami 138-9, 234-5
ortolans 167
Orwell, George 58
Osbourne, Ozzy 318, 319
The Osmonds 222
Oswald, Lee Harvey 91
Otis, Elisha Graves 309

P

Palme, Olof 336
Panama Canal 249
paper planes 234-5
Papillon (Henri Charrière) 34
parasites 92-3
Paré, Ambroise 211
parking meters 176
Parton, Dolly 101, 148
Pascal, Blaise 292
Pastrana, Travis 154
patents 122-3, 347
Pavlova, Anna 341
Pearce, Guy 181
Pearl Harbor 90
Peek, Tony 293
Pele 228
penknives 242-3
People Nation gang 300
peppercorns 150, 233
The Pet Shop Boys 57
Petit, Philippe 38
pets 20-1, 120-1, 268-9
Philadelphia Experiment 90
Phillips, Agnes 69
phobias 152-3
Picasso, Pablo 18, 249, 293
pigs 152, 268
Piltdown Man 51
Pink Floyd 56
Piquet, Nelson 311
Pitt, Brad 226, 227
planes see aircraft
Planet Earth
  7 wonders of the world 248-9
  60 seconds to save the world 260-1
  Acts of God 74-5
  Cloud spotting 270-3
  Death and disaster 78-9

Don't go there 14-15
The end is nigh 350-1
The eve of destruction
    162-3
I will survive 128-31
Introduction to Earth 6-7
Own islands 146-7
Plague of locusts 76-7
Plato 340
pogo sticks 39
Poitier, Sydney 33
polar survival 128
Poltergeist 171
Ponzi, Charles 106
Poppen, Sherman 53
potato chips 94
Presley, Elvis 32, 33, 269,
    318-19, 331
Principality of Sealand 146-7
Prosperi, Mauro 201
prosthetics 202-3, 211
punk rockers 246
Pythagoras 62, 111

Q

quicksand 128

R

rail disasters 79, 274
rats 269
Ray, Allan 317
Rebel Without a Cause 171
recycling 260
Redford, Robert 133
Redmond, Derek 172
Redneck Games 318
Rensenbrink, Rob 229
restaurants 94, 165
Reynolds, Burt 133
Richards, Keith 319
Rickenbacker, Eddie 201
riders 318
Rivers, Neal 28-9
roads 15, 46-7, 176, 176-7
roadsigns 220-1
robotics 210, 351
rock 'n' roll 318-19
rocketpacks 39
Rolling Stones 318, 319
Romero, Monseñor Oscar 337
Roosevelt, F. D. 90, 152
Roosevelt, Theodore 268
Rosemary's Baby 171
Rosicrucians 188
Roswell UFO 91
rugby 173, 209, 282
Ryan, Chris 200

S

safety
    airline 290-1
    home 156-7
Saffin, Jeannie 68
Salazar, Eliseo 311
salt 151, 233
SARS 91
sausages 18-19

Savage, Adam 140-1
scams 106-7
scarecrows 186-7
Scott, Lloyd 255
sea levels 162
sea survival 129
secret societies 188-9
self defense 131
serial killers 78
Seven Wonders of the World
    248-9
sex 16-17, 118-19, 134, 318-19
sex symbols *see* celebrities
Shackleton, Ernest 201
Shakira 277
sharks 101, 128, 140, 152, 170,
    263, 342
Sharp, Pat 181
Shepherd, Alan 255
Shields, Brooke 191
sign language 284-5
Simpson, Jessica 268
Simpson, Joe 201
Simpson, O. J. 337
Sinatra, Frank 291
Skull & Bones 189
skydiving 194-5
skyscrapers 308-9
snakes 71, 118, 129, 152, 269
snowboarding 52-3
soccer 88, 125, 173, 217, 228-9,
    255, 298-9, 311
Socrates 341
solar system 6-7, 209
songs 144-5
Sophocles 335
South Sea Bubble 107
souvenirs 184-5
space 82, 100-1, 302, 350
SpaceShipOne 296
speed cameras 177
speed dating 127
spices 150-1
Spiderman 22, 23
spiders 86-7, 123, 152
spies 178-9
spontaneous combustion 68-9
Sports & Leisure
    America's national pastime
        114-15
    Backhanders 168-9
    Bad sports 310-11
    Balloon sculpture 320-1
    Bar tricks 98-9
    The beautiful game 228-9
    Big feats 38-9
    Board sports 324-5
    Bull-riding 104-5
    Classic bout 28-9
    Contact sports 338-9
    Crash and burn 124-5
    Deadly sports 102-3
    Excess all areas 318-19
    Extreme endurance 192-3
    Extreme sports 322-3
    Horror movies 170-1
    Little soccer horrors 298-9
    New balls, please 88-9
    On the slopes 52-3
    Origami 138-9
    Paper planes 234-5
    Road trip 224-5
    Sports superstitions
        216-17
    The sweet science 26-7
    Trick cyclist 154-5
    United we fall 194-5
    Unlucky breaks 172-3

What's in a name 56-7
    Winners and losers 254-5
Sprague, Eric 244
Springsteen, Bruce 318
Stanley, Hans 242
Stone, Sharon 293
streakers 264
Strelzyk, Peter 35
Strutt, William 309
superheroes 22-3, 303
Superman 22, 23, 170
superstitions, sporting 216-17
surfing, big-wave 103
surgery 210-11, 244-5, 316-17,
    347
surveillance 58-9, 178-9
survival
    stories 200-1
    techniques 128-31
Sushruta 211
Swan, Joseph 275
Swiss Army knives 242-3

T

tail, losing a 130
Taipei 101 308
Tardelli, Marco 228
tattoos 212-15
Taylor, Elizabeth 73, 291
Technology
    Big Brother 58-9
    Come fly with me 290-1
    Emergency Room 316-17
    Happy accidents 314-15
    Hide and seek 178-9
    How to become a superhero
        22-3
    Human spares 202-3
    Human transporters 296-7
    Man on the moon 82-3
    Money, money, money
        232-3
    Natural remedies 264-5
    Not in real life 302-3
    Patent junk 122-3
    Pimp your ride 312-13
    Plane crash 238-9
    Plane spotting 236-7
    Reach for the sky 308-9
    Remote control 210-11
    Safety in the home 156-7
    Sharpest tool in the box
        242-3
    What to do with a spoon
        252-3
    World of war 196-7
teleportation 23, 90
tennis 89, 217, 311
Thatcher, Margaret 255, 346
Theismann, Joe 124
Thomas, Dylan 335
Thomas, Henry 69
Thrust SSC 297
Thurman, Uma 227
tigers 268, 342
tightrope walking 38
The Titanic 331
toasts 30-1, 165
toe wrestling 318
tools
    improvised 252-3
    for spies 178-9
toponyms 282-3
tortoises 235, 263, 343

Tour de France 172, 193
tracking devices 179
traffic regulations 176-7
Transformer Monster Truck 296
transportation 112-13, 260-1
Travolta, John 133
Triads 301
tricks, bar 98-9
Tsiolkovsky, Konstantin 83
tsunamis 74
turkeys 250-1
Turlington, Christy 279
turtles 263
Twain, Mark 341
Tyson, Mike 27, 268, 310

U

UFOs 91
unicorns 123
urinals 249

V

V-2 rocket 82, 100
vacations 14-15, 131, 184-5
Valens, Richie 291, 335
Valentino, Rudolph 279
van Gogh, Vincent 330
Van Halen 319
Varley, Isobel 214-15
vehicles 296-7, 302
    see also aircraft; cars
Versace, Donatella 245
Vesalius, Andreas 211
Vicious, Sid 319
vodka 165
volcanoes 74, 350
Voltaire 341
von Braun, Wernher 82
Vrba, Rudolf 35

W

walking tanks 298
Wallis, Barnes 253
The Waltons 222
war, nuclear 79, 351
Washington, Denzel 279
Washington, George 242
water
    saving 261
    walking on 38, 122
Watt, James 83, 309
Watts, Tonya 286
weightlifting 124
Wek, Alek 279
Welles, Orson 50-1
Welsh, Raquel 72
Westerns 303
Wetzel, Günter 35
Wetzler, Arthur 35
wheel clamps 177
whisky 165
White, Destry 125
The White Stripes 56
white-water rafting 103
Wildenstein, Jocelyne 245
William "the Silent" 55
wills 348-9

Winchester Mystery House 348
wine 30-1, 282-3
Wingdings 50
Winnebago 246
witchcraft 333
Witt, Dr. Peter 86-7
women's rights 16-17
Wood, Natalie 153, 171
World War I 79, 255
World War II 79, 82, 347
Wright Brothers 290, 347

Y

Yakuza 189, 300
Yardies 300
Yorkshire Ripper 25

Z

Zidane, Zinedine 311
Zodiac killer 337
zorbing 318

ACKNOWLEDGMENTS

Picture credits

The publisher would like to thank the following for their kind permission to reproduce their photographs:

(Key: a-above; b-below/bottom; c-center; f-far; l-left; r-right; t-top)

Christine Acebo: www.flickr.com/photos/lightlypaintedpixels/ 21crb; **Action Images**: 173bl, 229tr; BM/RCS Reuters 102tr; CP Reuters 103tl; JPP/ Reuters 229bl; KM/ Reuters 228r; Brandon Malone 52tl; Steve Marcus/Reuters 27tr; MSI 27br; Steven Paston Livepic 103bl; Patrick Price 104-105; CB/BM/CLH/ Reuters 173c; Peter Schols/ Reuters 311br; Sporting Pictures (UK) Ltd 228br; **The Advertising Archives**: 181bc, 181br, 181cb, 181cl, 181l, 226, 290c; **akg-images**: Musée Africain, Lyon 233crb; **Alamy Images**: Rubens Abboud 147bl; Allstar Picture Library 277c; Arco Images 93cl, 265c; Bill Bachmann 40cl; Suzy Bennett 166cla; Barry Bland 322tr; blickwinkel/Peltomaeki 119bc; blickwinkel/ Schmidbauer 342-343c; Steve Bloom Images 342c; Oote Boe Photography 221l; Oote Boe Photography 2 221crb; Mark Bowler Amazon-Images 92bl; Buzz Pictures 322br; John Cancalosi 119c; Frank Chmura 22br; Nic Cleave Photography 41tr; Bruce Coleman/Tom Brakefield 343cl; Wendy Connett 308l; Gary Cook 342fcl; David Crossland 40br; CuboImages srl/Damiano Zanderighi 89tl; David Cumming/Eye Ubiquitous 249br; Sue Cunningham Photographic 249cr; Martin Cushen 323c; DJ Dates 167cl; Phil Degginger 75tr; Matthew Doggett 211fbr, 221cra; Darroch Donald 210; Craig Ellenwood 21c, 21cb, 21tr; Simon Evans 309bc; FilterEast 167tr; Food Features 167cr; Global Images 39tl; Simon Grosset 322cr; Rab Harling 221br; Glenn Harper 278br; Mike Hill 221bc, 342cl; Ilianski 185tl; Jack Jackson/Robert Harding Picture Library Ltd 75br; Jam World Images 343r; Peter Jordan 166cra; Kolvenbach 89bl; Kraus/f1 online 193cr; Yadid Levy 213c; J Marshall - Tribaleye Images 167cla; Mary Evans Picture Library 26bl, 54, 69, 83ca, 83cla, 83tl, 88tc, 88tl, 101tr, 211cr, 287tc, 309tl, 332bl; Antony Medley/SIN 318; MJ Photography 167tl; Peter Mundy 167bc; North Wind Picture Archives 309tr; James Osmond 221c; Andrew Paterson 314br; Photos 12 32, 33bc, 73br, 302tl, 303cl; Pictorial Press 279tc; Pictorial Press Ltd 33c, 51c, 291cb, 291crb, 302cr, 303br; Wolfgang Pölzer 118bl; Popperfoto 13c, 27bl, 27tl, 89cl, 89cla, 168tl, 173br, 228bc, 228l, 229c, 300tl; Gene Rhoden 272-273; Pablo Ricardo 316br; RightImage 202 (back brace); Kevin Schafer 343c; Skyscan Photolibrary 297bl; Jack Sullivan 168tr; The Print Collector 211bc, 309crb; Miro Vrlik Photography 166fcl; Mark Wagner Aviation-Images 291br; Andrew Woodley 21fcr; **The Trustees of the British Museum**: 233cl; **China Foto Press**: 167fcr; **Corbis**: 22cb, 55cr, 191cr, 211br; Nogues Alain 317bl; James L. Amos 315bl; Bernard Annebicque 23bc; Richard Baker 142-143; Tiziana and Gianni Baldizzone 233tr; Dave Bartruff 333bl; Mariana Bazo/Reuters 102bl; Bettmann 26br, 26tr, 28-29, 50tl, 74tl, 78b, 100, 134cl, 134clb, 134tr, 135c, 211c, 211cl, 222br, 223tr, 255tr, 279fbl, 286tr, 291cl, 309c, 309clb, 312cl, 330cl, 331b, 331t; Mike Blake/Reuters 245crb; Gene Blevins 296-297b; Danilo Calilung 345bl; Philippe Caron/Sygma 248tr; CinemaPhoto 279tl; Andy Clark/Bettmann 124t; Envision 19tr; epa 210bl; Robert Eric 279bl; Deborah Feingold 190; Firefly Productions 140-141; Rufus F. Folkks 279bc; Owen Franken 167bl; Tony Friedkin/Sony Pictures Classics/ZUMA 103br; Al Fuchs/NewSport 154-155; Louie Psihoyos/Larry Fuente 312-313; Lynn Goldsmith 133tr, 180; Philip Gould 102cl; Neil Guegan/zefa 261tr; Pierre Holtz/Reuters 76-77; Hulton-Deutsch Collection 133bc, 255cl; Ed Kashi 202 (arm); Kelly-Mooney Photography 312bl; Igor Kostin/Sygma 79tr; JP Laffont/Sygma 73cl; Danny Lehman 41bl; C. Lyttle/zefa 40bl; . Wayne Lockwood, M.D. 119tl; Francis G. Mayer 330tl; Stephanie Maze 312c; Amos Nachoum 102br; Alain Nogues 238-239; Charles O'Rear 4-5; Gianni Dagli Orti 278tl, 278tr; Jose Luis Pelaez 338-339; Neal Preston 287tl; Roger Ressmeyer 203 (legs), 288-289; Reuters 75l, 277bl, 286br; Patrick Robert 245tc; Joel W. Rogers 294-295; Patrick Roncen 193bl; Anders Ryman 232; William Sallaz 296b; Schwarzwaelder 279cl; Erica Shires/zefa 102tl; Julian Smith/epa 342fcr; Joseph Sohm/Visions of America 186-187; John Springer Collection 33br; Rolf Vennenbernd/Epa 136-137; Patrick Ward 312tl; Michael S. Yamashita 218-219, 233b; **DK Images**: Geoff Brightling/Courtesy of Denoyer - Geppert Intl 202 (veins); Courtesy of ESPL/ Denoyer-Geppert 274bl; Courtesy of H Keith Melton Collection 179tr; Courtesy of the H Keith Melton Collection 178bl, 178c; Geoff Dann/The Wallace Collection, London 55tl; Chas Howson/The British Museum 150–151; Judith Miller/Lyon and Turnbull Ltd 88bl; Judith Miller/Wallis and Wallis 344tc; Andy Crawford/Courtesy of the Football Museum, Preston 88bc, 88tr; Shanachie 57cl; Sony BMG Music Entertainment 56bl, 56cr, 56tl, 57br; Wenger SA 242-243; Liz Wheeler 65br, 65tc, 66bl, 66br, 66tl, 66tr, 67bl, 67br, 67cla, 67cra, 67tr; **Durrat al Bahrain**: 147br; **Robert Estall Photo Library**: Carol Beckwith/Angela Fisher 352-353; **Dr. J Fletcher**: 213cla; **FLPA**: Hugh Clark 343cr; Panda Photo 118tl; **Getty Images**: 27c, 33bl, 82br, 101bc, 101bl, 181cr, 181ftr, 227clb; Evan Agostini 279tr; David Ashdown 124bl; Bongarts 229br; Boston Museum of Science 315br; Shaun Botterill/ Allsport 125l; Matt Cardy 41tl; Del Castillo 227cla; CBS Photo Archive 50-51b; Skye Chalmers 52-53; Ralph Crane/Time Life 250-251; Sam Diephuis 267bl; Stuart Franklin 168-169; Kent Gavin 228tr; Daisy Gilardini 118tr; George Gojkovich 124br; Sylvain Grandadam 249tr; Stuart Hannagan 168cr; Alexander Hassenstein 168bl; Paul Hawthorne 245bc; Mike Hewitt 125br; Dave Hogan 245l; Kevin Horan 192bl; Hulton Archive 279br; Chris Jackson 245br; Dr. Dennis Kunkel 92-93; Ross Land 168br; Oliver Lang 279cr; David Livingston 21bl; John Lund 213cr; Jim McIsaac 317br; Ryan McVay 29r; Frank Micelotta 330cr; John Moore 22tc; Chuck Nacke 300tr; Kazuhiro Nogi 213br; Scott Olson 296-297t; Gabe Palacio 125tr; Pascal Pavani 172r; Mike Powell 103tr; Patrick Riviere 191bc; H. Armstrong Roberts 232-233; Norbert Rosing 118br; George Silk 287b; Victoria Snowber 176-177; Jamie Squire 168cl; Justin Sullivan 21bc; Yoshikazu Tsuno 23cl; Art Wolfe 74r; **GrahamWatson.com, Inc.**: 224-225; **Jason Hawkes Aerial Library**: 146, 147cl; **Illustrated London News Picture Library**: 333tc; **Imaginechina**: 167br, 265bl; **iStockphoto.com**: William Berry 185br; Donall O Cleirigh 209bc; Rob Friedman 208r; Ethan Myerson 23t; Graeme Purdy 209r; Nuno Silva 208-209c; Kevin Su 209bl; Glen Teitell 164bl; **jupiterimages**: 221tc; Steve Vidler/ImageState 249tl; **The Kobal Collection**: 20th Century Fox 291tc, 303tl; ABC/Paramount 223l; Baywatch Co/ Tower 12 Prods 227tc; Cinema City Film Prod 301tl; El Deseo S.a. 277tc; Hammer 72; Imagine/Universal 227bl; MGM 222l; NBC-TV 222cr; Rank 33cr; Romulus/ Warwick 223cr; Warner Bros 222bl, 223bl, 227br, 302bl; Wolper/Warner Bros 223br; **Susan & Jason Larkins www.yoda-dog.com**: 1, 5, 20; **Lonely Planet Images**: Frank Carter 167ca; Peter Ptschelinzew 166crb; Oliver Strewe 166cr; **Mary Evans Picture Library**: 51tr, 89cra, 135bl, 333l; Ad Lib Studios 55cl; David Lewis Hodgson 332-333c; **NASA**: 39bl, 82, 82tr, 83, 147cr; **National Costume Doll Collection/Josien Buijs**: 64br, 64cl, 64cr, 65bl, 65cb, 65tl, 66cl, 66cr, 67c, 67cl, 67clb, 67crb, 67tl; **naturepl.com**: Mark Brownlow 96-97; **NewsCast photo library**: Smiths Group plc 202 (insulin pump); **Niagara Falls Public Library**: 38bl; **PA Photos**: 173tc, 173tl, 254br, 255cr; AP 79br; AP Photo/Alan Welner 38cr; Charles Doherty 310tl; Gerry Kahrmann 311bl; Tony Marshall/EMPICS Sport 254cr; Michael Probst/Ap 26tl; S&G 254tl; Amy Sancetta 311t; Jack Smith 310r; USAF/Abaca/ABACA 13ca; Henny Wiggers/ AP 194-195; **The Patent Office**: 122tl, 123br, 123tr; **Photolibrary**: Joe Blossom/SAL 342cr; David M Dennis 23br; Floyd Holdman William/Index Stock Imagery 249bl; Max Gibbs 93br; Jtb Photo Communications Inc 40tc; David Kirkland 213clb; Patti Murray 343fcl; Nonstock Images 213bc; Doug Scott/Mauritius Die Bildagentur Gmbh 119bl; Claude Steelman 22cl; Frank P Wartenberg 212; Ariadne Van Zandbergen 119tr; **PHOTOPRESS/ Victorinox**: 242cr, 243c, 243tc; **PunchStock**: 202, 202 (hand), 203 (hip), 203 (leg); **Redferns**: Action Press 181r; Sony BMG Music Entertainment 57tr; Sympathy 4 the R.I. 56c; **Rex Features**: 20thc.fox/Everett 276; 39r, 52cl, 53tr, 202 (head brace), 213bl, 245tr, 286l, 287tr, 322tl, 324-325; Stuart Atkins 277bc; Matt Baron 279c; David Batchelor 181tr; Bruce R. Bennett 322bl; Peter Brooker 21cl, 21clb, 21cra, 244; John Chapple 21tc; Crollalanza 227cr; Andre Csillag 181bl; Andrew Dunsmore 322cl; Jeremy Durkin 245c; Everett Collection 73bc, 73cr, 73tc, 73tr, 133bl, 133br, 133cl, 133tc, 191tc, 291bl; Albert Ferreira 277br, 277tr; Neale Haynes 53c; Annelisen Jackbo 255br; Richard Jones 343fcr; Pete Lawson 147c; MGM/Everett 191c; Ita Molin 181tc; David Muscroft 280-281; Paramount 191br; Paramount/Everett 133cr; Gary Roberts 322fbr; Roger-Viollet 79l; Sinopix Photo Agency Ltd 297tl; Sipa Press 21cr, 33tc, 191bl, 245cra, 277cl, 277cr, 290bl, 290r, 300-301b, 316bl, 316c, 316cb; SNAP 33cl, 33tr, 73bl, 191cl, 191cra; Michele Tantussi 227bc; J Tavin/Everett 73c; Sam Tinson 322fbl; Warner Br/Everett 132; Les Wilson 245bl; **The Ronald Grant Archive**: Columbia 303cr; **Science & Society Picture Library**: Science Museum 89cr, 102 (iron arm), 202 (fork hand), 202 (hobbs hand), 202 (hook), 202 (iron arm), 202 (noses), 203 (foot), 203 (roman leg), 213tr; **Science Photo Library**: George Bernard 271tc; Dr. Pete Billingsley, University Of Aberdeen / Sinclair Stammers 44-45; Eye Of Science 93cr; David R. Frazier 271br; Geoeye 147tc; Pascal Goetgheluck 210tr; Steve Gschmeissner 93bl, 93tl; Klaus Guldbrandsen 23cr; Adam Hart-Davis 152-153; Dr Najeeb Layyous 210br; Jackie Lewin, Em Unit Royal Free Hospital 93bc; London School Of Hygiene & Tropical, Medicine 93tr; John Mead 271bl; Pekka Parviainen 270cr, 270tl, 271cr; George Post 270br; Alan Sirulnikoff 271tr; Volker Steger 93tc; **Shutterstock**: Stephen Coburn 185cr; Vladislav Gurfinkel 184bl; Anton Gvozdikov 184bc; Jason 185bl; Antonio Lacovelli 185bc; Oleg Lazarenko 185clb; Neven Mendrila 185crb; **Burton Silver & Heather Busch**: 120, 121bc, 121bl, 121br, 121ca, 121cb, 121cl, 121clb, 121cr, 121tr; **SuperStock**: age fotostock 290cr; **Switzerlandshop.com**: 185c; **Tails by the Lake.com**: 21br; **TopFoto.co.uk**: The British Library /HIP 78tl; **U.S. Patent Office**: 122bl, 122br, 122tr, 123cl, 123cr, 123tl; **Isobel Varley**: Alexander Wehowski 214-215; **www.macgyveronline.org**: 243bc, 243bl

Jacket images: Front: **Susan & Jason Larkins www.yoda-dog.com**

All other images © Dorling Kindersley
For further information see: www.dkimages.com

Author's acknowledgments

With special thanks to Jeremy Beadle for moral support and access to his extensive library, Mitch Symons for sharing some gloriously quirky facts, Caroline Allen for her research assistance, Barbara Dixon for food facts, and Roddy Langley for soccer stats. And thank you to the team at DK, particularly Liz Wheeler, Jonathan Metcalf, Kathryn Wilkinson, and Vicky Short.

Thanks also to the following people and organizations for their help in researching *Take Me To Your Leader*: Simon Ager (www.Omniglot.com), John Allen, Kate Allen, Ashrita Furman, Lee Gluyas, Phil Harrison Rick Harrison, Rebecca Holmes (Norwich Union Insurance), Rébecca Käslin (Wenger SA), Thomas Keenes, Irene Knight (CN Tower), Kate Langley, Sally Lindsay, Tim McGee, William Parry, Tony Peek, Richard Penfold, Louise Prior, Mark Regan, Josh Risso-Gill, Barrie Singleton, Peter Tehan, Beyond Entertainment Ltd. (producers of Mythbusters) for the Discovery Channel, Village Books, Dulwich, UK, Pete Wilcock.

Publisher's acknowledgments

Dorling Kindersley would like to thank:
for illustrations: Dave Anderson, Container, Neil Duerden, Genevieve Gauckler, Clare Joyce, Tim Lane, Pablo Pasadas, Jo Ratcliff
for additional designs: Alison Gardner, Kenny Grant, Thomas Keenes, Simon Murrell, John Round
for additional design support: Elma Aquino, Adam Brackenbury, Mandy Earey, Philip Fitzgerald, Peter Laws, Heather McCarry, Adam Walker, Sara Oiestad

for editorial help: Angela Wilkes

Sarah and Roland Smithies for all their hard work on picture research.

for additional picture research: Lucy Claxton and Claire Bowers